RELIGION
and the
REBEL

RELIGION
and the
REBEL

— · —

by Colin Wilson

ASHGROVE PRESS, BATH

Published in Great Britain by
ASHGROVE PRESS LIMITED
4 Brassmill Centre, Brassmill Lane
Bath BA1 3JN
and distributed in the USA by
Avery Publishing Group Inc.
120 Old Broadway
Garden City Park
New York 11040

Originally published in Great Britain
by Victor Gollancz Limited

ISBN 0 906798 39 6

This edition first published 1984
Second printing 1988
Third printing 1992

Printed and bound in Great Britain by
Dotesios Ltd, Trowbridge, Wilts.

For

NEGLEY AND DAN FARSON

ACKNOWLEDGMENTS

THE SOURCES of all quotations, with author, publisher and, where appropriate, translator, will be found in the Notes (pages 323 ff.). I wish particularly to thank the Public Trustee and the Society of Authors for extracts from the plays and prefaces of George Bernard Shaw; Harcourt, Brace and Company, Inc., for extracts from T. S. Eliot's *Collected Poems;* Dodd, Mead & Company for extracts from *The Collected Poems of Rupert Brooke* (copyright © 1915 by Dodd, Mead & Company, Inc.), reprinted by permission of Dodd, Mead & Company; The Macmillan Company for extracts from the *Collected Poems of W. B. Yeats;* the Hogarth Press and W. W. Norton & Company, Inc., for extracts from J. B. Leishman's translation of *Sonnets to Orpheus* by R. M. Rilke; W. W. Norton & Company, Inc., for extracts from Rilke's *Duino Elegies,* translated by J. B. Leishman and Stephen Spender; Rupert Hart-Davis, Ltd., for extracts from *The Drunken Boat,* poems by Rimbaud translated by Brian Hill; the Oxford University Press, Inc., for extracts from *A Study of History* by Arnold J. Toynbee; Methuen and Company, Ltd., for extracts from *A Serious Call to a Devout and Holy Life* by William Law; New Directions for extracts from *The Crack-up* by F. Scott Fitzgerald (copyright 1945 by New Directions), reprinted by permission of New Directions; Nonesuch Press for extracts from William Blake's *Poetry and Prose;* and Penguin Books, Ltd., for extracts from Anthony Hartley's translation of "Le Cœur Volé" by J. A. Rimbaud in *The Penguin Book of French Verse: III.*

I am most grateful to Professor George Catlin, Mr. Hugh Heckstall Smith, and Dom Wilfred Upham for generous help.

C. W.

CONTENTS

A RETROSPECTIVE
INTRODUCTION

IT IS STRANGE to re-read a book after more than a quarter of a century. When *Religion and the Rebel* came out in 1957, it was hatcheted by the critics, and sank without a trace. As a result, I could never bear to re-read it. Doing so after twenty-seven years has been, on the whole, a rather pleasant surprise.

My first book, *The Outsider*, had appeared in 1956, and I was catapulted into an instant and rather unstable celebrity. Both in England and America, it stayed on the bestseller lists for week after week, and was quickly translated into a dozen or so languages. But the reasons for its success had very little to do with the book itself. One was that it appeared in the same week as John Osborne's *Look Back in Anger*, and the critics hailed us as England's new literary generation — the generation whose appearance everyone had impatiently anticipated since the end of the war. Added to this was the fact that I was 24 at the time of publication, and had never attended a university; popular journalists were impressed by the praise of 'intellectual' critics — like Cyril Connolly and Philip Toynbee — and I was compared to D. H. Lawrence, Byron and even, God help me, Plato. The publicity — associated with the label 'Angry Young Man' — irritated the respectable critics, who seized the first opportunity to retract their praise of myself, Osborne and various other young writers who had been tarred with the same brush. *Time* ran a gleeful full-page account of the slaughter of *Religion and the Rebel* with a headline 'Scrambled Egghead.'

When Robin Campbell of Ashgrove Press told me he wanted to reprint the book, I opened it for the first time since 1957, and started to read in the spirit of a bather dipping his toe into icy water. Within a page or two, the misgivings had vanished, and I was fascinated by this insight into the workings of my mind at 25. There was another bonus — for the first time I understood the miscalculation that had left me wide open to the barbs of the critics. I talk about 'the Outsider' as if he is a precisely definable type of human being, like an Eskimo or a cannibal. The truth is, of course, that most people contain an element of 'outsiderism' — a sense of alienation from society — and many people I discuss as Outsiders — Scott Fitzgerald, William Law, Bernard Shaw — could just as easily be labelled Insiders. For me now, this constant use of the term Outsider gives the book an element of oversimplification.

But in spite of that, there is nothing in the book that I now feel inclined to retract. Looking back on that self of almost thirty years ago, it seems to me that he was stating a real problem, and that his analysis was relevant and acute. I continued this analysis in another four books of the 'Outsider cycle' — *The Age of Defeat**, *The Strength to Dream*, *Origins of the Sexual Impulse* and *Beyond the Outsider*, while a postscript, *The New Existentialism*, forms a convenient summary of the basic ideas of the series. The debâcle of *Religion and the Rebel* at least taught me to stop throwing around the word 'Outsider'.

What I notice, the moment I begin reading, is that I then had a far more narrow and intense view of the problem than I have nowadays, and that this gives the book a sense of passionate involvement that is lacking in the later volumes of the series. I have only one minor rerservation. On Page 1, I state that what the Outsider is in rebellion against is the 'Lack of spiritual tension in a materially prosperous civilisation'. And throughout the book I am inclined to lay most of the blame at the door of prosperity and materialism, and to equate these with the 'decline of the west'. 'Outsiders appear like pimples on a dying civilisation'. Yet I also knew perfectly well that religious rebels like Pascal, Law, Kierkegaard and Newman were not simply 'virtuous men' who, like Noah, refused to be seduced into sin. They were contemplatives *by temperament*; they felt, like socrates, that the unexamined life is not worth living. And the people they disapproved of were usually people who just happened to have been born with a different temperament. This now leads me to feel that my attack on the 'sick civilisation' was a little too violent.

How, then, do I now see the problem? As a matter of *individual* discipline. I have recently written an enormous *Criminal History of Mankind*, and it confirms my feeling that the 'Outsider' is probably better off nowadays than at any time in

* In America *The Stature of Man* — the American publisher wanted an 'up-beat' title.

history. He may loathe western civilisation, but at least he can survive on National Assistance, and spend his days, if he is so inclined, reading Nietzsche and Kierkegaard and writing denunciations of materialism. But such negative exercises do not seem to me particularly useful. The real problem is to learn those mental disciplines that can raise us momentarily into states of 'mystical' perception — the insight that Chesterton called 'absurd good news.' In this book, I quote with approval the remark of shaw's Captain Shotover that the materialists — like Boss Mangan — strangle out souls, and that when we have the courage of our convictions, we shall kill them. I now feel that this is overstating the case. The Mangans might once have forced the 'Outsiders' to work sixteen hours a day for starvation wages, and so 'prevented them from having the aspirations', but those days are fortunately long past. For most modern 'Outsiders' — and I still know a great number of them — the real problem is to find the disciplines that will lead to self-transformation.

Two or three years after writing this book I became acquainted with the psychologist Abraham Maslow, and with his recognition that 'peak experiences' — the moments of 'absurd good news' — seem to happen frequently to people who are healthy and optimistic. The peak experience is a sudden glimpse of *objective* awareness, and it always takes the same form: a sudden recognition of *how lucky we are*. It confirmed what I had stated in my first two books: that one of the main enemies of the Outsider is self-pity, a tendency to look for somebody else to blame for his problems. Most of us spend our lives stuck in what I have called 'the swamp of subjectivity.' Crisis tends to jerk us out of the swamp, (as I discovered when I contemplated suicide — as described on P.16 of this volume.) It makes us aware that if we lack 'spiritual tension', the cause lies within ourselves, not in the 'botched civilisation'.

Maslow's concept of the peak experience was a milestone on my own road to the solution of the 'Outsider problem', and my discovery of the philosopher Husserl was even more important. They made me realise that a central part of the answer is to deliberately keep ourselves at a high level of motivation and purpose. It is recorded that when Samuel Beckett was a young man, he spent most of the day in bed because he could see no reason to get up. That is a fairly reliable formula for slipping into moods of 'life failure' in which you become convinced that all effort is futile. Our reaction to crisis shows us that the mind contains a kind of 'muscle', a 'contractile faculty', which tenses when we experience the sense of 'power, meaning and purpose'. This 'muscle' can be deliberately strengthened by concentration exercises. Graham Greene experienced the sense of absurd good news when he played Russian roulette with a revolver, and there was just a click as the hammer descended on an empty chamber. It *jerked* him into 'objectivity'. I have always found that if I try to imagine such an incident with enough force, I cause a contraction of that inner muscle, and an instant 'peak experience'. (I have spoken of this more fully in a recent small book, *Access to Inner Worlds*.)

An equally important insight came from a remarkable physician named Howard Miller (whose work I have described in a book called *Frankenstein's Castle*.) As a result of experiments with hypnosis, Miller came to the conclusion that what might be called the 'controlling principle' in man — the controller of intensity of consciousness — lies in the ordinary conscious mind, and not (as D. H. Lawrence thought) in the solar plexus or the instincts. This insight is closely connected to the recognition that has come about through the science of 'split brain physiology', that we have *two* people living in our heads, in the left and right cerebral hemispheres, and the person you call 'you' is the 'conscious self' living in the left brain. The right-brain self is a stranger, and is also the source of so-called 'psychic powers' *and* of the peak experience. Yet it is the left-brain ego, the conscious self, which is the controller of awareness. Why, then, can we not induce the peak experience at will? Because through some absurd misunderstanding, due to its narrowness, this 'controlling ego' *does not realise it is in control*. It believes itself to be passive and helpless, so it is inclined to lie in bed all day praying for peak experiences. In *The Outsider*, I quote Hemingway's story *Soldier's Home*, in which the soldier home from the war recalls those moments when, during crisis, 'you did the one thing, the only thing' and it always came out right. And this is because in moments of crisis, the controlling ego is *galvanised* into sudden wakefulness and suddenly remembers that *it* is in control, and can have peak experiences whenever it likes. Over the years, I have come to recognise that the real solution to the 'Outsider problem' is to induce that basic insight again and again until it finally takes root, and we grasp that we *already* possess the power. This is why the mystics felt that there is an element of absurdity in the visionary experience, a sudden realisation that made them want to kick themselves and shout 'Of course!' The solution lies in the recognition that the left-brain is the *gatherer of power*.

'Visionary consciousness' and the sense of 'absurd good news' is the starting point of *Religion and the Rebel*. And that is why when I re-read it, I was not upset by its crudities. It is true that I would like to rewrite it, removing 90% of its references to 'the Outsider'. And there are many pages that I would now like to re-cast: (for example, it seems to me that the facts about Wittgenstein's homosexuality that have emerged since I wrote the book explain a great deal about the self-hatred that resulted in the perverse 'reductionism' of his later work.) I also find that its romanticism is hard to take — its conviction that the Outsider is a lonely beacon of integrity in a sea of cheapness and futility: but that is surely inevitable when a man of fifty-two reads a book by a man exactly half his age. Still, on the whole, I find the speculations of that earlier self exciting, and his analysis of the problem basically accurate. It seems to me that he was correct in believing that mankind would develop a new religious consciousness. What he could not have foreseen was that it would happen so easily and naturally. By the mid-1960s, the works of Hermann Hesse — which were almost unknown in the English-speaking countries when I discussed them in *The Outsider* — had become best sellers again. A new generation plunged with enthusiasm into the disciplines of Buddhism, Hinduism, yoga, transcendental meditation and even ritual magic. No doubt many of these movements — like the psychedelic revolution — were mere fads, but there can be no doubt that the impulse behind them was a dissatisfaction with the quality of 'everyday consciousness', and the feeling that it ought to be possible to change it.

This, I suspect, will be regarded by historians of the future as the second great revolution of the 20th century, and one whose consequences may be far more important for man's future evolution than the one that took place in Russia in 1917.

AN AUTOBIOGRAPHICAL
INTRODUCTION

THE OUTSIDER was an incomplete book. It was intended to document and order a subject which, for personal reasons, I find particularly absorbing: the subject of mental strain and near-insanity.

Over many years, the obsessional figure whom I have called the Outsider became for me the heroic figure of our time. My vision of our civilisation was a vision of cheapness and futility, the degrading of all intellectual standards. In contrast to this, the Outsider seemed to be the man who, for any reason at all, felt himself lonely in the crowd of the second-rate. As I conceived him, he could be a maniac carrying a knife in a black bag, taking pride in appearing harmless and normal to other people; he could be a saint or a visionary, caring for nothing but one moment in which he seemed to understand the world, and see into the heart of nature and of God.

The more I considered the Outsider, the more I felt him to be a symptom of our time and age. Essentially, he seemed to be a rebel; and what he was in rebellion against was the *lack of spiritual tension* in a materially prosperous civilisation. The first nine books of Saint Augustine's *Confessions* are an Outsider document, and Saint Augustine lived in a disintegrating Roman society. It did not seem a bold step to conclude that the Outsider is a symptom of a civilisation's decline; Outsiders appear like pimples on a dying civilisation. An individual tends to be what his environment makes him. If a civilisation is spiritually sick, the individual suffers from the same sickness. If he is healthy enough to put up a fight, he becomes an Outsider.

The study of the spiritually sick individual belongs to psychology, but to consider him in relation to a sick civilisation is to enter the realm of history. That is why this book must attempt to pursue two courses at once, probing deeper into the Outsider himself, while at the same time moving towards the historical problem of the decline of civilisations. One way leads inward, towards mysticism; the other outward, towards politics. Unfortunately, I have almost no turn for practical politics, so the emphasis in this book is on religion and philosophy. Where the road disappears into the thickets of political theory, I leave it, and hope that someone less averse to politics than I am will press on where I have shirked the problem.

Various critics have objected — with some justification — that the term 'Outsider' is loose; that a word which can be applied to Boehme as well as Nijinsky, to Fox and Gurdjieff as well as Lawrence, Van Gogh and Sartre, is almost meaningless. But my use of the term 'Outsider' is deliberately vague. The ultimate question that, for me, lies behind the Outsider is: How can man extend his range of consciousness? I believe that human beings experience a range of mental states which is as narrow as the middle three notes of a piano keyboard. I believe that the possible range of mental states is as wide as the whole piano keyboard, and that man's sole aim and business is to extend his range from the usual three or four notes to the whole keyboard. The men I dealt with in *The Outsider* had one thing in common: an instinctive knowledge that their range *could* be extended, and a nagging dissatisfaction with the range of their everyday experience.

This, I must admit, is the urge that underlies all my thinking and writing. I state it here so that there shall be no doubt in any reader's mind about the central preoccupation of my book.

The publication of *The Outsider* brought me some interesting insights. It received more attention than I or my publisher had expected, and, quite suddenly, I became involved in all kinds of activities. For many months after it was published, I had almost no time alone, caught up as I was in a round of interviews by reporters, lectures, broadcasts, reading and answering letters, invitations to dinner, and so on. The result was exactly what I had been afraid of: I found myself losing the preoccupations that had led me to write *The Outsider*. Strangers who claimed to be Outsiders wrote me long letters explaining their symptoms and asking for advice, until I began to suspect parody. In this whirl, I discovered that I ceased to be aware of the states of consciousness that lie beyond my ordinary two or three notes. In my own terminology, I had started to become an Insider.

I record this because it is of central importance to the theme of this book. Most men I know live like this as a matter of course: working, travelling, eating and drinking and talking. The range of everyday activity in a modern civilisation builds a wall around the ordinary state of consciousness and makes it almost impossible to see beyond it. The conditions under which we live do this to us. It is what happens in a civilisation that always makes a noise like a dynamo, and gives no leisure for peace and contemplation. Men begin to lose that intuition of 'unknown modes of being,' that sense of purpose, that makes them more than highly efficient pigs. This is the horror the Outsider revolts against.

Some years ago, in Winchester Cathedral, I came across a pamphlet by Mr. T. S. Eliot; it was an address which Mr. Eliot had delivered in the Cathedral, and it had the unpromising title: 'On the Use of Cathedrals in England.' For three quarters of the pamphlet, Mr. Eliot talks like a studious country parson about the relation of the cathedral to the parish churches. And then, towards the end, he speaks of the position of the dean and chapter, and his pamphlet suddenly becomes an impassioned plea for leisure in a modern civilisation. He attacks the view that the dean and chapter should be general runabouts, preaching sermons all over the parish, and emphasises that good theological thinking requires quiet and contemplation. He adduces his own example to strengthen his point: he has always worked as a publisher to give himself the necessary leisure for writing, and any permanent value which his work may possess (he modestly claims) is due to the fact that he wrote only what he wanted to write, under no compulsion to please anyone but himself.

I remember being excited by this at the time. T. E. Lawrence had made the same point in *The Seven Pillars*: '. . . of these two poles, leisure and subsistence, we should shun subsistence . . . and cling close to leisure . . . Some men there might be, uncreative, whose leisure is barren; but the activity of these would have been material only. . . . Mankind has been no gainer by its drudges.'

For my own part, I found that I preferred working as a navvy or washing dishes to life in an office; for although I had no more than the normal reluctance to face hard work, I had a very real fear of that deadening of the nerves and sensibilities that comes of boredom and submitting to one's own self-contempt. I was sticking down envelopes with a damp brush one afternoon, when a young man who seemed to enjoy being a civil servant commented: 'Soul-destroying, isn't it?' A commonplace phrase, but I had never heard it before, and I repeated it like a revelation. Not soul-destroying, but life-destroying; the stagnating life-force gives off smells like standing water, and the whole being is poisoned. Desmond — that was his name — always looked well groomed and efficient, and I never saw him lose his temper. My own predisposition to boredom and irritable wretchedness inclined me to divide the world into two classes: people who disliked themselves, and people who didn't. And the former disliked the latter even more than they disliked themselves.

Such experiences were the groundwork of all my analyses, my starting point; and all my thought aimed at discovering some solution that would enable the people who disliked themselves to find reasons — or methods — of overcoming self-contempt, without numbing themselves into complacency. I called the people who disliked themselves Outsiders. Boredom, I knew, meant not having enough to do with one's life energies. The answer to it, quite simply, lies in extending the range of the consciousness: setting emotions circulating, and setting the intellect working, until new areas of consciousness are brought to life in the way that the blood starts flowing again through a leg which has gone numb.

That was just the starting point. It is not enough to have leisure; leisure is only a negative concept, the wide, clear space where one can build decent houses after knocking down slums. The next problem is to begin to build. I found it tiresome to work for an employer in a factory or laundry, and envied those men who can make a living by doing the things they enjoy. But closer acquaintance with such men — writers, artists, journalists — has usually proved to me that they have knocked down one slum only to build another — slightly more to their own taste, but still a slum. From the point of view of spiritual health, I do not think there is much to choose between the workman who has worked in the same factory for forty years and is spiritually warped and stunted in consequence, and the novelist who writes the same kind of novels for forty years and has a house on the Riviera.

It is unnatural to work for forty years in the same factory, but no more unnatural than it is to be born. Nature is dead; every act of will is unnatural, against nature. The more one has to fight against, the more alive one can be. That was why, for me, the problem of living resolved itself into the question of choosing obstacles to stimulate my will. Instantly, I came to recognise that our civilisation is flowing in the opposite direction; all our culture and science is directed towards enabling us to exercise as little will as possible. Everything is made easy; and if, after a week of office routine and travelling on buses, we still feel the need to work off excess energy, we can always enjoy ourselves playing all those games involving artificial obstacles, where the will is applied to beating another team of cricketers or footballers, or simply to wrestling with the imaginary Sphinx who sets the newspaper crossword puzzles. We have also invented a form of thought that fits in with this abdication of the will. We call it abstract philosophy. It is essentially the product of Western civilisation.

There was an element of disguised autobiography in *The Outsider*; obviously, since I spent most of the book calling on other men to bear witness to my own beliefs. Underlying the whole argument there was the belief that real philosophy should be the result of applying the analytical faculty — the mathematical faculty — to the stuff of one's own experience. Too much experience flows over us like water through a channel: it means nothing to us; we are unchanged by it, unconscious of it. For years before I wrote *The Outsider* I had kept a journal in which I had been mainly concerned with applying mathematical analysis to my own experience, and making a note when I read something that showed the same preoccupation. There was a slow, deliberate accumulation of material that I was able to transfer almost unchanged into the book. That material was chosen — naturally — to exclude my-self.

But it is time now, before launching into further analysis of other writers, to explain my own relation to my data. What I wish to give is as full an account as possible of how the problems of the Outsider came to preoccupy me. Some of the difficult issues to be found in the next three hundred pages of the present volume could easily become totally obscured without such a preface. Besides, my existentialist premises demand it. Philosophy is nothing if it is not an attempt to take one's own experience apart under a micro-scope.

When I was eleven years old, my grandfather gave me a tattered and coverless science-fiction magazine. (This was in the second year of the war, and I had never seen such a thing before.) It was here that I discovered a name of which I had never heard: Albert Einstein. It was difficult to determine, from the references in the stories, precisely what Professor Einstein had done, but every writer in the magazine mentioned him at least once, and the Letters to the Editor were sprinkled with his name.

The stories themselves excited me more than anything I had ever read. They were mostly about Experiments that got Out of Hand. There was one about a scientist who made a speck of grey proto-plasmic matter, which was somehow thrown into the sea and grew larger as it ate up the fishes, until finally it developed a habit of en-gulfing passenger liners or depopulating small islands. There was another about a scientist who made an Atomic Fire that was inextinguishable, and went on burning until it threatened to burn up the whole world.

I had never read anything like it. Compared to boys' papers and comics, it was erudite and intellectual. And one had a feeling of far more serious issues at stake than in stories about football games and ragging in the Lower Fourth. ('Yarroo, you rotter! I'll tell old Quelchy!') There was talk about positrons and cyclotrons and the theory of probability. Not to mention Professor Einstein.

I found Einstein's own little volume, *Relativity, the Special and General Theory*, and conscientiously plugged away at it, skipping the mathematics and wondering what the devil he meant by 'orientation.' But Sir James Jeans was easier; his explanation of the Michelson-Morley experiment simplified everything. From then on I thought I understood relativity. I enjoyed a certain amount of consideration among the boys at school as a consequence of tangling up the physics master on obscure questions about the speed of light in a moving co-ordinate system. They nicknamed me 'Professor,' and relied on me to waste as much of our physics lectures as possible by objecting that Newton was out of date and discredited. But secretly I admired Newton, for I imagined him as occupying a place in the hierarchy — Archimedes, Galileo, Newton, Planck, Einstein — which would one day include myself.

But my curiosity was not confined to purely scientific questions. Sir James Jeans begins *The Mysterious Universe* with a passage that might have been a sermon on Pascal's text: 'The eternal silence of these infinite spaces terrifies me.' This, and other passages of speculation, produced a sense of mystery that was so intolerable to me that I once wrote a twenty-page letter to Sir Arthur Eddington, asking him if he could please explain to me what the universe was all about. When I asked the local librarian where I could find his address, she told me that he had died earlier in the year. I was not wholly disappointed, since I had come to the conclusion that he was unlikely to know the answer anyway. This was in 1944.

I see now that it was Jeans and Eddington who were responsible for my sudden mental awakening at the age of twelve; at the time, I thought of Einstein as 'the master.' I believed that Einstein had taught me the impossibility of making a final judgement on anything. I tried to explain to school friends that space was infinite and yet bounded; and it seemed to me that the possibilities of human life were also infinite and yet bounded: that within its framework of endless repetition, anything could be done. It was to be another five years before I read *Zarathustra* and discovered that Nietzsche also recognised Eternal Recurrence as the foundation of an essentially optimistic philosophy.

But this notion was of secondary importance compared to that of the Will to Power. This is so central to my way of thinking that I should perhaps explain at some length how my ideas on the subject originated.

In some popular textbook of psychology, I had read summaries of the systems of Freud, Jung and Adler. Freud's insistence on childhood influences and the sexual urges seemed even then to be nonsense; Jung's theory of types struck me as equally irrelevant. But Adler's idea of the Power Instinct came to me as a revelation; it seemed to tie together all my observations of human beings, to add the final touch to the edifice that Einstein had begun. A great deal of a child's time is spent in being treated unfairly and wondering about the rights and wrongs of the case; also in observing that, although all adults seem to him to be equally self-possessed and balanced in judgement, yet there are some who are badly spoken of by others, or labeled as shifty, dishonest or stupid by one's parents. It is all very confusing. It leads the child to realise that he cannot leave the business of making judgements entirely to the adult world. And when such a child tries to form his own judgements, the real confusion begins. In most issues between adults, there seems very little to choose. It is less a matter of rights and wrongs than of individuals with their own will to self-assertion. So my summary of the situation went like this: 'right' and 'wrong' are relative terms; they have no final meaning; the reality behind human conflicts is only a will to self-assertion. Nobody is right; nobody is wrong; but *everyone* wants to be thought right.

Adler's use of the term 'inferiority complex' supplied me with my fundamental idea. I decided that the desire of every human being is to appear in as good a light as possible to himself. And since the opinions of other people affect the way we see ourselves, we seek to preserve our complacency by winning their respect or friendship. Of course, there is another way: to cut oneself off completely from the opinion of other people and build a wall around one's own self-esteem. The lunatic who believes he is Napoleon or Christ has done this — so I felt. The difference between the lunatic and the sane person is only that the sane person prefers to get other people to co-operate in maintaining his delusions.

There came a day when I took up a pen and settled down to writing a long essay about these ideas. I began it in a new school notebook that had written inside the cover 'Colin Wilson, Form 2C,' and underneath it, in block capitals printed in red ink: 'These notes are based on the relativity theory of Albert Einstein, and the system of Individual Psychology of Alfred Adler.'

The writing of that essay was an unforgettable experience. Years later, when I read in *The Varieties of Religious Experience* of Jouffroy's feelings of terror while analysing his own unbelief,* I remembered that night in 1944 when I wrote my 'Essay on Superiority' at a single sitting. It seemed that I had penetrated deeper into unbelief than any other human being; that by questioning too deeply, I had cut myself off from the rest of the human race. My brother came to bed in the same room while I wrote. Towards three o'clock in the morning, I turned off the light and climbed into bed beside him, feeling at the same time an awful fear that God would strike me dead in the night. I felt that I had destroyed in myself a certain necessary basis of illusion that makes life bearable for human beings. I had done this in the name of 'truth'; and now I felt no elation, only a sort of fatigue of the brain that would not let me sleep. Truth, it seemed, had no power of intensifying life; only of destroying the illusions that make life tolerable.

I still remember my surprise when I woke up in the morning and found I was still alive. God either didn't care, or didn't exist.

This was the beginning of a long period in which the key word, for me, was 'futility.' During this period, I felt that 'futility' was the final comment on human life. It was the worst and most depressing period of my life. It was not a case of my ideas depressing me; there was a social maladjustment for which the ideas provided the excuse. At thirteen I should have had friends — especially girl friends. Instead, I spent three years in my bedroom, reading and writing. The sexual desires I knew at the time were mere physical urges; there was no need or desire for friendly human intercourse. My admiration went to a certain ideal of cold brutality of intellect; while I wondered with despair where the motivation for such an attitude could lie, if not in the realms of delusion and self-assertion that I despised. When I read some sage or philosopher proclaiming that human beings are hopelessly deluded, I wondered what reason he had for saying so, other than a deluded wish to be admired for his cynicism. Human life seemed a vicious circle; the desire for life a delusion. I asked myself: Who made the delusion?

* *vide The Outsider*, pp. 123–4.

and decided that, whatever inscrutable aim inspired the Great De-lusion-Maker, it presupposed human futility and vanity. I was not ever certain that the Great Delusion-Maker himself might not be inspired by delusions.

Added to this was the exhaustion of reading and thinking too much; also, of course, the sexual unfulfilment. Shaw comments in one of the later prefaces that most young men need sex several years before it is socially convenient for them to have it. This, I think, is especially true nowadays, and the consequence is a residue of sexual hunger that may take years of libertinism to assuage. At all events, I believe that sex played as important a part as my eschato-logical doubts in making me wretched in my early teens.

I wrote as an antidote to misery or boredom. I became ashamed of the 'Superiority' essay, and wrote further essays in which I sought a more technical terminology. The central theme was always the same: that men are machines driven by emotions, that the 'desire for truth' is always some less creditable urge disguised by the emotions; that 'truth' would be as useless to human beings as bookcases are to cows. I find the two little notebooks of 'Sub-jective Essays' filled with speculations on the nature of human im-pulses, and can see now that these speculations were an attempt to track down the element of free will in man. In the essay on Fanati-cism, I state that the fanatic is the luckiest of all living beings, for he is driven by the most intense delusions. Somewhere — in Wells's *Outline of History*, I think — I have seen those huge Egyptian statues of Amenhotep III that are called the Colossi of Memnon; and in them I saw my symbol of the real philosopher, the man who could say that his reason was not prejudiced by emotion; huge, eyeless, immobile. Only in the dead, I felt, was there no emotional prejudice; consequently, only the dead may be called sane. And somewhere in the essays, I acknowledge that free will may exist, but in such a small degree as to be hardly knowable. I found my-self confronted by an urge to analyse my way to truth that con-cluded in a recognition that truth is of no use for survival.

I had other pursuits that kept me from complete abdication of will. From the age of eleven, physics and chemistry had been my major interests, and by the age of twelve I had made the spare room into a laboratory in which I spent most of my weekends and eve-nings; the pocket money I earned from a paper round was spent on chemicals. Then, in the August holiday of 1944, I conceived the idea of writing a book which would summarise, in formula and laws, all my knowledge of chemistry and physics. The scheme fascinated me so much that I soon made it more ambitious, and decided to write chapters on Astronomy, Geology, Psychology, Aeronautics, Philosophy and Mathematics. I had bought, at some church bazaar, six volumes of a self-educator with 'courses' on all these subjects. With the help of this and books from the local library, I began my attempt to summarise all the scientific knowledge of humanity. I wrote it in notebooks that held about fifteen thousand words each, and had filled six of these before it was time to go back to school. It was my first book, and I worked on it continuously and systematically — the best possible training for a writer.

In those years of the 'Subjective Essays,' the greatest impact on my mind was Bernard Shaw. I had seen Gabriel Pascal's film of *Caesar and Cleopatra* without being particularly impressed; it reminded me too much of Shakespeare, whom I had always found unreadable. But during the first week of the B.B.C.'s Third Programme, I switched on the radio one evening to hear Mr. Esmé Percy's voice declaiming:

> Friends and fellow brigands. I have a proposal to make to this meeting. We have now spent three evenings in discussing the question Have Anarchists or Social-Democrats the most personal courage? We have gone into the principles of Anarchism and Social-Democracy at great length. The cause of Anarchy has been ably represented by our one Anarchist, who doesnt know what Anarchism means. . . .[1]*

It was the beginning of the third act of *Man and Superman*. Even now, after more than ten years, I find it impossible to read this act without a curious feeling of awe. It was a totally new experience. I will not pretend that I was enthralled. I was not; I was partly bored, and could not follow a lot of it. But I was astounded that another man had actually thought and written about the problems that preoccupied me. Up till then, I had had a little private game with myself in which I examined everyone I met and tried to decide how close they were to seeing the world as I saw it; there was always an element of self-congratulation in the fact that I felt certain no one

* See Notes on pp. 323 ff.

ever had. I was already beginning to enjoy that first terror of feeling myself completely alone. It had become a commonplace of my
thinking that no man asked himself what life was about; or if he did,
answered with arrant nonsense or wishful thinking. (I once asked
my grandfather — during an argument about the existence of God
— if he understood the purpose of life, and he told me solemnly
that he did, and that he would explain it to me when I was fourteen. Nothing I could say would draw him out. Unfortunately,
he died when I was eleven.) Now I heard Shaw speaking quite
plainly about the purpose of life, and answering that it was a will
to self-understanding. It sounded plausible. It seemed paradoxical
enough. And the devil expressed my central obsession with the
idea of futility and purposeless repetition:

> ... Where you now see reform, progress, fulfilment of upward
> tendency, continual ascent by Man on the stepping stones of his
> dead selves to higher things, you will see nothing but an infinite
> comedy of illusion. You will discover the profound truth of the
> saying of my friend Koheleth, that there is nothing new under
> the sun. Vanitas vanitatum. . . .

And Don Juan interrupts impatiently:

> ... Clever dolt that you are, is a man no better than a worm, or
> a dog than a wolf, because he gets tired of everything? Shall he
> give up eating because he destroys his appetite in the act of
> gratifying it? [2]

I went to bed that night with a sort of mental numbness. I felt
that something of tremendous importance had happened to me,
something which I could not yet fully grasp. During the night, I
woke up and put out my hand to my brother; the bedclothes had
slipped off him and he was as cold as tin. For a moment I believed
him dead, and it seemed the natural and inevitable result of knowing
too much and prying too deep. It was an immense relief when I
covered him up and he grew warm again; and as much a surprise, in
its way, as the morning I woke up and found I was still alive.

I listened to the repeat of the play the following evening, all six
hours of it, and borrowed it from the local library and read it
through the day after that. I think that no other forty-eight hours

of my life has given me such a sense of a mental earthquake. Subsequently I read through all the plays (although not, at that time, the prefaces). The English master at school told me that an admiration for Shaw was something that often 'happens' in the teens, and disappears after five years or so. I find that, after twelve years, Shaw still seems to me the greatest figure in European literature since Dante.

Shaw was less of a mental tonic than might be expected. At that time, a sense of exhaustion and greyness seemed to wash around on the edge of my mind. I made a habit of wandering into churches and engaging the priest in arguments about the existence of God and the purpose of life. Sometimes, if the argument went on too long, I left the church feeling a little dizzy, and with an underlying certainty that stupidity and futility were the inescapable warp and weft of living. These periods of depression sometimes lasted for days. (One such priest, I remember, advised me to read nothing but newspapers for a year, telling me that I was suffering from mental indigestion from reading too much. I was delighted later when, in Fox's Journal, I read about the priest of Mancetter who advised him to take tobacco and sing psalms.*) I had passed beyond my period of militant atheism. The idea that there was no God no longer gave me a feeling of freedom. In my childhood I had been greatly given to praying mentally while I walked around; I was an incorrigible talker, and enjoyed keeping up a one-sided conversation when there was no one else to talk to, frequently apologising to God when my attention was distracted and I lost the thread of the discussion. Now I would have been glad to pray — except for the gloomy certainty that it would be mere emotional dishonesty. I had begun to read T. S. Eliot's poetry at this time, stimulated by some remark of the French master about his obscurity. In the first few lines I read, I found the words:

> And I pray that I may forget
> These matters that with myself I too much discuss
> Too much explain

and

> Teach us to care and not to care
> Teach us to sit still.[3]

* *The Outsider*, Chap. 8, pp. 209–10.

Immediately I felt I knew what he was talking about. After that, I tended to repeat *Ash Wednesday* as a form of mental prayer. It furnished a sort of antidote to depression and exhaustion that Shaw could not provide.

When I was sixteen, I left school, having passed my School Certificate. I had wanted to take some job where I could study for a B.Sc. (My chief ambition was still to be a scientist.) Unfortunately I needed five credits to be exempt from matriculation; I only had four, and had to take the maths exam again. In the meantime, I took a job in a warehouse; it involved weighing crates of wool when they came into the warehouse, keeping a number of girls and machines supplied with hanks of wool, and 'weighing out' the wool when it had been wound on to spools. I was not particularly miserable, but the hours were longer than any I had known before — from eight till six, with a break for lunch — and the work was heavier. After a while, the job began to bore me, and I tried various remedies to counteract my growing detestation for it. I read a great deal of poetry, because I found it relaxed me and refreshed me; I planned short stories and a long play while I worked, and wrote them in the evenings. After two months, I passed my maths exam with the necessary credit, and left the warehouse without regrets. I hated hard work.

In comparison, my job as a laboratory assistant at my old school seemed like a holiday. But I now found that I had lost all interest in science. I had written three acts of an immensely long play, designed as a sequel to Shaw's *Man and Superman*, and was convinced that I could make a living as a writer. I had my first short story published at about this time — it was in a factory magazine printed in Yorkshire. An uncle who worked in Durham had submitted the story for me, and the editor had written saying he thought I had talent, and would be glad to receive further contributions. The magazine collapsed about a month later, but by then I had conceived and begun to write another half-dozen short stories and some one-act plays. I wrote a long dialogue, set in the Temple at Jerusalem, between Jesus (aged sixteen) and a member of the Sanhedrin, putting my own arguments into Jesus's mouth, and the views of the priests with whom I had talked into the old man's. (I left this lengthy play on a bus shortly after I had finished it and never recovered it.)

I was causing an increasing dissatisfaction among the science masters at school. I spent most of my 'study time' in the library, writing plays and short stories, and most of my physics and maths lectures reading *The Pickwick Papers* under the desk. It is a sign of the patience and amiability of the headmaster that no one called me to account until the yearly exams made it impossible to ignore my complete loss of interest in science. Even then, I was exhorted to mend my ways, and told that I could stay on conditionally. I explained that I wanted to be a writer. They sympathetically paid me two months' wages and sacked me.

It would be untrue if I gave the impression that my term as a laboratory assistant was a period of peace and relaxation. I found too much leisure more of a nuisance than too little, and suffered agonies of boredom. I had a standing feud with one of the masters, who was adept at inflicting petty indignities and irritated me intensely. I frequently took days off, alleging illness, and spent them cycling out to Warwick or Matlock or Nottingham to work off my surplus energies. The periods of depression came more frequently and lasted longer. I had begun to keep a journal, inspired by some B.B.C. programme about Marie Bashkirtseff. Now I filled page after page every evening with expressions of my boredom and frustration, analyses of the books I had read (I had begun to read Ibsen, Pirandello and Joyce; I hated *Ulysses*) and diatribes against the people I disliked. Once, when an English master had been scathing about an essay I had written denouncing the concept of Shakespearian tragedy, I covered twenty pages of the journal before my indignation had subsided enough to allow me to sleep. I wrote the journal with the idea of ultimate publication, as I had no doubt that every word I had ever written would one day be of interest to students. I filled ten large-sized notebooks in just over a year, and then one day destroyed them all in a fit of disgust. I also had innumerable short stories and plays rejected by publishers, and finally stopped sending them out, finding that the remote possibility that they might be accepted scarcely justified the depression which I underwent each time they were returned. The underlying feeling of futility was still my major problem. My one-act plays were comedies, and most of the short stories owed their style to *The Pickwick Papers*, and I disliked myself for writing such stuff. Occasional attempts to write like Poe made me feel worse. I wrote with a sense of obsession, hating the medium. I also knew most of T. S. Eliot's poetry by heart now, but it had no notable influence on my style.

The worst insight came during the long Easter holiday of 1948. I had been reading far too much — out of boredom — and spent a whole day reading Janko Lavrin's little book on Russian literature. It is not very cheerful reading, with its descriptions of the stories of Chekhov, Saltykov's *Golovlyov Family*, Goncharov's *Oblomov*. I went into the kitchen to switch on the stove to make tea, and had a blackout. It was a strange sensation. I stood there, fully conscious, clutching the stove to keep upright, and yet conscious of nothing but blackness. There was an electric sensation in my brain, so that I could readily have believed that I had been given an electric shock. It was as if something were flowing through me, and I had an insight of what lay on the other side of consciousness. It looked like an eternity of pain. When my vision cleared, I switched on the kettle and went into the other room. I could not be certain what I had seen, but I was afraid of it. It seemed as if I were the bed of a river, and the current was all pain. I thought I had seen the final truth *that life does not lead to anything;* it is *an escape from something,* and the 'something' is a horror that lies on the other side of consciousness. I could understand what Kurtz had seen in *Heart of Darkness*. All the metaphysical doubts of years seemed to gather to a point, in one realisation: What *use* is such truth? Later in the day, I went out cycling; there seemed to be a supreme irony in every manifestation of life that I saw. Eliot's lines from *The Waste Land* ran in my head:

> On Margate sands.
> I can connect
> Nothing with nothing.
> The broken fingernails of dirty hands. . . .[4]

Later, I wrote about it in my journal, with a sense that the futility had now come its full circle; for until then, writing in my journal had been the one action that did not seem futile; now I was recording my certainty of the futility of *everything*. And yet I recorded it with a compulsive sense that everything should be told.

I think I recognised how far the source of these periods of exhaustion was physical. It seemed a further reason for nihilistic unbelief. All things depended upon mere physical energy. Therefore, there was no will.

I had seen the word 'nihilism' somewhere, and asked the English master at school what it meant. 'Belief in nothing,' he told me, and at once I thought I had found a name for my own state of mind. It was not just *lack* of belief in *anything* — it was active *belief in Nothing*. I cannot now understand the significance that that word 'Nothing' carried for me then. I remember, though, how I discovered the *Tao Te Ching* in a compilation called *The Bible of the World*, and read:

> There is a thing inherent and natural,
> Which existed before heaven and earth.
> Motionless and fathomless,
> It stands alone and never changes;
> It pervades everywhere and never becomes exhausted.
> It may be regarded as the Mother of the Universe
> I do not know its name.
> If I am forced to give it a name,
> I call it Tao, and I name it Supreme.
> Supreme means going on;
> Going on means going far;
> Going far means returning.

Therefore Tao is supreme; heaven is supreme; earth is supreme; and man is also supreme. There are in the universe four things supreme, and man is one of them.[5]

I was certain that 'Tao' was my positive principle of Nothingness. The line 'Going far means returning' I took to mean a recognition that all thought chases its own tail: *vanitas vanitatum*. As to the last section, with its 'Man is supreme,' my already Swiftian views on the stupidity and futility of human beings led me to decide that 'Man' was a mistranslation for 'I'; that, in fact, Lao-tse was merely expressing his inability to escape complete solipsism. I could not (and still do not) accept the view that Taoism is a humanism.

My solipsism I had arrived at by reading of Berkeley and Hume in some textbook of philosophy. I remember explaining to a group of friends in the playground at school why a bar of chocolate existed only in their own minds. Berkeley, added to Einstein and Eliot's *Hollow Men*, made a vertiginous mixture.

Then, quite suddenly, my 'nihilism' received a check. A day came when I seriously contemplated suicide. It was during the long, hot summer of 1947, when I was working as a laboratory assistant. I arrived home one evening in a state of nervous exhaustion, and tried to 'write away' my tension in my journal. I found writing simply an aid to reflection, a crutch for my thoughts. And after about an hour of writing, I found my resistance slowly returning. I thought clearly: This must cease immediately; *I will not go on living like this.* I was all too familiar with these revivals of strength that was sucked away again the next day. Then I saw the answer: Kill myself.

It cheered me immensely. I cycled to my evening classes with a feeling of having at last learned to master my destiny. I arrived late, and listened to the professor's sarcasms without interest. It was our evening for analytical chemistry practice. A glass tray contained a mixture of powders which we had to separate. I took some in my watch glass, sniffed it, tested it in a bunsen flame, and then went into the other room to the reagent shelves. Glass bottles contained cobalt chloride, silver nitrate, potassium iodide and various acids. In the middle there was a bottle of hydrocyanic acid. As I took it down, my mind made a leap, and for an instant I was living in the future, with a burning in my throat and in the pit of my stomach. In that moment, I was suddenly supremely aware that what I wanted was not less life, but more. The sensation of drinking the acid was so clear that it was almost as if it had actually taken place. I stood there for a second with the bottle in my hand, but the experience was so vivid that it seemed to last for hours. Then, as someone stood beside me, I put it back, vaguely, as if I had taken it by mistake, and reached down for the methyl red. In one second, I had seen something that I have striven to see all my life since.

My insight that evening did not last for long, perhaps because I was too anxious to cling to it. I remember the feeling of having been suddenly awakened to the possibilities of my own will power, and the dreamlike quality of the rest of the evening. And when I got home, I did not try to write about it. For the first time, I had a sense of something too real to write about. Later, when I came to analyse the experience in my journal, I recognised it as one of many such experiences which I had had, differing only in degree. I did not discover Hermann Hesse until six years later; I am certain that if I had, *Steppenwolf* would have become the bible of my teens. Hesse recognises these fluctuations of insight as being the very stuff of the artist's life. At any time in my adolescence, asked what is the final goal of life, I would have replied without hesitation: Insight. Later deliberations have made me less certain.

My year as a civil servant was the dreariest I had yet known. In my journal, I wrote that the chief qualification for a tax´collector is an ability to simulate work. I hated pretending to file Schedule A forms that did not need filing. I envied Shaw when I read in Hesketh Pearson's biography that he had been so efficient as an office boy that his employers had refused to accept his resignation. I was frankly incompetent and outspoken about my dislike of the job. I took half a dozen books to the office every day and read them when I had finished filing. In slack periods I slipped out to the local library and stayed there for hours at a time. I was an appallingly bad office boy. The head of the office was a pleasant, middle-aged Londoner; when he had nothing to do he asked me into his office, and 'talked philosophy' — which meant that he told me long, rambling stories about his life to illustrate his own incorrigibly optimistic point of view. Whenever I had to be reprimanded for some oversight or piece of incompetence — which was pretty frequently — he delegated the job to his second-in-command (a good-tempered Scot, who also took a lenient view of my inefficiency). After six months in the Inland Revenue office, I took the examination for establishment in the Civil Service. I can still remember my despair when I received the letter congratulating me on having passed. I celebrated my establishment by writing a long, pessimistic story about the end of the world; I produced it in a single eight-hour sitting one Saturday afternoon. No one ever liked the story, and I destroyed it later. It was distinctly indebted to Wells's *The Star*.

The only occurrence of importance in my year as a civil servant was my definite abandonment of Dickens as a master of style. One day, in a state of boredom and disgust, I began a story in the 'stream of consciousness' style and found that it expressed my emotions so well that from then on I experimented with it continually.

I had always detested the idea of National Service, but my period in the R.A.F. came as a relief. The first eight weeks of square-bashing were so hectic that I had no time to think, and my mental faculties enjoyed the vacation. This was followed by a tedious month spent in a Birmingham training camp, where I had little to do except learn to be a Clerk, General Duties. I had not chosen it myself — the clerking job — and I resented it. Finally, I was posted to a station near Nottingham, and given a little office all to myself, where I was as bored as I had been in the tax office. One day, in a state of wild irritation, I was thoroughly rude to the adjutant, who, instead of sending for the guard, asked me sympathetically why I disliked office work so much. He hoped to get me transferred to some medical unit where I might exercise my incompetence among malingerers who were hoping to escape parades. He had been un-lucky in having had a series of inefficient clerks whose oversights had brought unending complaints from G.H.Q., and hoped to exchange me for better or worse. Somehow, he overshot his mark, and a month later I found myself on my way home with my dis-charge papers. The whole story is unprintable. I left the R.A.F. with a delighted recognition that one's salvation can lie in proceed-ing to extremes of indiscretion and ignoring the possible conse-quences. It was the first time I had had a chance of putting Mr. Polly's advice into practice, and it had worked.

The sheer joy of walking out of the R.A.F. gave me a great sense of emotional release. I determined that I would never go back into an office. I sent in my resignation to the Civil Service, and received a long letter pointing out the gravity of what I was doing, and asking me to reconsider it. I stayed at home for a month until my discharge pay ran out, and then left home with a haversack and hitchhiked north. I had intended to find work, but found myself so reluctant to begin that I delayed until the last of my money was spent. Then I hitchhiked home again. In my fortnight's wanderings I had approached a dozen or so theatres with the idea of training to act in repertory. Luckily, no one had any time for me. At home I worked for a fortnight on a building site, and then set out again, this time travelling southward. I wanted to spend a night at Stone-henge — for no particular reason — and then head for Southampton, where I hoped I might be able to get a boat to India. Two R.A.F. policemen saw me emerging from a haystack wearing a grubby R.A.F. uniform (without shoulder flashes) and arrested me. I explained that I was not a deserter, but I had no discharge papers and they didn't believe me. I was sent home again.

I took a number of jobs in quick succession. I worked on a fairground, selling tickets for a gambling machine. I met a girl with whom I carried on an affair for the rest of the year. It was my first sexual experience, and it contributed to the tremendously optimistic state of mind that I experienced all that year. I took a building job that involved wheeling a thousand barrow loads of concrete a day up an inclined plank and along a trench to a half-finished building. After a week I handed in my notice and took a job in some government scheme for training farm labourers. For the rest of that summer, I worked on various farms in Leicestershire, learning to milk cows — electrically and by hand — make hay, shovel cow dung into barrows, harness and unharness horses, and dislike the English countryside intensely. Luckily, my dislike did not survive my period as a farm hand.

I had ceased to read Eliot; I even gave away all his works, alleging that he was 'morbid' and 'anti-life.' Instead, I carried Synge around with me, and read Herrick, Rabelais, Boccaccio, Blake — and, of course, Shaw. I preferred Joyce's Buck Mulligan to Stephen Dedalus. My interest in comparative religion also developed, and I read Buddhist and Hindu texts for the first time. My first reading of the *Bhagavad-Gita* was so important to me that I had my copy bound in leather and carried it around with me wherever I went. The idea of entering a monastery also became increasingly attractive. Not necessarily a Christian monastery — I did not count myself a Christian, in the sense of believing in redemption by Christ. Rather, the monastery symbolised serenity and time for meditation. Yeats's 'storm-beaten old watch-tower' would have done as well. My most acute problem, I felt, was to discover a means of escaping work, escaping the complications of having to find food and drink and a change of clothes. I started instruction in Catholicism, feeling that to become a Catholic would be the first step toward a monastery. But what I read of the strenuous life in monasteries discouraged me. My final disqualification, of course, was my failure to see any need for Christ. The need for God I could understand, and the need for a religion; I could even sympathise with devotees like Suso or St. Francis, who wove fantasies around the cross, the nails, and all the other traditional symbols. But ultimately I could not accept the need for redemption by a Saviour. To pin down the idea of salvation to one point in space and time seemed a naïve kind of anthropomorphism, like portraying Lao-tse's Unchanging with a beard and white hair.

The solution seemed simpler. As an adolescent, I had been puzzled and made wretched by a feeling that sudden moods of vision and insight — what Wordsworth calls 'the glory and the freshness of a dream' — could not be retained or recalled at will. The Buddhist and Hindu scriptures prescribed simple disciplines for retaining them. It was a short step from there to deciding that most men lead such dull and second-rate lives because the concept of a spiritual and intellectual discipline is so foreign to them. Even the men who talk about the need for discipline never practice it; at any rate, this was what I felt at the time.

By the time I had been back in civilian life for six months, I had begun to see my personal problems more clearly. Previously, my chief enemy had been boredom. I thought I had found an answer when I left the R.A.F. Hitchhiking into London from Wendover one day, lines from Rupert Brooke running in my head:

> Thank God, that's done! and I'll take the road,
> Quit of my youth and you,
> The Roman road to Wendover
> By Tring and Lilley Hoo,
> As a free man may do. . . .[6]

it had suddenly seemed that the answer was to keep on the move: never to stay anywhere long enough to get bored.* I felt that

---

* After writing this, I was interested to find a passage in Nietzsche's Morgenröte that expresses precisely the same attitude: 'I will rather emigrate and try to become master of fresh countries and, above all, of myself, changing my abode as often as any danger of slavery threatens me; not avoid adventure and war, and be prepared for death if the worst happens — but no more of this indecent serfdom, this irritation, malice and rebelliousness.'

nothing counted except to achieve the intensity of a visionary, and that the only way to do this was to care more about it than anything else; to be willing to sacrifice everything to the ideal.

It did not work out. Wandering entailed too much 'thought for the morrow'; it made life a perpetual anxiety. In its way, it was as bad as being drained of one's vitality in an office job. I wanted to be allowed to meditate and write; but wandering gave me no time or freedom to meditate, while working at a 'regular job' destroyed the inclination. The alternatives were equally poisonous. By the end of the summer, I had come to realise that the intolerable problem of subsistence was still unsolved. Of only one thing I was certain: it was no use staying at home and hoping. My will had to be constantly stimulated by new challenges.

In September 1950 I decided to go to France. It was not that I wanted to write in a garret on the Left Bank, or seek Murger's *vie de bohème* off the rue du Bac. My desire to write had almost died out, and I felt that intellect was a disease keeping me away from life. I was not sure what I hoped to find in France, but any movement was better than sitting still in Leicester. I set off to hitchhike to Dover, working for a week near Canterbury picking hops, and then for a fortnight near Dover, picking potatoes. During this second job, the farmer allowed me to sleep in an old cottage that he used for storing the potatoes; I slept in an upstairs room, settling myself in the corner of the floor that looked soundest. Most of the floorboards were missing in the rest of the room; I always installed myself before dark, and then refrained from moving in case I fell through into the cellar. At the end of the fortnight, I crossed to France.

Altogether, the two months I spent there confirmed my feeling that a life without security is dreary and demoralising. In Paris I lived for a time in the 'Akademia' of Raymond Duncan, brother of the dancer Isadora. He was a naïvely egotistic old American who printed his own Whitmanesque poems on a printing press that only had capital letters and issued a weekly newspaper called *New-Paris-York*, written entirely by himself in bad French. His long grey hair was fastened by a band around his forehead and he wore a toga and sandals. He preached a philosophy which he called 'actionalism,' which was a blend of Rousseauism and the commonsense practical beliefs of a self-made man who had once been a millionaire. He supported himself — like some mediaeval craftsman — by making things with his hands, and taught his 'disciples' (of whom I was enrolled as one) to do the same. He preached that a poet would be a better poet for being able to mend a lavatory cistern or dig a trench with a pick. For a few weeks I helped him to print his newspaper, and in exchange was given three vegetarian meals a day and a couch to sleep on (I had my own blankets). But he soon found me out — that the three meals a day meant more to me than the lectures which he delivered twice a week to selected audiences. He gave me a stiff dressing down, in which he told me that I was an adventurer and an impostor, and gave me twenty-four hours to find new lodgings. I was not resentful; it was true that my own approach had nothing in common with the diluted Platonism that he preached. When I had first come to the 'Akademia' I had hoped to interest Duncan in my own attitude; but it was useless. He was good-natured and easygoing, but old; too old to be interested in me; too old even to talk to me for more than a few minutes at a time. So, after a while, his hospitality began to weigh on my conscience, and the summary dismissal brought an element of relief.

I left for Strasbourg, where I had a pen friend with whom I had corresponded since I was fourteen. But my luck was no better there. Since I had last seen him, he had joined the Communist Party. In England, three years before, he had struck me as a fool. In three years, his Marxism had become an impregnable armour, and my own religious attitude had developed correspondingly. At first there was some talk of my staying in Strasbourg and working for his father — a rag merchant — but as our discussions became more heated and less friendly, this idea was dropped. Within a fortnight we could barely tolerate one another. One day, after a particularly sharp clash of our views, I went to the British consulate and borrowed enough money to return to England. Late the next day, I was back in Leicester. It was a few weeks before Christmas.

My three months' wandering, considered in retrospect, had given me a pleasant sensation of liberty, but I realised that none of my problems had been solved, and that I would never discover freedom by becoming a tramp. During the previous summer, when I had worked on farms, I had thought of certain poems of Synge, or certain pages in Hemingway — the El Sordo episode, for instance —

and had been possessed by an imaginative vision of freedom — a feeling that I could escape the prison of my own personality in the impersonality of other places, in the 'otherness' of the world. It was a romantic vision — it owed something to those last pages of *Ulysses*, where Mrs. Bloom suddenly becomes the earth spinning around the sun, and speaks of the 'flowers on her breast' crushed by her lovers. And it was hardly to be realised by crossing to France without money. But at least I had learnt that freedom could be discovered in retrospect, by 'recollecting in tranquillity' the episodes which had seemed so uninspiring at the time — such as reading the *Phaedo* while sitting at the roadside near Vitry-le-François, waiting for a lift. For a few weeks, I felt like a visitor in Leicester, and the place no longer oppressed me.

But not for long. I needed a job, and my father gave me a long lecture about wasting my time on manual labour; in his eyes, my resignation from the Civil Service was the most foolish act of my life. In deference to him, I again took an office job — this time in a large engineering works in Leicester. The pay was miserable, and after a few days, I began to hate the job as I have always hated work. Being in Leicester, working in a regular job, made me feel aimless, and robbed me of my sense of purpose. I have no doubt that I would have drifted back into my affair with the girl I had known previously, but while I was abroad she had thrown me over, and I was disgusted to find how much it hurt. However, I began to flirt with the works nurse, a slim, shy girl, ten years my senior, and I felt pleased at the way in which I appeared to have mastered my emotions.

The job followed the familiar pattern. The first few days there — the days I dreaded most — passed unexpectedly easily. Everything was new, and the office staff were pleasant. Part of my job involved walking around the works — they covered an enormous area — and delivering invoices to various departments. I liked to watch the red-hot metal being pounded by the steam hammer, or see long bars of it being cut into chunks. I especially liked watching it after dusk, when the great doors of the shop stood open, and the red glow made the half-naked men seem beautiful. In the shop where the white-hot metal was poured into moulds, it was necessary to stand near the doors, in case the splashes burnt holes in my clothes.

At the time, I was reading a great deal of Blake — I had only discovered him six months before, through reading Joyce Cary's *The
Horse's Mouth* — and the atmosphere of the Prophetic Books was
well suited to that of the engineering works, for they were also full
of talk of molten metal and hammers ringing on iron. I carried a
copy of Blake with me all the time, and repeated it to myself as I
walked around the works:

> For every Space larger than a red Globule of Man's blood
> Is visionary, and is created by the Hammer of Los:
> And every Space smaller than a Globule of Man's blood opens
> Into Eternity of which this vegetable Earth is but a shadow.[7]

It snowed a lot that December. Some evenings, walking around
the works, picking my way over girders covered with powdered
snow, moving towards the white glow that came from the welding
shops, the world would suddenly seem altogether good, no longer
alien, and my feeling of self-contempt would vanish.

All the same, I began to hate the job. As soon as I grew used to it,
I began to work automatically. I fought hard against this process.
I would spend the evening reading poetry, or writing, and would
determine that with sufficient mental effort I could stop myself from
growing bored and indifferent at work the next day. But the moment I stepped through the office door in the morning, the familiar
smell and appearance would switch on the automatic pilot which
controlled my actions. The longer I stayed in the job the more
impossible it became. Moments of insight became less frequent than
ever. Repetition makes one into a machine, and all responses become
automatic. But the important part of man — the creative part — is
the part that is spontaneous. To escape the feeling of being a machine — to try to jar my being out of its automatic responses — I
tried all kinds of exercise: getting up an hour earlier in the morning,
and going for long runs in running shorts and tennis shoes; sleeping
on the floor rather than in bed; sitting up in my bedroom half the
night, cross-legged, trying to concentrate until I had broken the
feeling of being merely another 'social animal'; staying out until
three o'clock in the morning and running all the way home. But the
longer I stayed in the job, the harder it became to escape the intoler-

able sense of being what society wished to make me, merely another human being in the human anthill.

Yet this problem of automatism is the problem of life itself. In childhood we respond freshly to everything, and nothing is automatic, but as we get older, life becomes more complex, and a part of our activities has to be handed over to the 'automatic pilot.' At first, new experiences stimulate us; after a while, no experience is new; it is intercepted by the automatic pilot. I am convinced that people die because they cease to want to live; what purpose is there in living when nothing challenges or stimulates us any longer, when everything is done by the automatic pilot? In my early teens, I had a terrible suspicion that wisdom meant becoming old and losing the desire to live; that the only way to live for a long time was to be so foolish that all sorts of trivial issues continued to excite one into old age, as an imbecile is excited by a child's playthings. It was not until I was eighteen, and read the *Bhagavad-Gita*, that this suspicion finally loosened its hold on me, and I recognised that the visionary disciplines himself to see the world always as if he had only just seen it for the first time.

At all events, the office job beat me. No amount of discipline could prevent me from feeling abysmally depressed within a minute of entering the office. Even my friendship with the nurse did not compensate for it; nor did the novel that I had begun to write, situated in Strasbourg and heavily indebted to Hemingway, nor the play inspired by Granville-Barker's *The Secret Life*, nor the half-dozen other literary projects I had started work on at this time. I stuck the job until shortly after Christmas and then gave in my notice. I visited the Leicester Corporation offices and got myself another navvying job, which involved travelling miles to work every morning, and then working knee-deep in mud, digging trenches. I had hoped the hardship would stimulate me, but within a day or two I disliked navvying as much as I had disliked the office. It was free time that I wanted. One day I suddenly conceived the idea of asking the Leicester Corporation whether they would object if I worked for only three days a week. It seemed a brilliant idea to me; it would have meant foregoing pocket money, but the amount of free time I should create for myself would more than compensate. At first, the Corporation agreed; then they changed their

minds, pointing out that the other men would object. In fury and
disgust, I gave the job up and took another in a chemical factory.

I had got into the habit of reciting poetry as I worked. I liked the
poetry of Synge, and that poem of Gogarty's that begins:

> I will live in Ringsend
> With a red-headed whore. . . .

It expressed my new anti-intellectual attitude. I liked also to
repeat the war poems of Wilfred Owen, especially 'Exposure' and
'Futility.' The active physical torment in the poems was a relief to
my feeling of being stifled in trivialities. For the same reason, I
looked at the painting of Van Gogh and read all I could find on his
life, and read Nijinsky's *Diary* continually. The concept of the
Outsider first began to form in my mind, and I started to use the
word in my journals. I had to concentrate on the idea of torment
and horror to obtain release from my sense of futility and pettiness.

But soon fresh complications were to alter my life completely.
It now becomes impossible to tell the story fully, for it ceases to be
my own story alone, and becomes that of myself and my wife — I
married in the June of that year. My marriage — to the nurse —
brought no answer to the problems; in fact, only intensified them,
since I was now forced to support a wife — and later a son — as well
as myself. There would be no point in telling of this marriage in
detail. For eighteen months I worked in factories in London, and
we moved from home to home with dismal regularity. The new
feeling of security, of having a wife and a home, stimulated me to
write, and I spent all my free time writing a novel about two Outsiders, one based on Nietzsche, and the other on Jack the Ripper.
At the end of eighteen months, we separated 'temporarily' while I
looked for another home for us; but the separation lengthened,
while I spent more time writing my novel and a play than looking
for rooms. I was working at this time as a porter in a hospital in
Fulham. Finally, I got sick of the portering job — which involved,
mostly, wheeling live patients to the wards and dead ones to the
mortuary — and went to Paris again. But the problem of working
for a living was not solved until the following year, when I had
returned to London. In a few months I went through a series of

jobs rapidly — a laundry, two office jobs (both firms sacked me), a plastic factory and a Lyons Corner House. Then, one day, the idea came to me that I was earning far more money than I strictly needed to keep alive. I earned £5 or £6 a week. Of this, 30s. was spent in rent, £2 or so on food, and the rest was sent to my wife, or spent on books and bus fares. I reasoned that of these, food is the only absolute necessity. One can buy a tent for 30s., and provide a roof over one's head. And a bicycle can make bus fares unnecessary. The tent idea excited me. It seemed a perfect solution — for summer, at all events. So I gave up my rooms (or rather, my landlady threw me out after a disagreement) and bought a tent. I did not give up work immediately: I was making a great deal of money by working overtime in a plastic factory in Whetstone. But I saved rent by setting up my tent at nights on a golf links opposite the factory. After a while, I realised that to put up a tent and take it down every day was an unnecessary labour. A waterproof sleeping bag would serve as well. So I bought one, together with an eiderdown sleeping bag, an immense army frame rucksack for my belongings, and a bicycle with a carrier on the back. In a few weeks, I had saved enough money to leave work with a certainty of not having to return for a few months provided my expenditure did not exceed £2 a week. I moved my quarters from the golf links to Hampstead Heath, and cycled down to the British Museum every day, to work from nine till five. I was making a determined effort to reduce some of the immense manuscript of my Jack the Ripper novel to publishable form. Mr. Angus Wilson, who at that time was an official in the Reading Room, noticed me writing furiously, and offered to read the manuscript when it was completed, and, if he liked it, to submit it to his publisher.

But sleeping out was a nerve-racking business. I did not dare to go onto the Heath until after midnight; there were too many young lovers about. The police patrolled the Heath, but they stuck to the paths and only occasionally flashed a powerful torch around. I sometimes slept till ten (the Heath is a surprisingly quiet place on weekday mornings), and was often wakened by someone's dog sniffing at my face, or voices in the distance. Usually, I had breakfast at a busman's café at the bottom of Haverstock Hill: they did a remarkably cheap slice of bread and dripping and an enormous mug of tea for 2½d. The day in the Museum usually went by too quickly; but the evenings were the difficult time. After eight o'clock all the libraries were closed; there was nowhere where one could spend a few hours in warmth and quiet until midnight. A girl whom I had met in Leicester the previous Christmas was also in London at the time. She kept all my books for me, and sometimes entertained me in the evening; but it was too much to expect her to have to put up with me every evening. Her help and sympathy were invaluable; but all the same, I always felt exhausted and ill at ease as I cycled around London with my sleeping bags rolled up on the back; it was a strange sensation, having nowhere to go, nowhere to retire to at nights, nowhere to spend the evening reading. Besides, the girl's landladies objected if I turned up too often; they left her little notes telling her not to let me use the bathroom, and that I had to be out by ten o'clock.

Occasionally during that summer I ran out of cash. Then I had to take a job for a few weeks: one in Lyons, one in a dairy at Chiswick. I continued writing the book well into the autumn. In early November the weather became so bad that I was finally driven indoors. I took a room at New Cross, and another job in Lyons. At this time I was seeing a great deal of another young writer, Stuart Holroyd, whom I had met the previous year. He talked vaguely of writing a critical book, and advised me to do the same; but I was too busy at the time, trying to finish the first part of my novel (it was to be in three short parts). I had heard a rumour that Angus Wilson intended leaving the Museum, and I wanted to be able to hand him the typewritten manuscript before he left. At Christmas that year I worked at the post office in St.-Martin's-le-Grand, sorting Christmas mail; by doing overtime, I made enough money to buy a secondhand typewriter. Over Christmas, alone in London, I finally completed the first part of the novel, and immediately settled down to typing it. A week later, lack of money made it necessary to find another job. There were long queues in the labour exchange, and only a few unskilled labouring jobs available. I accepted the first one they offered me — as I usually do — and the next day started to work in a laundry in Deptford. The job was so peculiarly detestable, and the conditions so appalling, that I overcame my usual laziness and cycled into London every day, trying to find evening work in a coffee bar. The laundry became completely intolerable to me when one day my journal was stolen out of my pocket. It had contained the entries of over a year past, and its loss enraged me. But the day after this happened, I found a job in a newly opened coffee bar in the Haymarket; I was the washer-up.

Compared with the laundry, conditions there were delightful. The kitchen was new and shiny and chromium-plated, and the food was unlimited and very good. I worked every evening from five-thirty till midnight, and had the day free to write. I finished typing the first part of the novel in a burst of energy, and handed it to Angus Wilson on the day he left the Museum. And then, suddenly, I felt a little lost. For many years, the novel had occupied my thoughts. Suddenly, it had gone out of my hands. If Angus found it bad, I would begin all over again. In the meantime, there was no point in going on with it. I began to wonder what I should do to occupy my days in the Reading Room.

It was at this point that Stuart Holroyd showed me the opening chapters of his *Emergence from Chaos*. Suddenly, I made a decision. I too would write a critical book — a credo. I would dash it off quickly, and then get back to the novel. In half an hour, one morning, I sketched out the plan of a book, to be called *The Outsider in Literature*. It would be a study in various types of 'obsessed men.' I immediately jotted down a list of the type of men who would interest me. Some immediately came to mind: Van Gogh, T. E. Lawrence, George Fox, Boehme, Joyce, Nijinsky (I had written a long essay on Nijinsky several years before, which I had sent to Madame Nijinsky. She had replied kindly to a preliminary letter of mine, but never acknowledged the essay.) There were obviously many different types of Outsider. Some were men of action, some were the very reverse. So there would be a chapter on Oblomov and Hamlet and Hesse's Steppenwolf and the Great Gatsby. These would be classified together as 'weak Outsiders.' Then there would be a chapter on Goethe's Faust, Mann's Doctor Faustus, and Dostoevsky's Ivan Karamazov, from whom Mann drew in his own scene between Leverkühn and the Devil. A great deal of the book would also be devoted to religious figures: Boehme, Law, Fox, Newman, Luther, Wycliffe — all rebels against their time. The Outsider shades off one way into the weakling — the Hamlet — and the other way into the Rebel. Then there were the French Existentialists, and Heidegger and Jaspers — and of course, Kierkegaard — and these pointed to a tie-up with Nietzsche, while the study of pessimism would link up with Schopenhauer and Spengler. As I jotted down names, and pushed them around to try to find some logical order for them all, I realised with growing despair that there was no order that would embrace *all of them* — or at least, if there were, the book would be so vast that it would involve ten years' work. There was no point in being overwhelmed by it and trying to see it as a whole before I began it. I had been doing that with the novel for years, and here, with over half a million words written, had only a hundred pages in their final form. I decided to begin the book that afternoon in the Museum. On my way down there, I remembered a volume which I had read about years before in the Everyman edition of *Le Feu* — Barbusse's *L'Enfer*. That would make a perfect starting point: the man who looks at life through a hole in his wall. In the Museum, I got the book and settled down to read it. In two hours I had finished it. It was within half an hour of closing time. Hastily, I looked up a striking sentence which I had noticed and copied it on to a sheet of paper: 'In the air, on top of a tram, a girl is sitting. . . .' I copied on hastily until the bell rang for closing time. The next morning, I wrote on to the end of my analysis of Barbusse, and without hesitation, plunged into H. G. Wells's *Mind at the End of Its Tether* (of which I had had a copy since I was sixteen).

Once I actually started, I wrote quickly. I had written as far as the Lawrence chapter before I stopped for breath. I then reread my manuscript, and decided that it began too abruptly and proceeded too fast. I wrote an introduction, which began by quoting T. E. Hulme's prophecy of the decay of humanism, and stating that this book was to be an attack on humanism and an attempt to base the religious attitude on reasonable foundations. Hulme had promised to write a defence of his religious attitude, but had been killed in the war. I stated my intention of attempting to write the book that Hulme had never written; my method would not be philosophical, but psychological; not an attempt to prove the existence of God, but a search for meaning in human life.

At about this time I was offered a daytime job that involved no more than sitting at a desk and answering a telephone if it rang. It seldom rang more than twice a day; and I sat there for four hours a day, writing furiously and being paid 3s. an hour for writing. In this early stage, the book was called *The Pain Threshold*. One day, I installed my typewriter in the office and typed the three chapters that I had written. When I had typed the Introduction (which did not appear in the published version) I sent it to a publisher. To my delight, he replied within twenty-four hours, expressing interest. I sent him the three chapters as soon as they were typed. This time, he took longer but finally wrote to say that he would definitely publish the book. I was delighted, but it was no time to give way to the pleasure of having been 'accepted.' I suspected that I could not finish the book as well as I had begun it, and that the publisher would change his mind when he read it as a whole. Now I had started typing the book, I became too lazy to write it first and type later, and began to use a typewriter all the time. Three months later it was finished. The advance which I received enabled me, for the first time in my life, to give up work and do nothing but write.

By this time Angus Wilson had returned the novel, with the comment: 'I like it. Go on and finish it.' But I found creative work appallingly difficult after the easy writing of the critical book. The writing of *The Pain Threshold* had not made the novel any easier; every section seemed to need a dozen rewrites. I struggled on slowly, and managed to finish it in six months. But having finished it, I could hardly bear to reread it, and decided to start from the beginning again. *The Pain Threshold* was due out in a month, and I had tentatively suggested calling it *The Outsider* (tentatively, because I knew of two other books with the same title — Camus's and Richard Wright's). Reading the proofs of *The Outsider* had made me terribly dissatisfied with it: I hadn't managed to put in half as many things as I wanted, or to pursue half as many lines of thought. It needed, I realised, the same care and patience as the novel. Besides, I had begun to read Arnold Toynbee's *Study of History* and a great deal more of Whitehead, and I saw that the argument could be developed much further.

The success of the book winded me, and made me more certain than ever that it should have been twice as long and far more carefully planned. I had believed passionately in the book, and had never doubted its importance as I wrote it. But it was intended as essentially a preliminary step towards a far bigger statement. After the delight of the first good reviews, and the knowledge that new impressions were being called for, I became aware of what had happened to the book itself. I was congratulated by critics on having started a craze, on inventing a new parlour game to replace Nancy Mitford's 'U and Non-U,' called 'Outsider or Insider?' The whirl and publicity went on for months, and soon I realised that I had become a stranger to my own book. The people in it, who for years had seemed to live with me, had suddenly become alien; a painting by Van Gogh no longer moved me; Nijinsky's *Diary* stayed on my shelf unread. It was interesting to hear people discussing me — as when a child falls into a doze at a party, and hears the grownups talking about him — but only because it was like seeing myself in distorting mirrors. Besides, after a while, people began attacking the book, and declaring that it had all been a mistake, and that I was not a 'promising young writer' after all.

No doubt they were right. Although I have always used writing as a medium to clarify my thoughts, I have never thought of myself as primarily a writer. Writing is an instrument of my main purpose, and that purpose is my own business and no one else's. I am convinced, like my 'Outsider,' that all men who have ever lived have been failures. As a child, I thought of every adult I met: *I* shan't waste my life like that. This problem is the impetus that drives my living, and my writing is merely one discipline for solving it. The answer seems to lie in achieving a certain state of mind called 'vision'; and above all other things I prefer to study the evidence that men have left of their moments of vision: Nietzsche's glimpse on the hilltop, Van Gogh's Green Cornfield, Pascal's *Memorial*, Boehme's 'pewter dish,' the moment of great insight in which the purpose of all life is seen. Ultimately, this is the only thing worth achieving. Yeats called life 'a vast preparation for something that never happens,' and yet one minute of such vision could turn all preparation into achievement.

These visions and the men who saw them occupy all my time and attention. To facilitate my own study of them, I wrote about them more or less consecutively in *The Outsider* (as I have been writing about them haphazardly for years in my journals). For myself, *The Outsider* and the present book are a sort of extension of my journals, a part of my working notes. I am grateful that their publication has made me enough money to allow me to continue to work on for a few more years; but their publication was not an essential part of my purpose. I am not necessarily a writer. The moment writing ceases to be a convenient discipline for subduing my stupidity and laziness, I shall give it up and turn to some more practical form. I wish this to be understood because I find that being regarded as a 'promising young writer,' or attacked as a charlatan or a woolly-minded freak, tends to destroy my certainty of purpose. The prospect of spending my life trying to make myself worthy of a few pages in *The Cambridge History of English Literature* seems to me a particularly dreary kind of treadmill. I see now that I must try to escape the subtle falsifications of my aims that the success of *The Outsider* caused. I must retrace my steps to the period before it was published, and begin working again from there. In those days, I had a plan for drafting a vast critical credo that should define the area of my interest, to be followed by a series of novels and plays in which the Outsider idea would be explored in all its existentialist implications. But the idea of writing books merely because I am now known as a 'writer' is repellent to me. Temperamentally, my sympathy is still with Novalis and Jean Paul Sartre and other deniers of the daylight, and to know that anything is expected and demanded of me is enough to make me detest it.

A few words should be said about the plan of this book. It has given me far more trouble to write than *The Outsider*, for the subject is far more complex. In the first chapter, I have tried to present the outline of *The Outsider* in a concentrated form, and to emphasise that what I mean by existentialism covers a broader field than what Kierkegaard or Heidegger or Sartre mean by it; my existentialism is closer to Goethe's idea of *Bildung*. I have tried to underline this by illustrating my thesis with analyses of Rilke, Rimbaud and Scott Fitzgerald; the last because he is, in all essentials, a man of the twentieth century.

In the second chapter, the central theme of this book appears for the first time: the decline of Western civilisation. The chapter is devoted to analyses of Spengler and Toynbee.

The second part of the book swings back to the problem of the Outsider, and his attempt to become an Insider by accepting a religious solution: Boehme, Swedenborg, Pascal, Ferrar, Law, Newman, Kierkegaard and Shaw are all examined and their solutions scrutinised. Shaw is deliberately included in the list of 'religious Outsiders' to emphasise that he is not quite the lone phenomenon that modern critics seem to believe, and to demonstrate his affinities with other anti-materialist thinkers since the sixteenth century.

In the final chapter of this book, the two lines of thought — the religious and the historical — converge in a consideration of the thought of two major twentieth-century philosophers — Ludwig Wittgenstein and Alfred North Whitehead, and the paradox that Wittgenstein was an Outsider in his life but not in his philosophy, while Whitehead led an Insider's life and yet created the only uniquely English brand of Outsider philosophy.

This book is still not a final solution of the problems that preoccupy me — how could it be? Rather, it is the opening of a new line of thought that increases the problems I have already raised in *The Outsider*. But at least I have tried to answer the accusation that the Outsider concept is just an intellectual fad, with no real relevance to the problems of the world in the twentieth century. The conclusions are pessimistic, as far as Western civilisation is concerned. And since the world is now a smaller place, where all civilisations are interwoven, it is difficult not to feel that this pessimism implicates the whole human race. Logically, this conclusion is difficult to avoid. Yet my own temperament has a vein of optimism that is not crushed by these reflections, although I am hard put to it to say why. Perhaps I have simply failed to grasp my own conclusions.

In any case, my business is clear: to present my vision as capably as I can, and then to carry my sense of urgency back into my own personal life. There is a limit beyond which discursive thought cannot go, and for the moment, I have reached my own limit.

PART
ONE

CHAPTER ONE

THE ANATOMY
OF IMAGINATION

THERE IS A CASE in Taylor's *Medical Jurisprudence* of a man who committed suicide by burning himself to death. He lay on a straw mattress, and lit a candle underneath. Periodically, he got off the mattress, and noted down his sensations on a sheet of paper on the bedside table. In the morning, when his charred body was discovered on the completely burnt mattress, the note was found. He wanted, he explained, to prove once and for all that suicides are not necessarily cowards. He had chosen this method to demonstrate it.

This is the image of the Outsider: a man whose passion for observation and experiment does not stop, even when it is a question of experimenting with his own death.

In Granville-Barker's *The Secret Life*, Strowde had quoted the words of Elijah: 'O Lord, take away my life, for I am not better than my fathers.' In that sentence is summarised what is, for the Outsider, the whole tragedy of living. Men come and go, and society changes; civilisations rise and fall, but men always remain as stupid. In a chorus of *The Rock*, Eliot asks:

Where is the Life we have lost in living? [1]

But for the Outsider, all men lose their lives in living them. All men are failures.

In *The Outsider*, I treated that consciousness of failure, of loss. Seven chapters of the book aimed at presenting and documenting, as fully as possible, the concept of the futility of human life, and also at trying to pinpoint the Outsider's occasional sense of a *way out* of the futility. In the two final chapters of the book, I tried to give a sketch of certain positive attempts to solve the problems of the Outsider. These attempts pointed to a religious solution, but one which was only outlined. In the present book, I hope to present such a solution more fully.

The Outsider, then, is a man who is haunted by a sense of the futility of life. Most of the modern Outsiders I dealt with felt that there was no way out of this impasse. But to some degree, a closer examination showed that this attitude is due to the peculiar conditions of our civilisation. Spiritual standards have almost ceased to exist, and Freud and Karl Marx have done a thorough job of convincing us that all men are much the same, subject to the same kind of psychological and economic pressures. If the modern Outsider finds the world an unrelieved prospect of futility, it is because his training and conditioning make it difficult for him to see any meaning in the notion of *increased intensity of mind*. And this is the key to all religion.

Like *The Outsider*, this book will be a case book. But most of the emphasis will no longer be on the sense of misery and futility. In *The Outsider*, a formula was arrived at: The Outsider's salvation lies in extremes. One could rephrase that: The Outsider only ceases to be an Outsider when he becomes *possessed*, when he becomes fanatically obsessed by the need to escape.

The Outsider could be compared to a man who has been hypnotised, and lowered into a cage full of apes. The hypnosis prevents him from understanding why he finds the apes disgusting and stupid. He only knows that he detests them. He believes he is an ape too. His solution lies in deliberately fighting the hypnosis, in telling himself: I am not an ape; I must be something more than an ape. A difficult matter if his hypnosis — his conditioning as an ape — inclines him to give up the struggle and become 'a member of the simian race' and a good citizen of the ape community.

The Outsider's despair, in fact, comes from his vision of the vast sea of mediocrity that makes up humankind, and his rebellion at the idea of belonging to it. The perfect example of this attitude is in Swift, whose loathing of human beings has frequently been called 'pathological,' insane, psychotic — although to any Outsider, it looks reasonable and normal enough. W. B. Yeats, who had profound insight into Swift (as his play *The Words Upon the Window-Pane* proves),* has characterised him in two lines:

> Swift beating on his breast in sibylline frenzy blind
> Because the heart in his blood-sodden breast has dragged him down
> into mankind [2]

When the Outsider is in his earliest stages — when he does not know himself or understand why he is 'out of harmony' with the rest of humankind — his hatred for men and the world makes him an unbalanced misfit, a man full of spite and envy, neurotic, cowardly, shrinking and wincing. His salvation depends upon the achievement of self-understanding, self-knowledge. It is only when he begins to find himself that he realises that his hatred is perfectly justified: a *healthy reaction* to a world of sick half-men.

But now there is an important new development, which I barely touched on in *The Outsider*. It can best be explained, perhaps, by referring to Peter Keegan, the Outsider priest in *John Bull's Other Island*. In this play, it will be remembered, Tom Broadbent, a typical bourgeois Englishman, goes to Rosscullen, in the west of Ireland, to take over some property from a landlord who cannot pay off the mortgage. He goes into a country of early-stage Outsiders, and Shaw's evocation of them is superb; Doyle, Broadbent's Irish partner, explains:

---

* This one-act play, which I have always considered to be Yeats's most powerful dramatic work, is about a seance in Dublin, in which the spirits of Stella, Vanessa and the Dean himself speak through the medium's mouth. Vanessa pleads with Swift to marry her and produce children; Swift protests that he believes he has inherited insanity, and has no wish to pass it on to a child. When Vanessa denies it, Swift cries: 'What do I care if it be healthy? . . . Am I to add another to the healthy rascaldom and knavery of the world?' And his total world-rejection is brought out by the last line of the play: Swift's: 'Perish the day on which I was born!'

Here [in England] if the life is dull, you can be dull too, and no great harm done. (*Going off into a passionate dream*) But your wits cant thicken in that soft moist air, on those white springy roads, in those misty rushes and brown bogs, on those hillsides of granite rocks and magenta heather. Youve no such colors in the sky, no such lure in the distances, no such sadness in the evenings. Oh, the dreaming! the dreaming! the torturing, heart-scalding, never satisfying dreaming, dreaming, dreaming, dreaming! (*Savagely*) No debauchery that ever coarsened and brutalised an Englishman can take the worth and the usefulness out of him like. that dreaming. An Irishman's imagination never lets him alone, never convinces him, never satisfies him; but it makes him that he cant face reality nor deal with it nor handle it nor conquer it: he can only sneer at them that do. . . . It's all dreaming, all imagination. He cant be religious. The inspired Churchman that teaches him the sanctity of life and the importance of conduct is sent away empty; while the poor village priest that gives him a miracle or a sentimental story of a saint, has cathedrals built for him out of the pennies of the poor. He cant be intelligently political; he dreams of what the Shan Van Vocht said in ninety eight. . . . It saves thinking. It saves working. It saves everything except imagination, imagination, imagination; and imagination's such a torture that you cant bear it without whisky. (*With fierce shivering self-contempt*) At last you get that you can bear nothing real at all: youd rather starve than cook a meal; youd rather go shabby and dirty than set your mind to take care of your clothes and wash yourself; you nag and squabble at home because your wife isnt an angel, and she despises you because youre not a hero; and you hate the whole lot around you, because theyre only poor slovenly useless devils like yourself. . . .[3]

This, it will be seen at once, is a perfect characterisation of the Outsider as I described him in the early chapters of that book: the Barbusse Outsider, the Axel: the whole subject of Goncharov's *Oblomov* (the Russian Hamlet who just cannot bring himself to do anything), and of all the work of Samuel Beckett from *Malone* (Beckett's *Oblomov*) to *En Attendant Godot*. (There is also, perhaps, an element of hitting-out at Yeats in this passage: Yeats of *The*

Land of Heart's Desire and the dreamy fairyland of the early poems. Shaw wrote the play originally for the Abbey theatre.)

In Rosscullen, Broadbent meets Peter Keegan, the strange, mystical priest, who spends his evenings dreaming by the Round Tower, and the conflict between their characters becomes, perhaps, the centre of the play. Keegan is generally supposed to be mad: the legend being that he once confessed a 'black heathen' on his death-bed, and that when the devil came for the heathen's soul, he took off Keegan's head and turned it round three times before putting it on again; and that Keegan's head has been turned ever since! In the scene in which Keegan and Broadbent meet for the first time, Doyle asks Keegan the true version of this legend. Keegan tells him:

> . . . I heard that a black man was dying, and that the people were afraid to go near him. When I went to the place I found an elderly Hindoo, who told me one of those tales of unmerited misfortune, of cruel ill luck, of relentless persecution by destiny, which sometimes wither the commonplaces of consolation on the lips of a priest. But this man did not complain of his misfortunes. They were brought upon him, he said, by sins committed in a former existence. Then, without a word of comfort from me, he died with a clear-eyed resignation that my most earnest exhortations have rarely produced in a Christian, and left me sitting there by his bedside with the mystery of this world suddenly revealed to me.
>
> BROADBENT: That is a remarkable tribute to the liberty of conscience enjoyed by the subjects of our Indian Empire.
>
> LARRY: No doubt; but may we venture to ask what is the mystery of this world?
>
> KEEGAN: This world, sir, is very clearly a place of torment and penance, a place where the fool flourishes and the good and wise are hated and persecuted, a place where men and women torture one another in the name of love; where children are scourged and enslaved in the name of parental duty and education; where the weak in body are poisoned and mutilated in the name of healing, and the weak in character are put to the horrible torture of imprisonment, not for hours but for years, in the name of justice. It is a place where the hardest toil is a welcome refuge from the

horror and tedium of pleasure, and where charity and good works are done only for hire to ransom the souls of the spoiler and the sybarite. Now, sir, there is only one place of horror and torment known to my religion; and that place is hell. Therefore it is plain to me that this earth of ours must be hell, and that we are all here, as the Indian revealed to me — perhaps he was sent to reveal it to me — to expiate crimes committed by us in a former existence. . . .

BROADBENT: Your idea is a very clever one, Mr. Keegan: really most brilliant. . . . But it seems to me . . . that you are overlooking the fact that of the evils you describe, some are absolutely necessary for the preservation of society, and others are encouraged only when the Tories are in office. . . . I find the world quite good enough for me: rather a jolly place, in fact.

KEEGAN (*Looking at him with quiet wonder*): You are satisfied?

BROADBENT: As a reasonable man, yes. I see no evils in the world — except, of course, natural evils — that cannot be remedied by freedom, self-government, and English institutions. I think so, not because I am an Englishman, but as a matter of common sense.

KEEGAN: You feel at home in the world, then?

BROADBENT: Of course. Dont you?

KEEGAN (*from the very depths of his nature*): No.

BROADBENT (*breezily*): Try phosphorus pills. I always take them when my brain is overworked. . . .[4]

This passage is supremely important in Shaw, because it so clearly defines the difference between the Insider's and the Outsider's positions. The Outsider was Shaw's lifelong preoccupation (as I shall try to show in a later chapter); in fact, the first use of the word 'Outsider' that I know (in the sense in which I use it) occurs in Shaw's preface to *Immaturity*. But most important is Keegan's doctrine of hell. Keegan's speech 'This world . . . is clearly a place of torment,' might have been placed in the mouth of Ivan Karamazov at the end of that terrible chapter in which he describes the torture and ill-treatment of children: *in fact, the belief that this world is hell is perfectly consistent with the Outsider's vision of it.* This was touched upon in *The Outsider*, where it frequently became apparent that the Outsider's vision of the world is a vision of torment, sordidness, misery, sudden death, and everlasting insecurity. (See, for example, Hemingway's works, and *La Nausée, Crime and Punishment*.) The Outsider's hatred of men, his contempt for 'the Life we have lost in living,' does not become *objective* until he realises that something is wrong *with the way all men live*. The ordinary businessman, the statesman, the professor, does not see man as a creature of possibilities. He sees other men as rather like himself — limited, narrow, but capable of minor achievements with more efficient business training, better social organisation, improved education. The Outsider, with his instinctive urge to become more-than-man (just as the hypnotised man wanted to become more-than-ape) feels the need to place man against some greater canvas than mere human beings — to see him in relation to his greatest spiritual possibilities. The Outsider's instincts, once he has got them disentangled from his misery and frustration, are the instincts of the spiritual explorer, the spiritual reformer.

Broadbent's vision is humanistic. He thinks in terms of education and liberalism — human progress through material prosperity. Keegan's is religious; he goes even further than the religious teachers who point out that it is a bad bargain to gain the world and lose your own soul; he claims that if you gained the world, you would only have gained hell.

It is true that his idea of hell is more like that of the Buddhist than the Christian. In the Buddhist doctrine, the penalty for sin and worldliness is to be reborn in a lower form of life — as an ape, for instance — and in this, the Buddhist shows a profound grasp of the reality of mental torment. Spiritual hell is to place a man of high abilities and great talent in a position where he will be frustrated and bored, denied self-expression. It is, in short, the Outsider's position in the world.

The idea of hell is fundamental to the Outsider's way of thinking. He lives in a world of apes, whom he detests. He is told that 'religion' consists in loving your neighbour as yourself, and in practising the virtues of patience and charity. The most the Outsider can say is that he dislikes his neighbour just a little more than he dislikes himself. Most human beings strike him as being so stupid that they might as well be dead; consequently, he has none of the 'respect for human life' that most religions enjoin. His credo is a doctrine of self-expression, and if self-expression means war and murder, he unhesitatingly prefers it to the doctrine of peace and goodwill towards men. By conventional standards, he is a dangerous and anti-social man who should be quietly exterminated for the good of society. This 'gospel of hell' is clearly expressed in William Blake's *Marriage of Heaven and Hell*, in such sayings as 'Drive your cart and your plow over the bones of the dead'; 'He who desires but acts not, breeds pestilence'; 'Sooner murder an infant in its cradle than nurse unacted desires.' Or, in a slightly different aspect, it can be seen in a parable like this, from Nietzsche's *Gay Science:*

A man holding a newly born child in his hands came to a saint. 'What should I do with the child?' he asked. 'It is wretched, deformed, and has not even enough of life to die.' 'Kill it,' cried the saint with a dreadful voice. 'Kill it, and then hold it in thy arms for three days and three nights to brand it on thy memory: thus wilt thou never again beget a child when it is not the time for thee to beget.' When the man had heard this, he went away disappointed, and many found fault with the saint because he had advised cruelty. . . . 'But is it not more cruel to let it live?' asked the saint.[5]

At first sight, in fact, it looks as if the Outsider's pessimistic vision leads direct to cruelty and anti-Christianity. Yet there is another aspect to this 'Outsider vision' of the universe: a profound awareness of misery and pain that is the very reverse of the ruthless concentration-camp mentality. It can be seen in Dostoevsky all the time, from *Poor Folk* to *The Brothers Karamazov*. On a first reading of Blake's Prophetic Books — especially the finest and most lyrical of them, *The Four Zoas* — the main impression the reader gets is of an enormous number of descriptions of misery and torment: passages like this are a commonplace:

The Spectre wept at his dire labours when from Ladles huge
He pour'd the molten iron round the limbs of Enitharmon.[6]

His personages are continually 'howling and wailing,' or 'writhing in torment'; the Prophetic Books are full of visions of winds shrieking through space, and red flames and smoke. Now it is evident that the motive underlying Blake's emphasis on pain is not sadism, but an Outsider's attempt *to underline the concept of hell.* He is simply striving for an intensification of consciousness through pain — the reaction of an Outsider in rebellion against the second-rateness of his time. For a full understanding of the Prophetic Books, they should be turned to immediately after reading Blake's *Island in the Moon,* the fragment of a satirical novel about the fashionable drawing-rooms of his day, with silly society women gushing, and detestable 'intellectual' men trying to be brilliant. One can see why an Outsider should turn with relief to the idea of pain; it represents an approach to reality.

The Outsider finds the concept of hell valuable, then, because pain is an antidote for human stupidity; it has the power of heightening consciousness, and the Outsider's deepest realisation is that his consciousness *needs* heightening. At the same time, the idea of ruthlessness is a relief when one has been overwhelmed by mediocrity.

The prevalence of the idea of strain and suffering in modern art is undoubtedly due to this basic Outsider consciousness: there is the gloomy atmosphere in the novels of Faulkner and Sartre, and the tension in the music of a composer like Alban Berg,* or in much of the painting of such men as Picasso, Ernst and Braque. But more than this, all Outsider art and literature has a sort of bias towards insanity. Blake says, in *The Marriage of Heaven and Hell:* 'As I was walking among the fires of hell, delighted with the enjoyments of Genius, which to Angels look like torment and insanity. . . .' This tendency could easily be labelled 'decadence,' but the label is meaningless. The truth is that the Barbusse Outsider (it will be recollected that Barbusse's hero spent his days looking through a hole in the wall at the life that comes and goes in the next room), the 'early-stage' Outsider, finds hell easier to comprehend than heaven. He finds insanity easier to comprehend than the supersanity of men of

---

* In fact, it has often struck me, in listening to the music of Berg, Schoenberg and Webern, that a good case could be made for calling twelve-tone music pure 'Outsider music' in its shunning of 'obvious' tonal values, its preference for an intellectually contrived set of atonal values — like the reversal of algebraic propositions in Hamilton's 'quaternions.'

genius — which is the only sanity that ultimately he *wants* to understand. For him, the 'sanity' of the bourgeois is not true sanity, any more than the stagnation of a swamp is true calm and serenity. But he knows no other kind.

The concept of hell is only important in so far as it points to a concept of heaven. The concept of insanity only matters because it is a step towards supersanity.

The second part of this book will be mainly concerned with defining these notions of 'heaven' and 'supersanity.' But before then, there are some important issues to be made clear. And the first of these is the question of the *real* meaning of *Existenzphilosophie* — the meaning that the Outsider attaches to it. And again, we must refer to this basic notion that all men have bungled their lives: Elijah's 'Take away my life, O Lord, for I am not better than my fathers.' The Outsider cannot help feeling that men do not learn from experience — not the really important things. When adulthood is reached, most men seem to reach a level of maturity at which they remain until their faculties begin to decay. There are, of course, some men who seem to squeeze the subtle essence from their experience and learn by it: the great poets and artists. The last quartets of Beethoven represent the accumulated experience of fifty years, and there seems to be no reason why he should not have gone on indefinitely — writing still greater music as he got older. But Beethoven is a rarity; he is more than a rarity, he is almost unique. How many other artists can be said to have gone on developing to the day of their death? Yet this is the essence of 'existence philosophy.' Philosophy means systematising one's knowledge of the universe; existence philosophy means systematising one's knowledge of how to live *by the most rigorous standards* — by the Outsider's standards. Very few men can serve as examples of this kind of development. It requires a peculiar sort of honesty. Among modern writers, W. B. Yeats, André Gide, Rainer Maria Rilke, possessed this honesty; Rilke especially deserves closer attention as the epitome of the existentialist poet.

Rilke's life is especially interesting because he was, in many senses, a failure. Yeats and Gide were both reasonably fulfilled men; but Rilke seemed never to find his feet. He was lonely and dissatisfied to the end.

The first sensation one is likely to have on reading Rilke is that he was far too sensitive; there was none of that tough-mindedness about him that one finds in Eliot or Hemingway. He is the sort of person that W. S. Gilbert might have satirised. What is one to feel about a description like this?:

> ... Through the crowd on the Graben [Prague's main street] a young man slowly makes his way, clad in an old-fashioned black frock coat, wearing a black cravat round his outmoded collar and a broad-brimmed black hat. This strange apparition holds a brightly coloured flower in his hand, a long-stemmed iris. He bears it along solemnly, as though he were carrying a blessed candle in a procession. . . . He seems to be looking for somebody that nobody has yet seen in these streets. . . . A group of quite young people have collected at a street corner and gaze ecstatically at the man with the flower. 'That was Rainer Maria Rilke,' one of them whispers . . . and all smile happily.[7]

This is an account of Rilke at twenty, by Steiner-Prag, a contemporary observer. In the same way, when one reads Rilke's letters — so many of them passionate effusions to older women — one cannot help feeling that he was a mother's boy, and never grew out of it. When one learns that his mother brought him up as a girl, dressing him completely in girl's clothes until he went to school, and even then playing games with him in which he would be 'little Sophie' (her 'sweet little daughter') one can only recoil, and turn hastily to Hemingway's stories of *his* early childhood in the Michigan backwoods.

But in spite of this, Rilke has a kind of toughness that is quite peculiar to him: a Baudelaire-like capacity to accept his own pain and transmute it; to hammer it into creation.

Rilke's father was a civil servant with some appointment on the railways, an Austrian whose family had strong military traditions, and whose own military career had been frustrated by ill health. He wanted his son to become an officer in the Austrian Army. So at the age of eleven Rainer was torn from his mother's petticoats and sent to the military school at St. Pölten. Until then, he had hardly mixed with other children; he had even been accompanied to and from school by a nurse. In the rough and noisy environment of the military academy he was thoroughly miserable, and may possibly have made himself more miserable by indulging in self-pity. He spent five years there; later he described himself as leaving it 'in a state of exhaustion, misused in body and mind,' and even went so far as to compare the academy with the prison camp of Dostoevsky's *House of the Dead!* It is, in any case, impossible to say whether the sudden harshness of his cadet experience did him more harm than good. Finally, at sixteen, he managed to get himself removed from the academy on grounds of weak health — or possibly the legend that he 'ran away' may have some substance. He studied in the commercial academy at Linz for a short time, and seems to have been a good pupil, and then, at the suggestion of an uncle, began to study law, with a view to succeeding the uncle in his barrister's practice. Probably Rilke accepted his uncle's offer to finance his education simply as an escape from the need to earn his own living. He seems to have been happier at Prague University than he had been in the academy: it gave him the leisure he wanted in order to write. For by this time, he had decided that he wanted to be a poet. He had always scribbled and sketched, ever since he was a child, and his parents had encouraged him in his early years. Now, at the age of seventeen, he began writing a great deal of bad verse, and fell in love several times. To one lady, he wrote no less than a hundred and thirty letters, which she later sold to the Prussian archive. (Rilke was always a prodigious letter writer; his collected letters occupy many volumes, and each letter is as carefully written as a poem.)

The remarkable thing about the young Rilke is not the excellence of his poetry; if he had died at the age of twenty-five, no one would have remembered him. It is the fact *that he so thoroughly dramatised himself in the role of poet.* The life of Rilke is an astounding case of *self-creation.* He has in common with his great contemporary Sibelius the fact that his early work showed no special talent; and it would have taken a person of extraordinary insight to distinguish young Rilke from the other young poets and writers he mixed with in Prague. His first volume of poems appeared when he was nineteen. It was published at his own expense; so was a curious little magazine called *Wild Chicory,* which he presented to hospitals and societies. There is a touching Shelleyan idealism about this last idea: writing 'songs for the people,' and giving them away free! He published more volumes of poetry in the next few years — an average of a volume a year. When he was twenty-two, he discovered the work of the Danish novelist J. P. Jacobsen, and was particularly influenced by *Niels Lyhne*, which is a sort of nineteenth-century version of Joyce's *Portrait of the Artist as a Young Man*. Rilke hardly needed confirming in his vision of himself as a poet; but Jacobsen's novel provided him with a warning, too. Niels's mother is a Madame Bovary figure, who has always lived in a land of dreams, and found reality too hard and coarse for her. She brings up her son with the idea of making a poet of him (we can see why Rilke was so struck by the book). Niels has the temperament of a poet, but not the strength for loneliness — that strength that makes the work of the deaf Beethoven so great. He keeps turning to people and to shallow ideals to relieve the tension. Finally, he becomes something of a drifter — a dissatisfied wanderer, like Shelley's Alastor — and joins the army in a war because he needs some external support for his own existence. When he is shot, and dies, the reader feels that it is not a moment too soon. He was weak.

Rilke took the lesson to heart; *Niels Lyhne* became his bible.

The uncle who had paid for Rilke's education in law died when Rilke was seventeen. He stayed in Prague for another three years, then moved to Munich, and announced to his disapproving father that he intended to follow a literary career. The allowance of his uncle was still continued. One suspects that he went to study in Munich because he wanted to get away from his family. At all events, he found himself a small room, and spent a great deal of his time in cafés, talking philosophy. He had discovered the work of Nietzsche at about this time, and it is evident that Nietzsche made an immense impact on him. He adopted the idea of the superman — the need to become greater than man — and even went further than Nietzsche in concocting a 'gospel of hate,' which he embodies in a short story *The Apostle*. In this story, a taciturn stranger excites the curiosity of the guests at a watering place; one day he is drawn out by a lady who asks him to contribute to a charity, and politely explains that he dislikes love and prefers hate. He then expounds the idea that the strong should build a new empire on the corpses of the weak and the unfit. It is evident that Rilke was in revolt against the feminine side of his nature, which his mother had helped to develop.

His three years in Munich seem to have been spent mostly in talking and meeting people. He met there Lou Salomé, the girl who had refused Nietzsche's proposal of marriage fifteen years before. (Nietzsche was still alive in 1897, but insane.) Lou was in her mid-thirties, and Rilke seems to have made a mother-figure of her, and written her (as usual) an immense number of long, confiding letters. She was now a happily married woman. In 1899, when Rilke was twenty-four, he went to Russia with Lou and her husband. This trip marks a turning point in his career. On his return, he spent several months studying Russian; he and Lou were the guests of a friend at Bieberstein. After this visit, Rilke dashed off in less than a month the twenty-six poems that make up his first really important volume of verse, *The Book of Hours*. Then, without pausing, he went on to write *The Love and Death of Cornet Christopher Rilke* — the first poem that was to bring him fame in German-speaking countries — and several short stories, including the haunting and grisly 'Annuschka,' about a half-imbecile country girl who is seduced, kills her baby, and then tries to compensate for its loss by buying a puppet theatre. There followed a second trip to Russia, longer than the first, on which he met Tolstoy. Relations between himself and Lou became rather strained on this trip, when she left him stranded in St. Petersburg. It is not certain whether Rilke had ever been Lou's lover; but certainly, after the second trip to Russia, he threw off her domination. He accepted the invitation of a friend to the village of Worpswede, where an artists' colony had been established, attracted, perhaps, by the austere beauty of the moors. There he became friendly with a group of young girls who were training themselves in painting and sculpture. One of them was Clara Westhoff, who not long afterwards became his wife. The young couple rented a farmhouse on the moors, and Rilke became a father. Finances were not easy. Until then, he had been receiving a small allowance from his father, but now his father wrote to say he could no longer afford it, and suggested that Rilke should come and take a job in a bank. The idea horrified him; he began to write frantically to all his friends, asking if they could suggest any literary work. Finally, someone commissioned him to do a series of monographs on the Worpswede artists, and the horror of working for a living was temporarily staved off. But life in the farmhouse was not easy. The baby screamed, and Rilke tried to write. Finally — probably to his immense relief — his wife went off to stay with friends in Holland, and he was invited to be the guest of a prince in a castle in Holstein. Rilke was never thereafter to settle down for a long period with his wife. It was an experiment, which had not worked particularly well, but his wife was of an independent temperament, and there was no quarrel.

In 1902, a year after his marriage, Rilke was commissioned to write a monograph on Rodin; he wrote, announcing his arrival, and then went to see the old sculptor in Paris. He detested the city; its misery and poverty appalled him. He wrote to Lou Salomé of 'a great terrifying astonishment,' and the 'horror at the prospect of all that, by some unspeakable confusion, is called life.' He saw Paris as a Waste Land, with 'hosts of invalids, armies of dying, nations of dead.' The book that grew out of these experiences, *Malte Laurids Brigge*, is one of the gloomiest books ever written. Like *Niels Lyhne*, it is the story of a young poet who is just not strong enough. It is written in the form of a journal, and interspersed with fictionalised bits of autobiography. Its atmosphere of misery and desperation is equalled by very little in modern literature.

On the other hand, Rodin was as salutary an experience as Russia had been. The powerful old man — he was then sixty-two — was a living example of the virtues of sanity and hard work. Russia had given Rilke's work a strong element of mystical religion; Rodin brought it back to earth and made its outlines sharp and clean. In 1905, Rilke acted for a time as his secretary, but the job bored him, and did not give him enough time for his own work. Finally, relations between them became strained, and they separated — although a friendship persisted. Rodin probably thought of Rilke as weak and oversensitive.

During the next eight years Rilke travelled around Europe, spending a great deal of his time as the guest of various members of the nobility. (There was an element of snobbishness in Rilke; he liked to believe that he was descended from Polish nobility, although his ancestors were actually German peasants.) He finished *Malte* very slowly, and it was finally published in 1910. More volumes of

poetry were published. *Cornet Christopher Rilke* had established
his European reputation in 1906 (some years after it was written);
the *Stundenbuch*, the *Buch der Bilder* (Book of Images) and *New
Poems* contained poetry that would add Rilke's name to the list of
great European poets. The most important friendship of these
years was with Princess Marie von Thurn und Taxis-Hohenlohe.
They met in 1909, shortly after he had finished *Malte*. She was
twenty years older than Rilke; immediately, he cast her for the
role of mother-figure, and she found it delightful. For the remaining years of his life, she supplied him generously with the sympathy
he needed — and also with moral and financial support. In 1912,
staying at the home of the princess, he began the first of his *Duino
Elegies*, his masterpiece.

The war came, and Rilke was called up for military service.
Three weeks of barrack life was enough to give him a breakdown,
and he was given a clerical job in the War Office. In 1916, a peti-
tion signed by numerous German writers secured his discharge,
and he returned to Munich. But the experience had shattered
him; it was too much like the military academy of his early years,
and the senseless horror of the war robbed him of creative ability.
As soon as the war was over, he escaped to Switzerland, where he
stayed as a guest with various friends. Slowly, he began to recu-
perate. His publisher was supplying him with an allowance (as he
had been for the past twelve years or so). Rilke moved to Paris for
a while, then into a castle that had been lent him for six months,
and finally, to the Château de Muzot, in the Rhone Valley. There,
in a sudden burst of power, he finished the ten *Duino Elegies*, and
produced the *Sonnets to Orpheus*, generally acknowledged to be
his other masterpiece.

It was as if the tremendous effort had exhausted him. For the
remaining five years of his life, he wrote very little: a few poems in
French, a few translations. His health was broken, and he died in
December, 1926.

From this brief account of Rilke's life, one might well ask: In
what sense was he an Outsider? There were certainly no strange,
catastrophic events, as in the lives of Nietzsche, Van Gogh, T. E.
Lawrence. If one wished to be unkind, one could say that he
solved the problem of making a living by bringing the art of 'guest-

ing' to perfection, and seems to have spent his life staying in castles
and châteaux borrowed from aristocratic friends. Yet a closer examination will show that, in a far deeper sense, he was even more of an
Outsider than Nietzsche or the others. For the simplest way to define an 'Outsider' would be to say that he is a man for whom the
world as most men see it is a lie and a deception. Blake, in this
sense, is the supreme Outsider. The fact that men need one another,
that they live in close contact, means that they all impose their way
of seeing on one another. This means that while a man is a member
of society, it is impossible for him to achieve any vision of the world
radically different from that of his fellow men. But Blake, with the
piercing insight of a visionary, wrote:

How do you know but ev'ry Bird that cuts the airy way,
Is an immense world of delight, clos'd by your senses five?[8]

and penetrated to the deepest root of the Outsider problem as only
a man of genius can. No man can become a superman in a world
of apes; it is impossible to be great among pygmies. And yet this is
the problem that drives the Outsider. In a passage in *Malte*, which I
have already quoted in *The Outsider*, Rilke asked:

Is it possible . . . that nothing real or important has yet been
seen or known or said? . . .
Yes, it is possible.[9]

In this long question-and-answer passage, Malte asks himself
many questions: 'Is it possible that, despite our discoveries and
progress . . . we still remain on the surface of life? Is it possible
that the whole history of the world has been misunderstood?'
And to each question, he answers himself: *Yes, it is possible.*

Complete isolation — that is what the Outsider is driving at. He
knows that, if he could only achieve it, there is a completely different way of seeing the world — a way so different that one might
almost say that it would no longer be the same world. *The Outsider's final problem is to become a visionary.* The first and most
obvious step is to cut himself off from other people, so as not to
be conditioned by their way of seeing. Malte's catechism is the
very essence of this attitude.

Rilke might almost be said to have made himself a poet by an act of will. As I have already mentioned, his early poetry shows very little talent; unlike a Rimbaud, a Hugo von Hofmannsthal, he did not create a great poetry at sixteen. He *envisaged* his ideal of the poet, and then quite deliberately *acted* the poet until he became one. He widened his receptive powers; and when the great experience of Russia came, he was ready for it. The broad rivers, the forests, the vast cathedrals and churches, the general feeling of a people untouched by Western materialism, produced a sudden heightening of his sensibilities, an ecstatic receptiveness. After the Russian experience, his work became 'saturated with religion.' The first two parts of the *Stundenbuch* (Book of Hours) are called 'The Book of Monastic Life' and 'The Book of Pilgrimage'; they are the meditations of a Russian monk on 'God, nature and human life.' J. B. Leishman has said that everything Rilke saw or felt in Russia was a revelation of God. It is quite clear that for the young poet, for whom the world up till then had been a gloomy, hostile, difficult place, Russia seemed like a spiritual Utopia. No doubt the Russia of 1900 was not quite the Russia that Rilke wanted to imagine; what matters is that the image of 'holy Russia' changed him from a mere poet to a visionary, and in doing so, made him into a far greater poet.

The next major experience — apart from the idyll with the *jeunes filles en fleurs* in Worpswede, and his marriage — was the other side of the penny: Paris, city of gloom, 'where ghosts in daylight clutch at passers-by.' After the spiritual release, back to the cage; the wheel turns again; the original vision reappears. The last book of the *Stundenbuch* is called 'The Book of Poverty and Death.' And the opening sentence of *Malte* is: 'People come here, then, to live? I should rather have thought they came here to die.'

Malte contains all that Rilke had learned in two decades about becoming a poet. It contains his denunciation of fame; the notoriety which can turn an Outsider into an Insider, and his warning against it:

> . . . fame, that public destruction of one in process of becoming, into whose building ground the mob breaks, displacing his stones.
> Young man anywhere, in whom something stirs that makes you

tremble, profit by the fact that no one knows you! And if they contradict you . . . if they would destroy you . . . what is this obvious danger, which holds you concentrated within yourself, compared to the later, subtle enmity of fame which leaves you harmless by scattering your forces?[10]

Malte is a great book because it is such an extraordinary evocation of a man on his own in a foreign city: the conflict between his certainty of his own power as an Outsider, and his feeling of being negated by the immense number of people who live their lives as if he did not exist. There are moments in it when Malte seems to achieve the power of insight that reconciled Hesse's Steppenwolf to his unfulfilment; the moment, for instance, when he passes the shop with the two masks hung outside the door: one of the drowned girl who was taken from the Seine, and smiles with such tranquillity; the other of Beethoven, symbol of the will to conquer:

> That hard knot of senses drawn tense; that unrelenting concentration of a music continually seeking to escape; the countenance of one whose ear a god had closed that he might hear no tones but his own, so that he might not be led astray by what is transient. . . .
> . . . who will now withhold you from lustful ears? Who will drive them from the concert halls, the venal company with sterile ears . . . ?[11]

If *Malte* is a less perfect book than *Niels Lyhne*, it is because Rilke lacked the staying power and detachment to shape the book as a novel. (After all, in Joyce's *Portrait* — *Malte's* closest relative — only the last few pages are in journal form, and these are the weakest of the book.) Yet because it is not a novel, there is a power of concentrated thought about it that makes it as unique as Sartre's *La Nausée*.

The fatigue and disillusionment that are visible in *Malte* were the next stages on the path from poet to visionary. Until then, the histrionic aspect of being a poet had kept Rilke too self-conscious to abandon himself to new stages of maturity. (As in earlier days he had carried flowers through the street, so now he wore black silk waistcoats, and douched himself in eau de Cologne.) Now he was universally recognised as a poet, but he had not much time to spare for basking in his fame; it would have meant ceasing to develop.

The first of the *Duino Elegies* came two years after he had finished Malte. The story of how the great first line was 'given' to him is well known. He was alone in Princess Marie's Castle Duino, near Trieste. One windy morning he received a business letter that worried him. With the oversensitivity of a poet, he allowed the problem to plunge him into an irritated despair, and went walking out along the battlements of the castle, with the sea roaring below. Suddenly, the lines seemed to come to him out of the sky:

Who, if I cried, would respond in the Order of Angels? *

It was the despair of a poet who felt that there *must* be some order of being more like himself than the apes who called themselves human beings. This 'higher order' of beings he called 'Angels,' although he might as well have called them Supermen (as Shaw or Nietzsche would) or gods (as the ancients would). He wrote the line down immediately in his notebook; hurriedly sent off the letter that worried him, and then completed the First Elegy. The second was written almost immediately, and the others sketched out in the same burst of creative power. The last Elegy was not to be completed until ten years later.

Since the *Elegies* might well be called the greatest set of poems of modern times, it would not be fair to try to give an impression of them here. They have had as much influence in German-speaking countries as *The Waste Land* has in England and America; although it would perhaps be more accurate to compare them to Eliot's *Four Quartets*. Their central theme is that of the angel: Rilke's certainty of the need for a higher order of existence. (It is significant that the *Elegies* were finally published at about the same time as *Back to Methuselah*.) Certain lines have a power that comes over even in translation:

* Literally: 'Who, if I cried, would hear me among the angelic orders?' [12]

> For Beauty's nothing
> but beginning of Terror we're still just able to bear.[13]

The idea that dominates the *Elegies* is the concept of human suffering, and the concept of a vision that makes human suffering seem unimportant. Yeats touched upon this many times in his later poetry:

> That some stream of lightning
> From the old man in the skies
> Can burn out that suffering
> No right-taught man denies. . . .[14]

But most important is the fact that Rilke's 'religion' in the *Elegies* is the Nietzschean religion. In a letter to the Polish translator of the *Elegies*, he makes this clear:

> Not, however, [religion] in the Christian sense (from which I more and more passionately withdraw), but in a purely mundane, deeply mundane, blissfully mundane consciousness. . . .[15]

In fact, the affirmation of Nietzsche's vision on the hilltop, of Van Gogh's *Starry Night*, of Beethoven's Ninth Symphony. There is also an element of the Goethean mysticism of the last words of *Faust:*

> All things corruptible
> Are only reflection.
> Earth's insufficiency
> Here reaches perfection . . .[16]

In the Ninth Elegy, this mysticism of the earth appears in the question:

> . . . Are we, perhaps, here just for the saying: House,
> Bridge, Fountain, Gate, Jug. . . ? [17]

And in:

> Earth, isn't this what you want: an invisible
> re-arising in us? Is it not your dream

to be one day invisible? Earth! Invisible!
What is your urgent command, if not transformation?
Erde, du liebe, ich will. . . .[18]

The last phrase must be left in German: the English 'Earth, thou loved one, I will!' hardly expresses its ecstasy of affirmation.

The opening lines of the Tenth Elegy are perhaps the greatest in all the *Elegies:*

Some day, emerging at last from this terrifying vision
may I burst into jubilant praise to assenting Angels!
May not even one of the clear-struck keys of the heart
fail to respond through alighting on slack or doubtful
or rending strings! May a new-found splendour appear
in my streaming face! May inconspicuous Weeping
flower! How dear will you be to me then, you Nights
of Affliction! Oh, why did I not, inconsolable sisters,
more bendingly kneel to receive you, more loosely surrender
myself to your loosened hair? We wasters of sorrows!
How we stare away into sad endurance beyond them,
trying to foresee their end! Whereas they are nothing else
than our winter foliage, our sombre evergreen, *one*
of the seasons of our interior year. . . .[19]

The concept that now grips Rilke is in the idea of super-consciousness, and the actual *using of his experience in a complete rebuilding of his being.* The passage above is pure existence-philosophy in the Outsider sense, for it shows Rilke reaching towards a new level of consciousness by the process of assimilating his most difficult experiences. Behind it there lies the feeling that men lose their experience because they turn away from it, shielding their heads with their hands, as if to ward off a blow. 'We *wasters* of sorrows' — we wasters of our own lives. This is Rilke's own way of phrasing, *and of answering*, Eliot's question:

Where is the Life we have lost in living?

When closely analysed, it becomes evident that Rilke's final philosophy is a philosophy of the Will. All experiences can be used as the building bricks of a visionary consciousness *if there is a conscious effort at assimilation.* It is not true merely of sorrows that we tend to 'stare into sad endurance beyond them, trying to foresee their end'; it is true of by far the greater part of our experience. Not being supermen, our brains are not big enough to contain all the world at once: we have to select what is to be remembered; and we remember only those experiences that we allow to penetrate our indifference. Rilke's *Elegies* are a plea for an effort of will to assimilate more; a plea for less indifference. The gloomy Fourth Elegy has the line 'Wir sind nicht einig,' 'We're never single-minded.' The whole of William James's chapter on 'The Divided Self'* is only a commentary on this line. Rilke felt, as Hesse did, that human life is spent in continual perplexity, continual boredom or misery or doubt. The moments of supreme detachment, when we stand above our own experience and somehow see a meaning in it, come too rarely. In those moments, we feel unified, and have a keener sense of being alive; the world no longer presses on us so that it seems to flatten us; it is withdrawn, at arm's length. Animals seem strangely at one with themselves; higher consciousness imposes new strains, and the men who have the greatest sensibility often wish they could get rid of it (like Whitman wishing he was a cow, or T. E. Lawrence envying a soldier caressing a dog). They are half afraid of it. They are afraid of insanity. But the strain occurs only in the halfway stage. Rilke recognised that what is needed is an *effort of affirmation.* Of course there is strain for a man standing between two stools. He must make up his mind which one he wants to sit on. If he decides for the lower one (as Lawrence did) he should sit on it. If he decides for the higher one, he should make the effort of will to achieve the new state of consciousness, and make an attempt to bully his experience, instead of allowing it to bully him. This may be an unpoetic way of expressing the philosophy underlying the *Elegies* (and an oversimplification, of course), but it is the language that precedes action, and Rilke's failure lies in the fact that he never tried to bridge the gap between words and action. Perhaps he loved words too much; and although this is fortunate for us, it made his life a tragedy.

Yet there are moments in Rilke's life of near-mystical experi-

* *Varieties of Religious Experience*, Lecture VIII.

ence. One of them he describes in a prose piece called *Experience*.
He had been walking in the garden of Castle Duino, reading a book,
and had leaned in the fork of a low tree, and suddenly felt

> . . . completely received into nature, in an almost unconscious
> contemplation. Little by little his attention awoke to a feeling he
> had never known: it was as though almost imperceptible vibra-
> tions were passing into him from the interior of the tree. . . .
> It seemed to him that he had never been filled with more gentle
> motions, his body was being somehow treated like a soul . . . he
> . . . asked himself what was happening to him then, and almost
> at once found an expression that satisfied him, saying to himself,
> that he had got to the other side of Nature. . . .[20]

There had also been another time, which he mentioned in a
letter to Princess Marie:

> . . . a morning hour, early on the second day, in the little draw-
> ing-room next to the billiard room; no one had yet come down;
> I was reading a hymn of some Poeta ignoto . . . and was full of
> concentration and pure mental composure. Outside was the park:
> everything was in tune with me; one of those hours that are not
> fashioned at all, but only, as it were, held in reserve, as though
> things had drawn together and left space, a space as undisturbed
> as the interior of a rose . . . a . . . space in which one keeps quite
> still. . . .[21]

This second experience is not a 'mystical' experience in the
accepted sense; its essence is the phrase 'full of concentration and
pure mental composure.' It is the sort of state that Sri Ramakrishna
strove to achieve by isolating himself and composing his mind; a
state which is difficult to attain in this complex modern age. But it
is the state in which mystical insight comes to birth; it will be necessary to say a great deal more of it in dealing with Swedenborg and
Boehme in later chapters. What is important to realise is that 'mystical' experiences are not experiences of *another* order of reality,
but insights into *this* order seen with extraordinarily clear vision
and greater concentration.

More important than Rilke's 'mystical' experiences are the conclusions that he drew from them. The essence of his philosophy

is contained in the phrase '*dennoch preisen*,' to praise in spite of. These two words contain the essence of Rilke's greatness. He admired Baudelaire's poem 'Carrion' because it faced unpleasantness and made poetry out of it: the poem is about a dead animal which Baudelaire came across on a walk. When Rilke first used that phrase 'to praise in spite of,' James Joyce's *Ulysses* had not been published, and Hemingway had not even begun to write. Yet the phrase defines the greatness of *Ulysses* and *A Farewell to Arms*. In *Ulysses*, the trivial and disgusting is dwelt on in considerable detail, so that the first half of the book usually repels readers who come to it for the first time. Then, with the Nighttown scene, a tremendous power begins to flow into it, and continues to rise as the Catechism chapter develops its God's-eye view of Dublin; finally, as Mrs. Bloom, dreaming of her past lovers, seems to change into the earth itself, spinning around the sun, the supreme transformation takes place: the great act of affirmation of all life, with 'yes I said yes I will Yes' — '*Erde, du liebe, ich will.*'

Rilke, too, was capable of envisaging such an act of complete affirmation; his 'Orpheus' of the *Sonnets to Orpheus* makes it all the time:

> Praising, that's it! As a praiser and presser
> he came like the ore from the taciturn mine
> Came with his heart, oh, transient presser,
> for men, of a never-exhaustible wine.
> Voice never fails him for things lacking lustre. . . .[22]

But Rilke could never make this boast of himself. Voice *often* failed him for 'things lacking lustre.' Like the early Yeats, he had all his life hated ugliness and misery and turned away from it. That effeminate, Jamesian prose was not the instrument for taking the worst reality by the throat; and could one honestly expect lyrical poetry to do all that Joyce did in *Ulysses*?

No, the truth is that, great as Rilke was, he reached his deepest insights in theory rather than in practice. Towards the end he *saw* quite clearly that the really great poet should be an Orpheus, living with such intensity that 'voice *never* fails him' — not for anything. But he did not put this into practice throughout his life. In the *Sonnets*, he strives to be Nietzschean in his refusal to shudder and turn away. In the ninth sonnet of the second part, he tells merciful judges not to boast of their humanity, and of the instruments of torture we no longer use, for men have not become greater by all this mercy and enlightenment. In the eleventh sonnet, he speaks of killing, and says that it is 'only another form of our wandering sadness.' (At this point, his English translator breaks into indignation in his notes, and demands whether one could murmur that sentiment over a Nazi murder camp!) This, of course, is pure Zarathustra — the man who has so far transcended his 'human-all-too-human' limitations that nothing horrifies him. But Rilke himself never achieved such greatness. He wandered from castle to castle, mansion to mansion, reading the bad poetry of rich women, and engaging in 'serious conversations' with all kinds of imbecilic members of the nobility. In between times he was a chronic hypochondriac, and something of a figure of fun in the Bunthorne manner. In short, after reading too many of the Letters, or one of the many biographies of him, one cannot help turning with relief to someone like Hemingway, who errs on the side of being thickskinned rather than oversensitive.

This is not intended as a literary criticism. The present chapter is not about literature, but about existentialism. Rilke's contribution lies in the fact that he did, actually, learn a great deal from his own life, and reached certain conclusions which, even if he didn't live up to them himself, are of inestimable importance in the search of the Outsider. It is important to realise that one cannot speak of Rilke the man and Rilke the poet as if they were one and the same. The poet was triumphant; the man was miserable. The poet seems to have achieved a peculiar self-mastery; the man was always subject to nervous prostrations and fits of hypochondria; he wasted his vital powers in worries and irritations.

Many 'Outsiders' might claim that this is quite inevitable — Hesse, for instance, who feels that the 'moments of ecstasy' are paid for by ennui and suffering; or Yeats, who wrote:

> The intellect of man is forced to choose
> Perfection of the life, or of the work.[23]

But the whole conception of the Outsider is a protest against this attitude. There was not this dichotomy in Chaucer or Villon or Rabelais; they were not haunted and miserable men because they were capable of creation. It is true that history may have deceived us, but they certainly give the impression of being men who knew how to live as well as to create. In the preface to his poems, John Millington Synge touches the question with finality:

> Many of the older poets, such as Villon and Herrick and Burns, used the whole of their personal life as their material, and the verse written in this way was read by strong men, and thieves, and deacons, not by little cliques only. . . .
> In these days poetry is usually a flower of evil or good; but it is the timber of poetry that wears most surely, and there is no timber that has not strong roots among the clay and the worms. . . . before verse can be human again it must learn to be brutal.[24]

It can be said that Synge, although he was writing twenty years before *A Farewell to Arms*, had anticipated the kind of existentialism that Hemingway brought back into literature, or that Joyce — apparently unintentionally — created in Buck Mulligan.

It is almost certainly true that the poetry of Rilke — 'the poetry of exaltation' — is higher than that of Herrick and Villon. The sensible assumption, then, would seem to be that Villon found it easier to make his life and his poetry commensurate because the poetry was nearer the ground, and that a poet like Rilke would require a far greater effort to live on the level of *his* poetry. This immediately disposes of that nightmare of the Barbusse Outsider, that life is bound to be a miserable failure for the sensitive man who sees 'too deep and too much.' The problem that is still left open is simply the question of how a poet like Rilke is to use the 'wisdom' of the poetry to direct his own life. It is the moral question that becomes an existentialist question only by the depth of the attempt to answer it: What shall we do with our lives? The Outsider's standards are unusually high. For him, 'success' and 'failure' have a completely new meaning. Ordinary 'success' seems particularly poisonous to him: the success of a film star or businessman or the author of a best seller. That is only a way of wading out into the world's stupidity and losing the possibility of vision. Yet this is no academic question, this question of purpose. The Outsider is only the ordinary man raised to an unusual level of perception; his conception of purpose is more exclusive than most men's. He crystallises it into a positive recognition of the need for an existence philosophy, *a science of living*. A 'science' only means an attempt to bring order and unity into a subject; the scientist's method is classification and comparison and experiment. That is the Outsider's method, too, except that his *subject* is the actual living stuff of experience, the raw material of the writer. This is why so much of the evidence examined in *The Outsider* came out of novels and plays and journals — especially journals. The art of the Outsider is essentially a movement towards a science of living. But only a move towards it. Human beings have not yet created such a science, but they may yet do so; it may be the peculiar achievement of Western civilisation to have brought to consciousness the idea of an existence philosophy. Such a philosophy has nothing whatever to do with any science that exists at present, and certainly has no relation to 'literary criticism' or to philosophy.*

The more vital the mind, the keener its sense of failure, of repetition and futility. A caretaker or charlady is content to sweep out an office every day, with the certainty that the job will have to be repeated within twenty-four hours. The man of genius demands that the work into which he throws his energy lasts as long as possible; the most casual conversation of a Johnson or a Goethe has a permanent value for posterity. So it is that the most simple 'Outsider' predicament is a question of futility, of frustration of an internal purpose. Most of us are driven by material anxieties and the need to work for a living. When, through material success or good fortune, the Outsider is freed from these casual obstructions, he is forced to scrutinise his sense of purpose more closely, to calculate how to use his opportunities to the best effect. He would like his life, seen in retrospect, to have the unity of a work of art, a meaning, so that he could point to it in answer to that question: Where is the Life we have lost in living? All the wisdom he gains through experience should be used as a tool to shape his life, not

* This, for me, was one of the most annoying misunderstandings of *The Outsider*: the attempts to classify it — and attack it — as something which it certainly did not set out to be.

merely noted in a poem or novel. The reason for Rilke's failure would seem to be a lack of will to do anything except write poetry (that is, to note down his 'wisdom,' and then forget it, or put it into cold storage until the next time he came to write); there was no will to shape his life by it. It was a failure to get his purpose consciously defined. Rilke synthesised his experience for the purpose of art, not for the purpose of wider and deeper experience.

It may be interesting, in this connection, to examine a poet whose vision was as profound as Rilke's, but whose conception of living was far more positive: Arthur Rimbaud.

Rimbaud was born in Charleville, in the north of France, in 1854 — only two years before Shaw. His father and mother separated when he was six. Madame Rimbaud, a hard-headed and determined woman, was left to bring up a family of four children on a minute income. She moved into one of the cheaper streets of the town, and kept aloof from her neighbours (she seems to have had something in common with D. H. Lawrence's mother, as described in *Sons and Lovers*). It would also seem that she was given to talking about religion and the conduct of life; her son irreverently nicknamed her *bouche d'ombre*.

But on the whole, Arthur was a well-behaved little boy; a good pupil at school, and obedient (except when he played with the scruffy boys in the street, whom his mother disliked). A photograph of him at the age of eleven shows a remarkably pretty, serious-faced boy with wide eyes and round cheeks. He read avidly and widely, and his schoolmasters predicted that he would be a prodigy; on one occasion, he produced a digest of ancient history, including Egypt, Syria and Babylon.* When he was fifteen, a young master named Izambard came to Rimbaud's school; he was only five years Rimbaud's senior, and immediately made friends with the star pupil, lending him volumes of contemporary French poetry. And in his fifteenth year, Rimbaud began to write poetry — poetry which, for precocious mastery, can only be compared to the early

* It is interesting to remember that the great archaeologist J. F. Champollion had first revealed his own astonishing mental powers by doing precisely the same thing at the age of twelve — producing a digest of world history 'from Adam to Champollion the Younger'!

music of Mozart. Izambard was the cause of this sudden creative
activity, for when he lent Rimbaud volumes of Hugo, Rimbaud
wrote poetry that echoed Hugo; when it was Banville or Verlaine,
he echoed Banville or Verlaine. Even so, these early poems show a
delicacy of ear, and an odd quality of self-examination; at fifteen,
he wrote a poem that began:

> At seventeen one isn't serious.
> A lovely night; beer-harvest, lemonade;
> The lighted cafés, dazzling, sumptuous;
> Strolls under lime-trees on the promenade. . . .

and containing the lovely line:

> on your lips a kiss
> Throbs pulsing, like a little animal.[25]

In the year he wrote his poem, he left school in a flurry of con-
gratulations and prizes. Izambard went home for the summer holi-
days; Rimbaud was sad to see him go. And then, quite suddenly,
the good pupil and obedient son started on a new course of conduct.
Perhaps it was the unrest of the war that affected him; the Prussians
were advancing on Charleville, and his elder brother had run away
and joined the army. He ran away from home and went to Paris.
He was arrested as he came off the train for having no money (or
that was the version he gave, in a letter to Izambard).

Izambard sent money, and a letter asking the prison governor to
send Rimbaud to Charleville, or if that was impossible on account of
the Prussians, to Douai. Douai is about a hundred miles northwest
of Charleville, and it was there that Rimbaud eventually turned up,
delighted to see his schoolmaster again, and rather pleased with
himself for his escapade. Madame Rimbaud was informed that her
son was safe; she immediately wrote demanding that he be sent
home, and ending her letter piously: 'May God not punish his wil-
fulness as it deserves.' The war made communication difficult, and
when Rimbaud eventually reached home, three weeks later, Madame
Rimbaud seized him by the ear and threw him in through the door,
and then turned furiously upon Izambard. He was glad to hurry off

back towards the railway station. However, a few days later he received a frantic letter from Madame Rimbaud telling him that Arthur had disappeared again, and begging his help. After his last encounter with her, Izambard was not enthusiastic, but he swallowed his annoyance, and set out to look for his pupil. The trail took him to Brussels, and then stopped. Defeated, Izambard went back to Douai — and found Arthur sitting in the parlour, copying out his poems. The fortnight of wandering had been, on the whole, thoroughly enjoyable. His poem 'Ma Bohème' tells the story; it begins:

> Fists probing my torn pockets, off I'd wander,
> My overcoat more holes than cloth and I
> Poetry's bondslave under the open sky. . . .[26]

But he couldn't stay with Izambard; this time, he was handed over to the police, who took him home. Izambard was not risking another abusive reception from Madame Rimbaud! At home again, Rimbaud wrote: '. . . I am dying and melting away in the dullness, the drabness and the foulness around me. . . .'

There was no school for the time being. Rimbaud spent his days reading books borrowed from the town library, writing, bored and unhappy. The Prussians occupied Charleville. The winter dragged by, and in February of the following year, school started again. But Rimbaud was determined not to return. Since he had left school the previous August, he had grown up a great deal. His mother found him unmanageable. His mind had suddenly matured. In Paris there were stirrings of revolution, and Rimbaud was impatient to enter the adult world and be done with the schoolboy's forever. Once again, he ran away to Paris. This time, he had a far less pleasant experience than before. He wandered around Paris for a fortnight without money, sleeping under bridges, eating out of dustbins. He seems to have spent a night in the army barracks, with humiliating results; it is not certain what happened, but the poem that was the outcome of the adventure makes it clear that he underwent some unpleasant sexual experience at the hands of the soldiers. Le Cœur volé is an extraordinary poem, almost untranslatable, but too good not to quote, at least in part:

Mon triste cœur bave à la poupe,
Mon cœur couvert de caporal:
Ils y lancent des jets de soupe,
Mon triste cœur bave à la poupe:
Sous les quolibets de la troupe
Qui pousse un rire général,
Mon triste cœur bave à la poupe,
Mon cœur couvert de caporal!

Ithyphalliques et pioupiesques,
Leurs quolibets l'ont dépravé!
Au gouvernail on voit des fresques
Ithyphalliques et ploupiesques. . . . *

This poem was the cause of Rimbaud's break with Izambard. He sent it to his former master with a letter that indicated how important he felt it to be. Izambard was not equal to the occasion; he did not realise what new worlds his pupil had become acquainted with since they had last met. He wrote a satire on the poem, and sent it to Rimbaud with the comment: 'You see, anyone can write nonsense.' It is hardly surprising that, from that time forward, Rimbaud offered him no more confidences. Nothing is more disconcerting to genius than to find itself outgrowing its elders in insight and intuition. But there is some exhilaration in the process; the contempt is a stimulus, the stupidity a steppingstone.

Once more Rimbaud was back in Charleville, and this time his mother did not seize him by the ear. It was less than six months since his last escapade, but in that time he had become uncontrollable. The things he had seen and felt had made him prematurely wise. He knew violence and death:

In a green hollow where a river sings,
Circling the grasses with specks of silver-white,

* The following is a literal translation: 'My sad heart slobbers at the stern, my heart covered with shag tobacco: they spirt soup over it, my sad heart slobbers at the stern: under the jokes of the crew, who utter a general laugh, my sad heart slobbers at the stern, my heart covered with shag tobacco!
'Their ithyphallic, barrack-room jokes have corrupted it! On the tiller one sees ithyphallic, barrack-room drawings. . . .' [27]

From his proud steeps the sun ascendant flings
Splendour. The valley scintillates with light.
Open-mouthed, capless, a young soldier lies
Where the fresh blue cresses cool his bare head;
Pale in the light raining down from the skies
He sleeps, stretched at length on his green mossy bed.
His feet bruise the iris where he takes his nap
Smiling like a sick child on its mother's lap;
He is cold. Earth, warm him! Cradle him to rest!
He heeds not the scents that rise about his head;
In the sun he dozes, head on quiet breast.
In his right side two bullet holes have bled.[28]

And now Rimbaud began to live in a manner deliberately conceived to shock Charleville. He refused to cut his hair or wash; he wandered around the town, smoking a dirty pipe with the bowl upside down; he lounged around in cafés, paying for drinks with lewd stories, or blasphemous comments on the Church and religion. He embarrassed the masters at his school by sitting on the wall where his former classmates could see him; all were shocked by the change that had come over the angelic-faced, well-behaved prize winner of the previous year. He still spent a great deal of time reading; now it was mostly books on black magic and Satanism, or the poetry of Baudelaire and Verlaine. He was in violent reaction against the years when he had been well-behaved and well-spoken, and besides, he was sexually frustrated and bored. He wanted an affair — that is to say, he simply wanted a woman; but the very intensity of the desire helped to frustrate it; his attempts to get on to close terms with the girls of Charleville usually ended in failure and periods of self-hatred. He was too full of lust and unsatisfied longing to make an irresistible, casual Casanova. The days were past when he could write of women with the gaiety of a Keats — as he had only a few months earlier:

Eight days I tramped, wearing my boots in holes
On flinty roads. I came to Charleroi where
At the *Cabaret-Vert*, I ordered buttered rolls
And fresh-cooked ham not cold yet. Sitting there
Contentedly, I stretched my legs out under

The painted table, studying the bits
Of simple wallpaper. Then — heavenly wonder!
A girl with roguish eyes and bouncing tits —

Not one to shy at kisses or such matter! —
Laughingly brought me on a coloured platter
The buttered rolls and ham streaked white and pink,
Ham warm and garlic-scented; from her jug
She filled with frothing beer a noble mug.
It caught a sparkle from the sun's last blink.[29]

And the idea of devil worship and blasphemy began to obsess him. He thought of Baudelaire as a man who had submitted himself to a forcing house of sin in order to make himself a great poet. In reaction against the small-town boredom of Charleville, Rimbaud dreamed of a continued exacerbation of the senses through lust, drugs, alcohol, suffering. Anything to drive away the second-rateness, the feeling of stagnation, anything to make the blood circulate again through those areas of his soul that seemed to go dead in the ennui of Charleville. The idea of becoming a drug addict, a physical wreck, a syphilitic, a dipsomaniac, did not worry him; it seemed a good exchange for boredom.

One should pause here to emphasise that it was *what was now going on in Rimbaud's mind that was the major event of his life*, not any mere physical happening. The real Rimbaud was born in those months of playing the roaring boy around Charleville. We are back again with the concepts I outlined in the Steppenwolf passage in *The Outsider*. The enemy was boredom and unfulfilment. The incentive was a feeling that *there should be some way of living life to the full*, and he didn't care what that involved. He thought he found a clue in Baudelaire — Baudelaire, the alcoholic, the drug addict, perpetually tormented, like Dostoevsky, by his own weakness and vacillation; it was in this man that Rimbaud thought he perceived a tower of satanic strength. For a while, Rimbaud became obsessed by the criminal, by debauchery and suffering. Like all true poets, he was 'of the devil's party.' Now, at the age of sixteen, he applied his mind to the problem of how to live life to the full. Charleville was as uneventful as a monk's cell; it was an ideal place for the hatching of great ideas. Like Mr. Polly, Rimbaud felt that men are imprisoned in paper walls, which they could knock down if only they had the courage. Like Novalis, he believed that the only thing that prevents men from being geniuses is laziness. He told Izambard, in a candidly brutal letter: 'You will end in smug self-satisfaction, *having achieved nothing because you will not have wanted to achieve anything.*' Meanwhile, he continued to shock Charleville. When someone tried to shame him for wearing his hair long by offering him threepence to go to the barber, he bowed mockingly, accepted the money, and went into the nearest shop to buy tobacco with it. In cafés, he took a delight in telling lewd stories in a loud voice, and was triumphant if people at the next table got up and moved further away. He attributed awful perversions to himself, claiming to have a predilection for dogs and cats. But when he was alone, he meditated on the Outsider problem, the problem of how not to take life for granted, how to uncover the hidden powers of the human spirit of which the average man is not even aware. He formulated his doctrine that the poet must be a *visionary* (not real-ising how close he was approaching to the thought of William Blake, who also paid full attention to the devil's side of the argu-ment). Rimbaud felt — like Blake — that one can train oneself to see visions, 'a drawing-room at the bottom of a lake, mosques instead of factories. . . . The poet makes himself a visionary by a long, im-mense and reasoned *derangement* of all the senses.' This could be done by upsetting the physical and emotional constitution by delib-erate exercise of asceticism or vice. Rimbaud must have recognised that there are certain times when the body is weak and fatigued — after a long illness, a hangover due to alcohol or drugs, or mere physical exhaustion — when a curious peace sweeps over the emo-tions. The mind becomes quite free in an altogether new manner; instead of being so distracted that it can hardly stick to the same thought or feeling for more than a minute at a time, it is relaxed and easy to handle; memory works with an amazing ease, and one's past is evoked — its actual smell and taste — by every chance thought or emotion. This is a sensation that every sick man, every de-bauched man, every despairing man, has known at some moment.

When he was seventeen, Rimbaud produced his greatest poem, 'Le Bateau Ivre' ('The Drunken Boat'). It is a long poem, in twenty-five four-line stanzas — a strange rhapsody, sung by a drifting ship after its crew has been murdered by Red Indians. The tense, beautiful language defies translation; something in the subject and verbal mastery remind one inevitably of *The Ancient Mariner*, but no comparison can suggest its uniqueness. For a boy who had never been near the sea in his life, it is a miraculous feat of visionary imagination.

It was through this poem that Rimbaud came to meet Paul Verlaine. He sent it, together with a letter, to Verlaine in Paris, and Verlaine replied with an enthusiastic letter, a railway ticket, and an invitation to come and stay with his family.

At this time, Verlaine was twenty-seven years old. He was already a well-known poet, having established his reputation with *Saturnian Poems*, published when he was twenty-two. He was a member of an influential group of French poets who called themselves Parnassians, and was highly thought of, in spite of his heavy drinking and sexual irregularities. He had been a member of the civil service, but lost his position, owing to a mixture of revolutionary sympathies and ordinary incompetence. He married a beautiful girl of seventeen, who came from a rich bourgeois family, and in the sheer physical ecstasy of the early married months, he became an excellent husband. He was weak, sensuous, good-natured and a master of delicate and exquisite verse that possessed a 'dying fall' — similar, in many ways, to the English poet Dowson.

At the time Rimbaud arrived, Verlaine was growing restive. His wife was expecting a baby, and they were living with her parents. He had told his wife and mother-in-law of the astonishing poet of Charleville (he thought Rimbaud was about his own age), and they both looked forward to meeting the discovery. When a tall, gawky boy, with long, dirty hair, filthy clothes, and a red peasant's face turned up in their drawing room, they were disconcerted. Verlaine welcomed Rimbaud warmly, but Rimbaud sensed the disapproval of the others. As always when he felt himself disliked, he set out to be offensive, took no trouble to hide his contempt for the *bourgeois*, and refused to be sociable. He went out of his way to scandalise, and it is hardly surprising that the place soon became too hot to hold him. Then he disappeared. Verlaine had been divided between enthusiasm for a brother poet, and embarrassment on behalf of his relatives. Now that Rimbaud had disappeared, his solicitude predominated, and he sought everywhere for the missing poet. A fortnight later, he finally bumped into Rimbaud in the street — an exhausted, sunken-cheeked Rimbaud who had been living off dustbins again and sleeping in doorways. With tears of pity, Verlaine bought him a meal and found him lodgings. However, Rimbaud was incorrigible, and before long he was in the street again. His unsanitary habits made him unpopular wherever he stayed. (It is said that Verlaine's wife went into the guest room to change the pillowcases, and was horrified to find the pillows swarming with lice; when told of this, Verlaine merely commented: 'Yes, he cultivates them to throw at priests when he passes them in the street!')

But the famous friendship between Rimbaud and Verlaine had now begun. It is true that the relation between them was homosexual, but it would not be true to suppose that it was *primarily* on a sexual level. Rimbaud had, for the first time in his life, found a brother spirit, a poet. At last he thought he had found a partner to accompany him on his journey away from the world. It meant that he had seen a way out of his Outsider problems: for the Outsider's deepest source of discouragement is his feeling that the world is his enemy, and he must fight the battle alone. For a while, Rimbaud laboured under the delusion that two Outsiders, in double harness, would stand a better chance against the world. Then he began to understand that he was mistaken. His immediate reaction was to treat Verlaine rather badly — to jeer at him, to quarrel with him. On one occasion, in company with other poets, Rimbaud asked Verlaine to spread out his hands on the café table; when Verlaine did this, Rimbaud drew out a knife and began stabbing at the table between the outstretched fingers.* Verlaine jumped up and left the café, at which Rimbaud followed him and began to slash at him with the knife.

This kind of antic reveals that Rimbaud was bored with his own

* This is a game that I have heard spoken of as being played among bored officers in the Occupation Army in Germany, the skill consisting in stabbing *between* the fingers at a tremendous speed. 'Russian roulette' is also played — twirling the chambers of a revolver containing only one bullet, pointing it at the head and firing. Both 'games' are obviously designed to release nervous tension.

attempts at vice, and was turning 'mean.' I cannot agree that he revealed hidden sadism; it seems more probable that the bursts of violence developed from an instinctive dislike of his own silliness and lack of discipline; for fundamentally, like all great men, Rimbaud was a puritan.

The scandal over the two men developed. Verlaine's wife was alarmed by the bad influence Rimbaud was exerting; one night, her husband tried to strangle her, and threw their baby against the wall. When he recovered from the hangover he sobbed with remorse, and promised to ask Rimbaud to return to Charleville. He did, and Rimbaud returned, cursing with rage. The few months at home were spent writing *Les Illuminations*, a slim work written in a mixture of prose and verse. It is significant that Rimbaud's finest work was written when he was away from Verlaine. The *Illuminations* record the result of months of discipline of the senses — more attempts to 'make himself a visionary.' The months of debauchery in Paris had only made him lazy, a drifter. Alone again, he made up for it. But soon Verlaine sent for him. He returned to Paris, and the round of vice and debauchery, absinthe and sodomy, began over again. Verlaine's unfortunate wife seems to have had a great deal to endure: Dostoevsky himself could not have invented a more pathetic tale. She had put up with beatings, drunken abuse, even attacks with a knife, and finally her husband left her for good and disappeared with his evil genius. Verlaine went to Brussels with Rimbaud, and his wife followed. When he met her, Verlaine was overcome with remorse; he made love to her and was reconciled; then, when she was dressed again, changed his mind. He accompanied her to the Belgian frontier, and hurried back to Rimbaud in Brussels. Rimbaud and he then crossed to England, and came to live in Soho. A sketch made by an artist friend at this period shows Verlaine, tall, skinny, helpless looking with his drooping moustache and spindly legs, and Rimbaud, slouching behind him, looking like a teddy boy with his long jacket, long hair sticking out from under his hat, and the foul old pipe in one hand. They wandered all over London together, drinking away the little money that was sent to Verlaine from France, wandering around the East End and the docks, or sitting in cafés all day. Verlaine's lovely poem 'Il pleure dans mon cœur' . . . commemorates a brief separation from Rimbaud:

Tears fall in my heart
Like the rain on the town
What is this dull smart
That pierces my heart?

O soft noise of rain
On earth and on roofs
For tired hearts in pain
The patter of rain. . . .

But still, the worst pain
Not to know why
Without love or hate
My heart has this pain.[30]

Later they went to Brussels again, and there the disaster happened. Rimbaud threatened to leave Verlaine, and Verlaine shot him through the wrist. Rimbaud made no complaint, but when, a little later, he set out for the station, Verlaine produced his revolver again, and Rimbaud took refuge behind the nearest policeman. Verlaine was arrested; Rimbaud was taken to hospital, where he spent a week in fever. When he finally got out, he was put on trial; the medical examination revealed recent practice of sodomy, and a thoroughly prejudiced judge sentenced Verlaine to two years in jail. The whole quarrel had been more Rimbaud's fault than Verlaine's, but it was Verlaine who paid the penalty.

Meanwhile, Rimbaud went back to Charleville. He arrived exhausted, with one arm in a sling, and immediately burst into tears. His mother was unexpectedly sympathetic, and even agreed to pay for the publication of the book he wanted to finish. The book was *A Season in Hell*, again a mixture of prose and poetry, an examination of his past life, his relation with Verlaine, the pride that had urged him on to excesses. His sister records that, while he wrote it, he could be heard groaning and cursing in his locked room. Finally it was completed and printed in a slim booklet. He sent copies to friends in Paris, and went to Paris to see how it was received. But the story of his exploits with Verlaine had preceded him; everyone thought of him as Verlaine's evil genius. He was universally snubbed. In a rage, he returned to Charleville and burnt all his papers, all his unpublished poems, all the copies of the book he could lay his hands on. He then returned to Paris, came to London and tried to make a living as a teacher, and finally went to Stuttgart to study German. There, Verlaine joined him again, but their second meeting was without success. Verlaine had attempted a reconciliation with his wife; when that failed, he tried entering a monastery; when that also came to nothing, he contacted Rimbaud. As usual, there was something about Verlaine that seemed to irritate Rimbaud — the weakness, perhaps. They staggered from café to café, drinking and smoking, and Rimbaud soon made Verlaine blaspheme against the religion he had embraced. One evening they had a quarrel by the river; Rimbaud knocked Verlaine unconscious and left him to lie there until the following morning. Finally, Verlaine returned to Paris; his road and Rimbaud's had separated for good. Verlaine now went quietly and gently downhill. For a while he taught in schools, then tried farming, then, with the death of his mother, simply allowed himself to drift; he drifted, on the whole, highly successfully for the next twenty years, in and out of hospital, always in poverty, always cheerful and gentle, until, by the time he died in 1896, he had a European reputation, and even England had received him with the respect due to a major poet.

After *A Season in Hell*, Rimbaud wrote no more — at least, none of his subsequent work has yet been discovered. If *A Season in Hell* is really his last work, there is irony in the fact that the book is a recantation of his previous 'errors,' and was intended to be a 'new beginning.' (It gives his poetic career a certain resemblance to that of Lautréamont — Isidore Ducasse; for Ducasse had also embraced a theory of Satanism, which he expressed in his long sadistic prose-poem, *Les Chants de Maldoror*, but recanted in the preface to an unwritten volume of poems which he sketched shortly before his early death.)

Rimbaud lived for another sixteen years, but there would be no point in tracing his wanderings in detail. He walked to Italy from Stuttgart, and worked as an unskilled labourer in the docks at Leghorn. He returned to Paris, and then enlisted in the Dutch army, to be sent abroad to the Sunda Islands. He deserted and went to Sumatra, and then to Java, where he lived for a while in the forest. Finally, he worked his way back to Cyprus, where he worked as a quarry hand for a while, and then moved on again, this time to Abyssinia. He set up there as a trader in coffee and perfumes, and later gold and ivory. For a long time he lived with the natives as one of them. His trading ventures were so successful that he was able to retire in 1888, at the age of thirty-four, and had a palace at Harar. During the next two years, he would seem to have played some part in international intrigue, and been in close relation with the King of Shoa. But in March, 1891, a cancer developed on his knee. He hurried to Europe for an operation, but got no further than Marseilles. There, his leg was amputated, and he died in hospital.

Meanwhile, in 1886, Verlaine had published Rimbaud's poems. Rimbaud, in Abyssinia, did not know it, but he had become famous. The aura of mystery attached to his name helped to make his fame; no one knew what had become of him, but it was assumed that he was dead. Many young writers were powerfully influenced by his work (the most important of these was Paul Claudel). The mystery is by no means cleared up today; there is still some controversy about whether *A Season in Hell* was really intended by Rimbaud to be his last work. (Miss Enid Starkie contends that it was not; if her supposition is correct, it is still possible that more works of Rimbaud may turn up out of the heart of Africa.)

Rimbaud reminds one inevitably of T. E. Lawrence. In both cases, there are the early, creative years, introspective, but full of will power and high-pressure development. Then the crises: for Lawrence, the desert war, for Rimbaud, the period with Verlaine; and after that, disillusionment and renunciation, the deliberate choice of oblivion; finally, accidental death, as if the fates had finally grown impatient about their failure to be creative. Both combined self-analysis with the mental make-up of the man of action.

Well, the key to Lawrence, as we saw in *The Outsider,* was that he thought too much; he could not stop thinking; thinking robbed him of all direct sense of the world and made him incapable of experiencing any other being but his own, a prisoner in his own rationality.

The same was true of Rimbaud, except that Rimbaud made war on his rationality. His perception was Blakean. In an early poem, he had written:

Notre pâle raison nous cache l'infini.

Reason for him, as for Blake, meant 'single vision and Newton's sleep.' He was far more positive than Lawrence, more wilful. He set about dominating his reason, with the sole aim of intensifying his intuitive experience:

> I accustomed myself to simple hallucination: I really saw a mosque in place of a factory, angels practising on drums, coaches on the roads across the sky; a drawing-room at the bottom of a lake: monsters, mysteries.[31]

But dominating the reason requires continual discipline — especially if one has the penetrating rational intelligence of a Rimbaud or a Lawrence. For a few years, Rimbaud was successful. Then, as practical questions began to demand his attention, his grip loosened. He restored the grip by wallowing in sensual practices, sex, absinthe, drugs — but it was not the same as in Charleville, when he had read treatises on magic. And finally, it would seem, he surrendered (although it might be as well to keep an open mind on this matter, in case Abyssinian poems *should* turn up). The early vision, the early certainty, disappeared. It has been said that Rimbaud was sustained by a satanic pride, but it was not mere pride. Ancient Egyptian noblemen boasted of being related to the gods; Rimbaud, too, began to create with this certainty, refusing to accept the common lot of mere humanity. It would seem to be a case of hard experience destroying the visions. He began by thinking of himself as a god; he ended by thinking of himself as human. That was his tragedy.

His achievement remains: it can be summarised in his phrase: 'One *makes oneself a visionary. . . .*' At the age of sixteen, he had seen all the way, to the end of the road; the final answer. But it was a goal which he was never to reach.

We have glanced at two 'visionaries,' and tried to pinpoint their inadequacy. Unfortunately, neither of them could be called 'twentieth-century figures,' in the sense that Lorca or James Joyce could be. This century has brought its own problems and complications; and above all, completely new conditions for the man of genius. The career of a typical twentieth-century Outsider might repay brief consideration. On a less serious level than Rilke or Rimbaud, the life of F. Scott Fitzgerald draws attention to new aspects of the problem.

Fitzgerald's life is the tragedy of a romantic Outsider in a mechanised civilisation. He was born talented, and with an incurably histrionic outlook on the world. Graceful language came to him as easily as to Oscar Wilde, and the power of evoking an atmosphere in a few words:

> One night ... I sat in a swaying motor-boat by the club-house pier, and while the moon beat out golden scales on the water, heard young Byron Kirby propose to Mary Cooper. ...[32]

The word-power comes out in descriptions of school friends whom he admired: Hobey Baker, the football captain at Princeton, 'slim and defiant'; 'the romantic Buzz Law, whom I had last seen one cold fall twilight in 1915, kicking from behind his goal line with a bloody bandage around his head'; his boyhood rival, Reuben Warner, sitting with 'aloof exhaustion' at the wheel of his Stutz Bearcat, and Fitzgerald's description of how he himself had 'slouched passionately' over the wheel of their family car in an effort to imitate him.

This is the interesting feature of Fitzgerald: the violent romanticism, straight out of Schiller or Hoffmann; the conviction that life *had* to offer him something fascinating. And it paid off. He canalised it into his first novel, *This Side of Paradise*, and the novel brought him fame at twenty-four; and more than fame, the dubious position of being regarded as a 'spokesman of the younger generation.'

The novel had been written under difficult circumstances; he had given up his job at the age of twenty-two, and retired, as he put it, 'not on my profits, but on my liabilities, which included debts, despair and a broken engagement.' To escape the pain of the broken engagement, he had stayed drunk for three weeks. Then he settled down to write. The girl had turned him down because he had no money or prospects. He was convinced he had genius. *This Side of Paradise* was written in three months and despatched to a publisher.* Two weeks later, it was accepted. He was so excited that he ran along the streets, stopping cars to tell friends that he was going to be

---

* Actually, it was revised and considerably lengthened from an earlier version called *The Romantic Egotist*.

published. He had no doubt the book would make his name. It never occurred to him that it might be forgotten in a week, like most modern novels. He informed his publishers airily that he would be satisfied with a sale of 20,000 copies — apparently unaware that he would be lucky if (as a first novel) it sold a quarter that number. Duly, it was published, sold 40,000 copies in a few months, and rocketed Fitzgerald to fame. Fitzgerald was the representative of a new generation and a new approach to life — at least, that was what the critics said. Fitzgerald says of it:

> . . . Petting, in its more audacious manifestations, was confined to the wealthier classes — among other young people, the old standard prevailed until after the war, and a kiss meant that a proposal was expected, as young officers in strange cities sometimes discovered to their dismay. Only in 1920 did the veil finally fall — the Jazz Age was in flower.[33]

And it so happened that Fitzgerald's manifesto, *This Side of Paradise*, was published in 1920 — the year when fashionable Europe and America went on what Fitzgerald has called 'the greatest, gaudiest spree in history.'

> A whole race going hedonistic, deciding on pleasure. . . . The sequel was like a children's party taken over by the elders. . . . By 1923 their elders, tired of watching the carnival with ill-concealed envy, had discovered that young liquor will take the place of young blood, and with a whoop the orgy began.[34]

Fitzgerald and his newly married wife, Zelda, were right in at the head of it. Both were physically beautiful; both had grace and charm. And Fitzgerald had $18,000 to spend. They rode on top of taxis, jumped into public fountains, tried to undress in restaurants, spun around in revolving doors for half an hour, drank phenomenal quantities of whisky and champagne, and rushed from party to party or city to city in a shower of enthusiasm and popularity like confetti. They got through the $18,000:

> The cashier had not even scowled at me. I had walked in and said to him: 'How much money have I got?' And he had looked in a big book and answered: 'None.'

That was all. There were no harsh words, no blows. And I knew there was nothing to worry about. I was now a successful author, and when successful authors ran out of money, all they had to do was to sign cheques. I wasn't poor — they couldn't fool me.[35]

In a burst of energy, Fitzgerald produced another novel, *The Beautiful and Damned*. Again, it was a considerable success. Again, Fitzgerald drew mainly on his own experience — this time his experiences since the publication of *This Side of Paradise*. It is hardly surprising that Fitzgerald later admitted to feeling nostalgic about the Jazz Age.

It bore him up, flattered him and gave him more money than he had dreamed of, simply for telling people that he felt as they did. . . .[36]

There was an extravagance about everything Fitzgerald did. In Paris, he announced to James Joyce that he intended jumping out of the window as a sign of his immense admiration for Joyce's genius. (*Ulysses* had barely been published at the time.) Joyce succeeded in restraining him, and afterwards commented mildly: 'That young man must be mad — I'm afraid he'll do himself some injury.' He played extraordinary practical jokes: one day he dumped a bin full of garbage over the hedge of a garden party to which he had not been invited by a society hostess. When he was approached by an old woman carrying a tray of imitation flowers, he 'gave it a sort of gay 'nineties kick and sent everything flying,' but was immediately full of remorse and desire to make amends. He and Zelda planned to saw a waiter in two with a musical saw ('to eliminate any sordidness'). On another occasion, at a farewell dinner given for the film star Grace Moore in Juan-les-Pins, Zelda jumped up, saying, 'What are words? Nobody has offered our departing heroes any gift to take with them'; she stepped out of her black lace panties and threw them on to the table. Grace Moore's fiancé announced that he must perform a heroic act in return, and jumped into the sea in his dinner jacket. When the excitement died down, they became aware of Alexander Woollcott, completely naked except for a straw hat and a cigarette, walking slowly across the garden and into the hotel, where he took his key from the desk and marched up to his room.

It is this age of fantastic parties that is conveyed in the books: there is an exotic, moneyed splendour about Fitzgerald's world. He gives the impression that the adults of the nineteen-twenties lived with the same exhilarated abandon as the teenagers of *This Side of Paradise*. There is a curious, dreamlike air about it all: like the party that occupies the third chapter of *The Great Gatsby:*

> A stout, middle-aged man, with enormous owl-eyed spectacles, was sitting somewhat drunk on the edge of a great table, staring with unsteady concentration at the shelves of books. . . .
>
> 'Absolutely real — have pages and everything. I thought they'd be a nice durable cardboard. . . . Pages and — Here! Lemme show you.'
>
> Taking our scepticism for granted, he rushed to the bookcases, and returned with Volume One of the *Stoddard Lectures*.
>
> 'See!' he cried triumphantly. 'It's a bona fide piece of printed matter. . . . What thoroughness! What realism! Knew when to stop, too — didn't cut the pages. . . .' [37]

It is a strange combination: the fairy-tale effect of the garden party in *The Man Who Was Thursday*, and an underlying exhaustion and unreality, as in Camus's *L'Etranger*. Gatsby is a symbol of Fitzgerald himself; his immense parties are only an attempt to impress a girl who rejected him once, a pathetic substitute for heroism. And Fitzgerald's drinking was a substitute for vitality; sometimes he was drunk for ten days at a time, and woke up in a strange town, unable to remember anything that had happened since he began drinking. There was the attempt at the heroic gesture, the Gargantuan hugeness; always, the sequel of headaches and hangovers, the sense of failure and the anxiety about money that was spent as fast as he received it from high-paying American magazines. Gertrude Stein coined the phrase 'lost generation' about the Jazz Age, but Fitzgerald was never morally lost; only an idealist could have lived as he did in the 'twenties. It was not boredom or despair that drove him on to dipsomania, that wrecked his wife's sanity: it was a lopsided idealism, a thirst for experience, that was derived from Rupert Brooke and the poetry of the 'nineties. In Brooke too there had been the hunger for all experience:

> It's the sort of day that brought back to me what I've had so rarely for the last two years — that tearing hunger to do and do and do things. I want to walk 1000 miles, and write 1000 plays, and sing 1000 poems, and drink 1000 pots of beer, and kiss 1000 girls. . . . The spring makes me almost ill with excitement. I go round corners on the roads shivering and nearly crying with suspense. . . .[38]

It is the same kind of generalised appetite for all experience that turns up again in Thomas Wolfe in the late nineteen-twenties — Wolfe's hero of *Look Homeward, Angel* who stands in the Library of Congress and yearns to read all the books, and know all the people who pass outside in the street. It was a poem of Brooke's that supplied the title of *This Side of Paradise;* a sensuous vision of heaven as a South Sea island. The same lust for experience and the intangible that drove Brooke from England to America, to the South Seas, leaving him always exhausted and disappointed, that fatigued and wrecked Thomas Wolfe in less than ten years after he had achieved literary fame with a youthful best seller, kept Fitzgerald and Zelda on the move. There is a startling similarity of temperament between Fitzgerald and Brooke; the letters of both are full of fooling and mock heroics:

> Please don't say you can't come the 25th but would like to come the 29th. We never receive people the 29th. It is the anniversary of the 2nd Council of Nicea when our Blessed Lord, our Blessed Lord, our Blessed Lord, our Blessed Lord ——
> It always gets stuck in that place. . . .[39]

And Brooke, in his teens:

> I am busy with an enormous romance, of which I have written five chapters. It begins with my famous simile about the moon ['the moon was like an enormous yellow scab on the flesh of some

leper'] but soon gets much more lewd. One of the chief characters is a dropsical leper whose limbs and features have been absorbed in one vast soft paunch. He looks like a great human slug,
and he croaks infamous little songs from a . . . round mouth with
yellow lips. The others are less respectable.[40]

But there was an intellectual seriousness about Brooke, and a quality of perception, that could have saved him from alcoholism in the
face of any disillusion. He could write in a letter to F. H. Keeling,
speaking of his own form of mysticism:

> It consists in just looking at people and things as themselves —
> neither as useful nor moral nor ugly nor anything else; *but just as
> being.* . . . I can watch a dirty middle-aged tradesman in a railway-
> carriage for hours. . . . I know their states of mind are bad. But
> I'm so much occupied with their being there at all, that I don't
> have time to think of that. I tell you that a Birmingham gouty
> Tariff Reform fifth-rate business man is splendid and immortal
> and desirable.[41] [Italics mine.]

Fitzgerald lacked this kind of perception, and as the idealism
leaked away, there was nothing to put in its place. Zelda had a
nervous breakdown and went into a mental home for a while. He
produced bad stories for commercial magazines, and drank. His
finest novel, *The Great Gatsby*, had been highly praised, but had
not sold as he had expected, and a few years after this, the demand
for his stories from the big magazines began to lessen. Other young
writers had arrived: Ernest Hemingway, Dos Passos, Wolfe, and
later, Faulkner. There was a period of self-pity, when he tended to
put the blame for his failure on his wife, and he dramatised the situation in his next novel, *Tender Is the Night*, in which a brilliant
and promising young psychiatrist marries a beautiful rich girl who
had been undergoing psychiatric treatment; he plunges into her
world of parties and summers on the Riviera, and ends as a dipsomaniac and a failure. The rich girl goes off and marries somebody
else. Fitzgerald was convinced that the novel would re-establish him
as the foremost writer of the time; he never recovered from the
blow of its complete failure. He was now forty. He and Zelda were

separated. His most serious and carefully constructed novel sold less than a quarter the number of copies of the first, carelessly dashed-off book. His nervous energy and self-confidence were badly sapped. And suddenly, he ran face-on into the basic experience of the Outsider — the devastation, the crack-up. He describes it in an essay called *The Crack-Up*: how he had been told by a doctor that he was tubercular, and had gone away and rested:

— And then suddenly, surprisingly, I got better.
— And cracked like an old plate as soon as I heard the news.

It was the moral exhaustion of the years of endless movement. Analysing it, he recognised:

. . . that in those two years, in order to preserve something — an inner hush maybe, maybe not — I had weaned myself from all the things I used to love — that every act of life, from the morning tooth-brush to the friend at dinner had become an effort. I saw that for a long time I had not liked people and things, but only followed the rickety old pretence of liking. I saw that even my love for those closest to me was become only an attempt to love, that my casual relations — with an editor, a tobacco seller, the child of a friend, were only what I remembered I *should* do, from other days. All in the same month I became bitter about the sound of the radio, the advertisements in the magazines, the screech of tracks, the dead silence in the country — contemptuous at human softness, immediately (if secretively) quarrelsome towards hardness — hating the night when I couldn't sleep, and hating the day because it went towards night. I slept on the heart side now, because I knew that the sooner I could tire that out, even a little, the sooner would come that blessed hour of nightmare which, like a catharsis, would enable me the better to meet the new day.[42]

It is to be noted that this experience is *the complete reverse* of Brooke's description of his feelings about businessmen in a train. It is the other side of the coin, complete apathy and dislike instead of vital insight. Fitzgerald has swung from the Rupert Brooke romanticism to a Chekhovian preoccupation with failure and collapse.

This, of course (although he never seemed to realise it), was what made *Tender Is the Night* so unpopular, and what would probably have made his last novel equally unpopular if he had ever finished it. It was full of brilliant observation, but depressingly unconstructive. By that time, Fitzgerald had made a sort of philosophy of failure. He was able to look back on his early life, and say of it:

> . . . [I believed] Life was something you dominated if you were any good. Life yielded easily to intelligence and effort . . . Life, ten years ago, was largely a personal matter. I must hold in balance the sense of the futility of effort, and the sense of the necessity to struggle; the conviction of the inevitability of failure, and still the determination to 'succeed'. . . .[43]

This was written four years before his death. He had steadily lost control. It was a long way from the best-selling young writer of 1920 (when a New York newspaper had run a headline: 'Fitzgerald knocks policemen other side of Paradise'), to this tired, defeated alcoholic of 1936. His marriage had broken up: partly because of his wife's temperament, her need to be more than the wife of a successful writer — to be herself successful and the centre of attention. His income was less than a third of what it had been in the years of his success. He felt he had sold out to commercial success. He had become nervous and bitter, often quarrelsome, frequently depressed. It seemed there was nothing left of the enthusiasm and vitality of the 'twenties. Like Vaslav Nijinsky, he began to see misery and tragedy wherever he looked:

> By this time, contemporaries of mine had begun to disappear into the dark maw of violence. A classmate killed himself and his wife on Long Island, another tumbled 'accidentally' from a skyscraper in Philadelphia, another purposely from a skyscraper in New York. One was killed in a speakeasy in Chicago; another was beaten to death in a speakeasy in New York and crawled home to the Princeton Club to die; still another had his skull crushed by a maniac's axe in an insane asylum where he was confined. These are not catastrophes that I went out of my way to look for — these were my friends. . . .[44]

He was writing better than ever before, and he knew it. Hemingway told him in a letter about *Tender Is the Night*, 'You are twice as good now as you were at the time you thought you were so marvellous.' Once, in exasperation at a young writer who praised *This Side of Paradise*, he said: 'You mention that book again and I'll slug you.' He was still making over $10,000 a year, but after what he had earned in the 'twenties, he felt poverty-stricken. He felt, like Axel, that the world is 'an old slave who promises us the keys to a palace of enchantment when he only clutches a handful of ashes in his fist.' The fun had gone; Zelda had gone — Zelda, who had once flung herself down a steep flight of steps in jealousy when Isadora Duncan had indicated that she would like to go to bed with Scott; who had been the symbol of his youth and success. He drifted towards Hollywood, and did some work on second-rate films. Budd Schulberg has described how shocked he felt when he met Fitzgerald in Hollywood — the writer he had always admired — and found him generally disregarded, patching up bad scripts. In his novel *The Disenchanted*, Schulberg gives a fictional version of how he started Fitzgerald on his last drinking session — inadvertently; at the time, Fitzgerald had been 'on the wagon' for several weeks, trying to finish his novel about Hollywood, *The Last Tycoon*. As a result of the session, Fitzgerald brought on a heart attack; he died in Hollywood in December, 1940. At the time of his death, none of his work was in print. He was buried quietly — according to his own wish — in Rockville, Maryland. As usual, critical opinion of his work began to rise after his death. The publication of *The Last Tycoon* fragment was the signal for a chorus of appreciation, and declarations that he belonged among the major American writers.

Now, seventeen years after his death, his position is secure. *The Great Gatsby* is generally recognised as one of the great novels of modern times; *Tender Is the Night* has received warm critical appreciation; most of his books are obtainable in cheap reprints; Professor Mizener's biography, *The Far Side of Paradise* (on which I have drawn largely for the present account), is exhaustive and unbiased, and is unlikely to be supplanted as the standard Life.

Consideration of Fitzgerald's life takes us to the heart of the problem to be dealt with in this book. He is a product of our modern civilisation, completely typical of it. His life was a mess. By material standards, he was a successful man:

It seemed a romantic business to be a successful literary man —
you were not ever going to be as famous as a movie star, but what
note you had was probably longer-lived — you were never going
to have the power of a man of strong political or religious convictions, but you were certainly more independent.[45]

Yet, without the convictions, he wrecked. Literary success *is* a
romantic thing — at least, it will always look that way to the average person, and no writer can deny that he wants an audience
above all other things. But Fitzgerald was not ready for it. He was
never sufficiently master of his own experience. He denied that
'life was something you dominated if you were good enough,' and
yet it was precisely this failure to dominate that Hemingway put
his finger on in that passage of *The Snows of Kilimanjaro:*

> Poor [Scott] and his romantic awe of [the rich] . . . he thought
> they were a special glamorous race, and when he found out they
> weren't, it wrecked him just as much as anything ·had wrecked
> him.
> He [Hemingway] had been contemptuous of those who
> wrecked. . . . He could beat anything . . . because nothing could
> hurt him if he did not care. . . .[46]

But perhaps diagnosing Fitzgerald's failure is not particularly instructive, after considering such men as Rilke and Rimbaud; it is too
elementary. He was a romantic, and he had considerable integrity,
which survived his success and period of literary prostitution un-
scathed. In the nineteenth century, he might not have come to a
great deal of harm; the penalties and temptations of success were
less great then. It is more interesting to wonder what would have
become of Rimbaud if he had been a young American in the
'twenties, and had made his type of 'rebellion' fashionable, as
Fitzgerald made *his* in *This Side of Paradise*. Fitzgerald's significance is to point out that the modern Outsider has a new problem
that did not exist in previous ages. In the past, the Outsider's chief
enemy was the indifference of his time, his failure to communicate,
failure to achieve self-expression. Ours is the first age in Western
history in which the Outsider has had to face the other danger —

horrifying because it is so insidiously attractive — of arousing too much sympathy and interest, of being paid and flattered by the age 'for telling people you feel as they do.'

The ultimate significance of Fitzgerald's predicament will emerge in the following chapter, in which this question of twentieth-century civilisation must be looked at more closely. For the moment, it can be observed that we have come a long way from the 'Outsider problems' with which this chapter opened: the Swiftian contempt for human beings, the man in the cage of apes. On the contrary, Fitzgerald was the dupe of his time; its appearance of riches and prosperity took him in. For all his talent, he was not big enough to be a representative figure of the twentieth century. He did not understand his own age.

I have stated that the Outsider's problems point to the 'visionary' way. That is only the answer for the individual. The avowed intention of this book is to say something about the need for a new religion in our time. And a religion is, by definition, a great deal more than a collection of religious individuals. It means a Church, and a communal form of worship. It is true that the individual Outsider arrives at a fundamentally religious solution when he recognises the need for a visionary and anti-humanistic attitude; but such a recognition is still a long way from belonging to a Church, especially in an age like ours, when the Church would seem to have lost all contact with the problems which beset us.

Ivan Karamazov argued that the State ought to be no more than a small corner of the Church. This is a view which is naturally sympathetic to the Outsider. If the Church represents spiritual reality (and the Outsider is interested in nothing if not in spiritual reality — even a man like Fitzgerald, with his continual juggling with emotions in his art, his refusal to be finally taken in by them), then certainly the State ought to be subordinate to it; for the State represents temporal expediency. But the moment the Outsider has been as bold as Ivan Karamazov, and made some statement which has a practical application, he has committed himself to a new type of problem. It is no longer the simple Outsider problem — the ultimate metaphysical problem of the unreality of life — but the practical problem of modern civilisation.

This is — and so it should be — the ground upon which the Outsider must justify himself in our century. There will always be men who will say: the Outsider is a stupid neurotic; his problems do not really exist; tell him to stop caterwauling and let us get on with solving the *real* problems of life.

But this argument is shortsighted. The real problems cannot be solved on this 'practical' basis, as the end of our Western civilisation may prove. They can only be solved on an Outsider basis. Two centuries ago, Blake stormed against abstract philosophy and materialism, and his protests have even more relevance today. The Outsider is the key to the decline of the West.

THE OUTSIDER
AND HISTORY

Towards the end of 1918, an enormous volume appeared on the bookstalls of Germany, with the provocative title: *The Decline of the West*.

For a few weeks, no one noticed it; it lay unbought in the shops. There were no reviews. Then, slowly, people began to feel curious about the immense tome whose first sentence declared:

> In this book is attempted for the first time the venture of pre-determining history, of following the still untravelled stages in the destiny of a Culture. . . .[1]

Perhaps this is the reason that the book began to sell in spite of the academic cold-shoulder: possibly its first audience consisted of the people who read 'What the stars say' in the Sunday papers. It was vast and ponderous and metaphysical, and had many footnotes and references to historians and philosophers; but it also professed to be a vision of the doom of our civilisation, a prophecy of the decline of the West. When the book became widely discussed, learned journals published attacks on it, and its sales rose steeply. It became something of a best seller, and the surprised publisher (who had printed only fifteen hundred copies) had to print a second and third and fourth impression in quick succession. Within ten years of publication, it had sold a hundred thousand copies. No one had ever heard of its author, Oswald Spengler. Subsequent publicity revealed that he was a former high-school teacher, with no special academic qualifications. The immense reading that supported the argument of *The Decline of the West* had apparently been done for his private pleasure. He was a frail, shortsighted man, with a tiny private income. Until 1910, he had been a teacher in Saarbrücken, Düsseldorf and Hamburg, teaching mathematics, biology, and even German, geography and history for a period. Teaching bored him; he wanted time to write and study (like another young writer of genius who had just thrown over his job as a schoolteacher — D. H. Lawrence). He began a book about politics, called *Conservative and Liberal* — the first version of *The Decline*. The legend has it that he saw a copy of Gibbon's *Decline and Fall* in a bookshop in Munich, and had his first ideas on how to re-shape his book on politics. Then the war came, and his modest income dropped below the level that means comfort even to an ascetic scholar. He was forced to take cheap rooms in a slum in Munich. He ate his meals in a workman's café. In his unheated room, he would pore shortsightedly over the manuscript of *The Decline of the West*. It is curious to remember that a quarter of a century earlier, Nietzsche had worked under exactly the same conditions, handicapped by myopia and headaches, the lower part of his body wrapped in blankets, occasionally laying down his pen to warm his hands at the oil lamp.

By 1917, the manuscript of the first part was finished. Then began the long business of submitting it to publishers, and having it returned regularly. All the major German publishing houses refused it. Finally, a small Austrian publisher agreed to risk an edition of fifteen hundred copies, and the book appeared in 1918.

There can be no doubt that it was successful for the same kind of reason that Eliot's *Waste Land* and Joyce's *Ulysses* were successful — because it expressed a new and pessimistic attitude towards life that had absolutely nothing in common with pre-war attitudes. It is interesting to realise that when Schopenhauer published his *World as Will and Idea* precisely a century before, his pessimism was so unfashionable that it took another thirty years for him to become known. Yet Schopenhauer's book and *The Decline* are so similar in attitude that they could almost be called literary brothers.

Probably after *The Decline* had been ignored for a few weeks,
Spengler began to wonder whether his fate would be the same as
Schopenhauer's. In some ways, he might have been better off if it
had been; for when he died, less than twenty years later, his name
had sunk into disrepute. In Nazi Germany, Nietzschean prophets
were not required.

What is it that makes *The Decline* such fascinating reading — as
fascinating now as the day it came out? First, because it is not in
any sense an 'academic' book. Spengler's intellect has a tremendous
range. On one page he is quoting Goethe or Bernard Shaw; on the
next, talking about Einstein and modern mathematics; on the next,
about Chinese art or Greek sculpture or the influence of the Mon-
gols on China. He is a poet who is fascinated by all kinds of subjects. (Again, it is interesting to note that *The Waste Land* and
Ulysses are remarkable for the breadth of their erudition.) One's
first feeling about *The Decline* is sheer admiration for the range of
this man who seems to know as much about art and music as about
biology and mathematics.

Later, one is impressed less by the literary fireworks than by the
depth of intuition, and the unified vision of history that Spengler
possesses. Spengler himself states in one place that he has been the
first to do for history what Newton did for mathematics, shaping
previously disconnected data into a coherent body of knowledge.
Before him, history had usually been regarded as a mass of odd
facts about the past. But Spengler advanced a surprising contention.
He claimed that civilisations are like human beings: they are
born, grow to maturity, and finally die out. Human beings are
made of biological cells. Civilisations are made of human beings,
who die out and are replaced by new generations just as the cells
of our bodies are completely changed every eight years. Progress?
There is no such thing. Just as every generation of human beings is
as stupid as the last one, so it is with civilisations. The aim? There
is no aim. It is just a biological process, like life itself.

Here we enter on the Outsider's ground. He is unwilling to
accept that life is just meaningless repetition of human futilities.
This is where the Outsider parts way with Spengler. But before
we insist upon this point, let us look more closely at Spengler's
method of arguing.

Spengler's basic method is to compare 'cultures.' It must be emphasised that he considered that history could be made into a *science*, like biology or physics. There is a branch of natural history called homology, which compares similar members and organs of various animals; for instance, the arm of a man, and the wing of a bird and a bat. Spengler applies the same kind of technique to history. The whole opening chapter of *The Decline* is devoted to numbers. Spengler claims that every 'culture' has had a different idea of mathematics. There is no such thing as 'mathematics' in the way that there is astronomy or chemistry; there are different kinds of mathematics in different civilisations, just as there are different arts — Egyptian, Greek, Babylonian, Arabian. The Egyptians had a strong sense of eternity — as their tombs prove; their idea of number was of pure, eternal entities. The Greeks were passionately devoted to the 'here and now' and never thought about eternity; their mathematics was devoted to the measurement of *things*, and was connected with the visible world. They invented geometry. Western man has a sense of time and change; his peculiar additions to mathematics are calculus, the mathematics of change, and per-mutations, the mathematics of chance.

This last paragraph can only give a vague idea of the way Spengler argues — the reason being that he does not really argue. He just states. Frequently, he does not bother to give a reason for some assertion. He admits this frankly, claiming that what makes the *real* historian — as distinguished from the academic dust-grubber — is his intuitive sense of the meaning behind events. It is the same gift that makes a great statesman or a great soldier. You cannot become a great statesman merely by studying the lives of Cato, Masaryk and Disraeli. You cannot become a great soldier by read-ing Clausewitz and Foch. The great statesman or soldier has a vital intuition which he combines with his practical capacity. So, Spengler contends, has the historian.

This view, of course, derives from Goethe. There is the famous story of Goethe and Schiller leaving a scientific lecture in Jena. Goethe said restively: 'There is another way of apprehending na-ture, *active and living*, struggling from the whole into parts.' Schiller replied mistrustfully: 'That's not practical; it's just an *idea* of yours.' Yet Goethe had put his finger on the central problem of the decline of the West.

Over a hundred years were to elapse before Alfred North Whitehead settled down to defining that problem in his book *Science and
the Modern World*. It is the question of the 'bifurcation of nature.'
Knowledge has come to mean something dry and static and logical,
and the poet's intuition is attacked by professors for not being
logically deduced from accepted premises. Yet, as Spengler knew,
even the great mathematicians are usually artists and not logicians
— Newton, Gauss, Riemann. (We shall later reinforce this point
in discussing Pascal and Swedenborg.) The mark of greatness is
always intuition, not logic. Our civilisation has unfortunately made
an imaginary distinction between the two, which is called 'philosophy.' Existentialism is a revolt against it.

It can be seen, then, that Spengler was actually a *historical existentialist*. This is his real importance. And although this is a very
difficult point — the concept of existentialism is as difficult for our
generation as relativity was for the physicists of fifty years ago —
it must be underlined here, for it is of major importance in the
problem of the Outsider. Let me be as explicit about this as I can:

The mediaeval Church believed that all history moved towards
the Last Judgement and the establishment of the Kingdom of God.
The monk Joachim of Floris, who divided history into three periods,
the ages of the Father, the Son and the Holy Spirit, won a large
following.

With eighteenth-century rationalism, the idea of the goal of
history disappeared. History simply meant a succession of events
in the past. Men were no longer considered so important; if human
history were to have a goal, there ought also to be a goal for dogs
and cats and frogs and fishes. The scientific attitude replaced the
religious attitude.

This was all very fine in a way. Such an approach disposed of
many superstitions. But it also implied: Human life is a journey
from nowhere to nowhere. Like Darwinism, it banished free will
from the universe.

Spengler's work is a rebirth of the idea of destiny and purpose.

There is an excellent proverb which says: Throw out your dirty
water before you get your clean. The eighteenth-century rationalists threw out the dirty water of mediaeval concepts of purpose and
man's place in the universe. For nearly two hundred years, the

bucket has been empty — although the rationalists were too de-lighted with their new toy, and too deficient in the Outsider's craving for purpose and meaning, to notice that they had no water. But with Nietzsche and Kierkegaard, there came a desire to get some clean water, a new concept of man's place in the universe, less naïve than the mediaeval concept, based on man's knowledge of the powers of his own scepticism. Dostoevsky recognised the need in *The Devils*, where Kirilov states the problem: If man says there is no God, he must face the implication that *he must be God himself*. But Kirilov was a spiritual giant. Most men are spiritual pygmies, and cannot see the implications of their own argument.

It is the same with modern philosophy. Mediaeval theology said: Man's purpose is salvation. Men must strive to be worthy of Christ's atonement; if they succeed, they go to heaven when they die; if not, to hell or purgatory. The eighteenth century dismissed all this, and stated: Man is plainly an animal, and his sins are not the result of free will, but of social pressure and conditioning.

Once again, the result was to destroy a number of naïve super-stitions. But it also destroyed the concept of a *moral purpose*. It failed to recognise that the problems we call 'moral problems' con-tinue to exist, even when we have dismissed the idea that sinners go to hell; that moral problems are actually *problems of vitality*. A man is more alive than a cow, just as a cow is more alive than a tree. A man's temperament gives him the power to become more alive or less alive. He can drift, give way to every sensual urge, and become little better than a cow; or he can discipline himself, exercise his intelligence, and raise himself to a higher form of life, automatically recognised by other men as a leader. A cow's temperament gives it less room to alter itself, but still — as every dairyman knows — there are stupid cows and intelligent cows. The tree has no power to alter itself at all. Morality, then, is the power of higher forms of life to achieve yet more life; sin is the *drifting* of higher forms of life towards an animal level. It is essentially the road of least resist-ance.

These definitions are implied in the work of Kierkegaard, Nietzsche, Shaw — even Mr. Eliot.* When the eighteenth century had thoroughly established the ideas of rationalism, the Outsiders

---

* 'Make perfect your Will.' *The Rock.*

began the existentialist revolt. The old religion was too naïve. But
so was the new rationalism. *They should never have become
divorced in the first place.* In the sages of ancient India and China,
great intellect and great religious urges co-existed in the same men
— Lao-tse, Chuang Tzu, Manu, Vyasa; the obvious necessity is that
the great artists and philosophers of the age should also be its
religious men and scientists. The scientist should be as capable of
attaining religious insight as the monk is of understanding the
quantum theory. The necessity today is obviously for a renaissance
of the idea of purpose — of the meaning of life. This is the basis of
the existentialist revolt. It is true, as Hulme pointed out, that we can
never return to the naïve religion of the Church of the Middle Ages.
Rationalism has increased man's stature. But it has also created
certain problems that threaten to wreck our civilisation. And now
we have arrived at the point where the Outsider and Spengler join
hands. For the Outsider's sense of urgency and approaching doom
is precisely the same sense as Spengler's. The Outsider only exists
because our civilisation has lost its religion. *The Outsider is the
result of Whitehead's 'bifurcation of nature,'* and Spengler's *Decline*
is a study of civilisation in which the Outsider has become the representative figure. The bifurcation of nature is the cause of the decline of the West.

Whitehead's philosophy will be more carefully examined in the
last chapter of this book. For readers who have never studied
Whitehead, it is not essential to understand the 'philosophy of
organism' at this point. All that matters now is to understand what
is meant by the statement that Spengler is an existentialist historian.
Existentialism is the revolt against mere logic and reason. It is a
plea for intuition and vision. It is a plea for recognising oneself as
being *involved* in the problems of existence as a participant, not just
as a spectator. All these things Spengler brought to the study of
history. He was a man who loved poetry and music, who quoted
Goethe and Nietzsche endlessly, who saw even mathematics and
science as a part of the battle of the human spirit towards greater
vision and deeper insight. Possibly his history lacks the precision
and sobriety of *The Cambridge Medieval History,* yet his contribution is far more important. Modern history moves towards the
breakdown. We cannot treat it as if we were eternal onlookers,
gifted with everlasting life, accumulating new bits of evidence like

Browning's Grammarian. Spengler's history has the nature of a
medical diagnosis. Admittedly, he regards our decline as inevitable
— just as any doctor regards death as inevitable. Yet, whether consciously or unconsciously, he has drawn attention to the problem of
the Outsider in civilisation. His very categories of history show this
existentialist approach; instead of dividing history into Ancient,
Mediaeval and Modern (as the Cambridge dons still do) he divides
it into cultures — Apollonian, Magian, Faustian. Our modern age
is the Faustian. It is significant that Spengler should choose the
name of Goethe's arch-Outsider to symbolise the West. Goethe's
Faust summarises the whole problem of the bifurcation of nature —
the division of intellect into science and art. At the beginning of
the poem, Faust stands precisely where the modern world stands.
He has followed the scientific method to its limit — studied philosophy, medicine, law, and now, he admits, he 'stands no wiser than
before.' (Recall Elijah's 'Take away my life, O Lord. . . .') His
knowledge is vanity and futility. It makes him cleverer, but no
wiser. His only way to escape is to summon up the devil, and ally
himself with him, *although he knows the devil is stupider than he is.*
Here is modern man — for all his scientific knowledge, as stupid as
his forefathers, and turning to all kinds of political charlatans for
leadership — wanting only to be *possessed*, possessed by anything,
by the latest politician or the latest crooner or film star — anything
to escape his own futility and emptiness.

It is impossible to give a summary of *The Decline of the West*
here. As many critics have pointed out, it is monstrously badly
written; repetitious, obscure, confused. And yet the clarity of
Spengler's mind emerges in spite of all these faults. Spengler the
existentialist is always making his attitude clear:

> Knowledge, for Kant, is mathematical knowledge. He deals
> with . . . the reason, but he never thinks of the wholly different
> mechanism by which historical impressions are apprehended.[2]
> . . . Newton, Gauss and Riemann were artist-natures, and we
> know with what suddenness their great conceptions came upon
> them.[3]

He announced with superb certainty: 'Systematic philosophy is
at an end,' meaning by 'systematic philosophy' what Blake meant

by 'abstract philosophy.' He is slashingly impatient with modern philosophers, and although his book appeared long before logical positivism or linguistic analysis, his criticisms might be aimed straight at Ayer and Carnap (not to mention Bertrand Russell):

> *A doctrine that does not attack and affect the life of the period in its inmost depths is no doctrine and had better not be taught.*[4]

Spengler was no escapist, no Barbusse Outsider who detested being forced to live. On the contrary, he embraced the complexity of modern civilisation:

> To me, the depths and refinement of mathematical and physical theories are a joy; by comparison, the aesthete and the physiologist are fumblers. I would sooner have the fine mind-begotten forms of a fast steamer, a steel structure, a precision-lathe, the subtlety and elegance of many chemical and optical processes, than all the . . . present-day 'arts and crafts'. . . . I prefer one Roman aqueduct to all Roman temples and statues. . . .[5]

This statement might have come from a Soviet 'realist' philosopher. Spengler's message is fatalism: it is Nietzsche's doctrine of *amor fati,* love of one's own destiny.

> . . . an irreligious time which coincides exactly with the idea of a world-city is a time of decline. True. But we have not *chosen* this time. We cannot help it if we are born as men of the early winter of . . . Civilisation. . . . Everything depends on our seeing our own position, our *destiny,* clearly, on our realising that though we may lie to ourselves about it we cannot evade it. . . .[6]

And Spengler prophesies an age of complete scepticism, which will be the last stage of Western civilisation. This he regards as the inevitable final stage of Western history, and, like H. G. Wells, believes that 'there is no way out or round or through.'

But let me repeat, the tremendous importance of *The Decline of the West* does not lie in its pessimistic conclusions, but in the luminous, vital intelligence of Oswald Spengler, who again and again makes statements of great importance to the Outsider. In a long footnote, for instance, he states that he owes the philosophy of *The Decline* to Goethe, and emphasises that Goethe is actually a philosopher of the first rank, although this is completely unrecognised today. He emphasises Goethe's kinship with Plato as an *anti-abstract philosopher* (he never uses the term 'existentialist,' but this is the nearest he comes to it!). *'Here we have intuition opposed to analysis.'* Plato, like Goethe, is as much of a poet and a playwright (or novelist!) as a philosopher. For Plato, it was as important to emphasise Socrates' *greatness as a man* as to show his brilliance as a thinker. This is existentialism, and in this sense, Shaw is the only other existentialist thinker of the same rank as Goethe and Plato. And this is the ultimate significance of the idea of the bifurcation of nature. If there are any readers who are still puzzled by the term, it is here that its meaning can be most clearly seen. The great man must be great in all things, not 'bifurcated'; not great in intellect alone, like Nietzsche or Lawrence, not great in intuition alone, like Van Gogh, not great in body alone, like Nijinsky, but all three at once. Only a great man is capable of great thought. Most Western philosophers have been spiritual cripples. The West has exalted the reasoning power above all other faculties, and the scientists and doctors can get away with anything. And yet we know that a man can have an extraordinary reasoning power, and still be a fool. For instance, there are certain men who are 'calculating prodigies.' One can ask them such questions as 'Give the square root of 3,748,289,' and the answer will be returned in a few minutes — sometimes a few seconds. Yet these calculating prodigies are often stupid youths, who grow up into completely untalented men. In the same way, some men show an unusual talent for languages, and can master dozens of languages in the time it would take a normal person to learn one, yet in other respects they seldom show any great intelligence. On the other hand, many men of acknowledged genius have confessed to having singularly slow brains. Shaw and H. G. Wells were both bad at languages. Thomas Mann protested that he had an unusually inefficient brain. Isaac Newton showed no sign of early mental development, and Beethoven never mastered the art of multiplying and dividing. What I wish to emphasise here is that a highly developed reasoning faculty has nothing whatever to do with genius. Nothing was ever *discovered* by logic. All things are discovered by intuition, as the lives of the great mathematicians and scientists prove again and again. Logic plods

after intuition, and verifies discoveries in its own pedestrian way.
Logic is a mere servant of the imagination. To exalt it — as modern
thinkers tend to — is to invite spiritual anarchy.

The importance of all this can hardly be exaggerated in an
examination of the Outsider. It is one of the basic causes of his
rejection of modern civilisation. Spengler realised this clearly.
The Outsider is a romantic and a mystic; and what is more, the
essence of Western civilisation — the 'Faustian culture' — is mystical and romantic. Western culture is the culture of Outsiders.
'Siegfried, Parsifal, Tristan, Hamlet, Faust are the loneliest heroes
in all the Cultures.' [7] The West is an Outsider culture, and an
attempt to analyse the Outsider's problems is an attempt to get
to the very heart of the problems of our civilisation. But even to
touch the surface of the problem requires unusual penetration and
intensity of mind. The Outsider is not a 'crazy mixed-up kid.' He
is not a bored and inefficient bank clerk. The essence of the Outsider problems lies in the need for self-transcendence. Spengler
quotes Part I of *Faust*:

> A longing pure and not to be described
> drove me to wander over woods and fields,
> and in a mist of hot abundant tears
> I felt a world arise and live for me.[8]

It is an experience known to a Rilke, a Rimbaud, a Goethe, an
Eliot, but hardly as common as some critics would have us believe.*

Spengler, then, stated the problem of the Outsider in historical
terms. Instead of comparing human beings, as I did in *The Outsider*,
he compares cultures, but the result is the same: a revolt against
'abstract philosophy' and materialism; an anti-liberal, anti-progress
attitude; an emphasis on the importance of Will. It is significant
that his conclusions are so close to Nietzsche's: a sort of 'eternal
recurrence,' the idea of *amor fati*, the anti-rational vitalism.

But Spengler, in many ways, was closer to Schopenhauer than

---

* Within a month of the publication of *The Outsider*, I received over
a thousand letters which began by claiming that the writer was an 'Outsider.' In many cases, this may have been so, but hardly in the sense that
I have implied above.

Nietzsche. His pessimistic view of history was not based on reason and observation; it was a temperamental bias, the vision of a prophet. And like most prophets, he was in reaction against his time, and driven to extremes by its shortcomings, by its spiritual laziness. Most prophets of a completely new idea tend to be extremists who deny the element of free will: compare Darwin, Freud, Marx, Gurdjieff.

As Spengler's views became more widely known, he founded a 'school,' and his followers tended to be less extreme in their pessimism. Spengler's fame did not last long in his own country. He showed himself to be anti-Nazi in his politics in the 'twenties, and when the Nazis came to power in the 'thirties, a cultural boycott began. He never again produced a work of the same magnitude and importance as *The Decline*, and his smaller works were either violently attacked, or ignored. Spengler didn't care; he had the Nietzschean power of aloneness, and worked on quietly on some gigantic metaphysical work that was never destined to see the light of day. He would undoubtedly have been held in high regard if he had chosen to support the Nazis, but he had the same sort of prejudice as Yeats about 'the rabble,' and preferred to hold it in scorn. His vogue with the general public had collapsed in the early nineteen-twenties, with the publication of a political tract, *Prussianism and Socialism*. Readers who rushed to buy it were disappointed, and declared that the author of *The Decline* was a mere journalist or crank. Later, as Hitler became more popular in Germany, Spengler made unflattering references to him; he commented that Hitler seemed less of a hero than a 'heroic tenor' from a Wagnerian opera! When the Nazis talked of the difference between Aryan and Semitic blood as the basis for their anti-Semitism, Spengler pointed out that it was actually the clash between the old Magian culture (the Jews) and the new Faustian. A second work, *Man and Technics*, was received without enthusiasm by the learned world, and a political volume, *The Hour of Decision*, was condemned and suppressed by the Nazis. When he died in 1936, his influence and reputation had almost disappeared; he was regarded as a crank and a reactionary. Foreigners tended to regard him as a supporter (and inspirer) of the Nazis, just as they regarded Nietzsche at the same time.

In retrospect, we cannot help feeling of him that he ought to have stuck to history and prophecy, and not meddled in politics. If he had done so, he might have lived many years longer. His political utterances now strike us as outdated or irrelevant. But *The Decline of the West* still remains one of the most significant books of the twentieth century:

> Each Culture has its own new possibilities of self-expression which arise, ripen, decay, and never return. There is not *one* sculpture, *one* painting, *one* mathematics, *one* physics, but many, each in its deepest essence different from the others, each limited in duration and self-contained, just as each species of plant has its own peculiar blossom or fruit, its special type of growth or decline. These cultures, sublimated life-essences, grow with the same superb aimlessness as the flowers of the field. They belong, like the plants and the animals, *to the living Nature of Goethe, and not to the dead Nature of Newton.* [My italics.][9]

It is his *living vision* of history that constitutes his greatness. It is an Outsider's vision, for the Outsider is in revolt against deadness and abstraction, which contradict the life he feels within himself.

To summarise, then: From Spengler, we learn that our culture is in decay, and that a symptom of its decay is 'abstract philosophy' which (as Blake knew) turns men into pygmies. Western culture is essentially Outsider culture (Faustian); our present-day materialism is a sign of its hardening arteries. But, according to Spengler, there is no escape. We are in the last stages of decay, and may as well take it for granted. There is no possibility of a new religion or a new philosophy. The soil of the West is 'metaphysically exhausted.' *Scepticism* is the only resource open to us; and scepticism, Spengler thinks, ought to be based on his *Decline of the West*. But then, he also believed that 'Mankind . . . has no aim, no idea, no plan, any more than the family of butterflies or orchids.' [10]

One tends to suspect that it is only Spengler's temperamental inability to conceive a purpose for all men which leads him to this complete pessimism and scepticism. At all events, the system of history that we are to examine — that of Arnold Toynbee — has all of Spengler's insight, without leading to the same pessimistic conclusions. It also treats the Outsider far more openly.

Spengler was not entirely without predecessors as a historian.

For the sake of completeness, it may be well to outline, very briefly, the ideas of some of these previous thinkers.

The first of importance is undoubtedly Giovanni Battista Vico, who was born in Naples in 1668. Vico's thought was directed very much along the same lines as the present book; he was equally interested in man as he *might be*, and man as he is — man as the Outsider conceives him, and man as history sees him. His two favourite authors were Plato and Tacitus, because they represent these two viewpoints. In his *New Science*, Vico propounds the idea of cyclic history, later thought of by Nietzsche. (James Joyce makes the idea the basis of *Finnegans Wake*.) Vico also recognised that civilisations begin with religious thought and progress to abstract thought. But, living in an age of 'progress,' Vico did not recognise as clearly as Spengler that the age of abstract thought precedes the downfall of civilisations. Nevertheless, in his major work, *Universal Law*, he attempts to show how an evolutionary force in man makes and changes laws, and how society depends upon the thought of its men of genius.

Nearly a century after Vico's birth, a great French thinker, Pierre Ballanche, was born in Lyons. Ballanche's way of thinking was even closer to Spengler's. His great unfinished book, the *Palingenesis*, has a tremendous sweep of ideas, ranging from man as he was before the rise of religion, to man as he might become in some ultimate state of perfection. The *Palingenesis* falls into three sections; the first, *Orpheus*, deals with man as he was in prehistoric times; the second, *The Formula*, covers the same ground as Spengler (although with far less power and insight): he tries to deduce 'laws of destiny' from the known facts of history. The third part (unfinished), *The City of Expiations*, considers what man *could become*. Ballanche's viewpoint was essentially religious. Like T. E. Hulme, he recognised the need for discipline and authority, and disliked the Rousseau notions of 'freedom' and 'progress.' The daring and breadth of Ballanche's vision has not been recognised in this country, or in the country of his birth. It is doubtful whether Spengler had ever read him.

Twenty years before Spengler began to write *The Decline*, two Boston brothers, Henry and Brooks Adams, were brooding on the laws of history. A young Frenchman, Alexis de Tocqueville, had

visited America for six months, and as a result of his examination
of the political scene, had written his famous *Democracy in America*,
in which, with the natural hauteur and detachment of an aristo-
crat, he had castigated the notion of mob rule. De Tocqueville admired the energy and 'push' of this new country, but he had seen
too much of political unrest in Europe not to ask where it was all
leading. Now, the Adams brothers, friends of the James family,
cultured Bostonians with the same mistrust of democracy, announced that Western civilisation was decaying, and nearing its end.
This was a startling conclusion to be reached in the midst of the
century of prosperity and progress, in a young and energetic
country. The Adams brothers did not become well known or
popular. Brooks wrote a book with the ominous title *The Law of
Civilisation and Decay*, which was mainly concerned with laws of
trade and population. Brooks claimed that the decay always
came about when 'surplus energy' created an unbearable internal
tension and pressure. This is as near to a *social theory of the Outsider* as any nineteenth-century historian approached. Materialism
increases, Brooks claimed, and imagination decreases; the result is a
failure of self-expression in society as a whole that is likely to burst
it apart. Brother Henry tried to be more precise about the decay
of the West, and tried to work out mathematical laws — which
strike modern readers in much the same way as Newton's scriptural
calculations of the age of the world, based on Archbishop Ussher
and the Book of Daniel. Henry had a temperament rather like
T. S. Eliot's; having rejected his own country and his own time,
he made the pilgrimage to Europe, and found solace in its cathedrals.
His finest and most beautiful book, *Mont-Saint-Michel and Chartres*,
is steeped in the atmosphere of the Middle Ages, and has the extraordinary serenity of a man who has at last found spiritual roots.*
He has remained best known for his autobiography, *The Education of Henry Adams*. But it is in his book *The Tendency of History* that he considers all the possibilities facing our civilisation,

---

* The relief with which he turned to mediaeval cathedrals may be
criticised as escapism — like Mr. Eliot's acceptance of the Anglican
communion — but I think that no one can read *Mont-Saint-Michel and
Chartres* without coming as completely under the spell of the Christian
Church in the Middle Ages as Henry Adams and Mr. Eliot.

and dismisses the idea that our materialistic 'progress' could continue indefinitely, or that world-communism could save us; and as to the idea of a new faith and a new religion, he states that this would be nothing less than committing suicide. The only hope might be for a 'science of history' to 'bring into sight some new *and hitherto unsuspected path for civilisation to pursue.*' The words have a Nietzschean ring — but Adams had nothing to suggest.

Two more thinkers of major importance should at least be mentioned in this brief account of Spengler's predecessors: Georges Sorel * and Vilfredo Pareto. They are both curious anti-revolutionary revolutionaries. Pareto jeered at Marxist ideology and its 'withering away of the state' (he caused Lenin some sleepless nights), and advanced his own thoroughly cynical view of history, in which the strong seized power because of their virtues of determination and ruthlessness, and then got lazy and guileful, to be eventually turned out by a new 'aristocracy' of strong and ruthless men. This was a new version of Nietzsche's 'master and slave' morality. Pareto had no political idealism at all; his approach was as realistic as Machiavelli's. Although, in his *Socialist Systems*, he dismissed all notions of a political Heaven on Earth, he had no positive religious ideals to advance in place of socialist systems. In his pessimism, he is very close to Spengler.

Georges Sorel was, in some ways, a greater man than Pareto, although his major work, *Reflections on Violence*, is only a volume of essays that hardly compares with Pareto's vast work. Sorel was a convinced socialist revolutionary who detested Marxist materialism, and insisted that socialism should have a religious basis, with a recognition of Original Sin and the need for discipline and authority. He had no particular party allegiance, and moved freely in and out of various parties, looking for real revolutionaries who might combine to get something done; he was, in fact, a thoroughly practical man, whose beliefs were entirely mystical. (We are reminded again of Shaw's Undershaft, the millionaire arms-king, who, when Barbara refers to him as a secularist, replies: 'On the contrary, my dear — a confirmed mystic!') Unfortunately, he never found his aristocracy of revolutionaries.

* The most easily available introduction to Sorel, for English readers, is the essay by T. E. Hulme, to be found in Appendix A of *Speculations*.

Other historians who should be mentioned in this connection are Jacob Burckhardt and Nicholas Danilevsky. Burckhardt was Nietzsche's friend at Basle university, but he became less and less friendly as Nietzsche elaborated his theory of the Superman. Burckhardt was as pessimistic about the future of the West as the Adams brothers. He is remarkable in having foreseen that the end would be preceded by an 'age of fuehrers,' and elaborated this idea in his political testament *Force and Freedom.*

Danilevsky was a biologist and a botanist who wrote a polemic called *Russia and Europe.* The thesis of this book was that Europe was on its way out, and Russia on its way in. Danilevsky's 'decline of the West' did not include the Slavic countries. But his analysis of the reasons for Europe's decline was reasonably thorough. His book was published half a century before Spengler's and stated that 'cultures' were like living beings, each with a definite life-span. Spengler had almost certainly never read him. One wonders what Danilevsky would have thought if he had foreseen the West-ernised modern Russia squabbling with America about a mere political ideology.

Arnold Toynbee's *A Study of History* is a record of one of the most extraordinary spiritual journeys of our time. (It is also the longest historical work of our time by a single author, its total length being a great deal over 5000 pages.) In spite of its length, and the impressiveness of its erudition, it is a far more personal work than the author is willing — at the outset, anyway — to concede. His first attempt to begin it, he admits, was cast in the form of a commentary on a certain chorus in Sophocles:

> Much is there passing strange;
> Nothing surpassing mankind.
> He it is loves to range
> Over the ocean hoar,
> Thorough the surgers' roar,
> South winds raging behind. . . .[11]

One penetrating observer, Mr. Albert Hourani, has commented that Toynbee's book is 'the product of a man of strange and power-ful imagination, haunted by echoes and visions.' In fact, the tenth (and last) volume of Toynbee's work is full of fascinating auto-biographical comments which show how far Toynbee's intuition and imagination were the sources of his *Study*. He describes, for instance, how

> . . . the writer of the present Study had an authentic minor personal experience . . . as he sat musing on the summit of the citadel of Mistra, with the sheer wall of Mount Taygetus bounding his horizon in the western quarter of the compass, towards which he was bound, and the open vale of Sparta stretching away in the opposite eastern quarter, from which he had made his way that morning.
>
> Though he had sat there, musing and gazing (and prosaically taking the edge off his hunger by consuming slabs of Pavlidhis' chocolate) through most of a long summer's day, till the gloom of evening constrained him reluctantly at last to move on in search of supper and a bed at Trypi, he cannot pretend he was inspired during his reverie on the summit by any strains from the throats of the nuns serving the church . . . for he had left this far below in his spiral ascent of the miniature purgatorial mount that the citadel crowned . . . The sensuous experience that activated his historical imagination . . . was the sight of the ruins among which he had wound his way upwards to the peak. . . .
>
> Mistra had continued . . . to reign for . . . six hundred years as the queen of the broad landscape that could be surveyed from her topmost battlements; and then, one April morning, out of the blue, the avalanche of wild highlanders . . . had overwhelmed her . . . and her ruins had been left desolate from that day to this.[12]

And Toynbee confessed that his feeling was 'a horrifying sense of the sin manifest in the conduct of human affairs.' It was this vision of 'the cruel riddle of Mankind's crimes and follies' that inspired *A Study of History*.

It is immediately observable that Toynbee is bringing a *moral sense*, a sense of meaning and purpose, to his study. In the first volume, he praises the ambitious scope of H. G. Wells's *Outline of History*, and attacks the 'historical specialists' who sneered at Wells's work, because it had achieved something 'which they themselves would hardly have dared to attempt.' Toynbee's own work, he implies, will have something in common with Wells's.

At once we recognise the similarity of aim to Spengler's book. There is no evidence that Toynbee was influenced by Spengler (his references to Spengler are, in fact, rather unfair), yet the same hostility to pedantry is apparent from the beginning. Toynbee's attitude, like Spengler's, was existentialist. He protested against those historians who write as if they are in some way standing outside history. This is precisely the same as the existentialist's dislike of philosophers who write as if they were standing outside life. One of the most important contentions of the *Study* appears in the section called *Challenge and Response*. Toynbee points out that so far, he had been using the 'scientific method' to examine the problems of civilisation. But this method contains a fallacy — the opposite of Ruskin's 'pathetic fallacy.' The pathetic fallacy means endowing a dead object with life — swearing at the bedstead on which you've stubbed your toe. The opposite of this is to pretend that a living thing is dead; to apply the 'scientific method' to something that is alive, and refuses to submit to scientific categories. Here again, we have existentialism. And immediately, Toynbee hits on a simile which describes civilisation — and also describes the Outsider: a sleeper who has awakened on a ledge of a cliff, and has started to climb the cliff face. Until he wakes up and begins to strive for higher things, he is safe. As soon as he begins to climb, he is in danger of falling. This was also Gurdjieff's image for human beings: they are safe while they are asleep, but when they wake up, the danger begins.

> In the language of our simile, Faust is saying: 'I have made up my mind to leave this ledge and climb this precipice in search of the ledge above. In attempting this, I am aware that I am courting danger and deliberately leaving safety behind me. . . . Yet, for the sake of the possible achievement, I am ready to take the inevitable risk.' [13]

This is close to Nietzsche's simile, comparing man to a tightrope stretched between beast and superman.

And at this point, Toynbee propounds his doctrine of Challenge and Response. His theory is a denial of Darwin's Natural Selection. He does not believe that men flourish under the easiest conditions. On the contrary, they flourish most under the circumstances that challenge them most. The greater the challenge, the greater the men who meet it. Toynbee cites a number of examples to prove his point that the hardest conditions produce the greatest men:* Rome and Capua, the Yellow River and the Yangtse, Attica and Boeotia, Byzantium and Calchedon, and many more, all offering the same contrast — the people under easy conditions who are weak; the people under difficult conditions who are strong.† To be spiritually and culturally great, a civilisation needs the challenge of a difficult environment.

Is it possible, then, to formulate a law: 'The greater the challenge, the greater the stimulus'?

No, not as simply as that. For after all, some civilisations respond successfully to certain challenges while others fail. The forests of Northern Europe baffled primitive man, yet the Romans built flourishing communities among them. The same is true of the white settlers in the forests of North America, who responded to the challenge where the Indians had failed.

What, then, makes the difference between a successful civilisation and an unsuccessful one?

And here Toynbee formulates one of his most valuable conceptions: that of 'creative minorities.' In this, he was influenced by Bergson, who, in his *Two Sources of Morality and Religion*, states his belief that civilisations progress because of *individuals*, not be-

---

* It is impossible not to be reminded of Yeats's passage in *The Trembling of the Veil* contending that great men are produced by 'crisis': 'They [the fates] bring our souls to crisis. They contrived Dante's banishment . . . and thrust Villon into the arms of harlots. . . . that Dante and Villon might become conjoint to their buried selves. . . .' And in language very close to that of Toynbee: 'They have but one purpose, to bring their chosen man to the greatest obstacle he may confront without despair.'

It is interesting to note how closely Yeats's 'cyclic' theory of the individual (in *A Vision*) corresponds to Spengler's cyclic theory of civilisation — and Vico's.

† Pareto, of course, made precisely the same observation in his *Socialist Systems*, published in 1902: the privileged classes become lazy, and are supplanted by tougher men who have been brought up under harder conditions.

cause of 'subterranean currents of thought' or 'the great unconscious soul of the race.' It is the conception which Harry Haller, the Steppenwolf, expressed: the Outsiders and men of genius are the spearheads of society; without them, society would fall to pieces.

Toynbee calls the Outsider 'the creative minority' (mentioning, at the same time, that it can be a minority of one). The creative minority is the few individuals who are capable of meeting the challenges that confront a society. How do they do this? Once again, the reason is of immense interest in a study of the Outsider: by a process of 'withdrawal and return.' These solitary creative individuals withdraw from society into solitude and there wrestle with the problems alone. There, in solitude their vitality and insight increases; and when they emerge, it is with the power to stimulate the rest of society to overcome the challenges.

And now an even more important problem arises. How does the man of genius persuade the uncreative majority to follow him? 'The direct kindling of creative energy from soul to soul is no doubt the ideal way,' but it is not practical — for those reasons that the wise Grand Inquisitor pointed out. The other way is by 'drill' — by laying down laws, and making sure that everyone follows them; by using all the powers of the leader and lawgiver: bullying, persuading, cajoling, legislating. All of this Toynbee calls 'mimesis.' Mimesis is the power used by the Outsider to persuade other people to follow his advice.

Toynbee has a long and fascinating section in his third volume, in which he analyses various great men — ranging from the Buddha, Saint Paul and Mohammed to Dante, Kant and Hindenburg — to show this movement of 'withdrawal and return' — a passage that might have been headed 'the Outsiders.' (It should be added that *A Study of History* is full of annexes on all kinds of subjects, ranging from ancient mythology to modern philosophy, and that these can be read almost like separate volumes of essays.)

But why, then, do civilisations decline?

Because the creative minorities fail them. And here again, we skirt the views of Spengler and Pareto. The man of genius must have the qualities of a leader. It was Spengler who complained that the modern thinkers and artists have no leader qualities. It was Pareto who pointed out that the 'ruling classes' decline as they allow themselves to relax and become decadent, effete.

Toynbee uses the Greek word for this, and calls it *hybris*, which can be translated pride, conceit, swelled-headedness, egotism. The very fact that a civilisation has met one challenge successfully means that it relaxes and gets out of condition, and probably fails to meet the next one.

Hybris, in one form or another, is the cause of the breakdown of civilisations. For instance, a nation that develops an effective army to meet the challenge of barbarians at its frontiers is likely to become militaristic, and the military mentality is invariably stupid. This stupidity prevents it responding to challenges that require intelligence, and also means that it suppresses Outsiders, and tries to drill them into a military mould. (The appalling results can be seen in the case of a Rilke.) Having crippled its Outsiders, it crashes. Modern Western civilisation is in this position.

It will be fairly apparent to most readers that this problem which Toynbee talks of in terms of civilisations is also the Outsider's problem. We considered an aspect of it in a writer like Hemingway, for instance, whose early books state important problems, and who seems to become less and less important as he becomes more successful. Later Hemingway seems to repeat the elements that made the early books successful — the violence and emotional tension, all conveyed by understatement — but it is only the hardened form of the earlier technique, and no new advances are made. Contrast this with someone like Yeats or Beethoven, who succeeded in developing right up to the end: there is an element of humility and self-examination in both of them.

What Toynbee has actually done is to make a major anti-materialistic statement. Not only do individuals depend upon moral vitality to create and evolve: civilisations need it too. It is pure anti-Marxism. Marxism states: Civilisations develop according to economic pressures; there is no free will. Toynbee states: Civilisations flourish or decline according to the moral vitality of the 'creative minority,' and the words 'moral vitality' would be meaningless if free will did not exist.

It is illuminating to see how Toynbee's revolt against materialism follows the lines of the Lamarckian revolt against Darwin.* Dar-

* This will be dealt with more fully in speaking of Shaw.

win's evolution was completely materialistic. If giraffes with the
longest necks are common today, it is only because giraffes with
short necks died out because they couldn't reach the highest trees,
and the long-necked giraffes mated and produced more long necks.
Darwin calls this 'the survival of the fittest,' or 'accidental selection,'
meaning that it is quite accidental which giraffes happen to be born
the fittest in the first place. Lamarck held that giraffes have long
necks because they *wanted* to develop them; that, as the food
became scarcer on the lower branches of trees, the giraffes strove to
reach the higher branches, and *willed* their necks to grow longer.

To any sensible person, Lamarck's plan is far more plausible. Obviously, one develops muscles — or any other faculty — when one's
survival depends on it. Difficult circumstances don't simply kill one
off — which is what Darwin implied happened to short-necked
giraffes; they represent a challenge to which one responds. This is
Lamarckian evolution.

Toynbee is to Spengler what Lamarck is to Darwin. For him,
there *is* a narrow possibility of the West surviving. But before we
speak of this, it is necessary to examine more closely Toynbee's
views of the disintegrating society.

Growth, according to Toynbee, means simply progress towards
self-determination. Self-determination means self-control and self-
discipline, and mastery of one's own problems. It is, in other words,
precisely what the Outsider is striving for.

But what does Toynbee regard as the central disintegrating force?

The answer is: Mimesis, that very power of persuasion or authority by which the creative minority established their own will. 'All
action that proceeds from Mimesis is essentially precarious because
it is not self-determined.' [14] This sounds rather obscure, and perhaps
an example will help to clarify it.

In his tract *The Perfect Wagnerite*, Shaw explains that Wagner's
Ring of the Nibelung is actually a political allegory.

Readers who know Wagner's music drama will remember the
story of how Wotan, the leader of the Gods, gives away one of his
eyes in exchange for Fricka. Fricka brings him, as her dowry, all
the forces of the Law.

Wotan is the pure force of creativeness; he is the poet, the visionary, the idealist, the man of genius through whose dreams and

visions all civilisation advances. He is a clear mirror in which the Will of the Life Force is reflected. But as a visionary, he has no practical power; his visions stay in his own brain. That is why he needs the alliance with Fricka, who brings him the power of the Law — the power to put his visions into practice. But in exchange for Fricka, he has to give away one of his eyes: that is to say, the man of pure genius has to compromise when he wants the power to put his ideals into action. When the philosopher is made king, he has to do all kinds of disagreeable things — like maintaining law and order by force, suppressing rebellion (although he may sympathise with the rebels), executing criminals. He has to make laws to suit the majority. He has to compromise, to consult *expediency*, instead of caring for nothing but his visions.

In Wagner's opera, we see how Wotan, the visionary, is forced to do more and more underhand things — to trick Alberich the dwarf out of the Rhinegold, to trick the stupid giants who build his Valhalla out of claiming Freia, the love-goddess, to kill his son Siegmund — until his compromises lead to his downfall, and the 'nightfall on the Gods.'

The moral of all this is clear. The moment the man of genius starts to put his visions into practice, he compromises his integrity, and a certain amount of 'dirty work' becomes inevitable. The moment the Outsider comes out of his cork-lined room and tries to realise his ideals, the compromise begins.

Wagner's *Ring* is a parable about Mimesis. Wotan is his 'creative minority.' The sin and brutality and folly of history are the inevitable results of the urge towards higher forms of life. Toynbee has reached the same conclusions about civilisation that the Steppenwolf reached about Outsiders: all life, after all, is a compromise between spirit and nature, and consequently the compromise begins the moment life begins:

> Every created thing, even the simplest, is already guilty, already multiple. . . . The way to innocence, to the uncreated and to God, leads on, not back, not back to the wolf or the child, but ever further into guilt, ever deeper into human life.[15]

And the same applies to civilisations.

The compromise — the creative minority putting their will into action — is all very well to begin with, for the minority are still fresh from their vision, full of integrity and determination. But sooner or later, their success leads them to 'sin' — that is, either leads them to become lazy and relaxed, or harsh and tyrannical. In either case, the breakdown begins.

Then, according to Toynbee, the creative minority becomes merely a dominant minority, holding power by privilege, no longer by genius. The Outsiders then tend to withdraw into their own ivory tower, and become what Toynbee calls an 'internal proletariat,' while the majority become the 'external proletariat' — dissatisfied and rebellious underdogs. This, Toynbee says, is the state of our society today.

These three groups — the Dominant Minority, the External and Internal proletariats — dislike one another. The leaders try to hold on to their power with more force than ever; the External proletariat reacts by rebelling, while the Internal proletariat becomes more internal and 'subjective' than ever. But in these last stages of society, the three groups sometimes achieve superhuman acts of creation. The leaders strive to create a Universal State; the Outsiders strive to create a Universal Church; and the proletariat often produces barbaric art, epic poetry, heroism.

In this stage, only the Universal Church may survive in the new civilisation that replaces the old one — *if* a new civilisation arises out of the chaos. In its last throes, the dying civilisation produces Saviours who try to lead it out of its impasse. But this only leads to a gigantic effort of recuperation which precedes complete collapse.

This, then, is Toynbee's vision of history — a vision to which he brings a tremendous wealth of illustration and example. It is true that many modern historians doubt the validity of Toynbee's demonstrations; one hostile critic has even gone so far as to refer to Toynbee as 'a reader of tea-leaves.' In general this would seem to be only another example of the hostility of mere academics to any work of creative imagination that trespasses on their domain of 'fact.' But, as I have summarised it, his theory leaves a lot of questions unanswered.

The ideal of a civilisation is to become 'self-determined.' But what then? It is like saying that the ideal aim of a man is to be perfectly self-controlled. But to what end? A man might strive for self-control in order to be a better soldier or thinker or artist or saint; but self-control is no end in itself.

In the first volume, Toynbee states his idea of the purpose of all this march of civilisation: it is the vitalist concept of 'the transformation of Sub-Man, through Man into Superman.' This idea underlies the whole work. But by Volume VI, when the basic ideas are all enunciated, the underlying religious notions have come to the surface. In the last four volumes — published twenty years after the first three — Toynbee's religious ideas are discussed openly and exhaustively.

It is true, perhaps, that the last four volumes are less readable than the first six; they are altogether heavier, more obscure. Yet from our point of view, they are the most fruitful volumes of the work. It should also be mentioned that the hostility to Toynbee in academic circles did not really begin until after the publication of these last volumes — and, of course, of the one-volume condensation of the first six that appeared shortly after the war. The general feeling seemed to be that if you are going to talk about history, you should talk about history, not about religion. But it is in these last volumes that Toynbee completes his concept of history. Now he is more candid about his notion that all history is the manifestation of God in matter. The aim for the individual — at any time and in any place — is the vision of God; the only thing worth striving for is sainthood. And it is significant that Jung's theory of 'psychological types' was one of the major influences on his religious thinking. Jung's psychological types correspond roughly to the three types of Outsider that I have named: the 'physical,' the 'emotional' and the 'intellectual.' The notion of hybris now becomes more precise; hybris is enclosure in the personality, and permitting the personality to take the place of the vital impulses. Man is a telephone line between God and the world, and his business is to be as receptive as possible.

This viewpoint is partly a contradiction of the views of the earlier volumes, where religion was regarded as simply a response to circumstances, a comfort in the face of death, a system of superstitions to explain the unknown destiny of man. Now, Toynbee's views have become wider and deeper. He sees the same essential truth in all religions — the same attempt to assert the reality of the spirit, the relative unimportance of the problems of our space-and-time world. The ultimate creative vision is a vision of love, of pure affirmation towards all existing things, and for this reason, Toynbee prefers Christianity to Buddhism.

Toynbee's religious doctrine is ultimately, perhaps, the same as Aldous Huxley's in *The Perennial Philosophy* — all religions are different ways to the same truth. This, I believe, is undeniably true — but it still leaves the real problem unsolved. The real problem is this: the element in any religion that makes it a *binding force* in a civilisation is an element of myth and dogma, not of 'universal truth.' For Christianity to be fully satisfying, the Christian has to believe that Christ *was* the incarnation of God, and that all men are redeemed through him. If the churches proclaimed tomorrow that Christ was no better than Krishna or Mohammed, the result would be a general falling-off from Christianity. It is a pity, but it is true — as the Grand Inquisitor knew. If it is to be as acceptable to the average navvy as to the saint and philosopher, religion must be more than the philosopher's perception of 'eternal truth' — it must be myth, dogma and ritual.

But there is no point in attacking Toynbee for these shortcomings. What is most impressive is the positive achievement of his work. Everything that Toynbee has learned or read or experienced goes into it sooner or later. It is the record of a spiritual journey — the spiritual journey of a modern man, equipped with the same weapons as John Stuart Mill or T. H. Huxley, and yet aware of the inadequacy of mere rationalism, and striving for a faith. The result of Toynbee's vision of history is a realisation that history is the attempt of spirit to conquer matter; and the question that it ends with is the same question that we arrived at in *The Outsider*: How does one become a visionary? Toynbee makes it clear that he feels that history leads towards vision:

. . . the historian's inspiration is preparing him for an experience that has been described as 'the Beatific Vision' by souls to whom it has been vouchsafed.[16]

There can, unfortunately, be no doubt that it is the nature of Toynbee's beliefs that makes him so unpopular among academic historians today. *A Study of History* begins and ends in moral concepts. A second reason is probably that there is so much of Toynbee himself in the book. The last volume (which no doubt most readers find the most interesting and readable section) explains at length how the book came to be written, and is also a sort of spiritual autobiography, Toynbee's *Ecce Homo*. The book's immense popularity (in America, for instance) is undoubtedly due to this strong personal element, and to the moral approach — the very reasons that lay Toynbee open to suspicion among his fellow historians.

Before we speak of this autobiographical element, there is an important question to be answered; a question that takes us back to the root of the Outsider problem. It will be remembered that Kierkegaard's detestation of Hegel was based on Hegel's attempt to tie up the whole universe in a 'System.' Kierkegaard protested, in effect: 'I will not be a mere element in *your* system; I *am*.' Now Hegel's major attempt at System-building is to be found in his two volumes *The Philosophy of History* and *The Philosophy of Religion*,* and in these two volumes, he does rather the same sort of thing as Toynbee: discovers a 'meaning' in history, declaring that all history moves towards the manifestation of God. Why, then, if we cannot accept Hegel, can we accept Toynbee?

There are two reasons. The first is that Kierkegaard had never read Hegel; he had only read interpretations of him.† Hegel's thought is actually more subtle than Kierkegaard ever gives him credit for. (In fact, it is likely that Hegel's final synthesis was based on some mystical experience; he is very far from being a mere philosopher.) But the second reason is more important: Toynbee always puts religion first; Hegel always thought that religion and art were inferior to philosophy to express man's relation to the absolute. For all his religious insight, he was heavily tainted with naïve rationalism. And now one can see more clearly why Toynbee's views are regarded with suspicion by other historians. The reaction against rationalism has not yet reached the academic world. The professors of England and America are mostly committed to nineteenth-century scientific attitudes. The existentialist revolt has not

---

* His most difficult book, *The Phenomenology of Spirit*, is an earlier stage of his 'System.'

† He attended Schelling's anti-Hegelian lectures in Berlin in 1842.

yet affected them. On the Continent, existentialism has been accepted since the early 'thirties; its time has yet to come in England and America.

In the tenth volume, Toynbee speaks of the personal experiences that lie behind *A Study of History*. What can be said of his approach? At the first glance, it would seem to be romantic and 'literary.' Almost every page has some quotation from the Bible, or Greek drama, or poetry, or the Church Fathers, and it would hardly be untrue to say that, wherever he can, he prefers to express a thought in somebody else's words rather than his own. There is an air of anthologising about the *Study*. (For instance, in the two pages that I happen to have open at the moment, I can count ten quotations from the Bible, two from Pascal, one from Plato, one from Rumi, one from Byron and one from Shirley.) This 'literary' element is apparent all the way through; the romantic element is less obvious until the last volume. There, he speaks of the inspiration of historians, and tries to show that almost every great work of history has been inspired by a sudden firing of the imagination. He tells how he himself had been impressed by hearing one of his schoolmasters at Winchester recount the life of Heinrich Schliemann, the father of modern archaeology and the discoverer of Ancient Troy. (Schliemann was the arch-romantic, who set out to find the ruins of legendary Troy on no better evidence than a passage in Homer, and a picture of Troy he once saw in some child's story book; the picture convinced him that walls so thick could never have been completely destroyed.)

Yet, as Toynbee shows, if this is romanticism, it is the inspiration of almost every great work that has ever been undertaken. It should be called, rather, 'imaginative vision.' In this form, it can immediately be listed among the answers to our question: How does one become a visionary? It is a deliberate discipline of the imagination to develop a sense of personal participation in history. It may take place in an obvious and simple way, as in the first example Toynbee gives:

'Mutilus, one of the proscribed leaders . . . succeeded, by muffling his countenance, in making his way undetected to the back of his wife Bastia's house — only to be refused admittance:

she taxed him with having a price on his head. His retort was to plunge his blade into his breast and spatter his wife's door with his blood.'

As the student read this quickening passage . . . he was transported, in a flash, across the gulf of Time and Space from Oxford in A.D. 1911 to Teanum in 80 B.C., to find himself in a back yard on a dark night witnessing a personal tragedy that was more bitter than the defeat of any public cause.[17]

It is interesting to note how Toynbee refers to himself in the third person as 'the student'; this modesty, this refusal to speak of himself in the first person, is apparent throughout the *Study*.

Toynbee gives five more examples of the same kind of experience in the pages that follow: reading Bernal Diaz on his first sight of the approaches to Tenochtitlán in Mexico, or Villehardouin describing his first sight of Constantinople during the Crusades, or a sudden vision of a battle seen on some battleground of the past, Pharsalus or Gettysburg. Once, in the theatre at Ancient Ephesus, the auditorium had seemed to become peopled with an angry crowd:

On each of the six occasions just recorded, the writer had been rapt into a momentary communion with the actors in a particular historic event through the effect upon his imagination of a sudden arresting view of the scene in which this long-past action had taken place. But there was another occasion on which he had been vouchsafed a larger and a stranger experience. In London in the southern section of the Buckingham Palace Road, walking southward along the pavement skirting the west wall of Victoria Station, the writer, once, one afternoon not long after the end of the First World War — he has failed to record the exact date — had found himself in communion, not just with this or that episode in History, but with all that had been, and was, and was to come. In that instant, he was directly aware of the passage of History gently flowing through him in a mighty current, and of his own life welling like a wave in the flow of this vast tide. The experience lasted long enough for him to take visual note of the Edwardian red brick surface and white stone facings of the station wall gliding past him on his left, and to wonder — half amazed and half amused — why this incongruously prosaic scene should have been the physical setting of a mental illumination.[18]

Toynbee's approach to history has something in common with Einstein's revolution in science. Einstein destroyed the idea of absolute measurements of space or time, and insisted on the part of the observer in scientific calculation. Toynbee's vision of history begins from the historian and his imagination. It is a denial of the abstract; an insistence on the personal. He sees history, not as a science, but as a mode of spiritual discipline. He insists that, in our present age, the thinker should remain uncommitted as far as possible. He quotes Melville in *Moby Dick* to this effect: 'All deep, earnest thinking is but the intrepid effort of the soul to keep the open independence of her sea,' and tells of a dream that he had once:

> . . . in a time of physical sickness and spiritual travail, he dreamed, during a spell of sleep in a wakeful night, that he was clasping the foot of the crucifix hanging over the high altar of the Abbey of Ampleforth and was hearing a voice saying to him *Amplexus expecta* ('Cling and wait').[19]

Toynbee's answer to the question: 'Can Western civilisation be saved?' is the answer that Shaw had propounded in *Back to Methuselah:* Only by a return to a religious attitude. But what religion? Toynbee's answer is vague. It would seem to be a sort of compound of all religions — like Huxley's perennial philosophy. Yet he is not pessimistic about our chance of survival:

> . . . in the second quarter of the twentieth century . . . Western Civilisation was perhaps the only extant representative of its species that did not show indisputable signs of being already in disintegration. . . . Western Civilisation . . . was apparently in the singular position of being the only one . . . whose present state and future prospects might still be open questions. While all the others were either certainly dead or almost certainly *in articulo mortis,* the Western Society alone was possibly still in its growth-phase.[20]

He asks the question: 'What were the Western Civilisation's expectations of life in A.D. 1950 or 1952?' and considers various answers.

The first is: Pretty small. Western Civilisation is just one of about thirty civilisations that have smashed and disintegrated; Nature has made thirty or so attempts, and Nature usually makes a thousand or so attempts before succeeding. But that is to assume that a civilisation and an individual species are subject to the same rules. A civilisation is a far more complicated thing than a plant or an insect; thirty experiments may not be such a ridiculously low figure. At all events, we cannot condemn our civilisation out of hand because it is only Nature's thirtieth attempt, and Nature usually takes several thousand tries to make a species worth perpetuating. The rules may be different. On the other hand, he quotes Gibbon and Paul Valéry as two types of 'feeling' about Western civilisation, Gibbon's optimistic, Valéry's pessimistic, and demonstrates that these 'feelings' are just as unreliable as statistics based on biology. He examines the state of the world in 1952 (the date of writing), speaks of the problems of atomic warfare, and raises the question of world government. It becomes evident by this time that he has taken the question as far as he is able — and this, throughout the ten volumes, has been an immense distance. He has no definite prophecy to make about the future of the West: only a feeling that it is just possible that the West may survive where other civilisations have failed. He points out that it is inconceivable what will happen if the West doesn't survive. In previous ages, some new culture emerged to replace the old one; but nowadays the world is a smaller place, and it is difficult to see where a new culture could come from. All the world is westernised. He raises also the important question of leisure in a highly civilised society, pointing out that leisure is usually a corrupting influence. To this purpose, he quotes the anonymous Greek work on *Sublimity in Style*, written at some time between the first and third century; the author's words could be applied to the twentieth century:

> One of the cancers of the spiritual life in souls born into the present generation is the low spiritual tension in which all but a few chosen spirits among us pass their days. . . .[21]

This was also written in a disintegrating civilisation in times of peace and prosperity; it enforces the point that all declining civilisations tend to divide into Outsiders and Insiders. Shaw, with his usual penetration, had summarised the whole of this problem in his preface to *Misalliance:*

> The secret of being miserable is to have leisure to bother about whether you are happy or not. The cure for it is occupation. . . . A perpetual holiday is a good working definition of hell.[22]

Toynbee states it in his own way:

> . . . Technology had inveigled her victims into putting themselves into her power by selling them new lamps for old. She had bribed them with 'the pictures' and 'the wireless' into selling her their souls; and the outcome of this ruinous cultural 'new deal' was the spiritual wilderness which Plato had dismissed as a 'Commonwealth of Swine,' and Aldous Huxley had satirised as a 'Brave New World.' [23]

At the end of the *Study*, Toynbee places his hope for the future of the West in 'a transfer of energy from Economics to Religion.' He does not say how this transfer is to be brought about. But he is certain that 'under the aegis of Religion, Western Man might find himself able to handle with spiritual impunity the material power thrust into his hands by the mechanisation of Western technology.' [24] It is Toynbee's own attempt to answer Evan Strowde's question: 'How can the spirit of man gain power over his prosperity?'

Toynbee has expressed the historical aspect of the Outsider problem so clearly that there is little more to say. Our society is spiritually rotten, and the Outsider is the lone individual who instinctively rebels against it. All living creatures live mainly by instinct, and man is no exception. But when a civilisation reaches its phase of disintegration, an instinct for health is not enough; intuition needs a spearhead of conscious intellectual effort. *The Outsider* was a study in many individuals who made that effort, and who, to a greater or lesser degree, recovered spiritual health. The Outsider usually begins as a romantic and a sceptic; and usually, he ends with neo-classic and religious convictions. In the twentieth century, this development is common to figures as diverse as Bernard Shaw and T. S. Eliot.

(Their similarity in this, and many other respects, is only just beginning to be observed.) It is a pattern so common that one could
venture a generalisation and say it is true of all Outsiders.

The implication becomes obvious: a healthy culture takes its religion and classicism for granted, and there are no Outsiders. (Can
the seventeenth century, for instance, produce any musical 'Outsiders' to compare with Wagner or Alban Berg?) In an unhealthy
(romantic) culture, the Outsider has to remake his own classicism
and religious attitude, and thus regains a certain degree of health. If
the whole civilisation began to feel the need to fight for a new lease
of life, it would have to follow the same path as the individual
Outsider.

Immediately, the objections raised by the Grand Inquisitor bulk
on the horizon. Society is not made up of Outsiders, and never has
been. When society has been most healthy, it has been in ages when
the Outsiders were the spiritual leaders, and the mass of the people
accepted them in the way that a modern man accepts the word of
Einstein or Planck for some scientific mystery he cannot understand. In our age, the Outsider is no longer the intellectual leader,
no matter how much society may admire the paintings of Van
Gogh, or the novels of Dostoevsky. The intellectual leader of the
twentieth century is the scientist, the psychologist, the statistician,
the positivist philosopher (consider the immense influence of Dewey
in America, or Russell in England), and these men are not Outsiders.
In former ages, the great churchmen were often Outsiders — there
are a hundred examples from Augustine to Newman. In the twentieth century, the religious man has neither authority nor credit,
and the occasional Outsider who accepts the authority of the church
— Berdyaev, Shestov, Eliot — thereby isolates himself and decreases
his sphere of influence. The most influential serious writers today
stand outside the Church, as Camus and Sartre stand outside; their
influence is largely due to the stoicism they preach, reminiscent of
Toynbee's dream with its 'Cling and wait.'

The Grand Inquisitor's logic blocks all hope of a return to
religion.* A new religion would mean the general acceptance of

---

* I am dismissing, of course, the 'religion' preached by 'hot gospel'
evangelists which causes periodic revivals of religious emotion. Religion
and religious emotion are not the same thing.

religious dogmas. Even if these dogmas were drawn up by an assembly of bishops — and this would be less difficult than it sounds — the problem would still be to get the half-educated modern man to swallow them. There can be no 'new religion.' A religion is not made by throwing ingredients into a cooking pot. And what the Outsider means by 'religion' is as incomprehensible to the average man as the quantum theory. A religion depends primarily on a climate of opinion which demands it, and that climate has not yet appeared in our civilisation. There are signs — it is true — that such a climate is beginning to appear; these signs are more apparent on the Continent, where questions of theology and philosophy are habitually discussed, than in England or America. But, so far, there is no indication that anything as universal as a religion is emerging.

The problem that confronts us is a problem of rebirth. Spengler declared that civilisations are never reborn. Toynbee is guardedly optimistic; his advice is summarised in his words 'Cling and wait.'

If our civilisation could survive — if any civilisation could pass beyond its danger-point without disintegrating — it would be by an effort of self-knowledge surpassing that of any previous civilisation: a sort of historical introspection that could be compared to Pascal's spiritual self-analysis. Re-creation by self-analysis is the most fundamental meaning of existentialism. Perhaps, as Toynbee suggests, the burden of re-creation will lie with a minority of Outsiders.

The conclusions of this chapter can be briefly summarised: Civilisations wreck when they lose control over their own complexity. And they begin to lose control the moment they begin to think in materialist categories; for ultimately, all power is spiritual power.

Western man — Faustian man — has always been inclined to lay too much emphasis on his intellect. This is the secret of his tremendous material progress; but it is also the cause of his downfall. He loses spiritual power — the vital sense that keeps species healthy. Without this vital sense, the word 'progress' is a mockery; it is like having a streamlined car, but no petrol to run it on.

This tradition of over-emphasising the intellect goes back to the Renaissance, when the humanist way of thinking first began to flourish. But it gained real power in the seventeenth century, with Galileo, Descartes, Newton, expanding through Locke and Hume, Kant and Hegel, until in the twentieth century it has invaded every branch of thought from philosophy to sociology, from physics to psychology. The full significance of this will appear when I speak of Whitehead in the last chapter of this book.

But there *is* another tradition of thought in the West — a tradition that has run parallel to 'abstract philosophy,' although its influence has never been so great. It is a religious tradition and — as I shall try to show in the following pages — an existentialist tradition. It is this tradition which I propose to examine in the second part of this book.

PART
TWO

THE MAKING
OF A RELIGION

I HAVE SAID THAT this book must be prepared to pursue two lines of argument at once. And the historical argument begins with this truism: Society must be held together by a discipline. This may seem so obvious as to be hardly worth saying, until we ask: *What* discipline? Society is a complex thing, and any man who is clearsighted enough to see where its good lies should obviously be given powers to put his insight into action; there are too few people with that kind of insight. But our knowledge of modern dictators is enough to make us recoil from the idea of political absolutism. It is true that a country, *as a whole*, is likely to work better under a political dictatorship. But the men of genius are never included in 'the country as a whole.' They do not fit easily into a political strait-jacket. And if a régime cramps its highest type of individuals, it may as well give up the ghost at once, for it cannot survive long.

We can formulate this rule, then: The ideal social discipline is the one that takes fullest account of the men of genius. When society no longer has such discipline, the men of genius become Outsiders: they feel lost; they no longer seem to fit into the social body. If this rule is true, no political totalitarianism can provide a lasting social discipline. It is only when a society is half-dead that people are stupid enough to think that it can.

But has there *ever* been a social discipline that fitted Outsiders perfectly?

Yes. Historical fact leaves no doubt that the Church of the Middle Ages provided such a discipline. It fitted everyone in society, from the highest intellectual types to the meanest artisan. And this has been true of every 'church' in history — Hindu, Buddhist, Zarathustrian, Taoist, Mahometan. When these churches were at the height of their health and strength, there were no 'Outsiders.' The men of genius were born into a thriving tradition; all of them — thinkers, painters, musicians, storytellers — created for the glory of the Church.

It is not difficult for us, in the twentieth century, to see what a desirable state of affairs this was. If we happen to have been brought up in some free-thinking or atheistic tradition, we may be inclined to sneer at the Church — whether in the tenth century or the twentieth. But that is only through lack of knowledge. No serious person could possibly understand the achievement of the mediaeval Church and still feel inclined to sneer.

The argument I am propounding is quite simple: Outsiders are a symptom of a dying culture. Without sense of purpose, there can be no life. Society *always* begins to die from the head downward. First, the men of genius lose their sense of purpose. When that happens, the decline has begun.

This position is anti-humanist. Humanism can be summarised in Rousseau's sentence: 'Man is born free, and yet is everywhere in chains.' The whole object of *The Outsider* was to prove that this is rubbish. Man is not born free; he is born in chains that are far more degrading and demoralising than loss of social liberty: the chains of boredom and futility. Without a discipline to give him purpose and save him from his own aimlessness, man is nothing.

But, it might be objected, man *has* a purpose that saves him from aimlessness: to feed and clothe himself and his family. Precisely: most men are saved from a sense of futility by mere physical demands. It is only the Outsider who resents this easy way of solving the problem of meaning. Eliot's 'Insider' Sweeney states:

> Birth, and copulation, and death.
> That's all the facts when you come to brass tacks:
> Birth, and copulation, and death.
> I've been born, and once is enough. . . .[1]

And this is true. On the physical plane, the plane of 'brass tacks,' life has no meaning. But the Outsider hates mere 'living' on this primary level; he infinitely prefers the 'secondary' plane of the imagination and the intellect. And you cannot live on that plane for more than a few hours before the problem of aim and purpose blocks the road.

There is a certain type of person who likes to declare that life *is* meaningless — usually as a justification for some hedonistic philosophy or just sheer empty-headedness. I have tried to argue that there is a meaning, and that it can be discovered by rigorous analysis and a *tremendous will to discovery*. (Without this latter, all the scepticism in the world is barren.)

What, then, is our position? Briefly summarised, it is this:

Society dies from the head downward — the head being the 'Outsiders.' Once the head is dead, the rest of the body has a limited life-span. And when I say that 'the head dies,' I mean that the sense of aim and purpose is lost.

But the 'head' can recover its sense of meaning. So it might appear that in solving the Outsider's problem of purpose we can solve the problem of his civilisation as well.

Unfortunately, this is not so. Before the head's sense of purpose can communicate itself to the rest of the body, it needs to be expressed in a form that the stupid body can absorb: I mean in a religion, in myths and parables and ceremonies. The essence of religion is eternal, but it is only the men of genius who can grasp it. The religion of the majority has to be simplified and coated with sugar. And the forms which a religion takes can survive only for a certain length of time. You may remember that in H. G. Wells's *The Invisible Man* his hero remained invisible as long as he was naked; as soon as he put on a suit of clothes, people could see where he was. We might liken the Outsider to a man who is so obsessed by the fact that he cannot see the Invisible Man that he develops a second sight, and can finally see him even though he remains naked. But for the common man, the Invisible Man must be persuaded to wear a suit of clothes if he is going to be seen. As long as the Outsider is interested only in seeing the Invisible Man for himself, it does not matter if he remains naked. But if the Outsider wants to convince the rest of society of the Invisible Man's exist-

ence, he has to persuade him to wear a suit of clothes. So it is that
for the Outsider who strives hard enough a sense of meaning becomes visible in life. But if he wishes to communicate that sense
of meaning to forty million of his countrymen, he must express it
in ways that are easy to understand. He must simplify it, and even,
where necessary, oversimplify it.

Of Christianity, the Outsider would state that every one of its
doctrines has two meanings: the ideas of Christ the Redeemer,
Heaven and Hell, Original Sin, can be understood in the obvious
physical sense — the sense in which most Christians have always understood them — and a spiritual sense, which is as elusive to the
ordinary person as the Invisible Man. The obvious physical sense
appears to the Outsider as no better than a fabrication of myths
and fairy tales; but the spiritual sense remains true.

Since five of the six great religious figures we are to consider in
this book were professed Christians, it might be instructive to examine the question: Can Christianity save our civilisation? And if
not, why not?*

It soon becomes apparent on reading the Gospels that Jesus was
of the type of the demagogue-artist; he had more in common with
Hitler than with Ramakrishna: a man of action with a distinctly
rough side to his tongue. There is no trace in the Gospels of 'gentle
Jesus, meek and mild' (although it would be a mistake to think of
him as always bad-tempered and impolite). He was not — like
many of the men we have examined — a mixture of mystic and poet;
in fact, he was not a mystic at all. He preaches in the same manner
as the Hebrew prophets. He threatens with hellfire (or at least,
with Gehenna, a place equivalent to our destructor of rubbish); he
adds to the demands of the Ten Commandments, strikes at sexual
looseness, and emphasises that the godly life must be a matter between a man and himself, not a concern of other people. He goes
to great lengths to emphasise the demand for unworldliness, telling
the people to think of nothing but God, and not to be anxious about
the morrow. The Sermon on the Mount is a demand for asceticism
and devotion to God. Jesus attacks hypocrites and worldly-wisemen, and demands a higher standard of conduct. Generally speaking, his attitude to the world is very like Nietzsche's — harshly criti-

cal, and based on a feeling that most men are only half-men, and
that they ought to spend all their time becoming whole-men.

On reading the Gospels, it becomes clear that Jesus's aim was the
aim of every prophet and artist — to make men *more alive, more
conscious;* a desire to get more life and more will out of a great
sea of half-dead matter. He teaches that the body is the temple of
the holy spirit, and the vehicle of the expression of the God-force.
Like Kafka and T. E. Lawrence, he advocates a recognition of the
difficulty of salvation, and comes close to saying with Kafka: In the
struggle between yourself and the world, always take the world's
side.

Such men as Jesus are always regarded as a nuisance by the 'average man,' the worldly-wisemen who consider that they are quite
good enough in their own fashion, and resent being asked to make
themselves uncomfortable. And it is perfectly true that this assertion 'Man is the temple of the spirit,' which is not 'religion' but
just common sense to the artist, is quite incomprehensible to the
average man. For the average man, the body's demands are common sense. The recognition of a permanent principle in man, of
an element which wars to impose its will on the body conditioned
by space and time, is reserved for the few who are awake enough
to be aware that time drags the body towards unconsciousness, that
'to be conscious is not to be in Time,' * that the aim of all religion is
increased consciousness. To devote the consciousness completely
to the demands of the moment (or of future moments) is to waste
it utterly.

This, then, is the essence of Christ's teaching: it is the will of the
life-force that men should strive for more consciousness and life
(or, as Jesus would have expressed it, it is God's will that men
strive to become more like Him). All men must be made to realise
that this is the single and sole aim. When they do so, they will
cease to bother their heads about trivialities; they will cease to be
petty and quarrelsome. Man will live in perfect fellowship with
his neighbour, because *in order to achieve his real aim,* he must not
waste time squabbling and bickering. Having ceased to be trivial
and shortsighted, having established a society on principles of com-
munism and mutual aid, and having outgrown such moral cancers

* T. S. Eliot, *Burnt Norton,* Section II.

as jealousy and possessiveness, man's feet are then at the foot of the stairway leading towards the primary aim of God — more life, more vitality, greater intensity of consciousness; for all life should aspire towards the godlike.

This can hardly be claimed as an exclusively Christian ethic: it has been the message of every great prophet and religious teacher since the world began. In preaching it, Jesus had not made any great departure from the message of Isaiah or Ezekiel or Micah. He had told them that 'the kingdom of God was within them,' and that men are gods (as the Eighty-second Psalm states) and must strive to 'have life more abundantly' by accepting greater responsibility for carrying out God's purpose in the world.

Now, as Dostoevsky's Grand Inquisitor was to point out, men do not want this kind of responsibility. The men who are willing to accept such a burden are rare. It is as if an art teacher were to tell every member of his class that their responsibility to God was to become Rembrandts and El Grecos, and that anyone failing to do so would be ostracised. Most people will claim that 'they know their own limitations,' although what they really mean is that they have no intention of paying the tremendous price of will power and sweat that makes a great artist. The moral teacher who tries to persuade men to stop looking for comfort and strive to become great is likely to find himself without an audience.

It is highly probable that this would have happened to Jesus, and that five years after his death everyone would have completely forgotten him. Jesus's teachings alone would not have preserved his memory beyond the end of the year in which he died. But there were other factors. To begin with, there were the miracles. He had some sort of strange power of healing (a power which is by no means as rare as we might suppose). Jesus himself never tried to use their power to reinforce his preaching, for he realised that the reputation of a miracle-worker would not make people take him any more seriously. Shaw makes this point brilliantly:

Jesus's teaching has nothing to do with miracles. If his mission had been simply to demonstrate a new method of restoring lost eye-sight, the miracle of curing the blind would have been entirely relevant. But to say 'You should love your enemies; and

to convince you of this I will now proceed to cure this gentleman of a cataract' would have been, to a man of Jesus's intelligence, the proposition of an idiot.[2]

But the miracles, irrelevant or not, helped to prevent Jesus being
forgotten as a hundred other prophets have been forgotten. This
was partly due to another factor — the 'divine mission' which his
disciples began to claim for him after his death, and towards which
they were able to adduce the miracles as evidence. Finally, when
the legend of Jesus began to spread throughout the Near East, it
was for reasons that had nothing whatever to do with his teachings.

Dr. Schonfield has given a vivid account of the situation after the
crucifixion,* with the disciples discouraged and frightened, and the
followers of Jesus breaking up and losing belief. Then the Resur-
rection was reported; the body had disappeared from the tomb.
People began to circulate stories about Jesus being seen in the
flesh. Jesus had prophesied the Last Judgement, and had declared
that it would take place within the lifetime of people then alive. He
himself would be the judge of the living and the dead. These
stories caught the imagination: the appalling death on the cross,
the reappearance as a living man for a few days; the prophecy of
the end of the world *within the lifetime of people then alive,* and
the Last Judgement with Jesus himself as judge.†

But there was an even more important factor in this growing
power of Christianity: the conversion of a former Jew and perse-
cutor of the Christians, St. Paul.

Paul, from all the evidence, was as different from Jesus as it is
possible to imagine. Jesus was a man of action, completely free
from a sense of sin or any other neuroses; a man like Isaiah and
Micah, impetuous, occasionally quick-tempered, sensitive, strong-
willed, driven by a need to impress his vitality on his age. Paul was

* *The Jew of Tarsus,* a life of St. Paul.
† It is interesting to compare this with the Jehovah's Witnesses, who
have also gained a large following by prophesying a Last Judgement
within the next few years. Their founder, 'Pastor' Russell, prophesied
the Judgement Day for some time early in the century; when the day
passed by uneventfully, the date was hastily revised, and declared to be
'within the lifetime of people alive in 1914.'

far more the thinker; he might have been a Kierkegaard — misshapen, unhealthy, intellectual, morbidly preoccupied with death, violence and pain, possessed by a sense of sin, perpetually tormented by self-criticism that could never stimulate his will to remake himself. In fact, Paul had practically nothing in common with Jesus; and neither had the religion that Paul invented and called Christianity anything in common with the teachings of its founder.

To begin with, Paul emphasised the idea of the end of the world and the Last Judgement. This view suited his way of thinking. A modern example of Paul's type of temperament would be Mr. T. S. Eliot: for all the preoccupations of *The Waste Land* and *The Hollow Men* are to be found in the Pauline Epistles. For Paul, as for Mr. Eliot, the past became a way of compensating for the present: the violent death of Jesus, his prophecies of the Last Judgement.

In saying this, I am not in any way trying to criticise Paul. To seek refuge in his own sense of inadequacy by viewing the world pessimistically is a perfectly valid way for an Outsider to escape from his plight. Paul only did what Hemingway and T. E. Lawrence and Dostoevsky did: concentrated upon the idea of pain and death and futility (which Paul called sin) until he felt he had gained power over them. And it was in this act that Paul conceived his greatest idea, which was to make Christianity a world religion: his idea that Christ died as a universal scapegoat for the sins of all men. After all, if the idea of the Crucifixion had helped Paul to gain power over himself, then it is obvious that, in a sense, Jesus had died to give Paul more intense life — a deeper consciousness of the meaning of life, a greater sense of purpose. And if Christ's death had saved Paul from his own futility, why should it not do the same for all men? This was the birth of the idea of the Vicarious Atonement: that Christ died to save men. With his Old Testament training, Paul was soon able to work this into an intellectually formidable doctrine. At the bottom of Paul's vision. lay his feeling that all men are born futile and stupid. The Old Testament gave him a reason for this: the disobedience of Adam (although actually, the purpose of the legend in Genesis is only to explain why there is pain and misery *in the world*, not to explain why *men themselves* are imperfect). Paul declared: It is Adam's fault that men are born in sin; but by turning to Christ, they can throw off all their sins and again become perfect.

This is all very well, but it has some obvious flaws. Paul felt that all men are futile and stupid ('in sin'). Before his conversion, he himself seems to have been a rather nasty little specimen; like Dostoevsky's beetle-man, lacking self-respect and certainty of purpose. Christ's death and his teaching gave Paul a sense of purpose and, with it, his self-respect. Paul then ceased to be a beetle-man, and entered the man-of-action stage — the Raskolnikov stage. Now for Paul, as for Jesus, the problem set by his vision of mankind was: Why are men not more like God? His answer was: Because of Adam's disobedience. But was it ever suggested that Adam was godlike? To the Outsider, Adam's existence in the Garden of Eden sounds rather dull — eating fruit and 'being happy.' The Book of Genesis nowhere states that it was Adam's business to use his brain in the work of helping God to create more life. And, as I have already pointed out, the Outsider's theology includes the belief that the Fall was necessary: that man would be little more than a vegetable if he had not 'eaten of the tree of the knowledge of good and evil.' So the Pauline doctrine of the Vicarious Atonement begins to look rather thin as soon as one examines it closely. As an account of man's position in the world, it has the virtue of assuming that man is essentially imperfect, and that the ideal aim would be to become godlike ('Be ye perfect as your Father in heaven is perfect'), but fails to recognise that (as Jesus saw) man can become far more godlike by his own efforts than he ever realises. All the same, it is this doctrine of Paul's that has become the centre of Christianity, and the backbone of the Church. It has also exposed Christianity to the complaint — voiced by Nietzsche — that it is a religion of lame dogs. Jesus's doctrine is essentially a demand for discipline and strength, but Paul turned it into the religion of refuge. The strong men who have gone into the Church — the St. Augustines, the George Foxes — have always done so for the opposite reason, because they are too strong and have nothing to do with their strength; they are like trees, overburdened with fruit. And this is the basis of the popularity of Christianity: the width of its appeal, to the weak and the strong, the underprivileged and the overprivileged, the 'poor in spirit' and the 'rich in spirit.' Nietzsche professed his respect for the founder of Christianity and his contempt for St. Paul, calling him 'the Jewish Pascal,' and referring to him as 'super-stitious and cunning . . . a man greatly tormented, greatly to be pitied.' Nietzsche's version of the revelation on the road to Damascus is as follows:

> And at last a rescuing thought, together with a vision (as was natural with an epileptic like him) flashed upon him: to him, the fierce zealot of the law, who, at heart, was wearied to death by it, there appeared on a lonely path that Christ with the radiance of God on his face, and Paul heard the words: 'Why pursuest thou me?' What really happened is this; his mind all at once had become enlightened. 'It is unreasonable' (so he said to himself) 'to persecute this very Christ. Here is the way out, here perfect revenge, here. . . . have I and hold I the destroyer of the law.' The sufferer from the most anguished pride felt suddenly restored, his moral despair was blown away, for the morals were blown away, destroyed — that is, fulfilled, yonder on the cross![3]

Nietzsche's account need not be taken merely as an attempt to debunk Paul; there is, at the bottom of it, a poet's perception of what went on in another poet's mind. It is not to Paul's discredit that he was mentally sick, and found an antidote in Christianity; if it were, the same objection could be applied to Nietzsche, who was sick when he was 'waylaid' by the idea of Zarathustra. Nietzsche only objected to the idea of the Vicarious Atonement — objected to it passionately all his life. His own great saviour-prophet, Zarathustra, tells his disciples to forget him and think for themselves; he does not want disciples and followers, but equals. Nietzsche, himself a prophet of the first rank, felt a tremendous objection to carrying the burden of his disciples' weaknesses (for that is what being a leader amounts to). The same is true of Christ, who declined to become the new Judas Maccabaeus, the leader-figurehead, and instead told his followers to go away and strive to be perfect as God is perfect.

But the Grand Inquisitor was right. Men do not want a religion on those terms. Tell them that they are morally free, and they will shrink from the burden. Not every man is capable of following the Outsider's hard road to belief. Men do not want 'moral self-leadership'; they want 'bread and circuses.' The men who are capable of carrying the burden of their own freedom are very rare. This is the observation which led Nietzsche to the doctrine that has made him most hated — his 'Master-and-slave' morality, which teaches that the human race is divided into masters and slaves: the masters capable of immense will power, immense suffering, immense self-discipline; the slaves too shortsighted to want anything except material necessities and a leader to obey. And yet Nietzsche's doctrine is no more than a flat statement of the moral hidden in Dostoevsky's fable of the Grand Inquisitor. The problem we face today is still the problem that the Grand Inquisitor stated: that Christ's teaching 'Be your own leader' will never suit the majority of men. Dostoevsky might equally well have substituted the Buddha for Christ in the parable, for the same objection applies; the Buddha also taught that men are answerable only to themselves for their moral well-being. He also warned men not to accept him as an oracle, but only to use him as a guide to find their own way. Yet Buddhism became a universal religion in precisely the same way as Christianity: by the formation of legends that changed the Buddha into a God, supplied his mother with a divine origin, and told of visions of angels, miracles, and a final chorus of the heavenly host to conduct him to heaven when he died. All this points to the truth of the Grand Inquisitor's argument, and to Nietzsche's Master-and-slave doctrine.

And this is the problem which now presents itself in our analysis of the Outsider. Let us summarise briefly:

Christ's teaching was the same as Nietzsche's and the Buddha's: Be your own master; strive to be perfect. On the strength of this teaching alone, Christ would have been forgotten nineteen centuries ago. But Christ died announcing the Last Judgement, *to begin almost immediately*, with himself as Judge. St. Paul made this the centre of his own version of Christianity, claiming that Christ had been sent by God to announce the end of the world, but that he had the power of remitting the sins of all who believed in him. In other words, Christ's teaching 'Be your own master' went overboard; in its place, St. Paul substituted a Christ who said: 'Regard *me* as your master, and I will do some special pleading for you on Judgement Day (by virtue of a bargain I made with my Father, that I should submit to the unpleasantness of dying in order to become your judge and advocate).' St. Paul's Christ had far more qualifications for popularity than Jesus himself ever had; and the consequence was a tremendous spread of 'Christianity.' After Paul, Christianity ceased to be the gospel of 'Redeem yourself' and became the gospel of 'Let me redeem you.' Shaw always referred to it as 'Crosstianity.'

For a long time after Christ's death, men waited patiently for the Day of Judgement. When it was delayed, they assumed this was due to God's mercy and patience, and regarded themselves as lucky. In any case, the Last Judgement soon ceased to be the centre of the Christian doctrine. Instead, Paul's idea of Christ as universal scapegoat took its place. The Last Judgement might be deferred to the remote future; in the meantime, the people who had believed in Christ would wait for it in Heaven. One believed in Christ in order to get to Heaven.

Undoubtedly, the Christian Church made for higher civilisation and culture. First, and most important, it provided men with a sense of spiritual purpose and direction. It emphasised the reality of the spirit. Its authority was entirely for the good, for it gave even the stupidest men a sense of being a part of a great universal scheme.

Moreover, it provided a refuge for Outsiders. The Outsider, I have said, is the prophet in embryo. When a man felt a stirring of those same urges that inspired Jesus — the need to seek for 'more abundant life' — he entered the Church, and was able to turn his spiritual energy to good purpose. The Outsider is the anti-world man and the Church which had always declared: 'My kingdom is not of this world' was the perfect home for him.

But naturally, things began to go wrong. As the Church grew stronger, it also grew more arrogant (Toynbee's 'hybris'), more authoritarian. The Outsiders began to find it more and more intolerable. The Outsider naturally begins as an anarchist; it is not until he has begun to understand his spiritual urges that he ceases to be destructive, and concentrates on creation. As the Church became more and more certain of its own power, it ceased to be so tolerant of that early anarchist phase in the Outsiders. In the eleventh century, a sect called the Paterines had objected to simony and other abuses, and the Pope had been glad enough to make use of them in his battle to prevent priests from marrying. A mere century later, Peter Waldo was excommunicated when he objected to the abuses of the Church. The Church was no longer willing to absorb Outsiders who would not knuckle under to its authority from the outset.

Waldo is an interesting figure who really deserves a chapter to himself.* He was a rich merchant of Lyons who suddenly sold all his goods and gave them to the poor. He then began to wander around, preaching. One of his first activities was to try to make the Bible accessible to ordinary working men. It was available only in a Latin version, and he paid for it to be translated. This immediately made him unpopular with the Church, which felt that its authority would be undermined. So Waldo was forbidden to preach, and, when he refused, was excommunicated. This did not worry him. He retaliated by answering that the true Church was carried in man's heart, and did not require priests to interpret it. The Church had made a stupid move in attacking him, and not trying to assimilate him. The attacks drove him much further than he would have gone otherwise; he finished by declaring that the Church was totally unnecessary. His followers increased (calling themselves the Waldenses), and a considerable anti-clerical movement began in France. Other sects sprang up: the Albigenses, the Cathari. All of them believed that oaths are forbidden, that capital punishment should not be allowed to the state, that any man is a priest if 'the spirit moves him,' and that the Roman Church was not the true Church. The Cathari actually declared that the Roman Church was the 'whore of Babylon' spoken of in Revelation. The Church attempted to stamp out the heresies by appointing inquisitors, who ruthlessly burned, tortured and confiscated property. The Waldenses retreated into Swiss valleys, where they were less accessible, and established contact with Swiss and German reformers.

The Outsider had become the Rebel, and the Reformation had begun. Three more centuries were to elapse before the Church received its greatest blow, from the hand of Luther, but in the meantime, it continued the same policy of oppression. John Wycliffe

* Interested readers will find an excellent chapter on him in Rufus M. Jones's *Studies in Mystical Religion.*

(1320–84), an Oxford scholar, came into conflict with the Church, and, like Waldo, refused to give way. As with Waldo, the Church drove him to greater and greater lengths of antagonism. He began by writing a pamphlet affirming that the Church ought to have no concern with temporal matters, and that the clergy ought not to hold property. But as the Church directed blow after blow at him, he went to greater lengths, and finished by denouncing the Pope as Antichrist, and declaring that transubstantiation (the changing of the bread and wine into Christ's body and blood) was nonsense. Like Waldo, he sent out lay preachers, and tried to make the Bible accessible to the average man. His various writings on theology had immense influence. He was lucky that the Church of his day was divided by squabbles, and that many powerful Englishmen felt that patriotism was at issue in the arguments between Wycliffe and Rome, and lent him their protection. Wycliffe remained free and unmolested, and died of a stroke at the age of sixty-four.

John Huss, the Bohemian reformer, was less lucky. He also began by having no intention of attacking the Church; he only called for its purification. He was an admirer of Wycliffe and a patriot, and taught at the University of Prague. The attacks of the Church led him to take a more extreme position, and finally he was excommunicated. This did not make him any less popular with the common people. Finally, he was lured to Constance with a promise of safe conduct. There he was arrested, tried and burned. His martyrdom caused tremendous anti-Catholic feeling in Bohemia.

The Church was to pay dearly for these attempts to stamp out heresy. A century after the martyrdom of Huss, a young German monk named Luther attacked the corruption of the Church. To begin with, he attacked only the abuse of indulgences — accepting money for forgiving sins — and nailed up ninety-five theses against it on the door of his church. The Pope ordered him to retract; Luther refused, and wrote a pamphlet called *Instruction to the People* denouncing various abuses. The Pope issued a bull of condemnation, and again called upon him to retract. Luther was a stubborn and pugnacious man, and he now began to go much' further than he had originally intended; he publicly burned the bull of condemnation. The Pope then used his last weapon — excommunication. He also called an assembly at Worms, at which Luther was asked again whether he would recant. Luther replied that he would not do so unless they could prove to him from the scriptures that he was in the wrong. The soldiers shouted: 'To the fire with him!' but Luther was under the protection of the Elector of Saxony, and was removed to his castle in Wartburg. The quarrel with Rome had gone on for four years, and a high proportion of Luther's fellow countrymen were behind him. He now translated the New Testament into German, and launched tracts and pamphlets from his castle. He later referred to the castle as his 'Patmos.' A year later, he returned to his own church in Wittenberg, and began the work of reformation there. The Emperor Charles had signed an Edict at Worms, condemning Luther and all his followers. But popular feeling was by this time so strongly roused that it was impossible to enforce the Edict. At last — after three centuries during which reformers had been suppressed or martyred — the reformation became too strong for the Church. All over Europe, the authority of Rome began to fail. In Switzerland, Calvin established the Protestant Church in Geneva. In England, Henry VIII snapped his fingers at the Pope, and dissolved the monasteries. The tide had turned.

It is noteworthy that the Reformation was not inspired by any dislike of Pauline Christianity; it was not a revolt in favour of Christ's exhortation to 'Redeem yourself.' On the contrary, Luther placed more emphasis on the idea of Christ as Redeemer than the Pope did. In his early days as a monk, Luther had been morbidly worried about his salvation, tormented by a fear that he was damned. His sexual urges were strong; he was — as history shows us — full of the faults of intolerance and pride; and he was self-critical enough to feel that he was extremely imperfect — which, in his terminology, meant damned. But one day the idea of 'justification by faith' came to him; that is to say, he suddenly felt: I am completely imperfect and sinful, but I believe in Christ and love him with all my heart; is not this enough to save me? He decided that it was; and 'justification by faith' became the cornerstone of Luther's teaching. It is open, of course, to the objection that it throws even more emphasis on Christ than St. Paul did (Nietzsche showed considerable penetration in likening Luther to Paul), and even less on man's ability to redeem himself by self-discipline. Luther removed the emphasis from self-discipline and threw it back on Christ the Redeemer. This, perhaps, is the reason why Protestantism is ultimately even less satisfying than Catholicism. Nothing is quite so bad for a religion as a man with an exaggerated sense of sin and a tormented conscience. Calvin — another sick man — also emphasised the idea of Christ as Redeemer. So the result of the Protestant Reformation was not a restoration of Christianity, but of Pauline 'Crosstianity.'

But a new revolution was about to begin — a revolution of far greater consequence than the Protestant Reformation. Luther, in one of his moments of asperity, commented: 'People give ear to an upstart astrologer who strove to show that the earth revolves, and not the heavens. . . . ' The upstart astrologer was Copernicus, who, in a book called *On the Revolutions of Heavenly Bodies*, had advanced the theory that the earth revolves around the sun, and not vice versa. The great figures of the Reformation — Luther, Calvin, Melanchthon — joined with the Roman Church in condemning Copernicus. Giordano Bruno, a Dominican friar, was imprisoned for seven years, and burned at the stake in 1600 for supporting the Copernican theory of astronomy. Both Protestant and Catholic appealed to the same source — the Bible — to prove that the earth was the centre of the universe, and the sun, moon and stars especially created to give it light. Galileo Galilei (1564–1642) the greatest scientist and astronomer of his age, was forced to appear before the Inquisition to withdraw his 'heretical opinion' that the earth revolved around the sun, and it was only by confessing that he had been in error that he escaped the fate of Bruno. Campanella, another Dominican, was imprisoned for twenty-eight years for his scientific thinking. Lucilio Vanini was burned at the stake for the same reason. René Descartes, the founder of modern philosophy and mathematics, was about to publish a book called *Le Monde*, based on the Copernican system, when he heard about the condemnation of Galileo, and hastily suppressed it. After his death, the book was placed on the Index.

In spite of all this, the age of rational thinking had begun. It gathered its strength from the intolerance of the Church — Protestant and Catholic (and the Protestant Church could be as intolerant as the Catholic; Calvin had Michael Servetus burned for denying the Holy Trinity). Descartes was the founder of modern rationalism. The fundamental principle of his philosophy was total scepticism. Descartes himself was a good Catholic, and took great care to doubt his way back to Catholicism. But later thinkers had no such prejudice, and allowed their principle of 'doubting everything' to mow down every sort of belief. By the age of Blake — a century later — scientific scepticism had become so popular that Blake reacted against it with horror in his poetry, claiming:

> If the Sun and Moon should Doubt,
> They'd immediately Go Out.[4]

Blake found the 'scientific way of thinking' so abhorrent that he attacked Newton and all the scientists and philosophers of his own day. But scientific scepticism had become the predominant way of thinking, and has continued to be so ever since. Blake's revolt against Newton and Hume was followed by that of Kierkegaard against Hegel and Kant, and that of Dostoevsky against the whole school of European scepticism. In our own day, Whitehead, Heidegger and Sartre have continued the revolt on different grounds. For better or worse, we are in a new age, an age of scepticism.

What I have tried to show in the course of the last ten pages is that Christianity was not built on the sound common sense of Christ's teaching — the teaching of an Outsider-prophet. It was built on a 'metaphysical' doctrine invented by St. Paul. This became the basis of the Catholic Church and also the seed of its corruption (for it was only one step from saying that Christ could redeem men from their sins, to saying that the Church could do so, and accepting money for it). When Luther rebelled against the corruption, he promptly reinstated the idea of Christ-as-scapegoat at the foundation of his new Church. But the scientific age was catching up on religion. In Blake's age, there was actually a movement among scientifically inclined people to declare that religion was scientific common sense, which they called 'natural religion.' Blake attacked it throughout his life; like Yeats, he considered it as the opposite of inspiration:

> . . . a levelling, rancorous, rational sort of mind
> That never looked out of the eye of a saint
> Or out of drunkard's eye. . . .[5]

And yet the 'natural religionists' were not so far from the truth; they wanted a religion, but didn't want St. Paul's mystifications.

This, then, is the situation with which we are faced today: on the one hand, the Church, still using the Vicarious Atonement as its cornerstone; on the other, the scientists and rational philosophers, very many of them men without imagination or inspiration. Between them stand the men who are painfully aware of not belonging to either great tradition: the Outsiders. To the Outsider, the *Weltanschauung* of the scientists is as absurd and over-simplified as the *Weltanschauung* of the Church.

And now we arrive at a crucial question: *Is the Outsider strong enough to create his own tradition, his own way of thought, and to make a whole civilisation think the same way?*

The Outsider's way of thinking is called existentialism. But it might as easily be called religion. It is a way of thought which, like the religious way, regards man as *involved* in the universe, not just a spectator and observer, a sort of naturalist looking at the universe through a magnifying-glass and murmuring: "Mmm. Most interesting.' Existentialism states that *the most important fact about man is his ability to change himself.* And it is just this fact that all the scientists and social reformers have failed to realise. They think that the only thing that needs to be changed is man's circumstances, his environment. This will lead to progress, and man ultimately becomes perfect.

The whole argument of this book and of *The Outsider* is directed towards showing that this is a shallow error. The only way in which this can be done is by directing the searchlight into the minds of Outsiders. It must attempt to show that the answer to the Outsider's problems is not a simple one, such as getting himself psychoanalysed, or joining the Communist Party. The Outsider is a man who struggles for power over his own complexity, over the civilisation which conditions him and tries to distort his identity. Hesse believed that the Outsider is the highest form of life that civilisation knows — next to the prophet. Nietzsche believed that the Outsider is a halfway house to the Superman. In Toynbee, the Outsiders are the men who solve the problems of a civilisation, and keep it alive. But while the Outsiders are a scattered and bewildered minority, without a tradition, without a philosophy, they are of no use whatever.

It is impossible to say at this point what might be the ultimate result of a concerted effort of all 'Outsiders.' The problem is even more complex than I have been able to suggest here. If man can 'change himself,' he must establish certain means to do so; he must work out a discipline. The moment we begin to consider the great Outsiders, or the saints and mystics, we are forced to recognise that man does not know who he is. And our materialistic civilisation, which seems so certain of itself and its aims, only helps to hide man from himself. The moment we consider men like Rimbaud or Rilke, we are aware of entering a *deeper intensity of life*, a level of life that is far more meaningful than the lives most of us lead. But Rilke and Rimbaud did not solve the problems that their deeper intensity implies — any more than Van Gogh or Nietzsche or Nijinsky or George Fox solved them.

In the next nine chapters, we must attempt to penetrate these problems. We must see if a fuller, more comprehensive answer cannot be given to the Outsider's problem. It is the problem of vision and intensity; the problem of how to become a visionary.

Only after considering this problem fully can we feel prepared to approach the other problem: the problem of the death of civilisation.

CHAPTER ONE

.

JACOB
BOEHME

Jacob Boehme, the greatest Protestant mystic, was born in 1575 — a mere decade after Shakespeare. His birthplace was a village near Görlitz, in German Silesia. Unlike Luther, he was the son of poor parents who could barely afford to educate him; he certainly never had Luther's chance of a university and monastic training. For much of his life he had to earn his own living. Yet in spite of this, he was to become — by the time of his death — an important figure with a European reputation.

This — as we shall see — is one of the surprising things about the great mystics: they seem to thrive *in spite of* the current of their time. Success never comes easily and quickly; they can never say, with Scott Fitzgerald, that they are paid for telling people that they feel like everyone else. A man such as Blake enjoyed scarcely any material success, yet he was indomitable. There is about these men some enormous strength that does not require the acknowledgement and recognition of the outside world. This is the sign of the true mystic.

In this sense, few of the men with whom I dealt in *The Outsider* were true mystics. Success would almost certainly have saved the sanity of Nietzsche and Van Gogh; on the other hand, can one imagine Dostoevsky managing to keep sane if he had not been sustained by his first great success with *Poor Folk?* Nijinsky might have stayed sane if people had recognised his extraordinary spiritual qualities, and not thought of him simply as a superb dancing doll. Success ruined Scott Fitzgerald, but failure would have ruined him even more quickly and completely. Rimbaud's career might have been a very different affair if recognition had come to him when he returned to Paris after writing *A Season in Hell.* All these men — except Fitzgerald — had some of the qualities of mystics. Yet that final touch of strength was not given to them.

Undoubtedly, it *is* a matter of strength. One recalls Marcel's friend in *Du Côté de Chez Swann,* who is unable to tell Marcel's father whether or not it is raining, being so absorbed in his interior world that his senses have ceased to inform him of what is happening outside. The mystic shares this attitude. It is the same as that of Axel in Villiers de l'Isle Adam's play: a lack of concern with the external world.

But this is only the negative aspect of the mystic. Before everything else, the mystic is a 'mental traveller' (to use the title of Blake's poem). His researches are carried out in strange regions of the human spirit. This is the most fundamental distinction between Insider and Outsider. The Outsider — as I have tried to show — is the man who strives to become a mystic.

In turning to the study of the mystics, we are definitely abandoning the whole viewpoint of the Insider. So far, I have kept touch with the Insider's point of view, and periodically contrasted it with that of the Outsider. But now the compromise is over. We plunge into the depths of the Outsider's inner-world.

In many ways, Boehme is the Insider's best approach to mysticism. He is not the type of mystic who completely abandons the material world, and speaks of a 'cloud of unknowing' and a 'death of the Will.' We might make the distinction more apparent by referring to a modern writer with a strong tinge of Boehme's type of mysticism — D. H. Lawrence. After a long chapter dealing with the sexual intimacy between Constance Chatterley and her gamekeeper, Lawrence describes her hurrying away:

> As she ran home in the twilight the world seemed a dream; the trees in the park seemed bulging and surging at anchor on a tide, and the heave of the slope to the house was alive.[1]

Lawrence does not mean that Lady Chatterley was suffering from delusions, and imagining the park 'bulging and surging at anchor.' The sexual ecstasy had *altered* her vision of the world, but not falsified it. It had simply made her aware of a living depth of instinct in herself — an instinct capable of *transforming her*, and her vision of the world.

In Boehme, we find this vision quite pure, unadulterated by the frustrated romanticism that made Mr. Eliot call Lawrence a 'heretic.' He was singularly free from the confusions and blind spots which seem to diminish the force of even the greatest twentieth-century writers.

Most of our knowledge of Boehme's life is derived from the introduction to the first edition of his collected works by von Frankenberg, his close friend. But the information Frankenberg gives is so sparse that we finish by knowing almost as little of Boehme as we do of Shakespeare. Frankenberg records that Boehme was a 'dreamy type' of lad, and that when he helped to herd the cattle, he was likely to go off into reveries. One of the legends has it that, on one occasion, he climbed to the top of a local hill called the Landeskrone, and found a cave with a vaulted entrance composed of four red stones. Beyond the brushwood that blocked the cavern entrance, he saw a 'great vessel' filled with money. He ran away in panic; but later, told other boys about it, and returned to the hilltop with them. The cave had vanished — and the money with it. Frankenberg interprets this episode as an omen of Boehme's 'spiritual entrance into the hidden treasury of divine . . . wisdom.' But this view seems a little far-fetched. The episode proves no more than that Boehme was an exceptionally imaginative child, with his head full of bandits and treasure-trove. He may well have invented the cave, and then talked himself into believing in it as he repeated the story to his friends.

Being too frail for agricultural labour, he was apprenticed by his parents to a shoemaker. Here again we have another of those equivocal legends about him. One day, when he was alone in the shop, a stranger came in and asked to buy a pair of shoes. Boehme did not want to sell the shoes in his master's absence, so he asked a price which he was certain would be too high. The stranger promptly paid it, and went out with the shoes. Then, from the street, he called 'Jacob, come out here.' When Boehme obeyed, the stranger looked deep into his eyes, and said, 'Jacob, you are small now, but a day will come when you will be great, and the world will marvel at you. So be pious, fear God, reverence his commands, and especially read the Holy Scriptures for comfort; for you will have to endure misery and poverty and persecution.' Again, this may or may not be an actual occurrence; with so little evidence to go on, it would be unwise to read too much into it.

Boehme followed the stranger's advice, and read the scriptures (Luther had translated them into German fifty years before). The scriptures were, of course, almost the only reading available to a poor shoemaker's apprentice with a taste for books. No doubt Boehme found his fellow apprentices as stupid and irritating as budding men of genius are likely to find their casual associates, and found their conversation and ideas of enjoyment tiresome and sordid. (One recalls the young George Fox in the tavern at Atherstone: 'And when we had drunk a glass apiece, they began to drink healths and call for more drink, agreeing together that he who would not drink should pay all. . . . I took out a groat, and laid it down on the table before them, and said: "If it be so, I'll leave you." ') His workmates and his master found him equally antipathetic, and he was finally dismissed on the grounds that they didn't want a prophet in the house! He was then about seventeen, and set out to wander around Germany as a travelling journeyman. It was a time of discord and suffering for the German people, with their Church divided, and the princes quarrelling. In his three years of wandering, Boehme began to form the same kind of antipathy to the established Church that George Fox had. He referred to it once as 'a spiritual whorehouse'! Finally, he returned to Görlitz, and married Katherina Kuntzschmann, the daughter of a butcher, who seems to have made him as excellent a wife as Catherine Boucher made the English mystic Blake. She was to bear him four sons.

When he was twenty-five, he had his first great experience of mystical insight. His gaze was attracted by a dark metal dish, whose polished surface reflected the sunlight; the brilliance of the reflection sent him into an ecstasy, and a strange sensation overpowered him; it seemed that he was looking into the heart of all nature, and could suddenly understand the world and the whole meaning behind it. He went out into the fields, and the same vision remained with him; he felt as if he could see into the heart of the trees and the grass, as if they were made of glass and lit from within.

Now he began to discipline himself deliberately to try to restore the same vision, and he actually succeeded in brief flashes. During the next ten years, his thoughts never left the problem of that insight — the sudden view of nature as a whole, and the sensation of being able to *affirm everything*. Paracelsus had taught that the essence of things could be seen by the visionary: 'we may look into Nature in the same way that the sun shines through a glass.' It may have been during these ten years after his 'vision' that Boehme first began to read Paracelsus; it is certain that the great physician and alchemist came to exercise considerable influence on Boehme's thought.*

At the end of the ten years — in 1610 — came his second great vision; † a sudden grasp of all his fragmentary insights, and a view of them *as a whole:*

> . . . the Gate was opened to me, that in one quarter of an hour I saw and knew more than if I had been many years together at a University. . . .²

The result of this vision was an impulse to write it all down — to try to express it all logically. He began to write in his spare time, and soon the manuscript started to swell to considerable proportions. He called it *Morgenröte*, and it would be too much to say that it manages to state Boehme's vision logically. Boehme confesses:

* Paracelsus was the self-conferred name of Theophrastus von Hohenheim (probably intended to mean as great as Celsus: Celsus was an early neo-Platonist philosopher). In 1526, he had lectured on medicine at Basle university, but enemies pointed out that he had no degree, and his 'system' aroused great antagonism. He died at the age of fifty-one, after falling down a steep slope during a drunken debauch. His medical teaching is a curious mixture of nonsense and inspired insight.

† Although Frankenberg mentions a much earlier experience when Boehme was 'translated into the Holy Sabbath . . .' and was 'enwrapped with the divine light for a space of seven days.'

Art has not wrote this, neither was there any time to consider
how to set it punctually down . . . all was ordered according to
the direction of the Spirit. . . .[3]

Boehme can be appallingly obscure; it is frequently impossible to
follow his meaning either intellectually, or 'intuitively.' Let me
quote a typical passage, taken at random from the *Signatura Rerum:*

Thus the compunction willeth upwards, and whirls crossways,
and yet cannot effect it, for the hardness, viz. the desire stays and
detains it, and therefore it stands like a triangle, and transverted
orb, which (seeing it cannot remove from the place) becomes
wheeling, whence arises the mixture in the desire, viz. the essence,
or multiplicity of the desire; for the turning makes a continual
confusion and contrition, whence the anguish, viz. the pain, the
third form (or sting of sense) arises.[4]

(It might be pertinent to add here that the *Signatura Rerum* is
perhaps the worst — the most discouraging — work through which
to approach Boehme.)

Yet, in this first book (later called *Aurora*), Boehme's obscurity
alternates with passages of penetrating insight expressed in clear and
precise language.* And before it was finished, the book was to
bring its author trouble. While he was still writing it, the manuscript circulated among various friends and acquaintances. A noble-
man, Karl von Endern, borrowed it and had several copies made.
One of these copies fell into the hands of the Lutheran pastor of the
town, Gregorius Richter. Richter was incensed: Boehme was
stating his own opinions and interpretations of the scriptures without worrying in the least whom he might contradict or offend.
Richter was enraged that this nobody — this shoemaker — should
declare that he was entirely independent of tradition and authority:

Though an angel from heaven would say otherwise yet would
I not believe it, much less understand it, for I would always doubt.

* *Morgenröte* (not to be confused with Nietzsche's book of the same
title!) has not been reprinted for many years, but there are many extracts from it in W. Scott Palmer's compendium, *The Confessions of
Jacob Boehme.* This volume is one of the best introductions, for the
modern reader, to Boehme's writings.

But when the sun goes up in my spirit, then I am certain.[5]

This is pure existentialism — in the sense in which I defined it in *The Outsider* — a flat refusal to accept anything on trust. As I shall try to show, Boehme is full of existentialism. (This is ironical, in a way, for historians of philosophy usually declare that Boehme was the father of German Idealism — especially Hegel's variety.)

One Sunday morning, as he sat in church, Boehme was startled to hear himself attacked by name by the pastor; it was a sermon on 'False Prophets,' and Richter pointed at Boehme, and poured scorn on him. Boehme, being the mild and good-tempered man he was, approached the pastor afterwards and expressed his willingness to be corrected where he had gone wrong. But the pastor screamed at him 'Get thee behind me, Satan!' and told him he had better leave the town as soon as possible. The next day, the magistrates summoned Boehme, and ordered him to leave the town immediately. He was refused permission to see his family and led outside the walls. No doubt he spent a gloomy night meditating on the persecution that can come to prophets of God. But the next morning, the council changed their minds, and let him come back. One commentator, Bartholomaus Scultetus (himself a pupil of Paracelsus and an alchemist) declares that Boehme spent the night in jail, but was released when the town council looked into the manuscript of his book and found nothing revolutionary in it. But Richter made it a condition of Boehme's return that he ceased writing in the future, and Boehme made the promise.

It is often suggested that Richter was getting his own back on Boehme for a rebuke Boehme had levelled at him some time before; the affair was about a relative of Boehme's whom Richter had cheated in some commercial transaction. But it is hardly necessary to look for ulterior motives behind Richter's persecution. The book itself was sufficient provocation. In spite of its tremendous obscurity, Boehme had some pretty sharp things to say about the Lutheran Church that were quite unambiguous. And he ended it by saying that if his religious views seemed to differ from those of Peter and Paul, it was because people did not 'lay hold of the heart of God' before they read the New Testament. Now this is the same sort of anarchic religion that made Peter Waldo and George Fox leave the

established Church, the religion of 'Let each man be his own conscience and his own Church,' and it is not surprising that the guard-
ians of the Church should find it horrifying. For it is not, and never
will be, a practical religion for every man; it can only work for
unusually gifted men. If every man tried 'laying hold of the heart
of God' and doing what he thought God had told him to do, people
with criminal inclinations would find God advising them to murder
and rob, while people with strong sex instincts would discover that
God ordered them to rape and fornicate. The thugs of India believed
that God had told them to kill as much as possible, while there is
an interesting case recorded of an American preacher who was
'ordered' by God to cut off his brother's head in front of his congregation, and then perform the miracle of sticking it back on again;
he was duly interned in an insane asylum, but his brother did not
recover his head. It is understandable that the Church should tend
to discourage 'individual revelation'; and even more understandable
in Boehme's day, when religion was universally accepted and
prophets were springing up constantly.

So Boehme had to refrain from writing for many years. He might
have kept his promise and never written another line, if he had
remained an unknown shoemaker; but fortunately, he had made
many influential friends with his first book, and they never ceased
to press him to break his word. Learned men, Paracelsian doctors,
noblemen who dabbled in alchemy, liberal clergymen, all came to
see Boehme and discuss his 'visions' with him, and to urge upon
him that he was committing a sin against God in refusing to employ
his extraordinary gifts. Luckily for us, Boehme was eventually
persuaded to take this view. It took five years for his friends to
alter his mind; but as soon as Boehme decided to write again, he
began to produce books like a machine. In the six years that remained for him to live, he produced a staggering number of works.
By this time, various wealthy friends were helping to provide for
him, and he frequently stayed at their houses. Argument with men
of fine intellect refined Boehme's own powers; it also made him
aware of his lack of education, and he made tremendous efforts to
pick up a knowledge of ancient languages, and to translate his own
insights into the fashionable scientific jargon of his day (which was
largely derived from alchemy). The results of this were not al-

together happy; if Boehme had intended writing scientifically, like Descartes, or theologically, like Melanchthon, he should have trained himself to it from an early age — preferably with a university education. As it is, his writing is least convincing where he is trying to write like a savant, and most convincing where he allows his own rough peasant voice to explain his meaning.

Boehme's insight amazed his learned friends. They soon discovered that he had the natural gifts of a true poet; he would startle the botanists among them by being able to tell them the properties of a flower merely by looking at it, or divining the meaning of a foreign word from its sound alone. This gift of his is important in understanding his 'philosophy of signatures.' By the 'signature' of a thing he meant its form and colour, through which the eye of the mystic could decipher its hidden properties. For Boehme, as for that great German thinker who has most in common with him, Nietzsche, the visible world is a deliberate deceit, hiding an internal reality which is so glorious that all men would be drunk with ecstasy if they could see into it. This internal reality is the purpose of the Life Force. Most of us are blinded by our moods and feelings, and have no sense whatever of inward reality. Our reaction to things and people — a gloomy day, our dislike of someone we have to work with — keeps us aware only of the surface of the world. But the great poet has moments in which people disappear as if they never had been, and his degrading membership of this club of squabbling, stupid schoolboys called the human race suddenly vanishes, leaving him aware of his own inward reality, and the reality of the force that drives all things. The Life Force has its own deep inscrutable aims and methods in this world of physical reality, but the mystic can discern its presence in the outward form of all things, just as an expert can find a criminal's fingerprint on every object from a glass vase to a human throat. This is what Boehme meant by 'signatures,' and it is the very essence of Boehme as a mystic. It is not ordinary mysticism — the mysticism of the East, which keeps men sitting cross-legged and immobile for twenty years; it is Nature-mysticism — the typical mysticism of the West, which sees the world transformed: 'If the doors of perception were cleansed, everything would appear to man as it is, infinite.'

Boehme was to live and write for only six years more after 1618,

and those last years were made comfortable and stimulating by the
friendship of the learned and the nobility. Yet even so, Boehme
managed to get into more hot water. Once again, though, it was
hardly his own fault. A friend of his had a few of his tracts printed
together in a volume called *The Way to Christ*. It was printed
without Boehme's permission, and was generally well received. A
copy came into Richter's hands, and once more he began to stir up
trouble. He launched fresh attacks from his pulpit, and published
a polemic full of abuse, containing the well-known gibe that
Boehme's work stinks of shoemaker's pitch and filthy blacking. In
the case of *The Way to Christ*, this is downright unfair (although
it might be excusable if levelled at the *Signatura Rerum*, where there
is an atmosphere of an alchemist's laboratory). As originally published, the book consisted of three tracts, *Of True Repentance*, *Of
True Resignation*, and the beautiful *Supersensual Life*; it was barely
a hundred pages long, and was completely free from obscurities.
But Richter made such a fuss that the authorities of Görlitz once
again asked Boehme to leave the town. This time, Boehme was not
destitute and friendless. He had good reason to be grateful to
Richter, for the first 'persecution' had made him famous and gained
him many friends; now the second resulted in an invitation to the
Prince Elector's court at Dresden, where he was questioned by many
eminent Lutheran theologians. With one accord, they declared that
Boehme's doctrines were too deep for them, but that they seemed
to be genuinely religious, and had no smell of heresy. His fame and
reputation were now assured. Eight months later, he was dead. He
died of gastric fever in Görlitz, in November 1624. Richter had
died a few months earlier, but his successor disliked Boehme just as
much, and feigned illness rather than preach a funeral sermon.
Finally, a man was found who was bullied into doing it; but he
began with a bad grace: 'I'd rather have walked twenty miles than
preach this sermon.'

After his death, Boehme's fame and influence spread all over
Europe; he was translated into many languages; societies of his
admirers were formed. In due course, his home town erected a
statue to him, and began to celebrate the centenaries of his death.
There have always been scholars and philosophers who have studied
him and spoken his name with respect. In our own day, Nicholas

Berdyaev, perhaps the greatest mystical philosopher of the twentieth century, acknowledged Boehme as a vital source of his thinking, and was about to write a book on Boehme when he died in 1948.

There is a question that we had better face squarely at this point, before going on to discuss Boehme's philosophy; the question of the obscurities. Is a great deal of Boehme's work simply too deep for everyone, and awaiting some giant brain to explain its meaning, or is it just badly written?

I am afraid that the answer, in all probability, is the latter. By this I do not mean that a passage like the one I quoted a few pages ago is necessarily meaningless, but that I suspect Boehme of an element of wilful obscurity. He was an uneducated shoemaker with the insight of a great poet, and the learned men of his day gasped with admiration at the quality of his intuitions. He had an agile brain, and he clearly enjoyed juggling with ideas put to him by his friends. He began to translate his own ideas into terms of the magic and alchemy which his friends discussed. (The most obscure paragraphs in Boehme are those in which he talks in terms of ideas that are not really his own.) If confusion resulted, Boehme let it stand; possibly because he felt that one confusion more or less would be put down to the depth of his thoughts, and remain unchallenged. In fact, I strongly suspect that in Jacob Boehme, the humble mystic of Görlitz, there was an element of the urchin schoolboy getting quite a kick out of being the centre of attention of so many eminent men. Let anyone who finds this view lacking in respect for Germany's great mystic turn to the *Signatura Rerum* and try interpreting its mixture of Lubets and Sulphurs and whirling centres and strange trinities.

What, then, is the reason for all this obscurity in Boehme? Is he, as many writers have affirmed, just a crank?*

For a modern reader, the most plausible answer is that Boehme was one of the earliest psychologists. He was aware of a great deal going on inside himself, and he was also aware, to some extent, of

---

* In 1899, Canon Bigg wrote an introduction to the Methuen edition of William Law's *Serious Call* in which Boehme is violently attacked. Bigg calls him 'a false, or bastard, mystic,' and refers sneeringly to him as 'the Görlitz cobbler.' This introduction is still included in the Methuen edition of *A Serious Call*, which has been reissued as recently as 1950.

how to travel from the ordinary, everyday state of mind into the mental state of the visionary. In other words, Boehme, as much as Rimbaud, set himself to discover how one becomes a visionary. He knew that, in certain moments, he achieved a state of mind completely different from his everyday state. He achieved this quite involuntarily — or perhaps I should say, by purely instinctive effort. He wanted to retrace his steps *consciously* and to try to understand them, so that he could achieve the same state — and explain to other men how to achieve it, too — by conscious effort. But there was no science of psychology in his day, and he had to invent his own language to describe what he saw. It is as if a man in the heart of some jungle were to discover a tribe with their own highly developed music, but had no knowledge of musical notation to carry his discovery back to civilisation. He might try to remember the music by ear — to learn to whistle it, for instance. But he would be more sensible if he invented a musical notation, and took down as much of it as possible. This, in a way, is what Boehme was doing. Three centuries before Freud, he was inventing his own terminology.

But there is one immense difference between Boehme's 'psychology' and the psychology of Freud and his disciples, and it must be emphasised here; we could even go as far as Gurdjieff, and say that *modern man does not know what psychology means.* The mystic's notion of psychology begins from the question: How does one become a visionary? Psychology, in this sense, is the anatomy of the soul. Freud's psychology, with its heavy emphasis on neurosis and abnormality, is at the very opposite extreme from Boehme's, which is essentially the psychology of supernormal people — i.e. *Outsider psychology.* Boehme's view — and that of the 'real psychology' spoken of by Gurdjieff — considers that there are as many different states of mind latent in man as there are streets in a large town. To some extent, a man learns to make his way from one state of mind to another; if he has had a hard day at work, he can go to see a musical show, or a crime film, and escape from the state of mind in which he left work. But the poet is aware of the possibility of far greater releases than these crude ones; sometimes, when his imagination is fired, he strays so far from his 'ordinary personality' that he becomes a person he can hardly recognise. Now it will be remembered that this was three quarters of the problem in *The Outsider*: the business of 'escaping oneself.' T. E. Lawrence wrote: 'I did not like the "myself" I could see and hear.' Tolstoy, in his *Memoirs of a Madman*, makes his madman say: '. . . it is myself I am weary of and find intolerable and a torment. . . . I cannot get away from myself.' And almost any poet or artist knows that struggle to escape one's fatigue and self-disgust. But it is not escape *from* something; it is escape *to* something — to greater power and ability to act, greater self-control and self-knowledge. If the mind is a 'town,' the poet or mystic is the man who wants to map the town so that he can find his way around it easily. States of mind are subtle things that cannot be easily re-created. One thinks that one has remembered every essential about some past state of mind, and suddenly a piece of music, or the scent of a flower, brings it back in all the poignancy of its former reality, and one realises that memory is not as accessible as all that. As the Steppenwolf sees in his moment of vision in bed with Maria, memory has enough accumulated material to make a man into a god — even the meanest and most degraded of men.

This is what interests the visionary above all else: the immense area of his own soul, the thousands of realisations and visions that are latent in it.

Having said this, we are now in a position to understand the obscurity of much of Boehme's work. In his day, there was no psychology; the only science was the rudimentary physical science of the period. He had not even read any of the other great mystics who are also psychologists.* He felt that he was moving on to entirely new ground, almost without precedent (and indeed, he can hardly even be said to have had any successor until Nietzsche).

As an example of what I mean by 'psychology,' consider this passage from the opening of *Six Theosophic Points:* †

* St. Augustine is an outstanding example. Consider, for instance, the use Wittgenstein makes of him in the opening paragraph of *Philosophical Investigations*.

† Some readers may be puzzled by the use of this word 'theosophy,' especially if they have had any dealings with the Theosophical Society, founded by Madame Blavatsky. But it should be pointed out that 'theosophy' in this sense means 'the philosophy of the religious life'; earlier

1. We see . . . that every life is essential, and find moreover that it is based on will; for will is the driving of the essences.

2. It is thus, as if a hidden fire lay in the will, and the will continually uplifting itself towards the fire wished to awaken and kindle it.

3. For we understand that every will without the awakening of the fiery essences is an impotency, as it were dumb without life, wherein is no feeling, understanding nor substantiality. . . .

4. Thus an unessential will is a dumb existence, without comprehension or life; and yet is a figure in the unfathomable eternal nothing, for it is attached to corporeal things. . . .

6. Thus life is the essences' son, and will . . . is the essences' father, for no essence can arise without will.[6]

Alter Boehme's terms a little, and this is comprehensible enough. What has been stated is this: Life is a fundamental issue, which cannot be further broken down or analysed, and life is based on will power. But will cannot operate without purpose, and the concept of 'purpose' belongs essentially to the material world. Without the material world to reflect it, will is nothing at all, unmanifest. So will requires a purpose to manifest itself. And life is the outcome of purpose (its son). So there is a sort of vicious circle: increased purpose requires increased *consciousness* (one cannot gain more purpose by becoming less conscious), but increased consciousness requires increased will power. And increased will power requires increased purpose, for without a purpose, the will is useless.

Now readers of *The Outsider* may recollect this proposition in the discussion of Camus's *L'Etranger*. It is, in fact, a proposition of fundamental importance in existentialism. When the existentialist says, 'Existence comes before essence,' he means that, before one can *make* anything (i.e. bring it into existence) one must have a plan of it in one's mind; this plan is what Plato called the 'idea' or essence of a thing. The idea of anything which one can make must precede

in this chapter, I should not have referred to Boehme's 'philosophy,' which is an inaccurate term, but to 'theosophy.' Berdyaev has an interesting chapter in *Freedom and the Spirit* dealing with the difference between modern Theosophy and the ancient Christian and Jewish theosophy, and insisting on the superiority of this older type.

its existence. But with man, this is not so. He is aware of himself as *being* — just being — before he is aware that he is being a man. If a magician changed him into a dog while he was asleep, he would have to open his eyes before he was aware he was a dog, but he would be aware that he existed before he opened his eyes. Yet human beings tend to take their existence for granted, just as they take the existence of tables and chairs for granted. *They believe they are static* — that 'they are what they are' — like tables and chairs. But the whole point about man is that he is not static; he has will power, and he can change himself, either for good or evil.*

In this form — the form that the French existentialists are inclined to emphasise — existentialism is a reaction against modern materialism. The typical figure of our day is the 'self-made' businessman. But such a man, although he may believe that in evolving from a newspaper seller to a millionaire he has become a completely different person, has not really changed *himself*. He has only changed his environment. The environmental change may be necessary (we shall return to this point in speaking of Shaw), but it is not nearly so necessary as the spiritual alteration from a lower type of man to a higher. Existentialism throws the emphasis on this latter kind of change. It is essentially a philosophy of the will, and its central thesis is that the highest purpose of the will is self-transformation.

And by this definition, Boehme is in every way an existentialist. If an architect wants to improve a town, the first thing he must do is to get a map of the town. If a man wants to change his own soul, the first thing he must do is to get a map of his soul. This science of the soul is called psychology.

And how does a man learn about his soul? By 'self-observation' and experiment, and by correlating what he learns scientifically. This is what Boehme attempts to do in all his books. As we read him, we discover that many of the things he says are not new to the

---

* Sartre's play *Le Diable et le Bon Dieu* brings this theme out clearly; its hero changes himself from a villain into a saint, then back into a villain again. It could be sub-titled: A Study in Self-transformation. Wells's *History of Mr. Polly* has exactly the same theme, and Mr. Polly's 'If you don't like your life you can change it' is the essence of Sartre's existentialism — if one adds: 'If you don't like yourself, you can change yourself.'

student of existentialism. There is frequently a Nietzschean note; what could be more Nietzschean than this?:

> If thou art not a spiritual self-surmounter, then let my book alone. Don't meddle with it, but stick to your usual affairs.[7]

In *Zarathustra*, Nietzsche had written: 'Not the height, but the drop is terrible. That drop where the glance plunges down and the hand reaches up. . . .' And in *Morgenröte*, Boehme writes:

> Now I am climbed up and mounted so very high that I dare not look back for fear a giddiness should take me. . . . When I go upward I have no giddiness at all; but when I look back and would return, then am I giddy and afraid to fall.[8]

And he states in his own words Blake's belief about 'the doors of perception':

> If man's eyes were but opened he should see God everywhere in his heaven; for heaven stands in the innermost moving everywhere.[9]

This term 'innermost moving' is Boehme's term for the depths of the subconscious mind. In other places he refers to it as 'the mind's third moving.' This 'third moving' obviously has something in common with Captain Shotover's 'seventh degree of concentration' in *Heartbreak House*.

In common with Jesus and Shaw and the Eighty-second Psalm, Boehme recognises the inner godhead of all men:

> For man is made out of all the powers of God, out of all the seven spirits of God, as the angels also are. But now seeing he is corrupted, therefore the divine moving does not always unfold its powers and operate in him. And though it springs in him, and if indeed it shines, yet it is incomprehensible to the corrupted nature.[10]

This last comment is particularly interesting. It is the complaint of every poet and mystic who has been overwhelmed by vision; when it disappears, one's ordinary state of mind has no power to summon it back, or even to begin to understand it.

And yet the point of the Outsider's question: How does one become a visionary? is the belief that these moments are not beyond reconstruction and comprehension. What is the essence of the 'moment of vision'? It would seem to be a sense of the multitudinousness of life, a release of energy into the brain (Nijinsky: 'God is fire in the head'; Yeats: 'Heaven blazing into the brain') which revitalises all the areas of one's memory. All sorts of other places and other times are suddenly revived. The essence of boredom and exhaustion is the narrowing of the brain, confinement, a sense of being imprisoned in time. This is its opposite: a sense of the immense strangeness and greatness of life, of 'unknown modes of being.' It is a tonic emotion that revitalises and creates courage. In which case the man intent on 'becoming a visionary' now has a definite aim: to learn enough about the structure of his own brain to be capable of flooding it with energy at will.

Boehme undoubtedly mastered this process, and this is what constitutes him a visionary. It will be remembered that Ramakrishna's visions were of the same nature — ecstasy flooding the brain and producing a sense of total universal well-being, which was often so exhausting that it knocked him unconscious. It seems to have much in common with the moments that Dostoevsky used to experience before falling into an epileptic fit. Boehme's descriptions of how he first attained a visionary state have a close resemblance to Ramakrishna's; Ramakrishna had fallen into despair, and begun to doubt whether God existed at all. In a moment of despair he seized a sword to kill himself, and at that moment, was overwhelmed with ecstasy so that he sank unconscious. Boehme tells how

when in this affliction and trouble I elevated my spirit (*which then I understood very little or nothing at all what it was*), I earnestly raised it up into God, as with a great storm or onset, wrapping up my whole heart and mind, as also all my thoughts and whole will and resolution, incessantly to wrestle with the Love and Mercy of God and not to give over unless he blessed me, that is, unless he enlightened me with his Holy Spirit, whereby I might understand his will and be rid of my sadness. And then

the Spirit did break through. But when in my resolved zeal I
gave so hard an assault . . . suddenly my spirit did break through
the gates of hell, even into the innermost moving of the Deity,
and there I was embraced in love as a bridegroom embraces his
dearly beloved bride.[11] [My italics.]

This passage leads into an important question which had already
begun to appear in *The Outsider*, that of the anti-Christian element
in the 'visionary' beliefs of Nietzsche, Rimbaud, and Shaw. How is
it to be reconciled with the definitely Christian element in such
visionaries as Boehme, Pascal, Law?

Partly, I believe, the answer is that there is no true contradiction,
only two widely differing approaches to the same problem. Christian mysticism lays great emphasis on the idea of submission and
humility, love and pity. Nietzsche and Shaw revolted against these
ideals. Nietzsche summarised his objections:

What is good? Everything that heightens the feeling of power
in man, the will to power, power itself.

What is bad? Everything that is born of weakness.

. . . Pity stands opposed to the tonic emotions which heighten
our vitality. . . .[12]

But it was not 'God' and 'Christianity' that Nietzsche was attacking; it was the unreal shadows of these things that passed for reality
in the Church of his day, and still pass today. What Nietzsche was
interested in — and Boehme, too — was ultimate reality. In the
moment of vision, the Christian God, whom Nietzsche calls 'God
of the sick, God the spider,' is eclipsed by a vision of reality, and
the whole world is seen as *physical reality*, an immense manifestation
of life, where 'everything that lives is Holy.' In his normal state of
mind, man lives in a mere corner of his being. It is self-knowledge
that is obliterated. His brain narrows until his consciousness is like
a dying candle. Having a 'vision' is like being connected with a
powerhouse; floods of energy and vitality sluice into the brain, and
the brain lights up, like a mansion in which every light in every
room has been turned on. This is the ectasy of self-knowledge.
Man suddenly understands that he is, as Boehme says 'made of all
the powers of God.' It is not original sin that keeps man unaware

of his own godhood, but his failure to connect himself with his own powerhouse; or rather, if original sin has a meaning, it is just this: that man is too lazy and unimaginative to strive for a continual state of insight. Life is a war — a continual spiritual warfare — as Father Lorenzo Scupoli, a contemporary of Boehme's, realised when he called his great devotional treatise *The Spiritual Combat.* (The monks of Mount Athos made this even clearer when they gave their translation of it the title *Unseen Warfare.*) Boehme knew this, and knew that the real enemy is the stupidity of the flesh:

> The soul liveth in great danger in this world; and therefore this life is very well called the valley of misery, full of anguish, a perpetual hurly-burly, pulling and hauling, warring, fighting, struggling and striving.
> *But the cold and half-dead body does not always understand this fight of the soul.* . . . It doth not understand the fight of the spirit, how the same is sometimes down and sometimes uppermost.[13] [My italics.]

It is this 'cold and half-dead body' which must be given consciousness of the 'wars of the spirit,' must be made to react immediately to spiritual needs. It is a mere instrument of the spirit, and it is the spirit's business to make it into a delicate and sensitive instrument, not to be bullied by its laziness and sensuality.

All this is very clear in Boehme's writing, just as it is clear in Nietzsche's and Shaw's. (Shaw has made it quite plain — dotting all the i's and crossing all the t's — in *Back to Methuselah.*) Yet it remains true that, in the moment of ecstasy, as one's mistaken vision of oneself is suddenly swept away by the flood of certainty, one's feeling is of complete humility, complete instrumentality, a strong desire not to allow any of one's stupidities, any of the corrupt, earthbound personality, to interfere with the cold wash of vitality. Prayer is the natural expression of the gratitude that rises; not prayer directed at anything in particular, at any personal God. It is simply that the sudden awareness is an awareness of one's own godhead, and therefore of kinship with God, of a close relation with God; it is this awareness that makes prayer the spontaneous expression of the vision. The remote God the Father, whom Nietzsche railed at (quite rightly), suddenly becomes an immediately sensed God the

Brother. The image of the bride and bridegroom also arises naturally, for the flood of energy is like an impregnation. It is distinctly
a physical sensation, and may not only be *likened* to the sexual: it
may actually contain a large element of the sexual.

It is difficult to discuss these matters freely, for we are still handicapped by a lack of psychological terminology. But it is now obvious, I hope, that the need for such a terminology is as acute today
as it was in Boehme's time. Psychology is still in as rudimentary a
state. All the contributions of the psychoanalysts have not made it
easier to discuss the mystics; in fact, modern psychology tends to
regard mystics as a distinctly cranky branch of the human tree.

Let me make my implications quite plain. In *The Outsider* I tried
to show that the kind of person I call an 'Outsider' is a *development*
of the 'ordinary man,' for the truth is that there is no such thing as
the ordinary man. It is like talking of 'the average healthy leper.'
If he is a leper, then he is not average or healthy. Neither is man
average or healthy. The Outsider is a man who has realised with
horror that all men are lepers — spiritually and morally. All are
corrupt.

Now I have tried to make it apparent where the road from corruption leads. The Outsider develops, by immense spiritual effort,
into the mystic. He does this by turning his life into a state of
warfare, and living with the mental alertness that is necessary to
warfare. The mystic's view of the world is a view that sees everything as beauty. This beauty is already beginning to be present in
the Outsider's way of viewing the world. The world may torment
him, and lead him to declare that it is a waste land or city of dreadful night (Keegan's view), but the very fact that his vision has
intensified it with revulsion means that he sees the world as more
vital. Terror is the beginning of beauty, for all crises lead to beauty.
Terror is not the opposite of beauty; both beauty and terror stand
at the opposite pole from boredom and, ultimately, death. When
a man begins his unseen warfare against the world, he becomes an
Outsider; if he fights long and hard enough, he develops into what
men call a mystic. But this is not an end in itself; a mystic is only
a man with a higher degree of perception and vitality.

The difference between the Christian and the Nietzschean ideals
— and their ultimate identity — can be seen by considering Kafka's

aphorism: 'In the struggle between yourself and the world, always take the world's side.' This is a completely Christian statement. It means: Where men humiliate you, allow them to trample on you; where they strike you, allow them to beat you into unconsciousness; where they constrict you, allow them to crush you. But the 'you' of whom Kafka is speaking is not that real self seen in visions; it is the superficial self, the worldly personality, the 'doors of perception' that shut out the eternal world with their grime and stupidity and pigheadedness. Our psychological language knows nothing of the extent of man, and the number of layers of his being that stretch from the material surface, whose rule is expediency, to the ultimate depth of purposive godhead. Nietzsche was naturally an ascetic, a man of tremendous self-discipline, who preferred to concentrate on the positive need to strengthen one's vitality rather than on the negative crushing of the personality by subjecting it to indignities. And yet he would have understood Kafka's viewpoint well enough. For Nietzsche, as for all great Outsiders, the passion for truth was a discipline — the discipline by which he became a visionary. (There is a revealing passage in *The Antichrist* in which he jeers at the freethinking of scientists and physiologists: '. . . they lack passion in these matters; they do not suffer [free thinking] as their passion and martyrdom.') The Outsider's greatest need is to find a way in which he can become a visionary. The Outsider is a freethinker because the only kind of thought worth anything is free thought. This means that he can accept nothing until he has proved it by his own direct insight, and that he can *never* accept unprovable things, such as the Vicarious Atonement. But he approaches freethinking with the saint's passion to find salvation, and the fanaticism of a martyr. And the result of his free thought is a totally religious position — although not necessarily a Christian position.

It is impossible here to examine Boehme's theology more closely; even full-sized volumes on the subject are difficult reading, and it would be impossible to explore further in such a brief exposition as this.* For readers beginning to study Boehme, W. Scott Palmer's

---

* The best accounts of Boehme in English are to be found in Howard Brinton's *Mystic Will* (Allen & Unwin, 1931) Rufus Jones's *Spiritual Reformers in the Sixteenth and Seventeenth Centuries* (Macmillan, 1914) and Bishop Martensen's *Boehme* (recently reissued — 1949 — by Rockliff). Alexander Koyre's biography (in French) is perhaps the best so far.

slim compilation, *The Confessions of Jacob Boehme* (Methuen, 1954), is perhaps the best introduction. We need only emphasise, in retrospect, that Boehme was an existentialist in the profoundest sense. He never ceases to tell his readers that merely reading him will do them no good — they will have to go out and *do*. 'You must follow the flights of my soul, not of my pen.' He hated abstraction and abstract philosophy as much as Blake did. Even to try to summarise his cosmogony would therefore be contrary to his own aims; he did not want to have the essence squeezed out of him and served up in university courses, any more than Gurdjieff did.

Bishop Martensen observed that Boehme is one of the few great mystics who lay emphasis on the glory of God. But he is not alone in this, for it is something which he has in common with all the Outsider mystics. In Dostoevsky, in Nietzsche, in Fox, in Blake, in Traherne, it is the poet's vision that is emphasised, not the philosopher's, and the poet's vision is of glory. Nietzsche asks: 'What is happiness?' and answers: 'The feeling that power is growing; that resistance is overcome.' When the Outsider momentarily begins to win his unseen warfare, and has that sensation of resistance overcome, his vision of the world becomes positive, and this positive vision is what Martensen calls 'the glory of God' — a vision that finds its finest expression in the poetry of Blake, or the great eleventh book of the *Bhagavad-Gita*.

This is the vision that is the beginning and the end of the Outsider's struggle. One glimpse of it is enough to make a man into an Outsider, perpetually dissatisfied with the ordinary world — like Yeats's 'Man who dreamed of Faeryland,' who could never again tolerate the 'common light of day.' This vision makes men into poets and romantics — but if it is strong enough, it pushes them into being metaphysicians and Outsiders, and from there into the hard road of spiritual discipline.

NICHOLAS
FERRAR

AT ABOUT THE TIME when Boehme was dismissed from his apprenticeship for being a 'house-prophet,' there was born in England a theologian whose life affords an even better example than Boehme's of an Outsider's retreat from the world. Nicholas Ferrar was not a mystic, and possibly his story is out of place among such men as Boehme and Swedenborg. Yet his solution is so relevant in a consideration of the religious Outsider that it would be inexcusable not to mention it briefly.

Ferrar was born into a wealthy family in 1592; his father was a prominent London merchant. From an early age he showed signs of such brilliance that his family anticipated a triumphant career for him. Both his parents were devout Anglicans, and Nicholas accepted the faith wholeheartedly; at the age of twelve, he seems to have had some religious experience which gave him an obscure sense of being dedicated to God. At fourteen, he went up to Clare Hall, Cambridge, and continued to impress all with whom he came into contact with the power of his mind. His tutor, Augustine Lindsell, who later became Bishop of Peterborough, used to say that his tutorship of Nicholas had taught him more than he had succeeded in teaching Nicholas. Inspector Lestrade is said to have thanked God that Sherlock Holmes was on the side of the law; the Bishop of Peterborough paid Nicholas Ferrar the same sort of compliment:

'If he should turn heretic, he would make work for all the world, such a head, such a heart, such prevalent arguments he hath . . . that I know not who would be able to grapple with him.' But Ferrar never turned his formidable intellect and sensibility against the Church of England, and the Bishop never had reason to complain. Instead, Ferrar travelled widely, and then took up a position in the Virginia Company, where he used his abilities to such effect that, when the Company was dissolved in 1623, people vied with one another in offering him appointments, ranging from a readership at Gresham's to a high civil service appointment and an ambassadorship. He declined all these, and entered Parliament; but he was not long in deciding that the political life was not for him. He was passing through the same kind of crises that affected Lawrence when he came back from the Peace Conference in 1922; an anti-world attitude was developing in him. He was sick of public life.

In 1625, the family bought a remote and dilapidated house in Huntingdonshire. It stood off the main road, in the middle of a field. In one corner of a field there was a farm; in the other, an old church which the farmer used as a barn and pigsty. The house was called Little Gidding. The whole family assembled there: Nicholas's mother, who was seventy-five years old, but vigorous and healthy, his elder brother John with his family, his sister and her large family of sixteen, and various other people — thirty in all. Across the fields, about two miles away, was the church of Leighton Bromswold, where George Herbert was appointed prebendary in the same year.

After Nicholas had been ordained deacon in Westminster Abbey by Bishop Laud, the family at Little Gidding rebuilt the church and the house, and immediately began to live a rigorously monastic life under his spiritual direction.

There were two aspects of life at Little Gidding. Part of the building was fitted up as an almshouse, where four poor widows were permanently housed; there was also a hospital, where Nicholas turned his medical experience to good account (at one point in his career he had studied as a doctor); a large pigeon house was converted into a schoolroom, and three masters were permanently maintained by the family. Finally there was a regular free distribution of milk and gruel for the local poor. But apart from all this, the centre of the life at Little Gidding was worship. Three times a day the family crossed the field to the little church — at six and ten in the morning, and at four in the afternoon for evensong. They crossed in orderly procession, the girls all wearing black habits and veils. Inside the church, the altar hangings and carpet, the tapestry cushions and all the other cloths had been exquisitely embroidered by the women.

On Sundays, the local vicar came to the church with his congregation to take the morning service; and in the afternoon, the whole family walked over the fields to Steeple Gidding for evensong.

In the house itself, on weekdays, a service was held regularly every hour consisting of a hymn and a reading from the Gospels; these services — which lasted a quarter of an hour — were not attended by the whole family, but were arranged in relays. Ferrar himself had compiled a 'harmony' of the Gospels — a continuous narrative composed of all four; and this was read right through once a month and then begun again. When King Charles I heard of it, he borrowed it, and returned it in due course with many marginal notes written in his own hand. (This volume is now in Harvard University library.)

Nicholas also arranged night watches; from 9 p.m. until 1 a.m., the Psalter was recited; and at 1 a.m., Nicholas was called; he then spent the rest of the night until dawn at his own meditations and devotions. He did this for two or three nights a week, and had only a minimum of sleep on these nights. In the autumn of 1637, when Nicholas was forty-five, he fell ill. He seemed to know that this was the end, although at first the illness did not appear serious. His last weeks were spent quietly and serenely disposing his affairs and preparing for death; he died on Advent Sunday, at one in the morning — the hour at which he normally began his vigil.

Little Gidding was to continue for the next twenty years under the guidance of Nicholas's elder brother John. In 1642, in the shadow of the impending civil war, the King visited the family. Four years later, he was back again — this time a fugitive from the triumphant Parliamentary forces — the 'broken king' of T. S. Eliot's *Little Gidding*. John Ferrar entertained him, and then escorted him across country by lantern light to the house of a Royalist at Coppingford. Three years later the King was executed, but Little Gidding suffered the consequences of its loyalty long before that. Only three months after that night of March, 1646, the house and church were looted by Cromwell's soldiery, and books, tapestries and furniture burned on a bonfire.

In spite of this, the Ferrars carried on the old way of life for another eleven years, until the death of John Ferrar. Then, with no leader to hold it together, the family broke up.

Today, the church of Little Gidding still stands in the corner of the field, but there is no sign of the manor house. Outside the church door stands the plain altar tomb of Nicholas Ferrar; there is no inscription on it, not even a name.

To many modern readers, the whole way of life of the Little Gidding community must seem incomprehensible and repellent, and the children of the Ferrar family martyrs to a fanatic's desire for sanctity. Yet to many, there must be a nostalgia in thinking of the serene, uncomplicated life of this family who had withdrawn from the world. Nicholas Ferrar had chosen one way out of the Outsider's dilemma; he had set his own little corner of the world in order, and lived in that corner as if the rest of the world did not exist.

It is true that the monastic temper is not a familiar one in the modern world and that, although millions of people may detest the routine of modern life and wish they could escape from it, they would hardly be willing to exchange it for the life of a monk. This is easy to understand. It is also easy to see how a Lytton Strachey — or any other modern 'debunking' biographer — could write about the life at Little Gidding in such a way as to make it appear grotesque and rather ridiculous. But could such a biographer, having dismissed Nicholas Ferrar as Strachey dismissed Thomas Arnold, then make constructive suggestions for solving the problem of a modern Nicholas Ferrar? Ferrar had the 'anti-world' temperament — the temperament that made Yeats want to start a community of poets in a 'Castle on the Rock' in Roscommon. It is, we may as well admit, a romantic temperament: but in this context, the word can be used without any suggestion of mockery. Consider, for instance, Yeats's own attempts to find a solution. In his *Autobiographies*, he speaks of his belief that 'whatever the great poets had affirmed in their finest moments was the nearest we could

come to an authoritative religion, and that their mythology, their
spirits of water and wind, were but literal truth.'[1] Yeats, like all
Outsiders of genius, felt the need to make a *way of life* out of
whatever truths the Outsider can affirm as ultimate. He felt that
the truths by which the 'average man' lives are half-truths, accepted
out of fear and laziness. In a memorable passage, he tells how once
'passing . . . by the new Law Courts . . . I grew suddenly oppressed
by the great weight of stone, and thought, "There are miles and
miles of stone and brick all around me," and presently added: "If
John the Baptist or his like were to come again and had his mind
set upon it, he could make all these people go out into some wilder-
ness leaving their buildings empty," and that thought, which does
not seem very valuable now, so enlightened the day that it is still
vivid in the memory.'[2] Why did that thought enlighten the day?
Because Yeats felt that civilised men live by watered-down standards
that are built on cowardice, and that all that was needed to make
them renounce their Tower of Babel was an Outsider prophet to
inspire them. Lawrence had written of the Arabs that they could
always be led to the ends of the earth by the prophet of an idea.
Yeats was 'enlightened' by his idea because it made him certain that
his hunger for a *more serious level* of living constituted him a poet
and a higher type of human being, and not a slightly mad Outsider.

This is what constitutes an Outsider. He is uncomfortable in the
world. To begin with he fears that this is only because of his own
inferiority as a human being. (The early heroes of Aldous Huxley
afford an example of this stage: the hero of the long poem *Soles
Occidere et Redire Possunt*, for instance, who is the prototype of
Denis in *Crome Yellow* and Gumbril in *Antic Hay*.) Later, he
decides that it is the world that is 'out of joint,' not himself. Then
he ceases merely to hate the world, and begins to condemn it. Yeats
admitted: 'In London I saw nothing good and constantly remembered that Ruskin had said to some friend of my father's, "As I go
to my work at the British Museum I see the faces of the people
become daily more corrupt." I was convinced myself for a time
that on the same journey I saw but what he saw.'[3] In the outer
world, the Outsider sees chaos and corruption. In his inner world
— at the times when he is most aware of his subjectivity — he sees
order and beauty and certainty. What is more natural than that he

should try to find a corner of the world over which he can have absolute control, and then organise that corner until it reflects his inner world? This is what Yeats dreamed of when he thought of instituting a mystical Order in his Castle on the Rock, and 'for ten years, my most impassioned thought was a vain attempt to find philosophy and to create ritual for that order.'

So it is that, for the Outsider, Nicholas Ferrar is more than a great Anglican. He is a symbol of one bold attempt at a solution of the Outsider's problems. We may feel that there is much to find fault with in the Little Gidding way of life. The objection to it is the same as the objection to Mr. Eliot's embracing of Anglicanism: that the Outsider must not surrender his reason to some 'historical' fact. For ultimately, history does not matter. History, as Stephen Dedalus says, is a nightmare; and it is a nightmare from which all humankind is trying to awake. This is the significance of the myth of the Trump of Doom, when the dead awaken. Ibsen was right. We are all dead, and the Last Judgement will be the day when we dead awaken. It will be the moment when the first human being breaks out of the vicious circle that makes us more animal than man. In such a moment — envisioned by Blake and Nietzsche — history will end, and real time begin.

CHAPTER THREE

BLAISE
PASCAL

Blaise Pascal is great for so many reasons that there is always an initial embarrassment in writing of him: the question of from what angle to treat him. A writer on mathematics begins a chapter on Pascal with the statement that he is one of the greatest might-have-beens in the history of mathematics, and adds that Pascal began to 'die off at the top' when he became interested in religion. A recent biographer begins his enormous study with the words: 'Blaise Pascal was simply one of the greatest men that have ever lived,' and then reels off a long paragraph of his achievements in science, mathematics and theology. Other writers emphasise his importance as a philosopher, and his influence on William James, Bergson and the modern existentialists. T. E. Hulme wrote that he considered all his work as a mere preface to the reading of Pascal.

But again, the simplest and most fruitful approach for our present purposes is to consider Pascal as an Outsider. He had a thoroughly scientific brain, united with the profound craving for meaning and certainty that characterises all Outsiders.

Pascal was born in the year before Boehme died, 1623, at Clermont. His father was an important government official of Central France, whose hobbies were physics and mathematics. Blaise had two sisters, both beautiful and talented, one older and one younger than himself.

From the time of his birth, the legends about Blaise began. He became strangely sluggish, and his abdomen swelled. Local gossip suggested that a spell had been put on him, and his father was sufficiently impressed by the rumours to summon before him the old woman who was supposed to be the author of the malady. When he raged at her and threatened her with hanging, she confessed to having put a spell on the child, in a fit of pique. Unfortunately, it was a death spell, which could only be removed by being transferred to some other creature. Etienne Pascal offered a horse, but the witch explained that a cat would serve just as well. This was duly supplied; but on her way downstairs with it, some friars spoke to her sharply, and the cat jumped out of the window and broke its neck. Monsieur Pascal had to supply another cat. She also required certain herbs, which had to be plucked before sunrise by a child less than seven years old. This was also done. The witch made a poultice of the leaves and applied them to Blaise's stomach. The result was that the child appeared to die; he ceased to breathe, and his limbs became cold. In a rage, Monsieur Pascal struck the witch to the ground, but she assured him that it would be all right. A few hours later, Blaise began to yawn and wake up. The illness had disappeared. Not long after, Monsieur Pascal returned from the law courts and found the baby pouring water from one glass into another. It is not recorded what happened to the witch, who was, apparently, an old woman who lived on the charity of Madame Pascal.

Blaise was never a healthy child, and his mother's death when he was three years old may have affected him severely. But he showed himself so intelligent and eager for his lessons that his father was in the strange position of having to prevent his son from working too hard. This may be to some extent the cause of his extraordinary precocity. For instance, his father refused to allow Blaise to begin geometry until he had mastered Latin and Greek. Blaise questioned his father's friends until he had learned something of the methods and aims of geometry. At this point his father intervened, and asked his friends not to talk to Blaise about geometry. So Blaise began drawing charcoal diagrams on his nursery floor, and tried to teach himself. He drew a perfectly round circle, with an equilateral triangle in it, and set out to prove that its angles equalled 180°. His father came into the room, stood watching his son's efforts, and then broke in and asked him what he was up to. Blaise explained his logic — a little apprehensively — using his own terminology of 'bars' and 'rounds' for lines and circles. Gilberte Pascal — the elder sister — finished telling this story with the assertion that from then onwards, Blaise was given full access to geometry books. Her further statement that Blaise rediscovered for himself the first thirty-two propositions of Euclid must be discredited, on the grounds that there is not enough logical dependence between them to allow the greatest mathematical genius in the world to 'rediscover' them for himself without some help. It is more probable that Gilberte meant that Blaise had rediscovered the thirty-second proposition, which is the famous one about the angles of a triangle equalling 180°.

The Pascal family bristles with legends. When Blaise was fifteen, his father incurred the displeasure of Richelieu over a matter of some bonds which had ceased to pay dividends, and went into hiding to avoid being thrown into the Bastille. Twelve-year-old Jacqueline was showing the same precocity as her elder brother, and was making herself known at Court as a poetess. One day, Richelieu's niece decided to present a play for the benefit of the Cardinal, and Jacqueline was asked to take part. The tragedy, Scudéry's *Love the Tyrant*, made the Cardinal scream with laughter; no doubt the sight of these piping cherubs declaiming about passion, poison and petrifaction affected him much as Daisy Ashford's *The Young Visiters* affected a later generation. Jacqueline's father was summoned from his hiding to be congratulated, and was given an important government post.

At this time Pascal was working at his mathematics; his interest centred on conic sections. But his brilliance was not confined to mathematics alone. He invented a calculating-machine to help his father in his work — he was twenty at the time — and flung himself into the discussions on the vacuum that were dividing the scientists of the age. He played a leading part in conducting experiments, and collaborated with many eminent physicists and mathematicians, including Descartes (twenty-seven years Pascal's senior), who seems to have shown a regrettable streak of jealousy of Pascal. I cite these activities, not simply to underline Pascal's genius, but to give some idea of the atmosphere in which he spent his teens: continual excited speculation, and the feeling that man was learning to discover the secrets of nature. It was, in many ways, a thoroughly 'modern' atmosphere, full of faith in science and progress; the favourite reading of cultured people were semi-Christian stoics like Montaigne and Du Vair — fashionable 'doubters' — and Pierre Charron; the popular poet was Corneille, with his Emersonian maxims: 'I am master of myself and of the universe.'

But Pascal was not a physically healthy person; unlike Leonardo, another many-sided man of genius, he did not possess a powerful physique to take the strain of his intellectual excitement. And it is possible that this explains their difference of temperament, and the fact that Leonardo never developed a particularly religious temper. Pirandello has pointed out that man accepts happiness and health unquestioningly; it is only in misery that he begins to question. Pascal was not a happy, single-minded scientist because his health did not allow him a eupeptic, optimistic temperament.

And when he was twenty-three, Pascal's whole mental life was suddenly reoriented. His father slipped on an icy road and dislocated his hip. Two bonesetters moved into the house in Rouen to keep in constant attention. They were named Jean and Adrien Deschamps, and both had recently been converted to a doctrine known as Jansenism. During the period which the bonesetters spent in the house, Blaise became completely converted to this doctrine.

'Jansenism' derives its name from Cornelius Jansen, bishop of Ypres. Some fifteen years before Pascal's birth, Jansen and another student named Jean de Hauranne, better known as Saint-Cyran, had talked together about the religious laxness of their age, and brooded on plans for reform. Saint-Cyran was a man of great charm who later developed a compelling personal power and eloquence; he became father confessor to the nuns of Port Royal, a convent fourteen miles south-west of Paris, and exercised immense influence over his charges. He and Jansen had been in correspondence for many years, and Jansen had been elaborating his beliefs in an analysis of St. Augustine, which he called *Augustinus*. Jansen died in 1638 — at the time when Blaise was busy with his treatise on conic sections — and his book was published — in Latin, of course — two years after his death. The central doctrine of the *Augustinus* is the doc-

trine of grace. But Jansen and Saint-Cyran saw the world from an
extreme Outsider's viewpoint, as a sloppy and irritating place full
of rogues and fools. They felt as Swift felt about human nature;
and on the question of salvation, they would have agreed with
Gurdjieff and T. E. Hulme: men are so stupid and lethargic that no
human being has *ever* been saved by his own efforts. With the
penetration of true Outsiders, they realised that men have far less
'free will' than they like to believe. They saw clearly what so many
Outsiders have stated: that no man who has ever lived has solved
the problem of living; that all men are failures.

But in that case, what about Christianity? What about Christ,
who gave his word that the faithful should be saved? Their answer
was that some of the faithful are saved — but not by their own
efforts. They are saved by the grace of God.

And how does one gain this inestimable gift?

One doesn't — this was Jansen's answer. One just has to hope.
Man has so little free will that he can *do nothing*. He can only
strain all his fibres to become worthy of grace.

Blaise was immediately converted to this doctrine, which corresponded to the way he saw the world. He was first and foremost
a psychologist — as most Outsiders are. His own insights into human nature tended to make him agree with Jansen. From the age
of twenty-three, he became a fervent Jansenist.

In becoming a Jansenist, Pascal became a rebel against the established Church of his day — like Boehme and Kierkegaard and Fox
and Blake — in fact, like most other Outsiders who embrace Christianity. For in Pascal's time, the Church had again become a lax
and easygoing institution, as it was when Luther had been provoked
to break with it. After Luther's time, it was the Jesuits who had
done most to restore the meaning of Catholic Christianity; who had
again raised standards to the rigour demanded by the early Church
Fathers. Now, in France, at the time of the boy king (the *roi soleil*
succeeded to the throne at the age of five, in 1643) the Jesuits were
all-powerful; most families of the aristocracy had a Jesuit father
confessor. And naturally, the Jesuits were forced to compromise a
great deal with their aristocratic charges, for the worldlings, the
wealthy politicians, the businessmen and merchants did not want a
confessor who would impose a rigid moral discipline on them and

refuse to wink at their minor sins. The Church was by no means in the same appalling state as in the days when Luther was a monk; but its compromise with 'the world' was enough to provoke such men as Jansen and Pascal to denounce it as utterly corrupt.

Blaise's conversion was complete and wholehearted. He studied Saint-Cyran's *Spiritual Letters*, and Arnauld's *Frequent Communion*, and suddenly it seemed to him that the mystery of life had been solved: the road to God lay before him; it was open, and all one had to do was walk. Nothing mattered except to be undivided in purpose. He converted Jacqueline, and persuaded her against marrying a counsellor. Together they converted their father, and his elder sister and her husband. Less creditable was Pascal's controversy with Saint-Ange, a Capuchin friar who held that the truths of Christianity may be proved by the reason alone. Pascal arranged a meeting with the Capuchin and subjected him to an inquisition. Saint-Ange replied good-humouredly, but his reasonableness was not enough to sway the newly converted heresy hunter, nor two friends who agreed with Pascal. Letters written to the Archbishop stirred up a scandal, and Saint-Ange was driven out of his benefice, and later out of a quiet village near Paris. The young heresy hunters were well satisfied with themselves; but after three hundred years, it is Saint-Ange who emerges from the episode with credit, while Pascal's admirers have to do their best to gloss it over.

In the year following this unpleasant interlude, Pascal's health collapsed entirely; he was forced to walk with the aid of crutches, and seized with cramps which modern experts diagnose as intestinal tuberculosis. His feet were always icy, and had to be warmed with cloths dipped in brandy. In spite of this, he continued his experiments with the vacuum. Early in the summer of 1647, Blaise and Jacqueline moved to Paris, and together attended the service of Father Singlin, the famous preacher who had been converted 'by grace' when he was a young draper's assistant. Singlin's eloquence moved them both deeply. Jacqueline decided there and then to become a nun; but her father opposed the idea strongly, urging her to wait at least until he was dead. She agreed to this. Blaise became more devout than ever, but could not bring himself to renounce science for the monastic life. Besides, his father's health was weak, and he had no wish to hasten a complete breakdown. He took his father into the country at Auvergne for six months in 1649, and his own health improved steadily. His doctors advised him to relax and lead an easy social life. For a while Pascal followed their advice. With his friend and admirer the Duc de Roannez he began attending social gatherings, gaming, and otherwise diverting himself. His intellectuality brought him much esteem and admiration in society. He fell in love and pursued a lady whose identity is not known (it may have been the duke's sister). Jacqueline was made miserable by this unexpected streak of 'worldliness' in her adored brother, and prayed for his 'conversion.' Soon there was more reason for friction between them; their father died in 1651, and Jacqueline decided to take the veil immediately. For some reason, Blaise asked her to delay for a year, but she refused him. She could hardly realise that Blaise was developing a deeper and wider knowledge of life and of himself, and that all experience was invaluable to him. His father's death caused him acute grief, but it did not keep him away from society for long. For three years he played the man of the world; yet he did not abandon himself entirely to pleasure, as Jacqueline was inclined to believe. Now his mind was full of the problem of the human will and its strength. He read Montaigne and Epictetus, Charron and Descartes. It was not that he had forgotten his original conversion; only that his conversion had taught him that the aim of human life is to strive towards the saintly or the godlike. And now all his curiosity as an Outsider was directed to finding shortcuts to this end. He allowed himself to become divided again. Sometimes he hated himself; frequently he hated his fellow men, and found them contemptible and trivial. Having deliberately divided himself, he now ceased to have the feeling of close contact with God, and his devotions became mere mechanical rites. In 1654, he wrote to Jacqueline confessing that he had reached an intellectual and spiritual impasse. He was thirty-one, and had all the Outsider's feeling that human life is a lukewarm half-measure.

After a year of deteriorating health and spiritual uncertainty, Pascal had a vision. It was on the 23rd of November, 1654. At half past ten in the evening — probably as he lay in bed — an overpowering sense of health and vitality suddenly swept over him, a feeling of complete and total well-being; a certainty so sudden and complete that, when he wrote about it, he headed the page: fire.

The sensation lasted for two hours, and he tried to capture it on paper. As he wrote, his feelings changed — no vision can be sustained for two hours — and he began to feel that he had sinned for the past few years. This is always the way with a vision. The first sensation is of vitality that makes one affirm all existence, and love, love of the world, of its physical reality. As this certainty dies away, one becomes aware of the need for discipline if it is to be recaptured, and of one's lack of discipline in the past. Pascal's *Memorial* begins:

fire

God of Abraham, God of Isaac, God of Jacob, not of the philosophers and scholars.
Certitude, certitude, feeling, joy, peace.
God of Jesus Christ.

and further on:

> Joy, joy, joy, tears of joy.
> I have been separated from him. . . .
> Let me not be separated from him eternally.

It ends with the lines:

> Let me never be separated from him.
> ' He is preserved only by the ways taught in the Gospel.
> Renunciation, total and sweet.[1]

At once, we can see that this vision has much in common with the vision of Boehme, and with Nietzsche's vision on the hilltop when the lightning and rain gave him an exalted sense of well-being; it is an experience that can be testified to by a dozen Outsiders: Nijinsky's 'God is fire in the head,' Yeats's 'heaven blazing into the brain,' the vision underlying Van Gogh's *Nuit Etoilée* and Rilke's Ninth Elegy with its affirmation 'Erde, du liebe, ich will,' the Steppenwolf's moment in which he could 'affirm everything.' Pascal called it 'inspiration,' and so it was; a violence of pure affirmation. From that time onward, Pascal never swerved in his intellectual certainty or in his religious vision.

His first desire was to retreat to Port Royal, and to submit his soul to the direction of Father Singlin. But Singlin was ill, and Pascal had to contain his impatience. His friend the Duc de Roannez returned to Paris, and was awe-stricken by Pascal's conversion; within a few days, he was converted too. This caused a little trouble; Roannez's family were plotting to marry him off to a wealthy heiress of peasant origin (his lands were all mortgaged; in seventeenth-century France, a marriage of this kind was known as 'manuring one's land'). After his conversion, Roannez changed his mind. His family were enraged, and rightly blamed Pascal, who was staying in their house at the time. One morning, the wife of the concierge took a knife and went to Pascal's room, having determined to kill him. He was out — contrary to his usual habits. When he heard of the episode, he did not return. Instead, he spent a few days in the country, and then moved into Port Royal.

Here, the third great period of Pascal's life begins. The man-of-the-world phase was over. He settled down to days of quiet study of the scriptures and the Church Fathers. He submitted himself to the rules of the house, which involved rising at 5 a.m., fasting, and keeping vigil. But his soul was now undivided, and his health thrived on the austere routine. In the *Memorial* he had written that the teachings of the New Testament are the only way of reaching union with God, and now he learned the Gospels by heart. The period now beginning was probably the happiest of Pascal's life. He had accepted the Nicholas Ferrar solution of the Outsider's problems. It suited him well. When trouble blew up for Port Royal a few months later, he was spiritually and physically refreshed, and ready to take up the cudgels in defence of his new home.

The trouble began when the Jesuits refused communion to a certain Duc de Liancourt because he was a friend of Port Royal. Arnauld of Port Royal attacked the Jesuits, and a correspondence began on the question of divine grace. The question was submitted to the Faculty of Theology for judgement, but the Jesuits had contrived to pack the court with Jesuits and Molinists. (Molina was a Jesuit who taught that predestination and free will are not incompatible.) Arnauld was condemned, and his condemnation filled Port Royal with apprehension. It was only one stage now to pronouncing Jansenism heretical and breaking up the Port Royal community.

Arnauld appealed to Pascal to exercise his immense intellectual powers in defence of Port Royal, and (after some hesitation) Pascal agreed. Early in 1656, a slim pamphlet entitled *Letter to a Provincial* appeared on the streets of Paris, and quickly sold out. It caused a sensation. It opens in an easy, conversational style: 'My dear Sir: Well, we were much mistaken. I learned the facts only yesterday. . . .' The attention was immediately captured; people read on. After all, the letter continued, it is a simple matter. Arnauld has been condemned for doubting that Jansen's book really contained five heretical propositions; well surely, the commonsense thing to do is to read the book and find out. Why don't the censors state *where* the five propositions appear in Jansen, and give people a chance to judge for themselves? The letter-writer then describes a visit to Dr. N., the anti-Jansenist theologian. Here, Pascal shows that he had the makings of a first-class novelist. He skilfully creates the character of an intellectually dishonest, dust-snuffling theologian, and describes his discussion with the letter-writer in detail. The writer professes to be completely bewildered by all this word-spinning, and goes off to see a Molinist theologian. And yet another Gogolian character is created in a few strokes. In this first *Letter*, Pascal poses as 'the man in the street' who only wants to get to the bottom of a difficult matter. He uses the same device as many modern journalists, although his effect is rather less nauseating.

All Paris talked about the *Letter*, and the police tried to trace it to its source. Five days later, another was on the streets. The police seized the printing presses normally associated with Port Royal. Nine days later, a third letter was being sold publicly. It was the joke of Paris, and the enraged Jesuits tried to discover who the author could be. Pascal was among those suspected, but his associates were too clever to let the suspicion become a certainty. Unfortunately, the letters did nothing to stay the persecution of Arnauld, and he was duly struck off the role of doctors of the Sorbonne. In the fourth *Provincial Letter*, Pascal drops his defence of Arnauld — which amounts to the statement that it was not Arnauld's ideas but just Arnauld's existence that was offensive to the Jesuits — and attacks the Jesuits' moral system. A Jesuit named Escobar had compiled an anthology from various Jesuit fathers; it was for the guidance of Jesuit priests on matters of casuistry. (Casuistry is the

discussion of whether certain actions are ethical or unethical, but its
aim is not, as modern readers might suppose, 'to make the worse
appear the better reason.' It is simply a practical necessity for any
hard-working priest.) The Jesuit Escobar was not a particularly
dishonest man, but many of his propositions looked as if they had
been invented solely for the benefit of hypocrites and the spiritually
lazy: Pascal's letter-writer has a discussion with a Jesuit about
Escobar:

> 'Tell me,' he continued, 'do you use much wine?'
> 'No, Father,' I said. 'I can't endure it.'
> 'I asked you that, to inform you that you could drink it in the
> morning and whenever you liked, without breaking the fast. . . .'
> 'That Escobar is a decent sort,' said I.
> 'Everyone is crazy about him!' replied the Father. . . .[2]

The examples become more outrageous; Escobar is quoted to support every sin from simony to murder. Pascal attacks the Jesuits
for having condemned Galileo; as the letters go on, he continually
assumes new positions from which to attack them. The *Letters* continued for a year, and then abruptly ceased; Letter Nineteen breaks
off in the middle of a sentence.

There was one event that occurred during the writing of the
letters which should be recorded. Pascal's ten-year-old niece Marguerite suffered from a large swelling at the corner of her eye that
discharged pus and a foul odour; over three years, the bone structure of the nose had been affected by it. On May 24, 1656, a
holy relic was displayed in the monastery — a thorn that was pur-
ported to come from Christ's crown of thorns. Marguerite's eye was
touched with this thorn, and within a few days, it was completely
healed. The miracle restored the faith of Port Royal; it restored
Pascal's faith in his opposition to the Church; and above all, it
brought to Port Royal an odour of sanctity which disarmed many
of its enemies. The miracle was made the subject of an ecclesiastical
enquiry, and a commission reported it to be genuine.

The miracle of the thorn and the *Provincial Letters* delayed the
downfall of Port Royal, but could not avert it entirely. In 1660,
the *Provincial Letters* were burned at the hands of the common

hangman (although the judges could not be persuaded to give up their copies, and the hangman had to burn some other book instead). In 1661, Jansen's book was condemned as being contrary to the doctrines of St. Augustine, and the leading spirits of Port Royal were made to sign the document condemning them. Pascal was so shattered by this that he had another breakdown in health, from which he never recovered.

But in the meantime, he had begun another great project — a project worthy of his immense powers. The Jesuits were not real enemies; they were only less religious than Pascal — which is only to say that they were not Outsiders, and were preoccupied about the good of the majority of Insiders. But already, in Pascal's day, the rise of science had brought a wave of humanism and atheism, which Pascal determined to attack.

This project — I have no need to point out — is very close to the Outsider's heart. All his life, Dostoevsky purposed to write an immense novel called *Atheism*. When he was killed, T. E. Hulme was planning to write a book that would overturn humanism from its foundations. Everything about the Outsider's state of mind is anti-humanistic, anti-materialistic. Atheism, in the last resort, means materialism. Let me, before I go on to discuss Pascal's *Pensées*, try to make this clear, for it is one of the most important points that arise in connection with the Outsider.

This division of the world into Outsiders and Insiders is obviously rough-and-ready, and not intended to stand up to close analysis. It is simply a convenient way of approaching an important subject. Outsider and Insider differ in degree, not in kind. But it is also true that the difference between the caveman and Professor Whitehead is a difference of degree; that doesn't make it any less real and important. The Outsider is the obsessed man — obsessed with the problem of where he is going and who he is.

But man evolves by being obsessed: Mahler became a great musician by being obsessed by music; to begin with, he was sentimental and banal. The same is true of many men of genius. Gauguin's painting is great, not because Gauguin is a *talented* painter, but because he cared so much about painting that his comparative lack of talent (in the sense that Ingres had talent) is unimportant.

The Outsider sees this as the final difference between men. Will power and obsession are all that counts. The obsessed man is great; the satisfied man is not. The Outsider's natural attitude to philosophy is this: Do not ask whether the philosophy is true; look at the philosopher and ask whether he is great. A man who is not obsessed cannot be great.

A doubtful proposition, perhaps, and one whose dangers I shall have to point out in the chapter on Shaw. But it is undoubtedly a valid starting point for an examination of Western civilisation.

Apply this criterion to materialism and atheism. What type of man is the materialist, generally? Sometimes, of course, a man who has been thrown into a frenzy of opposition to the religious viewpoint by some unfortunate experience with its representatives. (Graham Greene presents an example in his police captain in *The Power and the Glory*.) But this type of man is a rarity in the modern liberal country, no matter how common he may have been in Tsarist Russia. More commonly, the materialist is a shortsighted sceptic who has never undergone any deep emotional or spiritual experience (they are practically the same thing). He is the type of person that Blake satirises in *An Island in the Moon*. He is a man whose formative years were intoxicated with the idea of science, which can make man the master of the world and of himself (for of course, part of man's slavery to himself is really slavery to his cowardice — his fear of the external world, which science can teach him to master). The rationalist, then, is driven by a will to power over the world; a power which he is convinced that unending reason and logic can give him. But his defeat is the same as that of Alexander the Great: when all the world is conquered, what then? The rationalist has failed to recognise the most important fact about man: that reason and logic may give man power over the outside world, but no power over himself. They can make him into a dictator, but not into a genius.

But every poet knows that a man's real value is determined by the depth of his emotional experience. It is those deep insights into his own being that really give man mastery over himself and then over the world. Any young poet knows this, any adolescent intoxicated by reading Shelley and Wordsworth. The man whose mental life is restricted to meditating about logic and science is only a half-man, and will become mentally stunted. If he spends his time with his attention concentrated on the natural world and its laws, he will never explore the strange countries within himself. Blake's finest lyric is called *The Mental Traveller*, and begins:

> I travel'd thro' a Land of Men
> A Land of Men and Women too,
> And heard and saw such dreadful things
> As cold Earth wanderers never knew.[3]

Blake disliked Newton for being a mere 'cold Earth wanderer.' 'The further one travels, the less one knows,' states the *Tao Te Ching*. In the course of this long exploration of the Outsider, I have tried to show that man's evolution lies, not in science, but in knowing more of himself.

This does not mean that science is useless. On the contrary, it is the greatest instrument man could have developed for his evolution. Science means the conquering, compressing and ordering of knowledge. All that must be emphasised is that *natural knowledge* — the sort of knowledge with which physics and mathematics are concerned — is only a fraction of real knowledge.

All man's experience is emotional experience. Even the mathematician, plunged in his calculations, is undergoing emotional experience. His intellectual activity is accompanied by a pleasure and an excitement that is emotional, and it is this that makes him pursue mathematics. An electronic brain takes no pleasure in its calculating. All life is continual emotional experience.

It is also true that 'wisdom' (i.e. maturity) is an increasing control of one's emotional experience; an ability to cut out certain distracting types of experience so as to be better able to concentrate on others. Many emotional experiences are just repetitive, and teach us nothing new: jealousy, irritation, fear. The more mature the man, the easier he finds it to combat these experiences.

The other experiences — the more important experiences — must then occupy all the attention. Each strong emotion reveals a new area of man's being. For instance, Yeats and Rupert Brooke knew that a man can be introduced to himself in a moment of anger and courage:

> Know that when all words are said
> And a man is fighting mad,
> Something drops from eyes long blind,
> He completes his partial mind,
> For an instant stands at ease,
> Laughs aloud, his heart at peace.*

But freed from the bondage of the trivial and the immediate, man plunges into a world of new sensations and new self-discovery. This is the real meaning of the word education; the profoundest of all senses, in which Goethe uses it in *Wilhelm Meister*. Real education means existentialism, and existentialism means exploring one's inner world scientifically. This is why materialism and all its incarnations — Marxism, logical positivism, and the smirking Bertrand Russell type of rationalism — are so deadly. They make imprisonment in time, consciousness and personality — to which human beings are only too prone — seem quite natural and inevitable. And since this way of thought has become the prevalent way in our modern world, the Outsider must raise the banner of a new existentialism, and make war on civilised modes of thought.

It is this materialism which Pascal wanted to fight in his *Apology for Christianity*. He begins his argument from the same position that I began *The Outsider*: with the man who is obsessed by the search for truth. He writes: 'I can approve only those who search groaning,' anticipating Nietzsche, who was to write: 'I love only what a man has written with his blood.'

Pascal never finished his *Apology*, and its fragments — some nine hundred of them ranging from unfinished sentences to small essays — have never been arranged in satisfactory order. I do not intend to undertake a lengthy analysis of them; this is unnecessary. Most of what Pascal has to say about human nature has been said by the various Outsiders I have examined in these two volumes. There is the emphasis on human stupidity to be found in Nietzsche or Swift.

---

* Yeats, 'Under Ben Bulben.' In his sonnet 'Peace' Rupert Brooke thanks God for the war that has —
> ... caught our youth, and wakened us from sleeping,
> With hand made sure, clear eye, and sharpened power,
> To turn, as swimmers into cleanness leaping.

There is the distinction between the mathematical and the intuitive mind which is essentially the starting point of 'the attempt to gain control' — the difference between T. E. Lawrence and Van Gogh. The relativity of all human judgements is emphasised: 'All the false beauties we blame in Cicero have their admirers, and in great number.' Like Yeats and Nietzsche, he is aware that the poet and artist cannot be absolutists about truth, for chaos is usually more fruitful for the creator than order. Where Yeats had written 'What theme had Homer but original sin?' Pascal says laconically: 'A poet and not an honest man.'

In a summary of his plan for the *Apology*, Pascal wrote:

> *First Part:* Misery of man without God.
> *Second Part:* Happiness of man with God.
> Or: *First Part:* That Nature is corrupt. Proved by nature itself.
> *Second Part:* That there is a Redeemer. Proved by Scripture.[4]

We can see that this *First Part* covers the same ground as the existentialist Outsiders, from Sartre's Roquentin to Dostoevsky's Ivan Karamazov. It is the misery of the total sceptic — and not only his misery, but his terror. Once he has dismissed as unproved the notion that the universe has any total meaning, that life in itself is good, he finds himself facing 'the horror' of which Conrad wrote in *Heart of Darkness* and Andreyev in *Lazarus*: that life may not be a progress towards anything good, but an escape from something evil which waits on the other side of physical reality. It is Dostoevsky's speculation that eternity may be a corner of a dusty room covered with cobwebs — or that perhaps eternity is a spider. In a famous passage, Pascal speaks of the vastness of space, and then of the wonders of the world of minute organisms, and contrasts man, the 'thinking reed,' with the multiplicity of nature. Elsewhere, he speaks of man's need for constant diversion, his perpetual misery unless he is up and doing (which we have already seen emphasised by Strowde in *The Secret Life* and by Gurdjieff). He comes very close to saying with Gurdjieff, that man is a mere machine, completely at the mercy of his environment; that he has no free will whatever. But unlike Gurdjieff, he does not then go on to consider the question of how man might learn to create free will for himself, how he might cease to be a mere leaf, tossed about on the current of his environment.

But the second part of Pascal's argument is open to more doubt. A thing can only be 'proved' by referring it to something that is unquestionable, and showing that it is in agreement. By the Outsider's standards, it is no proof to refer to the scriptures. And this, perhaps, is the chief weakness of the *Pensées* from the point of view of the Outsider. Pascal simply tears away the veils from the world, and shows human nature in all its vagueness and laziness and lack of purpose — and he rightly calls this 'misery.' (Kierkegaard would later call it Anguish.) Having made human weakness so clear that it is self-evident and requires no further proof, Pascal then takes the next step and posits the need for a redeemer. Like St. Paul, he has rejected the imperfection of the world, and immediately created the need for redemption.

And we are back again at the most fundamental of human problems. The Outsider has accepted the existence of God — that is, of a force working through human beings and through nature, of a purpose greater than the purpose of any individual conscious human personality. A little discipline of poetic insight, a little 'mental travelling' can reveal the existence of levels of purpose that are deeper than our knowledge of ourselves. But the Outsider feels that evolution — man's spiritual progress — depends upon a deepening of this insight, and constant discipline of intuition. What has this to do with accepting a historical saviour?

On the other hand, how is this belief to be turned into a religion which can be generally accepted? The Outsider is a sort of spiritual graduate who can be trusted to pursue his own researches; but the average man needs a nursery discipline, and a nursery simplification of his problems. In fact — and this, we must agree, sounds most cynical and blasphemous of all — the average man needs to believe in a saviour as a child needs to believe in Santa Claus, and he must be assured of the existence of a saviour as the child must be assured of the existence of Santa Claus. The alternative will be a terrible impoverishment of his emotional life. A child has to be educated, and he cannot be educated by working on the assumption that he is an adult. The problem we are facing is, in fact, a problem of education. Existentialism means the ability to grasp the meaning of life. The Outsider is a graduate of the school; his knowledge of life is more complex than the average man's, just as Einstein's knowledge of mathematics is more complex than a schoolboy's.

Obviously, the notion of evolution is fundamental in this scheme. *Not* 'natural selection' — which means mechanical evolution — but the slow struggle of will to master life's complexities. This also means that Nietzsche's concept of the Superman has some relevance, even if we dare not yet formulate that relevance for fear of oversimplifying. One might even allow speculation to roam further, and think of the Outsider as occupying a position midway between man and superman, or at least between man as he exists at present, and some type of man with one degree more moral consciousness. The danger to be avoided, of course, is talking vaguely about 'the Life Force' as if it were some strange entity like the Iron Curtain. If existentialism has any meaning, it is expressed in the assertion: 'I *am* the Life Force,' or in Nijinsky's 'I am God.' It implies the necessity of immediate action — or at least, of immediate realisation of *involvement* — a complete abandonment of the attitude of being the uninvolved spectator (the philosopher's attitude), or the more human attitude of 'taking life as it comes,' which really means allowing life to take you where it wants, and drifting aimlessly.

These observations — which, no doubt, have the appearance of being an alternative second part of the *Pensées* — are not intended as a dismissal of Pascal's theory of redemption. Insight into the human situation will never cease to be valid — until human beings transcend their situation and make it redundant — and Pascal's *Pensées* can no more be discredited than Dante's *Commedia* or *Paradise Lost*. As an attempt to solve the Outsider's problems, they are self-complete and beyond criticism. I have only tried to point out that, under the premises we have developed in studying the Outsider, Pascal's Pauline solution cannot pass muster. It may have been valid for Pascal and for his contemporaries, but for civilisation in the mid-twentieth century it does not fit the facts. What are 'the facts'? A highly technical civilisation with a three-century tradition of freethinking behind it, and more leisure than it knows what to do with. And perhaps Pascal would not have expected it to fit the facts. The groundwork of the *Pensées* is essentially pessimistic. Like Pareto, Pascal would have considered Marxist ideology sentimental and shortsighted. In his day there was a Church; in our own — as Mann observed — human destiny presents itself in political terms. In solving our modern problems, the *Pensées* will take us so far and no further. What is important — what cannot be over-emphasised — is that in any civilisation that has reached our stage, political thinking must begin with the assumptions of Pascal's *Pensées* — with the Outsider.

An error must have time to grow and develop all its tendencies before it can be killed. Pascal came too soon; so did Blake, whose fragmentary *Pensées* begin with his pamphlet *Against the Deists*. The time had begun to be ripe when Hulme pointed out that romanticism is religion turning rotten. Now the error has developed to the full, but most of us are too closely involved in it to see it; only a few farsighted historians have recognised our true situation.

Pascal died in 1662, at the age of thirty-nine. His attempt to demolish the foundations of atheism was never completed; and it is doubtful whether it would have made any great impression on its age even if it had been; no doubt it would have become a classic, like Fénelon's *Existence of God* or Butler's *Analogy*, and made no impression whatever on the living thought of its time. Science was too young. It is true that Pascal himself was a scientist; so was Bishop Berkeley, who wrote a treatise on mathematics to refute a mathematician who claimed that no man could believe in both God and mathematics. There is a law of history which could be called the Law of Errors, and it is this: An error is unkillable until it has stopped growing (unless it is uprooted by the doubtful method of fire and sword). In Pascal's time, materialism was still young.

Pascal is, perhaps, the most important 'Outsider' we have considered so far in this study; more important even than Nietzsche and Dostoevsky, for they were both simply artists. Pascal was a scientist and a mathematician. Many Outsider temperaments loathe mathematics — Dostoevsky and Ramakrishna did, for instance — and a modern materialist thinker is inclined to explain the difference between the religious and the materialist temper as being merely the difference between superstition and logic. A figure like Pascal decisively disproves this. In all things he excelled. He had the practical ability of a statesman; he had a genius for friendship; his mathematics and physics show the mental power of a Newton; his *Provincial Letters* show the satirical talent of a Gogol or Fielding; his *Pensées* show an insight into the human heart that only Dostoevsky can equal, and an iconoclasm as deadly as Nietzsche's. It is difficult, in our age of dilettantism and specialisation, to comprehend his greatness; and impossible to pass judgement on it.

CHAPTER FOUR

EMANUEL SWEDENBORG

In spite of the immense differences between them, there is a curious similarity between Blaise Pascal and Emanuel Swedenborg. Swedenborg was also a man of scientific genius who is known to posterity by his religious genius. But Swedenborg lived more than twice as long as Pascal, and his mark on history is greater, for there exists all over the world today a considerable and flourishing church that preaches his doctrines. For a twentieth-century reader, this is enough to attach a somewhat doubtful odour to his name. We have had too much of cranky messiahs — Mary Baker Eddy, 'Pastor' Russell (of the Jehovah's Witnesses), Madame Blavatsky — yet the truth is that Swedenborg is a far greater figure than any of these. He also poses a perplexing and unsolved problem. Until he was almost sixty, Swedenborg was a scientist and mathematician; and when, at the end of the last century, his scientific writings were examined, it was found that he had been ahead of his time in almost every major department of scientific activity. His work on the brain anticipated modern physiology; his work on palaeontology anticipated later Swedish geology; he advanced the nebular hypothesis of the formation of the planets long before Kant or Laplace; his magnetic theory has much in common with Clerk Maxwell's; he was the first to try to create a science of crystals; he produced one of the earliest accounts of the phenomena of phosphorescence, was the first to use mercury in an air pump, and invented a method of determining longitude at sea by observation of the moon among the stars. As indubitably as Newton or Einstein, he had scientific genius. At the age of sixty, he began to study the Bible, and to write theological works. Very soon, he was claiming, in his calm and matter-of-fact way, that he had been allowed to make a tour of heaven and hell, and had conversed with angels and spirits of the dead.

Before we hastily dismiss this as senile self-deceit, let us glance at the three best-known cases of Swedenborg's unusual powers. First, there is the case of the Queen of Sweden. Count Höpken, a contemporary, describes it:

> Swedenborg was one day at a court reception. Her Majesty asked him about different things in the other life, and lastly, whether he had seen or talked with her brother, the Prince Royal of Prussia, He answered No. Her Majesty then requested him to ask after him, and give him her greeting, which Swedenborg promised to do. I doubt whether the Queen meant this seriously. At the next reception, Swedenborg again appeared at court; and while the Queen was . . . surrounded by her ladies of honour, he came boldly in and approached her Majesty. . . . Swedenborg not only greeted her from her brother, but also gave her his apologies for not having answered her last letter; he also wished to do so now through Swedenborg; which he accordingly did. The Queen was greatly overcome, and said: 'No one but God knows this secret.' [1]

This episode is well authenticated; it is said that for days afterwards, carriages rolled up to Swedenborg's front door, and nobles tried to persuade him to tell them what he had told the Queen that had affected her so greatly; Swedenborg, of course, refused. Many versions of the story became current at the time.

The second unusual occurrence is known generally as 'the Stockholm fire.' In Gothenburg one evening, as Swedenborg was about to sit down to dinner, he suddenly turned pale, and went outside. When he returned, he told the company that a great fire had broken out in Stockholm, and that his own house was in danger. Stockholm was 300 miles away. For two hours, Swedenborg walked up and down anxiously; then, at about eight o'clock, he said suddenly: 'Thank heavens, the fire is under control; it had almost reached my doorstep.' The news spread throughout Gothenburg, and the next day Swedenborg was summoned before the governor to describe the fire. It was not until the following day that a letter arrived from Stockholm confirming all that Swedenborg had said, down to the last detail.

The third case has something of the air of a detective story. Madame Marteville, the widow of the Dutch Ambassador in Stockholm, received a large bill from a goldsmith named Croon; it was for a silver tea service which she was convinced her husband had paid for. However, she could not find the receipt. Swedenborg was called in as a last resort, and asked to question the deceased husband next time he happened to meet him in the spirit world. A few days later, he came to the house when Madame Marteville had a company of friends with her. 'I questioned your husband. He confirmed that he paid for the tea service, and says that the receipt is in the bureau upstairs.' 'Impossible,' the lady answered. 'I've turned everything out of it.' Swedenborg then explained that there was a secret compartment behind the left-hand drawer of the bureau, which could be got at by pulling out the drawer and sliding a board aside. It also contained, Swedenborg explained, certain Dutch business letters. The whole company trooped upstairs. Swedenborg could hardly have asked for a better effect — and a search of the bureau revealed the receipt and letters just as Swedenborg had described them.

It should be added immediately that Swedenborg attached no importance whatever to these incidents. He seems to have had the same ironic attitude towards them that Jesus had towards the miracles; they were irrelevant and likely to get him the reputation of a charlatan.

Swedenborg was born nearly a quarter of a century after Pascal's death, in 1688. His father's name was Swedberg, and he was a bishop of the Lutheran Church. (Swedenborg was given a patent of nobility by Queen Ulrica which authorised him to insert the extra syllable in his name; it is equivalent to the German 'von.') Strangely enough, his maternal grandfather was called Behm, a variant of

Boehme.* Swedenborg passed through the usual tutelage and university training until he was twenty-one; little is known about his youth. He was known to his family as a poet, but his mind seems to have been as curious and as omnivorous as Leonardo's, and his interest in physics, geology, biology and mathematics was as great as his interest in literature. When he set out on his travels, at the age of twenty-two, he made a summary of the mathematical discoveries of the previous two centuries, to which he intended to add anything new that he might find on his travels. In London, he made a point of lodging with men of different trades — a watchmaker, a cabinet-maker, a mathematical-instrument maker — and learning all he could from his landlords. He also studied music, and learned to play the organ well enough to replace the organist in his local church. In 1710, he published his first book — a collection of poems in Latin. The next few years were a period of frustration for him; Sweden was a cautious, conservative nation, and young Swedenborg's many ideas for his country's scientific advancement were thwarted. He began a scientific journal to record the discoveries of his day, and dedicated it to the king. With his brother-in-law, he planned a great astronomical observatory. He spent another year at the University to study engineering. Finally, when he was twenty-eight, he was given the appointment of Assessor to the Swedish Board of Mines. To begin with, there was no salary attached to this post, but it fascinated Swedenborg's practical mind; so much so that he turned down a professorship of Astronomy at the University, and, a few years later, a professorship of mathematics. This latter he refused on the interesting ground that he thought mathematicians should not confine themselves to mere theory. All his life he was sturdily practical, and had no use for theory divorced from practice; this was as much the characteristic of his religious as of his scientific teaching. For him, thought was essentially the prelude to action; there was no such thing as abstract thought. His capacity was formidably demonstrated in 1718, when Charles XII was laying siege to the Danes in the fortress of Fredrikshald; he was given the task of transporting five ships across fifteen miles of country. The feat took seven weeks, but it was accomplished, under Swedenborg's direction.

* Boehme was also known as Behmen or Behm in England up to the beginning of the present century.

Swedenborg was also closely involved in the construction of the great docks at Karlskrona, and in the scheme for connecting the North Sea with the Baltic by canal (this was left unfinished when Charles was killed by a bullet in the campaign of 1718).

There is no point in following Swedenborg's quarter of a century as assessor in detail; it is enough to say that he gradually made himself invaluable to the Board of Mines, and helped to revolutionise mining in Sweden. He started to write an immense work on science, which began with a whole volume on the origins of the universe, and others on the practice of smelting iron and steel, copper and brass. His work on physiology — especially the function of the brain — advanced many views that were heterodox in his own day, but have since been proved correct: for instance, that the activity of the brain is synchronous with breathing, not with the beats of the heart or the motion of the blood.

Equally important, in periods of long, intense concentration, Swedenborg disciplined his body to make its presence almost imperceptible. He learned to work for long hours without mental fatigue, and his concentration was so great that at times his breathing seemed to stop. This, it may well be, was the really decisive factor in turning Swedenborg the engineer into Swedenborg the mystic. The variety and number of his works are bewildering: treatises on algebra (the first in Swedish), on economics, on salt mining, on the tides, on astronomy, on minerals, on anatomy and physiology. In France in 1736 he predicted the revolution of 1789. Early in the seventeen-forties, his first work on theology began to take shape, the *Hieroglyphic Key to Natural and Spiritual Mysteries*, in which he advances a theory that seems to have much in common with Boehme's 'signatures,' although it appears that he had never read Boehme.

The year 1744 was the turning point in Swedenborg's life. In April of that year he seems to have had some kind of vision; having retired to bed at ten o'clock, he heard a roaring noise like a high wind; when he jumped out of bed in alarm, the wind seemed to pick him up and fling him on his face, and he felt the presence of something 'indescribably holy.' He fell on his knees and, addressing Jesus, began to pray for grace. Suddenly he felt a hand seize his own; upon opening his eyes, he claims, he saw Jesus face to face.

Jesus then asked him the rather curious question as to whether he had a 'bill of health' (a document certifying the health of a ship's crew before it leaves port). Swedenborg answered in the affirmative, and the vision replied: 'Well then, do.' At this, Swedenborg woke up. This dream seems to have completely altered his mental life, giving him a sense of close contact with unseen powers. No doubt as a consequence of this new attitude, he began to have ecstatic trances, of the same type as Sri Ramakrishna's. In London, later that year, he was robbed of his gold watch while in a state of trance, and the thieves (who were employed in the house), when he approached them, tried to persuade him that he had thrown the watch out of the window in his ecstasy. He was unconvinced, but did not attempt to prosecute them.

One sign of his new attitude was his sudden loss of sexual desire. All his emotional energy was taken up by the visions and ecstasies, which became more and more frequent. He now no longer had to sleep to see visions; angels in the form of men appeared to him when he went into a state of meditation, and once a voice told him sharply to hold his tongue; he was writing, not talking, at the time, so possibly the spirit was irritated that Swedenborg's receptivity was being interfered with by his scientific labours. If this is so, it enforces the point that Swedenborg's visions and voices took place inside his head — in his imagination. But this is not to say that they were just self-deceptions; Shaw's Saint Joan commented that all visions come through the imagination, and certainly anyone who has had much experience of imaginative creation knows that the imagination's power lies in its receptivity, not in any power to 'invent.'

In 1747, Swedenborg resigned from the Board of Mines; he was fifty-nine at the time. For another quarter of a century he wrote the immense theological works upon which his living influence rests. The works were all published in Latin, and many were anonymous. Naturally, they caused no great sensation; in fact, it is recorded that only four copies of the first volume were sold in two months. But over the years, Swedenborg's reputation grew, and the established Church began to show its hostility to him. A Swedish bishop declared his work 'full of intolerable . . . errors' and heretical, but the royal protection did not fail, and Swedenborg was never actively persecuted.

His first religious work was published two years after resigning from the Board of Mines; it was the first volume of the *Arcana Coelestia*, an examination of the Book of Genesis (like Boehme's *Mysterium Magnum*). In it, he makes no bones about stating that he has been permitted to enter the spirit world and speak with angels and the spirits of the dead. This work extended to eight bulky volumes before it was finished. His next work, entitled *The Last Judgement*, was published in 1758, and maintained the startling thesis that the Last Judgement had taken place in the previous year — in the spirit world, of course — and that from then on, spirits would be judged immediately on reaching heaven. The reason, apparently, was that the evil spirits in the other-world had swelled to such immense numbers that their baleful influence was becoming dangerous for the earth. (It is interesting to note that the Jehovah's Witnesses hold the same kind of belief — that the kingdom of the devil came to an end in 1914, and that now — in the spirit world — Christ is king.) In *Heaven and Its Wonders and Hell* — his most immediately attractive work — he speaks of having been allowed to tour both regions, and even ventures upon some physical descriptions of them. For instance, some hells appear as holes or caves in rocks; others look like ruined cities, with streets and brothels: 'in the streets and lanes are robberies and plunderings'; others look like rude cottages. But the greater part of *Heaven and Hell* is taken up with analysis of the *state* of blessedness and damnation, and in many parts Swedenborg asserts that hell is a mental state, not a place.

This is the puzzle of Swedenborg's work; and so far, no one has been able to solve it finally. The great bulk of it consists of profound psychological observations in which the Outsider can discover his own insights reflected; the remainder describes conversations with angels, and details the spiritual state of man after death, and so forth. Obviously, this cannot be considered as 'truth' in the same sense as the psychology. For the existentialist, truth is subjectivity; external events are neither true nor untrue, but unimportant.

The basis of Swedenborgianism, of course, is the assertion that the 'spirit world' is the place to which men go as soon as they die. For the Outsider, this may be true or untrue, but it is completely irrelevant to the Outsider's problems. Wittgenstein summarised the Outsider's position at the end of his *Tractatus*, where he said: 'The meaning of life must lie outside life.' This means that there is no point whatever in deciding that the meaning of this 'earthly life' becomes defined by a continuation in a spirit world on the other side of the grave. Life is the interaction of spirit and matter. If 'truth is subjectivity,' then truth is approached by retreating from the region where spirit and matter interact (i.e. the world) and withdrawing into oneself: into what St. Teresa called 'the interior castle,' or what Captain Shotover called 'the seventh degree of concentration.' And Swedenborg's heaven and hell are irrelevant, whether they exist or not.

This also means that much of Swedenborg's teaching is irrelevant to the Outsider. (I do not mean, of course, that his writings are not worth study; on the contrary, they soon come to exercise an extraordinary fascination over the student. But it is the same fascination as that of Madame Blavatsky's *Secret Doctrine* — that of a vast, learned piece of mythology.) And yet his premises are Outsider premises. In the *Spiritual Diary* he writes, '. . . bodily concerns draw down the ideas of the mind and immerse them in corporeal things,'[2] and he emphasises the importance of getting free of worldly cares. He says penetratingly: 'A fallacy . . . *is a judgement of the eye, not of the mind';*[3] as human beings, we are bullied by appearances. But as soon as we begin to use our minds to penetrate the world, we find that appearances are deceptive, that our sensations are not to be relied upon. On a spring morning our senses tell us that 'God's in his heaven, All's right with the world'; a change of weather can bring a change of mood that gives us a completely different 'philosophy.' Our feelings are linked to the appearance of the world, and if we lived according to our feelings, we would be as unstable as weathercocks. Man ceases to be a mere animal by deliberately criticising everything his feelings — and his eyes — tell him. He becomes a more spiritual being by analysing continually, by total scepticism. But, as I have already pointed out, a sceptic must also be sceptical about his own scepticism; his own judgement is the first thing he should doubt. And scepticism must not be limited to logical propositions; it must be a continual sifting of all experience. The ideal philosopher would unite the visionary power of Swedenborg or Blake with the scepticism of Bertrand

Russell; anything less is inadequate. It is lucky that Swedenborg had had forty years of scientific training when he began to have his extraordinary experiences, but it is a pity that his training was not in philosophy; he might easily have established existentialism on a basis that would have changed the course of our civilisation.

Swedenborg's basic assertion, then, is the same as Blake's or Sartre's: that the mind must learn to be independent of the physical world. Sartre says of the café proprietor in *La Nausée*, 'When the café empties, his head empties too.' Shaw begins *The Apple Cart* with a scathing comment on a man who spent his life arranging pageants and believing in them, and who went insane when he was cast up on a desert island because he had no one to talk to. (Later in that play, when Boanerges accuses the king of wishing he could still have people beheaded, the king replies urbanely: 'Many people would not miss their heads,' and all Shaw's contempt is compressed into the sentence.) Men should not hold the physical world in contempt (which is blasphemy), but they should not be enslaved by it, either. Swedenborg, like Blake, has no use for the monastic ideal. Although he withdrew from the world to write, he regarded his own as a special case: men are *meant* to live in the world. He is in complete agreement with Hesse, who makes this the moral of most of his novels; man must become greater by living in the world with the moral strength of a saint and the will power and discrimination of a great artist. Steppenwolf's first comment in Hesse's novel is that when a man has embarked on the life of the mind, he has left the solid land of the physical world, and may easily steer himself into insanity. But the life of the mind, even if it brought about the Fall of Man, is the road to becoming more than man, and it must be embarked on. As opposed to the life of the body — life on a primary level of physical experience — it involves living in a different world — a world of spiritual perception.

And this, no doubt, is one explanation of what Swedenborg meant by his talk about exploring the spirit world; it may have been his way of trying to explore the truths of the mind and convey them to ordinary men living a purely primary existence. But this explanation is not very plausible — not in the face of the evidence. It *may* be true that Blake meant the 'spirit world' in this way, and that he talked about ghosts and spirits because that was the only way to

jar the philistines. (Yeats, of course, did precisely that; and admitted
it in his later years:

> Because there is safety in derision
> I talked about an apparition,
> I took no trouble to convince,
> Or seem plausible to a man of sense. . . .
> *Fifteen apparitions have I seen;*
> *The worst a coat upon a coat-hanger.*[4])

But Swedenborg asserted again and again that he meant the spiritual
world in a real, not an allegorical sense. His major work, *The True
Christian Religion,* has many passages labelled *Memorabilia,* which
begin 'One day, as I was talking with an angel . . .' or: 'As I was
walking around hell. . . .' (Blake satirised them in the 'Memorable
Fancies' of his *Marriage of Heaven and Hell*.) It is true that he
attaches a great deal of importance to the idea that all sacred writing
has two senses, one literal and obvious, the other spiritual and hidden, and it may well be that he means his more discerning readers
to ignore his talk about spirits and concentrate on the meaning of
what he is trying to convey by his allegories. On the other hand, it
is said that he was in the habit of entering some perfectly down-to-
earth argument with a comment like: 'As a matter of fact, I was
talking to St. Paul about that very subject only this morning. . . .'

It might be mentioned that, on the subject of St. Paul, Swedenborg also took the view that Paul's writings were not particularly
inspired, and that his doctrine of the Vicarious Atonement was
nonsense. In *The Doctrine of the Lord* he dismisses it incisively
(n. 18), and in the *Arcana Coelestia,* explains that the Saviour is a
symbol of Divine truth, and his power of saving mankind is simply
the power of truth.

One thing about Swedenborg is certain: that even if we choose to
dismiss the supernatural element in his teaching, the greatness and
insight of his works is not diminished in the least. He is not merely
a theologian; he is a psychologist, as Pascal was. Swedenborgians
believe that what distinguishes Swedenborg's writing from that of
Boehme or Blake or Fox is that he is writing at the dictation of
spirits. The ordinary mystic, they claim, is too much an erring

human being. But there is a fallacy here. Swedenborg himself asserts — with all the mystics — that in the heart of his being, man is really God. He recognises the immense difficulties that prevent men from defeating their human-all-too-human stupidity and penetrating to that still centre. But there is no such thing as 'dictation by spirits.' There is only dictation by the spirit, which lies at the centre of man. It is only loose thinking to call this 'the spirit of man' (as the humanists are inclined to). Man is simply a dirty filter through which the spirit has to penetrate.

To say all this is not to devalue Swedenborg. On the contrary, it is an attempt to rescue him from the pigeon-hole with Madame Blavatsky and Mary Baker Eddy to which the twentieth century has assigned him. He was far too gifted, modest and well-adjusted a man to be dismissed as a mere crank. Attempts to 'explain away' such thinkers as Pascal and Swedenborg by a glib use of the terms of psychoanalysis merely serve to indicate how much we need their insight, at a time when rationalism is dying on us, and almost crushing us. The teachers of the reality of the Will are relevant as never before.

CHAPTER FIVE

WILLIAM
LAW

THERE IS VERY little to tell of the life of William Law that could
not be compressed into two long paragraphs. We know nothing of
his inner life in comparison with what we know of Swedenborg's
or Boehme's; there are no dramatic documents, like Pascal's
Memorial or *Mystère de Jesus*, no crises or long illnesses or sudden
illuminations. In comparison with George Fox or John Wesley, his
life was flat and uneventful. For all that, he was one of the greatest
and most powerful minds ever produced by the Church of England,
and no examination of the mystics would be complete without reference to him.

Law was born in King's Cliffe, Northhamptonshire, in 1686, the
son of a grocer. He entered Emmanuel College, Cambridge, when
he was nineteen; he was a 'sizar,' that is, one who is partly supported
by the college funds, and performs certain menial services in exchange. By the time he was twenty-five he had become a fellow,
and seemed set for a quiet and retired life as a college don. Undoubtedly it would have suited him. But George I came to the
throne, and demanded an oath of loyalty from everyone in authority; Law supported the Stuart Pretender, and refused to swear. He
then resigned his fellowship in anticipation of being deprived of it.

The remainder of Law's life falls into two main periods: the first
from 1720 to 1740, during most of which time he acted as tutor to

Edward Gibbon (the historian's father) at Putney and wrote a number of controversial works; the second from 1740 to his death twenty years later, when he returned to his native village of King's Cliffe and lived a semi-monastic life, writing the great mystical books based on Boehme's teachings.

He first came to prominence as a writer in 1717, the year after he had resigned his fellowship. It was in a controversy with Bishop Hoadly, the Bishop of Bangor. Hoadly was a good-natured man, easygoing, charitable, learned — rather like a Peacock character — and his views were distinctly liberal and broad church. He had preached a famous sermon defending the interference of the state in Church affairs; where it was a question of Church and state, Hoadly said, the state should be master, and the Church stick to its own realm — the realm of the spirit. Law held Ivan Karamazov's view that the state ought to be no more than a department of the Church. He published his *Letters to the Bishop of Bangor,* which brought him the same kind of overnight celebrity that the *Provincial Letters* had brought Pascal (except that, in this case, there was no secret about the author's identity). Law was a formidable controversialist, and perhaps more than a little unfair. For instance, the Bishop had alleged that Roman Catholics must be excluded from the throne, not on account of their religion considered as such, 'but the fatal, natural, certain effects of it to our destruction.' This is a straightforward enough proposition; a good parallel would be to say that one could not allow a Negro on the throne of England, not because of any objection to the colour of his skin, but because it would cause complications in British West Africa. But Law chooses a less fair parallel:

> As for instance your Lordship may mean thus: if a man of a great estate dies, he loses his right to his estate; not upon the fatal account of death, considered as such, but for the certain fatal, natural effect of it upon himself. Or, suppose a person be excluded for being an idiot; it is not for his idiocy, considered as such; but for the certain, fatal, natural effect of it upon himself to our destruction.
>
> My Lord, this is prodigious deep. . . .[1]

Law's argument is, of course, unfair, but it takes several minutes' thought to see where it is unfair, and most of his readers did not bestow that much time on it.

Five years after this first controversial masterpiece came a second one; his reply to Mandeville's *Fable of the Bees*. Bernard de Mandeville's book was written in doggerel couplets, and advanced a sort of Marxist thesis that religion is a fiction invented to help govern society, and that only the vices of men tend towards progress, since they stimulate the circulation of capital. Law's reply is a superb piece of caustic and vigorous prose that does not lose by comparison with Swift or Voltaire. (Being an English masterpiece, it has naturally been out of print in England for the past hundred years.)

His most startling work — in the eyes of the modern reader — is his pamphlet *The Absolute Unlawfulness of Stage Entertainments*, in which he makes an even more violent onslaught on the theatre than Collier had made in his famous pamphlet of thirty years before. Law attacks the theatre, not for its immorality, but because he found it a silly waste of time (as Dr. Johnson found the opera). His condemnation is so violent — as violent as Pascal's in the *Pensées* — that most writers on Law have felt it necessary to try to excuse him. Yet his attitude is hardly surprising, in an age when the comedies were usually cheap farces and the tragedies rehashed versions of Elizabethan plays. Even without this justification, his attitude should be easily comprehensible to the modern world, where there is still the same division between serious-minded and cheap entertainment, and the latest jazz singer or film star is idolised by millions.

But the essential William Law emerged fully in *A Serious Call to a Devout and Holy Life*. This work exercised immense influence on its own and succeeding ages, and is still the only work of Law's which is easily obtainable today. Dr. Johnson, who disliked Law because he was a non-juror, and because latterly he was influenced by Boehme (whom Johnson regarded as 'crack-brained'), called it 'the finest piece of hortatory theology in any language,' and confessed: 'When at Oxford, I took it up expecting to find a dull book, and perhaps to laugh at it. But I found Law quite an overmatch for me.' The book was a powerful influence on John and Charles Wesley and George Whitefield. Even the sophisticated agnostic Gibbon came under its spell. There is a famous story of Froude and Keble which shows the influence of the book over a hundred years after its publication. Hurrell Froude (elder brother of the historian) was waiting to see Keble to his coach. Keble seemed to have something on his mind. At the last moment, Keble blurted out: 'Froude, you said you thought Law's *Serious Call* a clever book; it seemed to me as if you had said the Day of Judgement will be a pretty sight.'

Like Pascal's *Provincial Letters*, *A Serious Call* maintains its thesis by using a novelist's devices; its argument proceeds with a series of vignettes. For instance:

> Julius is very fearful of missing Prayers; all the Parish supposes Julius to be sick, if he is not at Church. But if you was to ask him why he spends the rest of his time by humour and chance? why he is a companion of the silliest People in their most silly pleasures? why he is ready for every impertinent entertainment and diversion. If you was to ask him why there is no amusement too trifling to please him? why he is busy at all balls and assemblies? why he gives himself up to an idle gossiping conversation. . . .
>
> If a man was to tell Julius that there was no occasion for so much constancy at Prayers, and that he might, without harm to himself, neglect the service of the Church. . . . Julius would think such a one to be no Christian, and that he ought to avoid his company. But if a person only tells him, that he may live as the generality of the world does, that he may enjoy himself as others do, that he may spend his time and money as People of fashion do, that he may conform to the follies and frailties of the generality, and gratify his tempers and passions as most People do, Julius would never suspect that man to want a christian spirit, or that he is doing the devil's work.
>
> And yet if Julius was to read all the New Testament from the beginning to the end, he would find his course of life condemn'd in every page of it.[2]

This is clean, hard-hitting prose. In its clarity, it has something in common with Shaw; certainly much in common with Pascal. Law might be that 'inspired churchman' of whom Larry Doyle speaks in the passage from *John Bull's Other Island* that I have quoted. But observe also the firm Outsider-Insider contrast in the paragraph. Having said this, I have made my most important point about Law: that although his life gives us no reason to bracket him with the 'Outsiders,' yet the content of his writing very emphatically does. Law seems to have been lucky enough to have found his place in the Church without much difficulty; but if he had been born two hundred years later, his attitude towards society would almost certainly have been the same as Rimbaud's or James Joyce's or D. H. Lawrence's. What is expressed most clearly in all this early work of Law is not a specifically Christian attitude (as in St. Francis or Suso), but the attitude of a man with a hunger for reality, a desire that his life should be far more serious than other people's, a man with all the Outsider's hatred of triviality and purposelessness. On the title page of Law's works, the statement, 'The Outsider's salvation lies in extremes,' would not be out of place. It is not a specifically Christian viewpoint that Law is trying to enforce; it is the Outsider's viewpoint. It is a question of existentialism: that is to say, a question of *living*. Law calls it 'the right use of the world':

> It is this right use of the world, that I would lead you into, by directing you to turn your eyes upon every shape of human folly, that you may thence draw fresh arguments and motives *of living to the best and greatest purposes of your creation*.[3] [My italics.]

He understands the Outsider's concept that man is his own enemy: that all men are murdered by an enemy they carry around inside them, and that all men's lives are robbed of meaning by self-division. The answer is discipline and asceticism:

> If religion requires us sometimes to fast, and deny our natural appetites, *'tis to lessen that struggle and war that is our nature*.[4] [My italics.]

His picture of the religious man, translated into twentieth-century terms, is a portrait of the Outsider. His rule for judging whether men are religious is to ask: 'Do they live as if they belonged to different worlds, had different views in their heads, and different rules and measures of all their actions?'[5] Apply this standard to Lawrence, Nijinsky, Rimbaud, Van Gogh; it fits them as well as it fits Fox or Nicholas Ferrar; '. . . *as if they belonged to different worlds.*' There is the Outsider's strength and the Outsider's detachment in Law; passage after passage sounds like an Outsider's credo: '. . . to renounce all its goods, to fear none of its evils, to reject its joys, and to have no value for its happiness.' [6] This might have been taken from Stephen Dedalus's 'credo' at the end of the *Portrait of the Artist as a Young Man*. And Law faces the usual complaint that the Outsider takes life too seriously:

> Some people perhaps object . . . that by depriving ourselves of so many . . . innocent pleasures, we shall render our lives dull, uneasy and melancholy. To which it may be answered: First, that these rules are prescrib'd for, and will certainly procure a quite contrary end. That instead of making our lives dull and melancholy, they will render them full of content and strong satisfactions. That by these rules we only change the childish satisfactions of our vain and sickly passions, for the solid enjoyments and real happiness of a sound mind. [7]

In the silly essay which I have already quoted, Canon Bigg has made at least one good comment on Law; that he was 'a real man insisting on reality.' And this is precisely what the Outsider is: a rebel against inanity.

The more one reads Law, the more he reminds one of Bernard Shaw. *A Serious Call* is an optimistic book; it produces an effect of balance and infectious common sense, and one feels that Law knows what he is about. If one could speak of hortatory theology as one can speak of poetry, one could say that its merit lies in inducing a *state of mind* in which everything looks cleaner and harder. No doubt if Law had written in the twentieth instead of the eighteenth century, he would have had the same accusation flung at him that Shaw had: that he was 'heartless,' a 'walking brain-box without feelings.' *A Serious Call* and the third act of *Man and Superman* have exactly the same attitude towards the 'world' and the life of drifting self-indulgence which 'civilisation' calls pleasure.

Law even has some of Shaw's faults as a dramatist: he conjures up people who fail to gain the sympathy of the reader; he is inclined to underestimate the reader's intelligence. Among the people in *A Serious Call* there are an awful pair called Flavia and Miranda; one a scatterbrained society woman, the other a model of Christian womanhood. Both alienate the reader thoroughly, and there are other couples who have the same effect: Leo and Eusebius, Sussuras and Matilda. But this is not an important flaw in a great book, where there are ten successes to every failure. Here is a further example of Law's character-drawing; the business tycoon:

> Calidus has traded above thirty years in the greatest city in the kingdom; he has been so many years constantly increasing his trade and his fortune. Every hour of the day is with him an hour of business; and though he eats and drinks very heartily, yet every meal seems to be in a hurry, and he would say grace if he had time. Calidus ends every day at the tavern, but has not leisure to be there till nine o'clock. He is always forc'd to drink a good hearty glass, to drive thoughts of business out of his head, and make his spirits drowsy enough for sleep. He does business all the time that he is rising, and has settled several matters before he can get to his compting-room. His prayers are a short ejaculation or two, which he never misses in stormy tempestuous weather, because he has always something or other at Sea. Calidus will tell you with great pleasure, that he has been in this hurry for so many years, and that it must have kill'd him long ago, but that it has been a rule with him to get out of town every Saturday and make the Sunday a day of quiet and good refreshment in the country.
>
> He is now so rich, that he would leave off his business, and amuse his old age with building and furnishing a fine house in the country, but that he is afraid he should grow melancholy, if he was to quit his business. He will tell you with great gravity, that it is a dangerous thing for a man that has been us'd to get money, ever to leave it off. If thoughts of Religion happen at any time to steal into his head, Calidus contents himself with thinking that he never was a friend to hereticks and infidels, that he has always been civil to the Minister of his parish, and very often given something to the charity schools.[8]

Note the fine touch about Calidus not giving up business 'because he is afraid he should grow melancholy,' and its implication that this man has learned to master a fortune and is still a slave to

his own moods — mentally as soft as putty. Law knew about the
Outsider's problems as well as Pascal or Gurdjieff. His *Serious Call*
is summarised in his injunction: . . . 'let us judge ourselves sincerely,
let us not vainly content ourselves with the common disorders of
our lives.' [9] Alter this last phrase to 'let us not vainly content ourselves with the common futility of our lives,' and again Law has
paraphrased the Outsider's aim: the need for self-analysis, sincerity,
a sense of purpose and reality.

It was in or about 1737 that Law first read Boehme; perhaps the
most important single event of his life. At some time between 1738
and 1740, he retired to King's Cliffe, and settled down to studying
the works of Boehme in the original. (He is said to have translated
some of Boehme; the *Dialogue on the Supersensual Life*, to be
found in the Everyman edition of the *Signatura Rerum*, is ascribed
to Law; if so, Law not only translated, but added greatly to the
original, as comparison with the recent translation by J. J. Stoudt
will show). There he was joined by two maiden ladies, who accepted him as their spiritual director. For the last twenty years of
his life, the routine at King's Cliffe resembled in many ways the
routine of Little Gidding, with devoutness and prayer, almsgiving,
the building of a school, care of the local poor, and so forth. In this
period, he produced the works which are now generally recognised
to be his greatest: *The Spirit of Prayer* and *The Spirit of Love*. In
these works, the Shavian controversialist has completely disappeared.
The atmosphere is one of devoutness and humility. Having withdrawn from the world, Law tried to see a total order and meaning
in it. His 'philosophy' was Boehme's in every detail, except for his
toning-down of Boehme's harsh doctrine of damnation. All the
emphasis is placed on learning complete non-attachment; it could
be summarised in Blake's lines:

> The Angel that presided o'er my birth
> Said, 'Little creature, form'd of Joy and Mirth,
> 'Go love without the help of any Thing on Earth.' [10]

One might make against Law the objection that he had a great
deal to 'help him to love': a quiet, easy life, enough money, a high
reputation. It is Swedenborg's objection, that man is intended for
life in the world, not for solitude and withdrawal. But perhaps

Swedenborg's excuse applies to Law too: that he had a special mission to fulfil. The great mystical books of his last period are their own justification; an extraordinary serenity breathes through them. One gets the same satisfaction from them that one gets from a philosophical 'system' like Hegel's or Kant's: all discords seem to be resolved; the difficulties of the world have disappeared. But one never feels that Law has accomplished this by shutting his eyes and inventing a fool's paradise. The 'sense of reality' does not desert him. As with Shaw and Nietzsche, immense emphasis is placed on Will. Man fell from divine perfection by deciding to follow his own miserable, shortsighted will instead of the Will of the power that created him. In doing this, he lost his will power, lost his sense of godhood, became a shortsighted, self-seeking flea, like Nietzsche's last man. Regeneration can come by striving with all his mind and heart to escape the narrow vision of a mere man: trying to comprehend the Will of the power that drives him, and to turn his own will into that greater Will. In describing this state, Law uses the same phrase that Shaw used in the last speech of *Back to Methuselah: 'no life is any longer a burden.'* This what the Outsider is seeking. His life is a burden; moments of vision tell him that life need not be a burden, but an ecstasy of will power and love. This is the vision that fills the work of Law's last twenty years. Unfortunately, it is almost impossible to represent this prose by quotation; its characteristic is the tightness of its structure, the closeness of its argument. Paragraphs occur far less frequently than in the earlier work. It is as if Law knew precisely where he was going, and needed no breaks to relieve his thought. Undoubtedly, it ranks with the greatest prose of its kind in our language, which makes it all the more regrettable that it is almost unobtainable today.* Law, the greatest of the English mystics, is virtually unknown in England, and it has remained for a Frenchman to write the first book on his greatness as a stylist.†

* The only edition I know is Stephen Hobhouse's excellent anthology *Selected Mystical Writings of William Law* (Rockliff), which, as well as long extracts from Law's major mystical writings, contains several lengthy essays by the editor which cover every aspect of Law's theology. Its companion volume is Bishop Martensen's book on Boehme.

† *William Law*, by Henri Talon (Rockliff).

Law was not a mystic in the popular sense: a man who was continually seeing visions and plunging into trances. Late in his life, he confessed that he was 'a stranger to revelation.' This is because he was a man of great intellect, and his self-discipline was too great to allow those moments when the will is overthrown and the senses reel. All his revelation came through the intellect; and (as I commented in *The Outsider*) the intellect is made drunk with its own power far less readily than the body or the emotions. Law was great because he was not an emotional man. He did not take trips to the spirit world, like Swedenborg, nor sink into *samadhi* like Ramakrishna. More than any other great mystic, his bent was intellectual; and it is this which gives him his importance in a study of the Outsider's problems. His kind of greatness is the kind needed most urgently in a declining civilisation. He was religious in the most essential meaning of the word; not out of any emotional need or human weakness, but out of sheer strength: the craving of a powerful mind and a vital will for still greater health, and deeper consciousness and vitality.

CHAPTER SIX

JOHN HENRY NEWMAN

With the exception of William Law, all the religious figures with whom I have dealt so far have been 'Outsiders' in the obvious meaning of the word — strangers in society. Neither Law nor Newman — the subject of the present chapter — are Outsiders in that spectacular sense; neither of them had visions, turned their backs on society, or behaved in an extraordinary fashion. Why then, one might ask, bother to deal with them at all?

Part of the purpose of this book is to try to show that the solution reached by Law and Newman is valid for the Outsider generally. I do not mean that Law and Newman provided a positive and final solution — no one has ever done that — but that, in different circumstances, both of them might have been Outsiders as completely as Dostoevsky or Nietzsche or George Fox. They were both lucky enough to belong to Churches whose teachings justified their anti-social feelings, with the paradoxical result that instead of becoming tormented misfits, they were valuable members of society.

Newman was born in 1801, the son of a London banker. We know little about his childhood, except that he seems to have been a frail, shortsighted child, fond of his parents and of reading. He was given to daydreaming, and particularly interested in stories of magic or ghosts (he remained interested in ghosts all his life). Descriptions of Newman as a boy bring to mind James Joyce's self-portrait in his *Portrait of the Artist* — the delicate health, self-isolation from other children, the sensitivity and precocious intellectualism. His parents were proud of his precociousness, and encouraged it by praise and attention. At seven he was sent to a school in Ealing, and soon became the most promising pupil in the school. He was always shy and solitary, but his brilliance brought him admirers — even worshippers — and he never developed a strong sense of 'apartness'; throughout his life, he never lacked for close friends. At fifteen came his first 'conversion'; this seems to have been due more to his own precocious meditations than to the influence of any particular person on him — although he speaks of the influence of a clergyman named Mayers. In the following year he went up to Trinity College, Oxford, and continued his brilliant scholastic career. At twenty, he sat for his degree, and failed spectacularly; he was (as Sir Geoffrey Faber observes) 'incapable of doing anything by halves.' He had worked too hard and was mentally stale. For a year he relaxed, pottered around amusing himself with mineralogy and chemistry, and studied mathematics to discipline his mind. Then he decided to stand for an Oriel fellowship. On this occasion he had no time to get himself worked into a 'state,' and sailed through the examinations easily. The legend has it that the butler who brought the news to the successful candidates found Newman playing the fiddle. In his facetious way, the butler announced that he had disagreeable news to impart. Newman went on fiddling. 'Mr. Newman has been elected a Fellow of Oriel, and his presence is required by the Provost.' Newman had no sense of humour, and merely nodded, and went on fiddling. As soon as the butler had disappeared, he threw down his violin and rushed out of the room as fast as his legs would carry him. One wonders whether Sir Arthur Conan Doyle had this story in mind when he endowed Sherlock Holmes with his passion for the violin! Portraits of Newman's pale aquiline face irresistibly recall that of the great detective.

As a Fellow of Oriel, he was shy and gauche, and worked harder than ever. Two years later, he was ordained, and became the curate of St. Clement's, Oxford. When he was twenty-seven, he became vicar of St. Mary's. Now began the period of Newman's greatest influence at Oxford.

He had been a tutor at Oriel for two years; naturally, his pupils came to hear him preach. Until then, very few undergraduates had attended services at St. Mary's. But Newman proved to be an extraordinary preacher. He did not shout and threaten fire and brimstone; he talked quietly and hesitantly, and with penetrating psychological insight. He had some sort of hypnotic power as a preacher. Students came to hear him, and were disappointed, having been told to expect something extraordinary. But they came back the following week out of curiosity, and Newman's strange charm had them bound hand and foot. He had a light, silvery voice, and a habit of talking slowly, with long pauses, until his own words seemed to carry him away, and his conviction was transmitted like a warm current into the audience. Soon, Newman had become one of the most influential men in Oxford. Before he had been appointed to St. Mary's, he had achieved complete sway over the minds of his pupils at Oriel; now his pulpit brought him a host of disciples. A few years later, the Provost of Oriel showed his apprehension of this power of Newman's, and deliberately tried to weaken his influence; Newman resigned his tutorship and went for a long holiday in the Mediterranean. In his five years of preaching from the pulpit at St. Mary's he had demonstrated that his genius was the genius of a George Fox or a T. E. Lawrence — the power of binding other minds by his conviction.

On his return to England, Newman became associated with an enterprise which was to make him even more influential than he had been before: together with Keble, Hurrell Froude and Pusey, he initiated the Tractarian Movement — better known as the Oxford Movement. Newman wrote the first of a series of tracts which, like Pascal's *Provincial Letters*, gained an astonishingly wide audience. John Keble — the author of *The Christian Year* — was the real originator of the Oxford Movement. He was several years older than Newman, a quiet little man who looked more like a schoolboy than a religious reformer; but his conviction that religion was dying out in Victorian England was deep-rooted and passionate, and he had the power of communicating it to his pupils. Hurrell Froude, brother of the historian, decided that Keble's beliefs must be made more public: that they made good 'fighting talk.' Newman fired the first shot. His aim was fundamentally the same as Pascal's in the *Provincial Letters* — to attack laxness and worldliness in the Church.

Finally, Newman's belief was as extreme as Ivan Karamazov's — he wanted to see the Church given complete power over the State. Pusey was another powerful ally — a scholar who had studied German philosophy, and who felt that his mission was to fight intellectual atheism. Together, the 'Tractarians' constituted an aggressive younger generation (Keble, the eldest, was only in his forties), asserting a standard of values that the nineteenth century had almost forgotten. When the first tracts were collected into a volume, it promptly became something of a 'best seller.'

Newman should have been born in the Middle Ages. The Church he longed for was the intellectual citadel of St. Bernard and Aquinas; not the poor, battered, dismembered Protestant Church of the nineteenth century. In the tracts, he tended to develop his conception of an ideal Church — much as H. G. Wells developed his notion of the ideal State sixty years later; it was nostalgic daydreaming. And naturally, since the Church for which Newman longed was the Catholic Church of the Middle Ages, his dream-picture in the tracts began to look more and more like the Catholic Church of his own day. Finally, in Tract No. 90, Newman argued that the Thirty-nine Articles of the Church of England were in no way incompatible with the creed of the Roman Catholic Church.

Immediately, the storm broke. Roman Catholics were not popular in England — they had been completely suppressed for a long period, and were still a suspected minority. Newman's enemies were convinced that he had been won over to Rome. Churchmen all over England were indignant. The Bishop of London declared publicly that nothing on earth would induce him to ordain a man who held the opinions of Tract No. 90. Newman's own bishop rebuked him, and Newman accepted the censure quietly. He withdrew to Littlemore, to a quiet, monastic retreat which he and a few friends had built; there they lived a life of great austerity and prayer. A year later, he published an anonymous retraction of all the hard things which he had said formerly against the Catholics, and in 1845, when he was forty-four, he was received into the Church of Rome. His period of retreat at Littlemore had caused almost as much public gossip as T. E. Lawrence's later retreat into the R.A.F. was to cause; he was a leader, a man of considerable influence, who suddenly turned his back on public affairs. Now, when he became a Roman Catholic, Mr. Gladstone expressed his horror, and a long wail went up from his many admirers.

There followed a long period of obscurity for Newman. He went to Rome, where he was ordained priest, and studied quietly for four years, returning to England as an Oratorian. When he was forty-nine, he delivered a series of lectures on Catholicism in England, during one of which he attacked a certain Dr. Achilli, a former Dominican friar who had turned to denigrating the Church of Rome. Achilli sued Newman for libel; anti-Catholic feeling was strong at the time, and Newman was found guilty, and ordered to pay damages of over £14,000. The sum was raised by English Catholics; but it was an unpleasant defeat for Newman, who had been used to having the taste of victory in his mouth. It must have seemed to him that the fates had turned against him since he had entered the Church of Rome. Four years later, he was invited to become rector of the newly established Catholic University of Dublin. But once again, he was frustrated; he put up with four years of irritating and trivial complications, and then resigned. He subsequently proposed to found a 'House of the Oratory' at Oxford, but Cardinal Manning opposed the idea, and it fell through. It seemed that Newman's lot had become perpetual defeat.

At least one good thing had come out of his Dublin period: a series of lectures on university education, published in pamphlet form as *Discourses on University Education*, and later enlarged and re-titled: *The Idea of a University*. Important as it was, this work excited no great sensation when it came out, and Newman reacted to increasing public neglect by retreating more and more into his own self-made corner of the world at Birmingham, to the Oratory of St. Philip Neri, where he had his own school.

His opportunity came unexpectedly, six years later. Charles Kingsley published an attack on him in *Macmillan's Magazine*, casting doubt on his intellectual honesty and on that of the whole Catholic priesthood. Newman felt that the easiest way to vindicate his attitude would be to recount with complete sincerity how he had arrived at his beliefs. He published a pamphlet which began boldly:

It may easily be conceived how great a trial it is to me to

write the following history of myself; but I must not shrink from the task. . . . I was brought up from a child to take great delight in reading the Bible. . . .[1]

He went on to describe his 'conversion' and the origins of the Oxford Movement, and promised further pamphlets to complete the story. These pamphlets enjoyed an immediate and immense success, and they were soon republished in book form, under the title *Apologia pro vita sua*. The modern reader may find it difficult to understand why the *Apologia* won such success and re-established Newman's reputation so quickly; to do so, we must see the book in the context of its age. In 1860, four years before Newman published the *Apologia*, there appeared a volume called *Essays and Reviews*, a collection of essays about the Church and modern science, with one essay by Jowett, the translator of Plato, mildly supporting the cause of science against the dogmas of the Church. The subsequent sensation was comparable to that created by *Ulysses* or *Lady Chatterley's Lover*, and Jowett was reviled by the orthodox. *Essays and Reviews* was widely read because it tried to let a little light and air into the question of religion, and Newman's book attained popularity for exactly the same reason. In the Victorian age, frankness and intellectual honesty sent the public scurrying to the bookshops. Unless this is realised, it will be difficult to come to any understanding of Newman's life and work, and impossible to understand our own position, in the mid-twentieth century. Newman had an Outsider's appetite for seriousness of purpose, like Law and Ferrar and Pascal. But his precursors were not Outsiders in the modern sense of the word — the sense of being completely out of sympathy with their time. When they attacked irreligiousness, they were listened to respectfully. When Newman attacked it — as in his controversy with Dr. Achilli — he was jeered at and accused of dishonesty. He was an Outsider in conflict with Insiders. The same is true of Kierkegaard, Newman's junior by twelve years (of whom I shall speak in the next chapter), and of Nietzsche. Half a century later, Shaw and Dean Inge — two of the outstanding religious teachers of their day — were forced to adopt the tactics of Insiders — journalism and wit — to make themselves heard at all.

This is the importance of the *Apologia*. It is one of the earliest

Outsider documents of modern times. Law wrote a Serious Call
to religion; Newman had to write an apology for it. The Insider
temper had begun to dominate the age.

The *Apologia* not only re-established Newman as an influential
public figure; it also gave a tremendous impetus to the cause of
Roman Catholicism in England. Unlike his contemporary, Cardinal Manning, Newman did not adopt the irritating tone of a man
who 'knows he is saved'; instead, he talked with the hesitant, self-
analytical tone of a great artist, more concerned with expressing
himself than with converting others. The result was a formidable contribution to the intellectual traditions of the Catholic
Church.

Newman was already sixty-three when the *Apologia* appeared,
but he had another quarter of a century of life in front of him: the
studious, uneventful life of an introspective artist. He published
one more book of the first rank: the *Grammar of Assent*, written
when he was sixty-eight. Ten years later, Pope Leo XIII made him a
Cardinal, an appointment which was received with acclamation by
Catholics and non-Catholics alike. By this time, Newman was tired:
he was old, his health was poor (he had always been frail), and
the journey to Rome might easily have been his last. Instead, it
seemed to give him new life; after a serious illness in Rome, he returned to England, and again took up residence at the Oratory in
Birmingham. During the last ten years of his life, he made many
visits to London, and continued to preach and write until his death
at the age of eighty-nine.

I have said that Newman's chief significance, in this context,
is that he was the first English religious figure to be sniped at by
Insiders on definite anti-Outsider grounds. The decline of Western civilisation becomes recognisable in Newman's time. Newman recognised that decline early in his career — although, not
being a historian, he did not recognise the parallel with previous
civilisations. In 1841, he wrote a series of letters to *The Times*,
published in book form as *The Tamworth Reading Room*, in which
he attacked the idea that mere knowledge makes men greater.
Sir Robert Peel had made a speech about the establishment of a
library at Tamworth, in which he had expressed his faith in scientific knowledge, and its power to make men rise to higher things.
Newman asks 'how wonderful moral effects are to be wrought

under the instrumentality of physical science,' and goes on to con-
tend that the idea is an impossibility. Lord Brougham had expressed the same faith in the power of science, and Newman
answered him, as well. 'Human nature wants recasting, but Lord
Brougham is all for tinkering it.' [2] Brougham and Peel both felt
that man could become religious merely by contemplating 'the
immense mystery of nature.' Newman's objection is the same as
that of the Grand Inquisitor: 'Only *great* men can. What about
the others?' In these letters of Newman's, there are two important
strands which were never to disappear from his outlook: contempt
for logic, and a feeling that religion begins with instinct, conscience, a hunger for meaning. Like Boehme, his religious attitude
is existentialist; in the sixth letter of *The Tamworth Reading Room*,
he states:

> *Life is for action.* . . . Life is not long enough for a religion
> of inferences. . . . To act, you must assume, and that assumption
> is faith.[3] [My italics.]

Newman believed, as F. R. Cronin has written, that 'certitude is
is for the intellectual *élite.*' In other words, the Grand Inquisitor's
master-and-slave morality underlies Newman's religious doctrines.

Newman's novel *Loss and Gain* has something in common with
the Cranly pages of Joyce's *Portrait*: it is about a young man becoming a Catholic; but its long arguments are not, like Stephen's
arguments, an escape from Catholicism, but a movement towards
it. Newman's hero, Charles Reding, is sent down from Oxford for
doubting the Thirty-nine Articles. One of the men who lead him
to doubt the Church of England is a Dr. Brownside, a liberal
divine, for whom Revelation 'instead of being the abyss of God's
councils, with its dim outlines and broad shadows, [is] a flat sunny
plain, laid out with straight macadamised roads.' [4] Obviously, Newman's feelings about life are closer to Dostoevsky's than to Dr.
Brownside's; he detests two-dimensional logical thinking as much
as Dostoevsky's beetle-man, in *Notes from Under the Floorboards*.

In *The Outsider* I cited the key passage from the last chapter of
Newman's *Apologia*, but it is too important not to quote again:

> Starting, then, with the being of God (which, as I have said,
> is as certain to me as the certainty of my own existence. . . .) I

look out of myself into the world of men, and there I see a sight which fills me with unspeakable distress. The world seems simply to give the lie to that great truth, of which my whole being is so full. . . . If I looked into a mirror, and did not see my face, I should have the sort of feeling which actually comes upon me, when I look into this living busy world, and see no reflection of its Creator. . . .

To consider the world in its length and breadth, its various history, the many races of man . . . the disappointments of life, the defeat of good, the success of evil, physical pain, mental anguish, the prevalence and intensity of sin . . . the corruptions, the dreary hopeless irreligion . . . all this is a vision to dizzy and appal; and inflicts upon the mind the sense of a profound mystery, which is absolutely beyond human solution.

What shall be said to this heart-piercing, reason-bewildering fact? I can only answer, that either there is no Creator, or this living society of men is in a true sense discarded from his presence. . . . And so I argue about the world: *if* there be a God . . . the human race is implicated in some terrible, aboriginal calamity.[5]

This is the *grimmige Einsicht* that Rilke spoke of, the terrible insight, the feeling of *Malte Laurids Brigge.* It is obvious, from this passage, that Newman was no Blakean visionary. When Boehme or Van Gogh looked at the 'living world,' they were dazzled by the reflection of its Creator. Newman never knew this experience, which perhaps accounts for his comparative failure as a poet. His best-known poems are *The Dream of Gerontius* (from which the lovely hymn 'Praise to the Holiest in the Height' comes), and the three stanzas of 'Lead, Kindly Light.' The language of Newman's poetry is commonplace; 'Lead, Kindly Light' is as commonplace as the rest, but was written when Newman had half made up his mind to become a Catholic, and was tormented by doubts: it is a striking proof of Yeats's theory that the most moving poetry is written out of a sudden intense emotion, which does not depend upon great language for its effect.*

Newman's most important work — certainly the work which gave him most trouble — is the *Essay in aid of a Grammar of*

* *Reveries,* Section XXX.

Assent. The title is deliberately modest (Eliot followed its example in *Notes Towards the Definition of Culture*), which, considering the magnitude of the subject, is hardly surprising. Newman's aim is the same as Pascal's in the *Pensées* — to justify religion to unbelievers. The book is extremely difficult reading; it is obviously intended to browbeat the sort of philosopher who thinks that Hume and Mill have said the last word about religious belief. Newman simply wants to show how it is possible to assent to religious belief without falling into intellectual dishonesty. It cannot truthfully be said — even by Newman's greatest admirer — that he succeeds. He sets out to analyse the question of assent in the manner of Mill's *Logic*. Now one can anticipate the whole enquiry by asking a simple question: Can logic lead to religion? The answer (as Wittgenstein and Whitehead asserted) is: No. Nevertheless, many valuable ideas are enunciated in the *Grammar*, and it will justify a closer analysis, in this chapter, than any of Newman's other works.

Newman begins with a simple distinction: between real assent and notional assent. Real assent is the assent one makes with the *whole being*, not just with the intellect. He then passes to the question of the existence of God, and attempts to show that the existence of conscience — of a sense of moral law — points to the reality of God. He attempts to show that the reality of God is at least as certain as the reality of the physical world; for we infer the physical world from the fragmentary impressions which our senses fling at us, and we infer the existence of God from the fragmentary twinges of our conscience or sense of moral purpose. An imbecile never draws any conclusions from the world around him; a man of scientific genius never ceases to draw conclusions about it. So a moral imbecile learns nothing about the laws of his spirit; the prophet and saint (and, we might add, the Outsider) observe the operation of a need for greater intensity of life in themselves, the need for purpose, the need to understand, and try to imagine, to envision, what man would be like if he could follow this urge to its utmost limit.

Part II of the *Grammar* asks how mere inference can lead to assent, and answers: By the balance of probability. A sufficient number of probabilities, all converging, constitute a certainty. Newman invents the term 'Illative sense,' which is man's ability

to weigh up probabilities and extract a certainty from them. Some
people have more of this Illative sense than others. For instance,
Newton had an extraordinary gift for sensing where lines of
thought converged, and 'intuiting' a conclusion where a lesser
man would have been hopelessly confused. This is the power possessed by the great religious minds; but in their case, the 'facts'
are not physical phenomena or numbers, but *psychological* facts —
the facts of man's spiritual life. Newman anticipates Sartre by
denying that Man is a universal idea, of which all individual men
are examples. All men are individual things, independent, incom-
municable. He comes very close to saying, with Hesse, that 'man
is a bourgeois compromise' — there is no such thing as 'man,'
only individual men. In other words, although Newman did not
realise it, he was propounding the fundamental idea of existentialism: In man, existence precedes essence. Newman announces
his lack of faith in formal logic; formal logic uses words which
are divested of their historic and poetic association. This can only
lead to abstraction, and religion is *not* abstraction. Man's business
is to use his logical faculty to get to the concrete, and to do this,
he must think in terms of the concrete. It is no proof of religion
to talk about 'man,' or to try to prove God by algebra; one must
talk about individuals: about individuals under spiritual strain.
(Newman does not take the next step and admit that the best
person to do this will obviously be the novelist or poet, not the
philosopher.)

It will be seen, by this time, that Newman has not succeeded in
producing a logical proof of religion, or a logical justification of
assent. Although he has written a book which seems logical in
its method, he has actually declared in it that logic is no final
guide: one abstraction can only lead to another. Man's business
is to try to weigh up the world; and the world is not just the
universe around him, it is the universe behind his eyes. What man
wants is an assumption upon which he can act: *a belief that will
give him purpose.* And the final criterion of the value of a belief is:
How long can a man go on acting by it? Alexander had a belief
that gave him a tremendous sense of purpose; his belief that it was
his destiny to rule the world. But when he had conquered the
world, he asked despairingly: What now? That is the test of any
belief. If a sense of purpose can come to an end, then it is not one

of real purpose, of ultimate purpose. But religion is supposed to supply man with a sense of ultimate purpose, a purpose which would not fail him even if he lived to be a million years old.

Newman ends the *Grammar* with a passage explaining why, for him, Christianity has enough 'converging probabilities' to constitute a certainty. He speaks of the Messianic prophecies of the Old Testament, the strange history of the Hebrew nation, the power that the early Christians gained from their belief in Christ, and so forth. He concludes ' . . . either Christianity is from God, or a revelation has not yet been given to us.'[6] This, of course, is no final proof. He might as well have said that Beethoven's Ninth Symphony moved him more profoundly than any other work known to man, and concluded that Beethoven must have been the Messiah foretold by Isaiah. (Newman was, in fact, passionately fond of Beethoven's music.) He is arguing, in the final analysis, from the observation made by Mencius: 'Those who follow the part of themselves that is great are great men; those who follow the part of themselves that is little are little men.'[7] Man does not know the extent of his own greatness until he has been introduced to it through some intense spiritual experience, which has the effect of freeing him from his own stupidity, from his personality. Newman says, in effect, that Christianity has introduced him to the greatest heights he has known; consequently, Christianity must be God's greatest revelation in the world. Possibly, if Newman had been a Hindu or Buddhist, the concept of Brahman or Nirvana might have made him aware of new areas of his psyche — perhaps of higher areas of his being than Christianity revealed — in which case, his Illative sense would have led him to make an ultimate act of assent to Vedantism or Buddhism.

Newman's significance lies in the fact that a sensitive, highly self-critical and self-analytical nature was able to find complete balance and self-expression in accepting Catholic Christianity and returning to the mediaeval Church. Yet at the same time he went beyond a mere 'personal' solution to the Outsider's problem. He was aware of the greater problem — the problem of making religion valid for a civilisation. In the sixth letter of his *Tamworth Reading Room*, he says:

People say to me, that it is but a dream to suppose that

Christianity should regain the organic power in human society which once it possessed. I cannot help that; I never said it could. I am not a politician; I am proposing no measures, but exposing a fallacy . . . do not attempt by philosophy what once was done by religion. The ascendancy of Faith may be impracticable, but the reign of Knowledge is incomprehensible. The problem for statesmen of this age is how to educate the masses, and literature and science cannot give the solution.[8]

This was written before he became a Catholic. Ten years later, in his famous sermon *The Second Spring*, he states his feeling that the Catholic Church may again become universal, and regain the power which it held in the Middle Ages. This, of course, is still theoretically possible; but in our world of hydrogen bombs and conflicting ideologies, it no longer seems likely. But what conclusion does this point to? That Newman was wrong? That the problem of 'the reign of Knowledge' will not be solved by a new Christianity? The problem is still 'to educate the masses'; but the masses cannot be educated to think like the Outsider, any more than they can be educated to understand quantum mechanics. The whole Outsider theory can be reduced to certain simple religious facts: Original Sin, escape from personality, the reality of Will, the existentialist statements that truth is subjectivity, that there is no such thing as man, that existence precedes essence. Newman accepts all these facts; but he knew of no way to teach them to a man who would not make the effort to follow him step by step.

In the twentieth century, all the problems which Newman treats are still with us, and our civilisation declines steadily because they remain unsolved. Under the circumstances, Newman has one thing to teach us. It is the answer suggested by Rilke in *Malte*: that the individual who understands the problems must attempt to bear them on his own shoulders. Even if he is completely alone, he must make the effort. Newman's example proves how great can be the influence of one man's attempt to shoulder the problems; his strength became the strength of a whole generation. If the twentieth century could produce even a few men of Newman's stature, the whole course of history might be changed.

CHAPTER SEVEN

SØREN
KIERKEGAARD

Even for a philosopher, Kierkegaard led a singularly uneventful life. In fact, there are really only two striking events in it: the Regina Olsen episode, and the attacks published on him in *The Corsair*, a Copenhagen newspaper. He always had enough money to live quietly and write his books; and on the day he went to the bank to draw out the last of his money, he collapsed in the street and died. He was forty-two at the time.

But it is impossible, when reading any biographical study of Kierkegaard, not to feel that he was a frustrated man. He remained unmarried, but not necessarily through choice. In some ways his life reminds one of a short story by Chekhov. There are hints in it that he was sexually incapable, either for psychological reasons (like Carlyle), or from some physical cause. He was a skinny, undersized misshapen man, lame in one leg. His childhood was a thoroughly bad one from the point of view of his mental health; his father was already an old man when he was born, but a strange, melancholy, strong-willed old man, who was haunted by the fact that he had once cursed God as a child. He treated Søren like an adult; encouraged his precociousness, stimulated his imagination, and 'discharged his melancholy' on the boy's head. Kierkegaard's mother was a maidservant whom his father had made pregnant and decided to marry, another fact which preyed on the old man's conscience.

In his youth, Søren is supposed to have led a somewhat disorderly life — though it is hard to guess what the morbidly religious Kierkegaard would have regarded as disorderly. The prospect of the fortune he would inherit from his father made him something of a social lion, and he soon gained a reputation as a wit in Copenhagen. He studied at the University of Copenhagen, but without great diligence, and quarrelled with his father about his debts. Then, when he was twenty-five, he had a reconciliation with his father; and a few days later, a sudden religious experience which completely converted him from his old way of life. In his Journal (May 19, 1838) he describes it as a sudden intense experience of joy, 'a heavenly refrain which suddenly breaks in upon our ordinary song, a joy which cools and refreshes like a breeze. . . .'[1] It would seem to be the experience which Nietzsche described happening to him again and again during the writing of *The Gay Science* and *Zarathustra*. With Kierkegaard, it was the rarest of experiences.

A few months later, his father died, and left him a considerable fortune. He returned to his study of theology at the University, and passed his examinations two years later.

When his father died, he had been in love for a year. The girl was only fourteen at the time; her name was Regina Olsen. When she was seventeen, he began the active pursuit of her; a few months later, he proposed to her, and she accepted him. But he was too much the tumultuous romantic to accept his conquest and enjoy it; like the narrator of *Wuthering Heights*, the slightest sign of success in love was enough to make him change his mind. At first, Regina seemed to take the engagement lightly; she once even said that she had accepted him out of pity. He set to work to make her take him seriously, and was soon successful; she seemed to surrender herself completely to him and become his slave. Immediately, he began to feel trapped, and decided to break off the engagement. When he sent Regina her ring back, she was frantic, and begged him to change his mind — the worst possible tactic. He withstood her pleas, and those of her family, and went off to Berlin for a holiday. There he wrote most of his first book, *Either/Or*. This book contains the famous short novel, *Diary of the Seducer*. The seducer is called Johannes (i.e. the German form of Juan or Giovanni), and a quotation from *Don Giovanni* serves as an epigraph: 'His ruling

passion is the fresh young girls.' The seducer sees a young girl
alighting from her carriage, and decides — quite arbitrarily — to
seduce her. He finds out that her name is Cordelia (Regina's
younger sister was named Cornelia) and turns all his energies to
making her acquaintance, and then to becoming a regular visitor at
her house. It would be tiresome to describe in detail the various
steps which he takes to become engaged to her, then to persuade her
to break off the engagement, then to regain her and seduce her. The
Diary is a prodigiously long work, and ends with the hero declaring
that now he has possessed her fully, he no longer has any interest in
her.

It is a nasty piece of work — a gloating on the sense of power
that the Regina affair had given him. It is prolix, and its emotion
is rather juvenile. Luckily, *Either/Or* is not entirely of this quality.
There is some penetrating criticism of the age. There is the witty
essay called *The Rotation Method*, with its famous thesis that boredom is the root of all evil (with which most Outsiders would agree
completely):

> The gods were bored, so they created man. Adam was bored
> because he was alone, and so Eve was created. . . . Adam was
> bored alone, then Adam and Eve were bored together; then Adam
> and Eve and Cain and Abel were bored *en famille;* then the popu-
> lation of the world increased, and the peoples were bored *en
> masse.* To divert themselves, they conceived the idea of con-
> structing a tower high enough to reach the heavens. This idea
> itself is as boring as the tower was high, and constitutes a terrible
> proof of how boredom gained the upper hand. . . .[2]

He goes on to point out that boredom is not to be combated by
frequent diversion, but by deliberate self-limitation. He recalls how,
at school, one could amuse oneself throughout a tedious lesson by
playing with a captive fly in a nutshell. He goes on to outline an
Epicurean plan for living: the discipline of one's power of remem-
bering and forgetting, and the avoidance of friendship ('A friend is
the superfluous third') and of marriage. It is obviously the work of
a young man who is well pleased with himself; who feels that he has
mastered the circumstances of his life, and gained the power of

detachment over them. It is witty and complacent. An essay on
Mozart begins with the words:

> Let others complain that the age is wicked; my complaint is
> that it is wretched, for it lacks passion. . . . Men's thoughts are . . .
> too paltry to be sinful. For a worm, it might be regarded as a sin
> to harbour such thoughts, but not for a being made in the image
> of God.[3]

The essay is a rhapsody built around *Don Giovanni*. It ends with
Kierkegaard describing how the gods offered him any gift he
wanted: youth, beauty, long life, women, and so on. He answered:
'I choose . . . that I may always have the laugh on my side.' It was
a request that was not granted to Kierkegaard in real life; later,
children would jeer as his stooped, black-clad figure passed them
in the street.

A second part of *Either/Or* deals with the ethical life. Kierkegaard ceases to be the Oscar Wildean aesthete, and speaks of religion
and morality. This is the meaning of the title: Either/Or. But it
cannot be said that he makes the moral idea as attractive as the
aesthetic. Nevertheless, he shows that he, Søren Kierkegaard, was
not deceived by his own juvenile Epicureanism. But there may be
another reason for the moral element: *Either/Or* was written to
make Regina understand him; it may have been deliberately conceived as illuminating the other side of his nature.

Kierkegaard decided that his treatment of Regina had some parallel with Abraham's treatment of Isaac: he was placing his love of
God above his personal feelings. In *Fear and Trembling* he wrote of
the sacrifice of Isaac, and allowed himself to indulge in the hope
that he might yet have Regina restored to him, as God had restored
Isaac to Abraham. But the real subject of *Fear and Trembling* —
the subject which transcends his relationship with Regina — is the
strange need of the artist and saint to do things that are paradoxical,
that are just not 'common sense.' *Fear and Trembling* could be
sub-titled 'The Defeat of Common Sense.' Like Dostoevsky's *Notes
from Under the Floorboards*, it is about the irrational, the anti-
world impulse. But as a treatise on the irrational, it is certainly not
as impressive as Dostoevsky's book.

The Regina problem continued to buzz in his mind. Having written *Either/Or* and *Fear and Trembling* in the same year, he wrote a novel called *Repetition*. It is about a young man who gets engaged, but is tormented by a tendency to melancholy, and breaks off his engagement by pretending that he has other mistresses. By the time he had written *Repetition*, Kierkegaard had begun to feel that maybe he could marry Regina after all. But just then, he received the news that Regina had become engaged to someone else. He changed the end of the novel, and made his hero announce his delight that all this trivial human problem had been finally solved, and he could devote all his time and energy to being a poet, a creator. Like Marchbanks at the end of *Candida*, he evidently felt like congratulating himself that 'they did not know the secret in the poet's heart' — the secret of his superior strength as a poet and philosopher. But this does not ring quite true; one feels that Kierkegaard was trying to compensate himself for what must have been a crushing disappointment. On the other hand, it is difficult not to feel a certain satisfaction — a sense of 'It served him right.' Kierkegaard certainly made far too much song and dance about the Regina affair; he made a fool of himself about it, and behaved like a sulky schoolboy. Unfortunately, most of his biographers have solemnly followed his lead, and referred to it as 'the deep tragedy of Regina,' etc. But the simple truth seems to have been that Kierkegaard was emotionally immature, no matter how mature he may have been intellectually. His jilting of Regina was not a 'sacrifice of Isaac,' but a piece of schoolboy emotionalism. The three books which came out of the affair were Kierkegaard's attempts to avoid facing the fact that he had behaved like a sulky child. He had been brought up in an atmosphere where he was thoroughly spoiled, but the shock of losing Regina helped to mature his emotions. The books that follow are far more important than the Regina books.

Kierkegaard was thirty when he finally lost Regina. In the remaining twelve years of his life, he produced such a prodigious volume of work that one would guess that he had little else to do but write. First came the *Philosophical Fragments*, in which it is apparent that the emotional immaturity has disappeared from Kierkegaard's make-up. He is considering the question of the truth of Christianity. He cites Socrates, who believed that man contains truth — the mystical belief that, in his depths, man is God. Socrates argues this in the *Meno*, where he makes a slave solve a geometrical problem, and thus shows that the slave contained the power to solve it within himself, but was too lazy to develop it without Socrates' prompting. Socrates' inference is that all men would have the power to become gods, if only they had the strength of Will to mine it out of themselves. In other words, *if* man is in original sin (as the Outsider tends to believe) his power of redemption lies within himself. Socrates thought of himself as a midwife, whose only job was to bring truth to birth in other people, not to make them a present of it.

Kierkegaard states, quite correctly, that to accept Christianity (by which he means St. Paul's version) involves rejecting this view. For in Pauline Christianity, Christ *does* make man a present of redemption. Kierkegaard then does some skilful arguing to justify the Pauline view. He invents a parable of a great king who wants to marry a humble maiden. But the king, although he is in love with the girl, is afraid that she will continue to regard him as a monarch, and herself as just a very lucky girl, and that this will completely wreck their relation, which depends upon her feeling equality with him. What is he to do? He cannot raise her to his level, and convince her that she is a queen. But he *can* lower himself to her level, and convince her that he is a humble lover, as well as a king. And this, Kierkegaard concludes, is just what God did when He came down to earth and allowed Himself to be crucified.

Kierkegaard does not finally accept this view himself in the *Philosophical Fragments;* he presents it as an enviable state of belief that he has not been able to achieve.

A work called *The Concept of Anguish* followed the *Fragments.* But it is not one of Kierkegaard's most important works: its main thesis is expressed much better in *The Sickness Unto Death,* where the word 'despair' is almost synonymous with 'angst': 'Anguish is the possibility of freedom; only this anguish is . . . absolutely educative in that it consumes everything finite, discloses all the illusions of the finite.' [4] It is the 'anguish' which Nietzsche understood so well: '. . . I doubt whether such pain "improves" us, but I know it *deepens* us.' [5]

In 1846, the year which saw the publication of his most important work, the *Concluding Unscientific Postscript to the Philosophical Fragments*, Kierkegaard became a Copenhagen celebrity in a way that was not pleasant for him. *The Corsair*, a comic paper, took offence at the way in which Kierkegaard had written about a member of its staff, and published a series of satires and cartoons on him. *Either/Or* had made him famous in Denmark; now *The Corsair* made him a laughingstock. Kierkegaard launched a vigorous counteroffensive, and succeeded in doing some damage to the journalist who had caused the trouble, but the whole affair upset him greatly. The trouble actually arose over a hostile review of Kierkegaard's *Stages On Life's Way*, a successor to *Either/Or*. In a long section called 'Guilty? Not Guilty?' Kierkegaard again analyses the Regina Olsen affair. Copenhagen naturally felt that this was in rather bad taste, since the story was well known; and the journalist in question felt that it was a dreary subject to treat at such length, anyway. No doubt he was right. At all events, *The Corsair* attacks seemed to cure Kierkegaard of his adolescent tendency to brood on his affair with Regina.

The *Unscientific Postscript* is a gigantic volume, and it is as obscure and unreadable as most of Kierkegaard's philosophic ventures. Nevertheless, in its eight hundred long-winded pages some extremely important ideas are formulated. Kierkegaard repeats the question: What does it mean to be a Christian? Hegel, it will be remembered, found a convenient little niche for Christianity in his System. It was this element in Hegel that Kierkegaard hated most. For him, religion was the final, most important element of man's spiritual life; not just a part of a great philosophical synthesis, to be given a condescending pat on the head like a well-behaved schoolboy.

The idea developed in the *Postscript* is that truth is not a formula or a system. Truth is the spiritual intensity of the man who apprehends it. 'Truth is subjectivity.' Kierkegaard was attacking Hegel because he seemed to be a great top-heavy intellect, a bloodless half-man. For Kierkegaard, Hegel was not a half-man because he lacked the sex impulse or any physical intensity (the indictment which D. H. Lawrence or Walt Whitman would have pinned on him); he was a half-man because — as Kierkegaard expressed it in *Either/Or* — he 'lacked passion.' And passion, for Kierkegaard, meant religious passion: the Outsider's craving for a sense of purpose. In the *Postscript* Kierkegaard launched his attack on 'mere intellect,' and contrasted the logical approach with the *existential* approach. It was the first use of the word existentialism in modern times. In the conclusion of the *Postscript*, Kierkegaard sums up: a man might be a Christian because he accepts certain doctrines (the Protestant way), or because he is baptised (the Catholic way), or he might be a Christian because of the intensity with which he feels the truth of the New Testament. This is Kierkegaard's way. In a later book, *Training in Christianity*, he goes even further, and says that true Christianity means living as if you were one of the twelve apostles.

Kierkegaard wrote many more books in the remaining nine years of his life, but there would be no point in referring to them all here. (I have already omitted reference to several of his volumes — mostly sermons and 'edifying discourses.') Only one of them is of great importance for the present purpose: the slim volume called *The Sickness Unto Death*. This is crucial because it formulates one idea which lies at the bottom of the whole Outsider problem. That idea, as Kierkegaard states it, is this: Every human existence *that does not know itself as spirit* is in despair. And what is even more important, a man who is in despair need not know that he is in despair. He may think himself perfectly happy.

This is not really such a startling concept as it sounds. Pascal talked about the 'misery' of man instead of 'despair,' but he emphasised that the men who seek most feverishly after pleasure — the men who look as if they are most happy — are actually the most deeply miserable.

This idea of Kierkegaard's — that a man's despair may be unknown to him — is of inestimable importance in the study of the Outsider. For the retort of the Insider who dislikes being told that he ought to be an Outsider is: Let me alone; I'm happy enough. His challenge tends to be: If I'm happy as an Insider, can you give me a single good reason why I should be an Outsider? For Kierkegaard, this is tantamount to saying: If I am suffering from a deadly disease without knowing it, can you give me any good reason for being healthy? He actually states that a sense of fundamental uncertainty, of chaos, is common to all men: but in some it is conscious, in some, unconscious. The Outsider is the man in whom it is conscious. The sense of chaos, despair, lies in the Insider too, but he is not conscious of it. He prefers to live in the comfortable daylight, pretending that the whole universe is as neatly ordered as his own little corner of it. In *The Sickness Unto Death*, Kierkegaard comes to the conclusion that I restated in the first chapter of *The Outsider:* The Outsider is the man who has faced chaos. The Insider is the man who blinds himself to it.

Kierkegaard, of course, knows nothing of these labels 'Outsider' and 'Insider.' In his own terminology, the true Christian is the man who has faced his own despair, and has defeated it by an act of faith. I only wish to draw attention to the fact that, by 'Outsider,' I mean precisely what Kierkegaard meant by the religious man.

The Sickness Unto Death was received, like most of Kierkegaard's major works, with complete incomprehension: an incomprehension that was partly his own fault, for in spite of his dislike of Hegel, he has one irritating quality in common with him, a most obscure and prolix literary style. It is true that his style is not always obscure; but he usually reserves his wit and clarity for his least important works. His last work, the *Attack Upon 'Christendom,'* has an aphoristic brilliance worthy of Nietzsche, but serving no other purpose than to attack the Protestant Church of Denmark.

The *Attack* was published in a series of pamphlets. Its original occasion had been a sermon preached by Bishop Martensen on his predecessor, Bishop Mynster. Mynster had been an unusually good bishop, but for some reason, Martensen's generous praise of him excited Kierkegaard to fury. He did not actually go as far as Shaw (in the preface to *Androcles and the Lion*) and assert that the Christian Church had chosen Barabbas; but he certainly felt that the Church was not Christian in the sense in which he understood Christianity. The *Attack* contains some of Kierkegaard's most amusing and readable writing — he was a master of satire when he chose to be. The pamphlets of which it is composed caused a sensation when they were published in 1854 and 1855. But nine months after they first appeared, Kierkegaard collapsed in the street when returning from the bank with the last of his money. Two months later, he died in hospital of a vaguely diagnosed malady. He himself told his doctors that the real illness was psychological. He refused to receive the sacrament from the hands of a priest, declaring that only a layman was worthy to administer it. At his funeral, students formed a guard of honour, and there was a riot which was checked in its early stages; there was also a last-minute outburst at his graveside from a sympathiser who accused the Church of hypocrisy in claiming the rebel who had denounced it.

For nearly half a century after his death, Kierkegaard remained unknown outside Denmark. Then, slowly, his reputation filtered through to other European countries, and his writings were translated into French and German. The result was the Continental Existentialist movement; Heidegger, its major German exponent, laid great emphasis on the idea of death, and the concept of unconscious despair. When Sartre and Camus called themselves Existentialists — Sartre more or less following Heidegger, Camus following a line of his own derived from Kierkegaard's idea of 'the absurd' in *Fear and Trembling* — Kierkegaard's name began to be bandied around among intellectuals in the same way that the names of Nietzsche and Bergson had been at the beginning of the century.

Now that Existentialism is ceasing to be a subject of such heated discussion, it is perhaps time to recognise that Kierkegaard may have been overrated. Nietzsche once said that he owed his penetration as a thinker to the fact that he never wasted his time on imaginary problems or pseudo problems. Kierkegaard cannot make the same boast. He wasted a great deal of his time by exaggerating his personal problems out of all proportion. He also lacked Nietzsche's healthy scepticism and his impatience with organised religion. It is interesting to wonder where Kierkegaard would have found himself if he had lived twenty years longer; his rejection of the Church might have led to some constructive results. As it is, the final judgement on him is likely to run: A man of superb intellect, and great spiritual strength, but a lopsided, tragic figure.

CHAPTER EIGHT

BERNARD
SHAW

In writing about Shaw, it is time to be frankly personal, for my attitude towards Shaw aroused more comment and opposition than any other point in *The Outsider*. It is my own opinion that Shaw's reputation will increase with time, until it is seen that his position in relation to Western thought is as important as that of Augustine or Aquinas to mediaeval thought. For me, the Outsider is the symbol of the whole problem of Western civilisation in the past five centuries of 'Faustian culture.' Shaw once said that he had solved every major problem of our civilisation, and that people still go on propounding them as if they are unsolved. This seems to me to be true. Shaw touched on the Outsider problem at almost every point, and came closer to providing a complete solution than any other thinker. It is his relation to the Outsider that I wish to make clear in the following chapter. The space is, of course, inadequate; and yet it is necessary that Shaw should be treated in this context — in relation to Newman, Law, Kierkegaard. Only in this way can his full significance be seen.

The impact which Shaw made on the generation who grew up between 1900 and 1920 is irrelevant; it was a mere impact of new ideas, and has nothing to do with Shaw's true stature any more than Goethe's *Sturm und Drang* period has anything to do with his. Ideas are fashionable, and then become unfashionable, and this is

unimportant; it matters as little as that the headlines of the newspapers change every day. The standards by which we judge a
Shakespeare or Dante are the real and important standards. Unfortunately, these do not apply to Shaw, either. Neither do the
standards that apply to Aristotle or Hume as revolutionaries of
thought. Shaw is far more difficult to classify, and I believe that it
is this which explains the present incomprehension and underrating
of his work. Shaw belongs to a rare class of men which also includes Plato and Goethe: in the profoundest sense of the word, he
is an existentialist thinker. And existentialism begins with the Outsider, and ends . . . no one knows where; but its road lies *through*
religion. Religion is not the end; it is only a rest-house on the way.

In saying that Plato, Goethe and Shaw were existentialists I mean
that all three were thinkers for whom thought and life are inseparable. Now the only other type of man for whom thought and
life are inseparable is the artist: his art is the result of the impact
of life on his sensibility. But normally he spends all his time acting
as a good recording-machine; his aim is usually to keep the 'receiving' surface of his sensibility as impressionable as possible. This
is what Keats meant when he talked of 'negative capability' as the
most important quality of a poet. When the artist begins to record
the impact of life on his sensibility, he has begun thinking: even if
his formula for art is as simple as Monet's: 'An eye, a brush.' Thinking is a movement of analysis, and an artist could not create unless
he analysed. But an artist is rarely outstanding for both his sensibility *and* his powers of analysis. He usually excels in one field or
the other, as a Shakespeare or a Kant, a Dante or a Hegel.

But occasionally there are men who go beyond the mere artist or
thinker. The artist fails to cultivate his analytical faculty; the
thinker fails to cultivate his sensibility. But certain thinkers have
believed that life itself is the stuff of philosophy — the living, raw
impressions which the artist puts into his art. They do not believe
that the artist's passive acceptance of his experience — the 'negative capability' — is the sole necessity. But neither do they believe
that the thinker's ability to roll the universe into a (theoretical)
ball is of primary importance. Philosophy should not be built with
thoughts and analyses, any more than houses should be built with
cards; it should be built out of living experience. Plato is fascinated

by mathematics, but he is equally interested in the mind of Socrates or Protagoras, and the psychology of Miletus and Xanthippe. He is, in fact, one of the earliest novelists in history. The same is true of Goethe; he is known to posterity as poet and lover, yet he had the restless analytical mind of a philosopher and scientist. Rudolf Steiner performed an invaluable service in editing Goethe's philosophical and scientific works, and revealing that Goethe the poet has obscured Goethe the philosopher from posterity.

Goethe revived one great concept that was already present in Plato: the idea of *Bildung,* or education. Not academic education, but the real education in living that makes for maturity: the education of the sage and saint. *Wilhelm Meister* is about a young man *learning* from his living experience. And this is of obvious importance to the Outsider, whose chief observation about human beings is that they never learn from experience; Evan Strowde's indictment: 'Now take away my life, O Lord, for I am no better than my fathers.'

But it is an immense and perplexing problem. For sensitivity — essential to maturing — means relaxing the will, making the personality transparent, becoming completely receptive; and analysis means essentially reacting, using the will, strengthening the personality. Which means that a man who wishes to develop without cramping his faculties must achieve complete control of this Caliban, whom Blake called the spectre. There is an unending warfare with this spectre; the spectre is the Enemy. Blake wrote:

> Each Man is in his Spectre's power
> Untill the arrival of that hour,
> When his Humanity awake
> And cast his own Spectre into the Lake.[1]

The ideally great existentialist, then, would have the ability to use his will power in analysis, and yet at a moment's notice to become completely negative, transparent and receptive. There would, that is to say, be complete *self-control.* And here we see that the concept of existentialism involves inevitably the idea of self-discipline and self-transformation — the *religious* idea. For the existentialist, then, thought can never be 'abstract'; it is always involved in a concrete situation. He never treats the universe as if he were sitting apart from it all, in a celestial armchair, 'logicising' about it. When the field of his own immediate being is no longer in question, he ceases to think and again becomes the receptive artist-poet. For the existentialist, the only form of abstract thought which is not unutterable nonsense is mathematics, and that is because mathematics is the dumbbell exercise of the existentialist, his mental gymnasium. But essentially, existentialism is not the building of an intellectual system. It is the building of an insight, a building of many insights into a total vision, an attempt to extend the consciousness,* to extend the sphere of the living being into the unliving. It is made of moments of insight of the kind that come to the poet. (It is the essence of Eliot's praise of Donne in his essay on the Metaphysical poets: 'A thought to Donne was an experience . . . When a poet's mind is perfectly equipped for its work, it is constantly amalgamating disparate experience; the ordinary man's experience is chaotic, irregular, fragmentary.' [2]) Yeats knew many such moments. In speaking of a waterfall, he writes:

> I would have touched it like a child
> But knew my finger could but have touched
> Cold stone and water. I grew wild,
> Even accusing Heaven because
> It had set down among its laws:
> Nothing that we love over-much
> Is ponderable to our touch.[3]

Here a physical experience has been translated into thought in a manner which is far more than ruminating: it is the immediate expression of an insight. The poetry of Rupert Brooke is full of this kind of insight. For instance, in the lines:

> and I should find
> Soon in the silence the hidden key
> Of all that had hurt and puzzled me — [4]

the poetic experience — the 'negative capability' — is conceived as an indirect means of conquering his experience. It is necessary to say all this to make clear what I mean by 'existentialist' — which

---

* I should mention that when I use the word 'consciousness,' I intend it to embrace the whole area of living consciousness in any form: i.e. the consciousness of an amoeba, or the so-called 'unconscious mind' of a human being.

is the indispensable preliminary to speaking about Shaw. We have been thinking about Shaw for so long as a political thinker or a propagandist-playwright that a major engineering operation is required if we are to overthrow irrelevant standards, and begin judging him without prejudice.

To summarise: the existentialist is the artist-philosopher, and his natural medium is the *Bildungsroman:* the novel or play which is about the maturing of its central character through the impact of his experience. Examples of this are *Wilhelm Meister*, *The Brothers Karamazov*, Meredith's *Ordeal of Richard Feverel*, Mann's *Magic Mountain*, Hesse's *Demian*, Sartre's *Chemins de la Liberté*, Hemingway's *Farewell to Arms*, Joyce's *Portrait*, Shaw's *Immaturity*. I have lumped the major with the minor here to emphasise the breadth of this category. Let me finish by dogmatising: In the twentieth century, the only serious form of literary art is the *Bildungsroman*.

Half of Shaw's greatness is symbolised by his love of Mozart. In Mozart, for all his depth, there are no self-conscious explorations of the tortured mind, and for all his vision, it never overwhelms the listener as if with a sudden and startling revelation. In his work, it is life that is glorified, life as such, without distinction between its surface and its depth. In *The Magic Flute*, the last opera, written after years of disappointment and suffering, he makes life seem transient and yet permanent; it would seem almost as if he were saying: Life needs no deeper meanings to make it beautiful and eternal; for all its torture and uncertainty, it is divine. The opera is 'lighter' and more delicate, and yet more profound, than anything Mozart had written before.

This vision of life is the true poet's vision: it is the vision of Keats and Shakespeare and Villon and Synge; it glorifies life without any attempt to find 'reasons.'

This vision is found in the two greatest writers of the early part of our century: Shaw and Wells. (It is also found in Chesterton and Belloc, and it is by recognising how little these latter achieved in comparison with Shaw and Wells that one realises how dangerous this capacity can be in the hands of a non-thinker.) It is the sheer vital energy, the love of life in all its manifestations, which makes Shaw and Wells so attractive. They had about them what Chester-

ton called 'a wild gaiety.' And in Shaw, this gaiety is closely connected with the influence of Mozart. One of Shaw's earliest musical
experiences was to see *Don Giovanni*. He was a romantic and imaginative boy, and *Don Giovanni* contributed to forming his picture
of what adulthood ought to be. The Don adores life and its perpetually renewed manifestations so much that he changes his mis-
tress every other day (or even more frequently, if Leporello's cata-
logue song is accurate). Naturally, this requires considerable heartlessness. The Don is not shown as a particularly cruel or unpleasant
man; consequently, there must be some remorse involved in breaking off an enjoyable human relationship for the benefit of another;
yet his love of change is so great that he apparently cultivates this
callousness in himself. His excuse is a delight in women which is
as promiscuous as a bee's delight in flowers. In order to indulge
this delight to the full, he has become completely 'heartless'; to keep
his aesthetic delight in women separated from his human interest in
them. Inhumanity is a condition of delight.

No doubt this made a deep impression on a romantic boy —
especially as the Don is represented as having all the romantic virtues
except fidelity: courage, wit, courtliness, and an irresistible attractiveness to women. The philosophy of Don Giovanni is the philosophy of Kierkegaard's seducer; but it also has elements of the philosophy of Plato and the Upanishads: that the fullest enjoyment of
life demands complete non-attachment. In his odd way, Don Giovanni is genuinely non-attached.

Beyond doubt, the young Shaw was the complete romantic. His
home life was admirably suited to his development in this direction:
his parents believed in letting him alone, and there was no attempt
to impose a Victorian discipline. We know too little about Shaw's
childhood: and yet he is the very man of genius who should have
written a full account of it, like Tolstoy's great book, for the Shaw
we know is a mature Shaw, the skilled controversialist, the lucid
reasoner, and *no* man could have developed such powers without
a long period of agonising immaturity. His very strength makes
him unpopular and remote; he showed penetrating insight into this
in *Back to Methuselah*, where he quotes Wells's parable *The Food
of the Gods*, in which a chemical food makes some people grow
to tremendous size, and the rest of the human race develops a pas-

sionate hatred of the giants and tries to destroy them. If Shaw had revealed more of his own weakness, as Joyce and Gide did, he might have had more defenders today.

But we know that Shaw was more fond of art than of life: that he wandered around the Dublin art galleries, went to the theatres and the opera whenever he had the opportunity, and was deeply impressed by Mozart's *Don Giovanni* and Gounod's *Faust* (in which he admired Mephistopheles for his arched eyebrows — a feature he himself was later to develop). And we know that he detested Dublin as much as the young James Joyce was to detest it thirty years later. In the preface to *Immaturity*, he says of *Ulysses:*

> James Joyce . . . has described with a fidelity so ruthless that the book is hardly bearable, the life that Dublin offers to its young men. . . . No doubt it is much like the life of young men everywhere in modern urban civilisation. A certain flippant futile derision and belittlement that confuses the noble and serious with the base and ludicrous seems to me peculiar to Dublin; but I suppose that is because my only personal experience of that phase of youth was a Dublin experience; for when I left my native city I left that phase behind me, and associated no more with men of my age until, after about eight years of solitude in this respect, I was drawn into the Socialist revival of the early eighties, among Englishmen intensely serious, and burning with indignation at very real and fundamental evils that affected all the world. . . .[5]

So, in fact, when Shaw left Dublin at twenty — having been a highly efficient and successful clerk for six years — he plunged into a strange city — London — and into relative solitude. And as he himself says in the same preface, he became an Outsider:

> When I had to come out of the realm of imagination into that of actuality I was still uncomfortable. I was outside society, outside politics, outside sport, outside the Church. If the term had been invented then I should have been called the Complete Outsider.[6] *

* I must confess that it was from Shaw's use of the term in this passage that the term Outsider (with a capital O) crept into my own vocabulary at about the age of sixteen.

Shaw was the most basic type of Outsider, the romantic Outsider. 'When I had to come out of the realm of imagination into
that of actuality . . .': it is the problem of Hanno Buddenbrooks
that Thomas Mann described in his first novel. And in *John Bull's
Other Island*, Shaw puts his hatred of Dublin into Doyle's mouth:

> And all the while there goes on a horrible, senseless, mischievous
> laughter. When youre young, you exchange drinks with other
> young men; and you exchange vile stories with them; and as
> youre too futile to be able to help or cheer them, you chaff and
> sneer and taunt them for not doing the things you darent do
> yourself. And all the time you laugh! laugh! laugh! eternal de-
> rision, eternal envy, eternal folly, eternal fouling and staining
> and degrading, until, when you come at last to a country where
> men take a question seriously and give a serious answer to it, you
> deride them for having no sense of humor, and plume yourself
> on your own worthlessness as if it made you better than them.[7]

Shaw wrote this nearly thirty years after he had left Dublin;
the clearness with which he remembers the humiliation of being
sneered at for being 'too serious' makes it apparent that it cut deep.
The whole meaning of this paragraph takes us back to the problems
I examined in the second chapter of *The Outsider*, in writing about
Camus's *L'Etranger* and Hemingway's *Soldier's Home*. Krebs, the
soldier who comes home from the war, remembers glimpses of the
heroic state of mind when 'you did the one thing, the only thing'
with calm and discipline, and hates the dullness of his home town
where the men play pool, and hang around telling stories; he hates
it because, having glimpsed a higher intensity of living, he now
longs for the heroic and detests the trivial. Strowde in Granville-
Barker's play threw away a political career because he had glimpsed
this higher intensity, and no longer had patience with politicians.
It is a romantic attitude — Yeats caught it perfectly in 'The Man
Who Dreamed of Faeryland' and 'Fergus and the Druid.' It is not
actually a distaste for living; it is only a distaste for the dilute,
gritty soup which gets fed to us under the name of 'living' in the
modern world. In *Peer Gynt*, Ibsen showed his romantic young man
prepared to accept the Troll King's ugly daughter as a ravishing
princess, and the pig he rides on as a magnificent white charger,

rather than face the dreary reality. It is a longing for the heroic, for a greater seriousness of life than ordinary human beings know about. And when a man has this appetite for seriousness, and cannot see it reflected in any of the human beings he knows, he must either submit to their standards and forget his dreams, or deliberately cut himself off from them — make himself an Outsider — until he has found a way of thinking and living that gives him scope for his deeper seriousness. Works of imagination will inspire him — especially works about ambitious young men struggling to escape their circumstances, like Stendhal's *Le Rouge et le noir* or Joyce's *Portrait*. It is this longing for the heroic that makes the Outsider; and his greatest enemy is 'nausea': discouragement, boredom, and the pettiness of so much modern life.

A romantic distaste for Dublin and a craving for seriousness kept Shaw in solitude for many years. In this solitude, his main solace seems to have been in the realm of imagination: in music, literature, art. On first coming to London, he went to see *Carmen* again and again; he soaked himself in Shakespeare and Dickens; he became as familiar with the London art galleries as he had been with the Dublin ones. And he also discovered Wagner.

Wagner's work is the apotheosis of the heroic ideal. From *Rienzi* to *Parsifal*, heroes occupy the centre of his stage. In his greatest and most significant work, *The Ring*, Wotan (symbolising the intellectual leader of men), brings a curse on the gods, which can only be removed by the rise of a higher type of man than the intellectual leader — the hero, Siegfried. It is hardly surprising that the young Shaw at once became 'the perfect Wagnerite.'

Shaw's training in being an Outsider was unusually long and complete; for years he had no field of action, nothing to occupy his attention except art. He was lucky enough not to have to work; like all true artists, he hated work, and refused to do any, allowing his family to supply his meals and a roof, and spending his days at the British Museum writing his five novels. In these eight years, he developed an immense romantic appetite for heroic achievement, and acquired vast erudition in the course of his long quest to find satisfaction in the realm of literature. The novels are all poor, but it is not easy to say why; mainly, perhaps, because Shaw had no deep interest in their central characters. The hero of *Immaturity* is a sort of self-portrait, but it is a curiously objective, unromantic self-portrait, with no appreciable element of self-pity or dramatisation; and the hero's name is — Smith! Before the end of the first chapter, Smith, newly arrived in London, has met an attractive girl named Harriet; but no romance develops; instead, he teaches her French. At the end of the book, Smith is as celibate as at the beginning. Harriet marries someone else. Smith's only achievement is to become a highly efficient private secretary. The interest in the novel has centred around Harriet and her painter husband as much as around Smith.

It would, of course, be a mistake to expect Shaw to have written his own *Portrait of the Artist* in the seventies of the last century; Joyce was unborn, and Shaw's reading had been limited to Dickens and Charles Lever. His tendency was naturally to try to tell a story, and to ignore psychological analyses.

In his next three novels, there is not even the suggestion of a self-portrait. *The Irrational Knot* is about a hard-headed engineer who marries a 'lady' but finds the insipidity of the life she expects to lead intolerable. *Love Among the Artists* has a composer, Owen Jack, as its central figure; he has a pock-marked face and the waspish temperament of a Beethoven, but a whole gallery of lesser figures get an equal share of the author's attention, and the result is not absorbing. *Cashel Byron's Profession* is about a young gentleman who runs away from school and becomes a prizefighter; then falls in love with a bluestocking named Lady Lydia Carew, whom he finally marries. The various complications that make the plot of the novel are weakly contrived, and there is an uncomfortable feeling that the novelist does not know exactly what he's about.

An Unsocial Socialist is undoubtedly the best of the five novels. Shaw was twenty-seven when he finished it, and the central character has strong elements of self-portraiture. Here, for the first time, Shaw's innate romanticism, bequeathed him by Mozart, appears with its own peculiar identity. The book's original title was *The Heartless Man*. Trefusis is heartless — as heartless as Don Giovanni — but he has also grown beyond the stage of finding any excitement in a series of sexual intrigues. He is thoroughly romantic, but his romanticism is revolted by the reality of the male-female relation. When the book opens, he has deserted his newly married wife, leaving her a note telling her that she is ravishingly beautiful and sensually satis-fying, but that the atmosphere of billing and cooing and making love is stifling him. Shaw then involves him in a hilarious and highly improbable adventure in a girls' school. It is all as involved and confusing as *Immaturity*, but this time, the character of Trefusis gives it unity and holds one's interest. He is shown as having Don Giovanni's attractiveness to women, but preferring socialism. At the slightest provocation, he makes long speeches about the oppres-sion of the working classes. It is his combination of romanticism and intellectualism that makes him heartless; he finds the reality of hu-man relations uninteresting by comparison.

The five novels did not find a publisher, although *Cashel Byron* was later a fair success. *An Unsocial Socialist* was published in a small monthly magazine; it had no success, but made Shaw known to William Morris, at whose house Shaw became a frequent visitor. For many years he had been interested in socialism, and had read Marx's *Capital* in the Museum. In the year after he wrote *An Un-social Socialist*, he joined the Fabian Society, and immediately be-came one of its moving forces, speaking on street corners and in Hyde Park, and writing pamphlets. He had been speaking in public since he was twenty-three, when he stood up at the meeting of the 'Zetetical Society,' tense with nervousness, and opposed the speaker. He always managed to cover his timidity with an air of self-confi-dence which often aroused violent hostility. ' . . . I had an un-pleasant trick of contradicting everyone from whom I thought I could learn anything in order to draw him out and enable me to pick his brains . . . I think I must have impressed many amiable persons as an extremely disagreeable and undesirable young man.' [8] When he was twenty-six, he fell in love with one of his mother's singing pupils, a nurse, but the affair came to nothing. He was still a virgin at twenty-nine, when finally another of his mother's pupils decided to seduce him, and met with no objection. Shaw then proceeded to make up for lost time, and had a series of affairs which continued until he married fifteen years later. The *Immatu-rity* preface contains a delightful portrait of the Shaw of the pre-Fabian period:

Clever sympathetic women might divine at a glance that I was mortally shy; but people who could not see through my skin, and who were accustomed to respect, and even veneration, from the young, may well have found me insufferable, aggressive and impudent. When a young man has achieved nothing and is doing nothing, and when he is obviously so poor that he ought to be doing something very energetically, it is rather trying to find him assuming an authority in conversation, and an equality in terms, which only conspicuous success and distinguished ability could make becoming. Yet this is what is done, quite unconsciously, by young persons who have in them the potentiality of such success and ability. . . .

The truth is that all men are in a false position in society until they have realised their possibilities, and imposed them on their neighbors. They are tormented by a continual shortcoming in themselves; yet they irritate others by a continual overweening. This discord can be resolved by acknowledged success or failure only: everyone is ill at ease until he has found his natural place, whether it be above or below his birthplace. . . . Besides, this finding of one's place may be made very puzzling by the fact that there is no place in ordinary society for extraordinary individuals. . . .[9]

The young Shaw was, emphatically, an Outsider, and what he has described is the position of every young man of genius before he has convinced himself or anyone else of his genius. There *is* no place in society for the extraordinary individuals, and neither should there be; all their power and importance lies in their being outside society. It is a pity that Shaw knew nothing of the equally great problem — Scott Fitzgerald's problem — of sudden overwhelming success, and the curious way in which success makes for a quite different kind of isolation in modern society.

I began *The Outsider* by denying that the Outsider is simply the misunderstood man of genius. This is true in the sense that genius means some extraordinary ability to create. Even a stupid and untalented man — like Barbusse's hole-in-corner man — may be made into an Outsider by some great suffering which cuts him off from his fellow human beings. But such suffering makes for the development of an intelligence which is halfway towards genius; so I must qualify my statement by an admission that the Outsider problem and the problem of genius striving for self-expression are closely connected. And in the *Immaturity* preface, the Outsider is simply the frustrated man of genius — of the same type as the angry and frustrated young man whom James Dean has made fashionable in the 'fifties.

But Shaw's interest in the Outsider theme was not limited to the frustrated-genius type. I have already spoken of Keegan, in *John Bull's Other Island*, who is an Outsider because of his Swiftian loathing of human cruelty and folly. Keegan was a late development, and there are many stages of the Outsider between Trefusis, the Heartless Man, and Keegan's almost Buddhist attitude. (There are so many, in fact, that I might well have written a book about the Outsider in Shaw, instead of tracing Outsiders from Barbusse to Ramakrishna and Hulme.)

Trefusis is Shaw's first Outsider, and he is an Outsider in the simple sense of being a rebel against the established order. He is also a symbol of Shaw's revolt against Victorian sentimentality, and the nineteenth-century emphasis on 'humanity' (the inevitable outcome of its materialism and agnosticism). He is heartless because he has the Outsider's consuming desire for seriousness of purpose, and a consequent horror of human entanglements. His heartlessness is of the same origin as that of St. John of the Cross or Eckhart. But his socialism does not make him simply an 'angry young man'; he has too much faith in the power of his enthusiasm, and he also has a sense of humour. He lusts for purpose and direction, but this does not turn him into a monk; there is a strong element of Mozartian love of the world in his make-up. All this becomes even more apparent in a short story which Shaw wrote a few years later called *Don Giovanni Explains*. In this story, a young girl returning from a performance of *Don Giovanni* meets the ghost of the Don on the train; he then tells her the *true* story of his life: the romanticism that made him into a lover, and the disillusion that made him turn away from sex — unfortunately at a time when his legend had made him so attractive to women that he spent his time trying to escape advances from them. The story of Mozart's opera is retold, but this time the Don is not shown as a rake, but as a fastidious artist and thinker with a strong leaning to asceticism. In the *Killing for Sport* preface, Shaw has the sentence: 'It all comes back to . . . appetite for fruitful activity and a high quality of life,' [10] (which makes the basis of his objection to killing animals). This phrase explains the whole aim of Shaw's life and work. Differently worded, it is the Outsider's question of how to live as fully as possible, or Eliot's question: 'Where is the Life we have lost in living?' Writing about Hamlet in 1897, Shaw said:

> Hamlet is not a man in whom 'common humanity' is raised by great vital energy to a heroic pitch. . . . On the contrary, he is a man in whom the common personal passions are so superseded by wider and rarer interests, and so discouraged by a degree of critical self-consciousness which makes the practical efficiency of the instinctive man . . . impossible to him, that he finds the duties dictated by conventional revenge and ambition as disagreeable a burden as commerce is to a poet.[11]

This is as penetrating an analysis of the Outsider as anyone could ask: '. . . discouraged by a degree of critical self-consciousness . . .'; this is T. E. Lawrence and Nietzsche. But Shaw's analysis goes even deeper than this; he goes on to say:

> And, indeed, there is a sense in which Hamlet is insane; for he trips over the mistake which lies on the threshold of intellectual self-consciousness: that of bringing life to utilitarian or Hedonistic tests, thus treating it as a means instead of an end. Because Polonius is 'a foolish prating knave,' because Rosencrantz and Guildenstern are snobs, he kills them as remorselessly as he might kill a flea . . . anticipating . . . the whole course of the intellectual history of Western Europe. . . .[12]

Shaw has diagnosed the Outsider's torment as the inevitable period of maladjustment on the threshold of intellectual consciousness; and he has also seen beyond the fascist error — the error attributed (quite mistakenly) to Nietzsche, and about which Dostoevsky wrote in *Crime and Punishment*: that the 'masters' — the Outsiders — should have power of life and death over the slaves. In the Postscript to *Back to Methuselah* (1944) he repeats his earlier diagnosis of Hamlet, and adds 'Had Shakespeare plumbed his play to the bottom, he would hardly have allowed Hamlet to send Rosencrantz and Guildenstern to their death. . . .'[13]

In his first critical book, *The Quintessence of Ibsenism*, written after he had been a journalist and reviewer for ten years, Shaw has already grasped his own task as a writer: to attempt to restore unity to the conception of nature. In his examination of Ibsen's *Emperor and Galilean*, he attacks Darwinism and materialism, and quotes Butler's dictum that Darwin had 'banished mind from the universe.' The full significance of this would not be understood until Heidegger in Germany and Sartre in France began the task of trying to 'restore mind to the universe.' Julian the Apostate tries to restore paganism, because he feels that the Christian ideal is decadent. But he tries to impose paganism by force, and fails. Maximus the Mystic, the strange old man who inspires Julian, predicts that both Emperor and Galilean shall be swallowed up by something that shall supersede both:

> Both shall succumb; but you shall not therefore perish. Does not the child succumb in the youth and the youth in the man: yet neither child nor youth perishes. You know I have neveι approved of your policy as emperor. You have tried to make the youth a child again. The empire of the flesh is fallen a prey to the empire of the spirit. But the empire of the spirit is not final, any more than the youth is. You have tried to hinder the youth from growing: from becoming a man. Oh fool, who have drawn your sword against that which is to be: against the third empire. . . . [14]

It is the truth which T. E. Hulme recognised: that although mediaeval religion gave way to humanism, the answer is not simply to put back the clock. For Western civilisation, the Church was the first empire — an empire of blind faith. It was replaced by an empire of free thought. One type of man alone in our civilisation has recognised that free thought leads back to religion — if it is free enough and ranges far enough: the Outsider. Unfortunately, neither Shaw nor Ibsen recognised that civilisations smash after the second empire. The problem of the third empire still stands, immense and unsolved: the problem of how to make our whole civilisation think like the Outsider.

But this is to anticipate the ideas of the later Shaw. In the eighteen-nineties, Shaw had recognised that life is a lust for wider and deeper self-consciousness, and that the Outsider is a man standing in bewilderment between two worlds. But when he began writing plays, he made no attempt to dramatise Outsider problems. *Widowers' Houses*, his first play, was produced in 1892; its message is completely socialistic, although, as with all Shaw's plays, the dialogue is so vigorous that it is preposterous to try to dismiss it as 'a socialist tract.' His second play, *The Philanderer*, returns to the Don Giovanni problem; its hero, Charteris, has much in common with Trefusis, except that he is altogether more amiable and more susceptible to women. His complaint is that of Shaw's Don Giovanni in the short story: '. . . whose fault is it that half the women I speak to fall in love with me?' [15]

The Philanderer is an attempt to depict a rising generation at the end of the last century, and as such has something in common with Michael Arlen's *The Green Hat* and John Osborne's *Look Back in Anger*. But the Ibsenite young people are rather dreary; the plot is as complicated as *Love Among the Artists*, and the over-all effect is one of confusion. But this is the last appearance in Shaw's work of such an effect; all his subsequent plays have a firm sense of direction.

A number of lighter plays were written during the next ten years. *Mrs Warren's Profession*, in spite of its subject — the white-slave trade — is witty and amusing. *Arms and the Man* makes fun of nationalism and patriotism; it is Shaw at his best in his anti-sentimental vein, but whereas other opponents of the army have raged and sneered about it, Shaw makes fun of it with the cool superiority of a man who has more serious things to occupy his mind.

The Man of Destiny introduces two elements into Shaw that were to appear again and again; one good, one bad. The good one is his tendency to portray great men — Napoleon in this case — as good-tempered and humorous; the bad one is his tendency to exaggerate the stupidity of some of his characters until they become almost village idiots. In this play it is a young lieutenant; his kind of imbecility reappears many times in the later plays, and gives the reader an irritated feeling that he is being underrated.

Candida is altogether the most important play of this period; it is a parallel study in an Outsider and an Insider. The Insider is a

socialist clergyman, witty, urbane, tolerant; the Outsider, a young
poet, uncertain of himself in all social relations, but supremely certain of his ideas as a poet. When the poet tells Morell, the clergyman, that he is in love with his his wife Candida, Morell kindly
warns him that he is making a fool of himself, and Marchbanks
launches a superb attack:

> Oh, do you think I dont know all that? Do you think that the
> things that people make fools of themselves about are any less
> real and true than the things they behave sensibly about? They
> are more true: they are the only things that are true. You are
> very calm and sensible and moderate with me because you can
> see that I am a fool about your wife; just as no doubt that old man
> who was here just now is very wise over your Socialism, because
> he sees that you are a fool about it. Does that prove you wrong?
> Does your complacent superiority to me prove that _I_ am
> wrong? [16]

This magnificent scene is more than an Outsider attacking an Insider; it is the first important appearance in Shaw of a device which
was to become the dramatic centre of all his later plays: the clash
of wills. He puts two people of strong character on to the stage,
and the audience watches with fascination for the explosion. He
had tried out this device for the first time with Vivie Warren and
her mother. It appears again in the court scene between Dick Dud-
geon and General Burgoyne in _The Devil's Disciple;_ it gives pi-
quancy to the relation between Caesar and Rufio in _Caesar and Cleopatra;_ it provides the comedy in _Man and Superman,_ and the
tragedy in _Saint Joan._ A theme which runs through all Shaw's
work is this theme of the will to power, the refusal to be brow-
beaten, moral courage. In _Major Barbara,_ the interest is provided
by the conflict between the strong-minded Lady Britomart and her
equally strong-minded daughter Barbara; between the armament
king Undershaft and Cusins, the Professor of Greek. In _The Apple
Cart,_ the self-made politician Boanerges is the first important character on stage, threatening to bully the king, and immediately the
audience waits for the clash of wills. It is never an obvious, brutal
crash: usually it involves the skilled fencing of intelligent antago-

nists. And just as Rufio, the bodyguard, has treated Caesar with rough familiarity, so Mrs. Basham treats Isaac Newton, and George Fox treats the king, in *In Good King Charles's Golden Days*, written forty years later. Throughout his work, Shaw plays with the idea of the defiance of authority, and rebellion, in one form or another, is the theme of all his major plays. Now the Outsider is not necessarily the rebel, but the rebel is undoubtedly a most important type of Outsider. The rebel attempts to assert that existence comes before essence, that will comes before authority. In another form, this existentialist theme is presented in Bergson in the opposition between 'open and closed religion.' Open religion is the inspired religious insight of the prophet and saint; closed religion is the ritual and law of a Church. On any level, this opposition between the living force and the forms which it puts on like garments, implies existentialism. And all forms of this opposition are present in Shaw's work (*Saint Joan*, for instance, is about 'open and closed religion'). It is not too much to say that all Shaw's central themes are existentialist.

However, I have left my attempt to trace the Outsider theme in Shaw's development. After *Candida*, its next major expression is in *Caesar and Cleopatra*.

Shaw's Caesar is an Outsider for the very reasons which made Shaw declare that Hamlet was an Outsider; because he has evolved a stage beyond his fellow men, and is quite alone among them, alone and incomprehensible. His opening speech expresses his isolation. He speaks to the Sphinx, alone in the desert:

> Hail, Sphinx; salutation from Julius Caesar! I have wandered in many lands, seeking the lost regions from which my birth into this world exiled me, and the company of creatures such as I myself. I have found flocks and pastures, men and cities, but no other Caesar, no air native to me, no man kindred to me, none who can do my day's deed, and think my night's thought. . . . Sphinx, you and I, strangers to the race of men, are no strangers to one another.[17]

It may be that Shaw had Marcus Aurelius in mind in creating Caesar:

POTHINUS: Natural! Then you do not resent treachery?
CAESAR: Resent! O thou foolish Egyptian, what have I to do
with resentment? Do I resent the wind when it chills me, or the
night when it makes me stumble in the darkness? Shall I resent
youth when it turns from age, and ambition when it turns from
servitude? To tell me such a story as this is but to tell me that
the sun will rise tomorrow.[18]

But later, when Cleopatra has had Pothinus murdered for revenge,
and defends herself against Caesar's condemnation, the tone ceases
to be merely stoical:

CLEOPATRA: Listen to me, Caesar. If one man in all Alexandria
can be found to say that I did wrong, I swear to have myself
crucified on the door of the palace by my own slaves.
CAESAR: If one man in all the world can be found, now or forever, to know that you did wrong, that man will have either to
conquer the world as I have, or be crucified by it.[19]

Shaw is expressing the essence of Christianity; but Caesar's preference — and Shaw's — was all for conquering the world by moral
greatness, not dying for it. And yet Shaw did not imply a condemnation of the Christian morality of self-sacrifice. In *Methuselah*, the
two human creatures whom Pygmalion creates each beg that the
other be killed, until the Ancient lays her hand on them and raises
them to a higher level of life, when they each ask to be killed, but
beg that the other be spared.

In his Preface to *Caesar and Cleopatra*, Shaw directed his famous
criticism against Shakespeare — that he understood human weakness
without understanding human strength. (It should be observed, at
the same time, that Shaw never denied Shakespeare's greatness as a
poet and playwright.) This criticism contains the essence of Shaw,
and it also contains the essence of the Outsider's position. For the
Insider, moral and intellectual ideas are unimportant in comparison
with aesthetic satisfaction. But for the Outsider, nothing matters
but moral heroism. The Insider does not mind people being trivial
and unheroic because life is still good. The Outsider cannot begin
living until he has solved the question of *how* to live; like Ivan
Karamazov, *he rejects the world*, he rejects life if it must be lived
trivially. He craves greater intensity of life. In the twentieth cen-

tury, the Insider's position is the philosophy of our civilisation —
the 'go-getter' utilitarianism. That is why, for any Outsider, all
that matters is that men should *become bigger;* that is why the
Outsider is the heroic figure of our time, and Outsider tragedies —
those of Nietzsche, Lawrence, Van Gogh, Nijinsky — are the great
tragedies of our time. That is why the great bulk of modern literature must be detestable to the Outsider: for, like Shakespeare, it
cares only about human weakness; it looks at human beings through
a microscope, not a telescope.

After *Caesar,* Shaw felt that it was time to make a more general
statement of his philosophy. He does this in his most brilliant play
— and perhaps his greatest — *Man and Superman.*

Superficially, this play is on the theme that it is the woman, not
the man, who does the wooing. This theme need not be taken too
seriously. After all, Shaw set out to write a play about Don Juan,
and the essence of Shaw's interpretation of the Don Juan legend was
that the Don was chased. (Observe that Shaw had written about
this theme in *An Unsocial Socialist* before he had his first affair.)
No doubt Shaw was right in a sense: in the sense that it is the
woman's job to continue the race, and the man's job to build civilisation; even the most ardent feminist would not deny that her child-
bearing function acts as a brake on her intellectual and moral pursuits. But the truth is that the higher form of life will always be
chased by the lower. The woman with elements of greatness will
always be chased by men; the man with elements of greatness will
always be chased by women. And the man or woman who becomes
great in a public as well as a private sense will always be chased by
people of both sexes who hope that by contact with him they can
escape from their own insufficiency.

Man and Superman is about a socialist intellectual, John Tanner,
who is made the guardian of Ann Whitfield, a girl who is in love
with him. In one of the earliest speeches in the play, Tanner summarises a trend which has become the theme of hundreds of twentieth-century novels and plays: the theme of social inferiority and
shame:

> . . . even I cannot wholly conquer shame. We live in an atmos-
> phere of shame. We are ashamed of everything that is real about
> us; ashamed of ourselves, of our relatives, of our incomes, of our

accents, of our opinions, of our experience, just as we are ashamed of our naked skins. Good Lord, my dear Ramsden, we are ashamed to walk, ashamed to ride in an omnibus, ashamed to hire a hansom instead of keeping a carriage, ashamed of keeping one horse instead of two and a groom-gardener instead of a coach-man and footman. The more things a man is ashamed of, the more respectable he is. . . .[20]

When Tanner finds out that Ann is in love with him (and it takes him two whole acts to do it), he hastily leaves the country and flies to Spain — only to be captured by the 'love-sick brigand' Mendoza, and held for ransom. That night, asleep in Mendoza's camp, he has the dream which constitutes the heart of the play. Tanner dreams that he is his ancestor, Don Juan, and in hell. But hell is not a place of fire and torment: it is an Outsider's hell of triviality and endless pettiness. Hell is the home of Insiders. Shaw does not divide the race into the good and the wicked: he divides it into Outsiders and Insiders, and the Outsiders go to heaven, the Insiders to hell. Hell is a place of eternal pleasure, eternal frivolity, eternal silliness — everything to revolt an Outsider with a lust for seriousness of purpose. Don Juan has been sent there by mistake. Soon Doña Ana arrives to disturb the Don in the solitude in which he has taken refuge, and shortly after that, the Devil (Mendoza in disguise) and the Statue from Mozart, who is Ana's father. Now begins the long discussion which I have always felt to be the greatest scene in Shaw, and one of the pinnacles of English literature. Doña Ana (Ann) has to have it explained to her why hell is not a place of eternal torment. Her father (the Statue) has come from heaven to live in hell; he is tired of the dullness of heaven. The Devil explains the dullness of heaven by analogy: in England (the country where he has the greatest following — no doubt America would compete nowadays) there are halls where classical concerts are held, and there are racecourses. Nothing prevents the lovers of racing from going to the classical concerts, and the concerts are acknowledged to be a higher, more spiritual form of entertainment than horse-racing. Nevertheless, the lovers of racing do not flock to the concert halls. Neither do the inhabitants of hell flock to heaven. Then a long argument develops, in which the Outsider Don Juan tries to explain why he is a 'social failure' in hell. The Life Force in him makes him uncomfortable when he is forced to sit around doing nothing but amuse himself. Life, he explains, strives towards the complete conquest of matter by the spirit. Matter and spirit are enemies. Man has a certain mastery over his body — he can make it stand up or sit down or turn somersaults — but he cannot prevent it from catching diseases or dying. And he cannot guard against accidents, or against being killed by a lower form of life: an Archimedes can be killed by a stupid Roman soldier. Man's way towards the conquest of matter is through spiritual discipline, striving to become a higher form of life. It is a development of consciousness. *The Aim of life is to understand itself.* Don Juan speaks then of his disappointments in love, and of how his romanticism was destroyed by his fastidiousness. He anticipates D. H. Lawrence's sexual mysticism when he tells how his conscious criticism of a woman would destroy his desire for her until 'Life seized me and threw me into her arms as a sailor throws a scrap of fish into the mouth of a seabird.' [21] And when the Devil objects that here, in hell, he has everything he ever wanted — music, painting, sexual adventures, and so forth, Juan states his Outsider's credo:

'I tell you that as long as I can conceive something better than myself I cannot be easy unless I am striving to bring it into existence or clearing the way for it. That is the law of my life. That is the working within me of Life's incessant aspiration to higher organisation, wider, deeper, intenser self-consciousness, and clearer self-understanding. It was the supremacy of this purpose that reduced love for me to the mere pleasure of a moment. . . .' [22]

Shaw, in other words, was 'heartless' and uninterested in human weaknesses for the same reason that all Outsiders are: through a passionate desire to create, to strive for greatness. It is a heartlessness of which the Outsider can passionately approve.

The 'higher form of life' that Don Juan strives to create is the Nietzschean Superman. Shaw felt obscurely that man is on the threshold of a higher form of life; either that, or the Life Force may scrap him and try something new. He was right, but not wholly: *man is always on the brink of a higher form of life when a civilisation reaches its stage of decline. The decline is a challenge to raise the standard of conscious life; otherwise it must smash.* Man evolved from the ape by developing a religious consciousness. He then evolved from the mere superstitious tribesman by developing his reasoning power. Before he can develop to a still higher stage, he must restore the religious consciousness: nothing else will hold society together. And while religion means 'closed religion,' mere ritual and superstition, then reason makes its existence impossible. Religion must become what the Outsider understands by it: a body of truth about man's purpose and relation to God. For a whole civilisation to think in Outsider terms would probably mean the total disappearance of Insiders. And the price of failing to meet the challenge need not be the scrapping of the human race; it may mean only the scrapping of all that we understand by civilisation. The alternative is a universal effort to create 'open religion,' and perhaps, eventually, a new 'closed religion.'

Don Juan launches a tirade against Insiders which is more devastating than anything in Swift:

> In this Palace of Lies a truth or two will not hurt you. Your friends are all the dullest dogs I know. They are not beautiful: they are only decorated. They are not clean: they are only shaved and starched. They are not dignified: they are only fashionably dressed. They are not educated: they are only college passmen. They are not religious: they are only pewrenters. They are not moral: they are only conventional. They are not virtuous: they are only cowardly. They are not even vicious: they are only 'frail.' They are not artistic: they are only lascivious. They are not prosperous: they are only rich. They are not loyal, they are only servile; not dutiful, only sheepish; not public spirited, only patriotic; not courageous, only quarrelsome; not determined, only obstinate; not masterful, only domineering; not self-controlled, only obtuse; not self-respecting, only vain; not kind, only sentimental; not social, only gregarious; not considerate, only polite; not intelligent, only opinionated; not progressive, only factious; not imaginative, only superstitious; not just, only vindictive; not generous, only propitiatory; not disciplined, only cowed; and not truthful at all: liars every one of them, to the very backbone of their souls.[28]

And he gets up and goes off to heaven. At this point, Tanner awakes, to find the police swooping on the brigands, and Ann

Whitfield looking for him. A socialist through and through, he explains to the police that the brigands are his escort. In the last act, Ann finally persuades him to marry her after a dialogue which has overtones of Don Giovanni's last wrangle with the Statue:

> TANNER: I will not marry you. I will not marry you.
> ANN: Oh, you will, you will.
> TANNER: I tell you, no, no, no.
> ANN: I tell you, yes, yes, yes.
> TANNER: No.
> ANN: Yes. Before it is too late for repentance. Yes.[24]

Which recalls:

> THE COMMANDANT: Pèntiti!
> DON GIOVANNI: No.
> THE COMMANDANT: Pèntiti!
> DON GIOVANNI: No!
> THE COMMANDANT: Sì!
> DON GIOVANNI: No!
> THE COMMANDANT: Sì!
> DON GIOVANNI: No!
> THE COMMANDANT: Sì, sì!
> DON GIOVANNI: No, no!
> THE COMMANDANT: Ah! tempo più non v'è! [25]

And Tanner marries Ann, who is a very ordinary Insider for whom he is just a talker.

So the ghost of Don Giovanni disappears from Shaw's work. From then on, the Outsider theme becomes even more clearly defined. The next play, *John Bull's Other Island*, centres around the Jansenist priest Keegan, and the triumph of the typical stupid Insider, Broadbent. Shaw is not terribly hostile to Broadbent, who is a well-meaning fool — but a materialistic fool, unable to realise that fundamentally the artist and poet are opposed to all that materialism stands for. In *Heartbreak House*, Shaw takes an altogether sterner stand.

Shaw's next play, *Major Barbara*, also throws new light on the

Outsider theme. The important characters in this play are Cusins, the young Professor of Greek, and Andrew Undershaft, his prospective father-in-law. Undershaft's daughter, Barbara, is a major in the Salvation Army. Undershaft is an armament king, whose faith can be summarised in two words: Money and gunpowder. Yet Undershaft has much of Shaw's Caesar about him; he has the gentleness of a man of immense strength. He and Cusins soon come into conflict on the question of religion. In their first discussion, Cusins quotes Euripides to the effect that most men squabble and seethe, but the only happy man is the man who knows that merely to be alive is to be happy (the position of Kirilov in Dostoevsky's *Devils*, it will be remembered, and of William Blake). Undershaft counters by saying that to know that living is happiness requires money enough for a decent life, and power enough to be your own master. (Later, in *Heartbreak House*, Shaw makes Ellie state the same position:

> ELLIE: A soul is a very expensive thing to keep: much more so than a motor car.
> SHOTOVER: Is it? How much does your soul eat?
> ELLIE: Oh, a lot. It eats music and pictures and books and mountains and lakes and beautiful things to wear and nice people to be with. In this country you cant have them without lots of money: that is why our souls are so horribly starved.[28])

It is, in fact, the need for leisure of which I spoke at the beginning of this book. It is Undershaft's reason for preaching a gospel of power. If the Outsider hates modern civilisation for its brutal materialism, his answer is not to retreat from it and go into an ivory tower, but to seek for power over it. Steppenwolf declared that Western civilisation fosters the very delusion of personality from which Eastern civilisation has tried so hard to escape, and his unspoken conclusion is that the Outsider should turn away from our hurly-burly of a civilisation to solitude and contemplation. Shaw implies, like Toynbee, that the Outsider must create the power to revitalise his civilisation. Undershaft has, in fact, anticipated Sartre's doctrine of 'commitment' — it is the essence of all he has to say. Not retreat from the world, but engagement, commitment. If ultimately the aim of spirit is to gain power over matter, then it must face the responsibility of action, and not spend its time complaining that the world is out of joint. Undershaft's positivism is the positivism of the *Bhagavad-Gita*. It will be remembered that in the *Gita*, Arjuna, the hero prince, faces his foes in a chariot, and suddenly decides that fighting is futile — *in fact, reaches the stage of the Hamlet Outsider.* Krishna, his charioteer, tells him not to make a fuss about nothing, for life and death are just a part of a great cycle of the soul; death is not to be considered as a final plunge into blackness, but as a minor inconvenience to be suffered before rebirth into another body. 'There never is a time in which I did not exist; nor is there any future in which we shall cease to be.' [27] And his exhortation reaches its climax in the words: 'Go out and fight. . . . These men are already slain by me,' implying that the actions of gods and heroes are predetermined by a universal law. It is to be observed that Undershaft's positivism is not just the philosophy of a blunt businessman. When Barbara introduces her father to Peter Shirley, the down-and-out Bradlaughite, she says: 'This is my father: I told you he was a Secularist, didnt I?' and Undershaft, shocked, replies: 'Not the least in the world: on the contrary, a confirmed mystic.' Undershaft, has, in fact, advanced to the position of the *Gita* — perhaps without knowing it.

Undershaft presents the Salvation Army with a cheque for £5000, and Barbara leaves the Army in disgust at having to accept the profits of war and murder. But later in the play, she has to face an even greater problem when Cusins, the man she is about to marry, decides to accept Undershaft's offer to go into the armament business as his successor. Then the great argument begins — between Undershaft and Cusins, on the ethics of making weapons of war. Cusins feels that he can salve his conscience by selling guns to any good cause, but Undershaft will have none of this; being an armourer, he says, involves selling to anybody who will pay cash. His morality is a morality of power — but only because he believes that all power is spiritual power. If men are to give spiritual power to the human race, they must begin by having some sort of political power. But not the power of governments or dictators; the power of money and prosperity. Undershaft declares that he is the hidden arbiter behind governments: 'You will make war when it suits us,

and keep peace when it doesnt. You will find out that trade requires certain measures when we have decided on those measures.' [28]
His is very clearly the Nietzschean Master-and-slave morality, but
only because he realises that before the slaves can become Masters,
they must first accept the leadership of the Masters, as a pupil can
only become a teacher by going to school. Undershaft has faced the
Outsider's second problem. The Outsider's first problem is: How
can I acquire spiritual power for myself? and for that purpose, he
retreats into solitude. His second problem is: How can I acquire
spiritual power for a whole civilisation? He may try to solve this
problem as George Fox or John Wesley or Savonarola tried to solve
it. But in a civilisation as complex as ours, a materialist civilisation,
the preacher's effect is inevitably limited, and has to compete with
the cinema and television and cheap literature. The only way left
is Undershaft's way: to strive to become a moving force behind society; to acquire power for one's fellow men by becoming a power
among them.

But Shaw does not make it clear how Undershaft and Cusins will
work to create spiritual power. Cusins summarises his reasons for
accepting Undershaft's offer:

> Cusins: You cannot have power for good without having
> power for evil too. Even mother's milk nourishes murderers as
> well as heroes. . . .
> Barbara: Is there no higher power than that? (*Pointing to a
> shell.*)
> Cusins: Yes, but that power can destroy the higher powers
> just as a tiger can destroy a man: Man must master that power
> first. I admitted this when the Turks and Greeks were last at
> war. My best pupil went out to fight for Hellas. My parting gift
> to him was not a copy of Plato's Republic, but a revolver and a
> hundred Undershaft cartridges. . . . That act committed me to
> this place for ever. Your father's challenge has beaten me. Dare
> I make war on war? I dare. I must. I will. . . .[29]

In other words, if the corruption of our society is to be fought,
the Outsider must fight it from inside, not outside.

This is not to be taken as Shaw's last word on the subject. All that he has expressed, through Undershaft, is the doctrine that the Outsider must leave his ivory tower when the time comes. The time is not ripe until he has achieved spiritual power over himself. And an Outsider might well feel, with Gurdjieff, that his degree of power over himself is always so tiny that he should stay in solitude all his life.

After *Major Barbara*, Shaw produced a whole series of light plays: *The Doctor's Dilemma, Getting Married, Misalliance, Androcles and the Lion, Pygmalion.* In the ten years after 1905, when *Major Barbara* was written, Shaw's disciples had reason to suppose that the Master was growing frivolous in his old age. *Androcles* has a magnificent preface examining Christianity (to which I am indebted for many of the ideas expressed in the introduction to Part Two of the present book). But the play itself is a salt-and-sugar mixture of farce and seriousness which produces an impression of cheapness. The important second act has the Heidegger-like theme of the 'glimpse of reality' experienced while facing death:

> LAVINIA: . . . my faith has been oozing away minute by minute whilst Ive been sitting here, with death coming nearer and nearer, with reality becoming realler and realler, with stories and dreams fading away into nothing.
> THE CAPTAIN: Are you then going to die for nothing? . . .
> LAVINIA: I dont know. If it were anything small enough to know, it would be too small to die for. I think I'm going to die for God. Nothing else is real enough to die for.
> THE CAPTAIN: What is God?
> LAVINIA: When we know that, Captain, we shall be gods ourselves.[30]

After this, the dancing lion is an altogether irritating piece of buffoonery.

Heartbreak House, the next major work, is an unsuccessful attempt to write a Chekhovian play. Chekhov's method depends on understatement, suggesting the tensions and tragedies beneath a surface of futility and inaction. But Shaw is not an emotional writer, and he does not succeed in conveying the hidden torment of his characters. In spite of this failure of conscious intention, *Heartbreak House* still succeeds in being one of Shaw's best plays. Written two

years before *The Decline of the West* was published, it nevertheless captures the atmosphere of that book. The play is about a
houseparty at 'Heartbreak House'; the guests are a cross section of
English society: Mangan, the businessman, Ellie, the girl who is
going to marry him for his money, her father, a helpless idealist who
has been swindled by Mangan, Lady Utterword, the typical English
lady, wife of a colonial governor and a lover of horses, Randall, a
useless man-about-town. But more important than any of these are
the residents of 'Heartbreak House': Hector Hushabye, the ro-
mantically handsome liar, his wife Hesione, and Captain Shotover.
Shaw rightly considered Shotover one of the greatest characters he
had ever created. Shotover is a strange old man, a retired sea captain, who is the only person in this houseparty of Insiders who has
any sense of reality. He spends his days trying to achieve 'the
seventh degree of concentration.'

This is an idea of primary importance for the Outsider, and Shotover's statement of it is perhaps the clearest single statement of the
Outsider's ultimate aim which we have yet encountered. After all,
consider almost any Outsider who has been mentioned in this volume or its predecessor: their problem is always the fact that the
world is 'too much with them.' What all Outsiders have in common
is a desire to escape the endless confusion of the outer world and
retreat deep into themselves. Truth is subjectivity, and is therefore
to be achieved by becoming concentrated in oneself. Ordinarily,
when a man concentrates on a problem, he only retreats into the
conscious area of his brain, the reasoning area. But there are deeper
areas — the areas where all the past is stored up, the areas from which
those sudden bursts of complete ecstasy flood up into consciousness.
By lowering himself down into himself, as into a deep mine-shaft,
man discovers the source of the secret life, the wellspring of life
ecstasy which drives him on in spite of the difficulties of the exterior
world. All life is a struggle to reach this inner power, and to assimilate the endless complexities of the outer world, which sap the
energies and destroy the appetite for life. The misery of the Barbusse type of Outsider is due to his having been trapped in that
surface world of consciousness, and separated from the inner love
of life. All the work of D. H. Lawrence is about the sudden contact with that flood of inner ecstasy achieved in sexual union. When

Ramakrishna seized a sword to kill himself, his spirit concentrated into a tight ball inside him and suddenly made him recognise that he contained a powerhouse of life energy: a powerhouse which he could only describe by speaking of 'a great sea of life'; this was his first 'vision' of godhead. Van Gogh was in contact with this inner powerhouse many times, and so was Nietzsche. Rimbaud achieved inner concentration by dramatising himself as the arch-Outsider and anti-social being, and thus freeing his consciousness from the feeling that he owed the outer world his attention. All genius springs from this ability to concentrate.

Even so, no man has ever achieved complete concentration. A poet's moments of ecstasy are nothing compared to the powerhouse of vitality which he contains within himself. Most poets achieve the first degree of concentration. A saint like Ramakrishna might achieve the second degree. Shotover spoke of seven degrees, and strove to achieve them all.

He doesn't, of course. He is too old. Yet the mere fact that he has had the idea makes him great, and his greatness is the greatness of *Heartbreak House*. His son-in-law, Hector, is an altogether lower-stage Outsider. Hector is a complete romantic who lives in a dream world of heroic actions. One of the most amusing passages in the first act is when Hector, alone, begins to strike attitudes, kiss imaginary women, duel with imaginary opponents; suddenly, Shotover walks in, and Hector has to account for his tense attitude by pretending that he is doing exercises. There then ensues a dialogue which is of great importance to Shaw's Outsider-position. Shotover is carrying dynamite, and he says it is to kill fellows like Mangan. He will make a dynamite that Mangan and his like cannot explode — when he achieves the seventh degree of concentration.

SHOTOVER: We must win powers of life and death over them. . . . I refuse to die until I have invented the means.

HECTOR: Who are we, that we should judge them?

SHOTOVER: What are they that they should judge us? Yet they do, unhesitatingly. There is enmity between our seed. They know it, and act on it, strangling our souls. They believe in themselves. When we believe in ourselves, we shall kill them. . . .

HECTOR: . . . I tell you I have often thought of this killing of human vermin. Many men have thought of it. Decent men are like Daniel in the lion's den: their survival is a miracle; and they do not always survive. . . . Give me the power to kill them, and I'll spare them in sheer. . . .

SHOTOVER (*cutting in sharply*): Fellow feeling?

HECTOR: No. I should kill myself if I believed that. I must believe that my spark, small as it is, is divine, and that the red light over their door is hell fire. I should spare them in simple magnanimous pity.

SHOTOVER: You cant spare them until you have the power to kill them. At present they have the power to kill you. . . .

HECTOR: They are too stupid to use their power.

SHOTOVER: Do not deceive yourself: they do use it. We kill the better half of ourselves every day to propitiate them. The knowledge that these people are there to render all our aspirations barren prevents us having the aspirations. . . .[31]

It is true that at the end of the play, it is Mangan who is blown up by the bomb, trying to save his own skin, and the others, who flood the house with lights so the raiders will see them, who are spared. But the moral is not that we should simply leave it to providence. Once again, Shaw is advising engagement: the Outsiders must achieve political power over the hogs. In *Man and Superman*, Don Juan had pointed out that although the Life Force is stupid, the forces of death and degeneration are even stupider. This can be immediately applied to the Outsiders, and the Insiders who are the leaders of society.

Ellie is also an Outsider in the sense of not knowing what she wants out of life except 'freedom.' Shotover tells her:

You are looking for a rich husband. At your age I looked for hardship, danger, horror, and death, that I might feel the life in me more intensely. I did not let the fear of death govern my life; and my reward was, I had my life. You are going to let the fear of poverty govern your life; and your reward will be that you will eat, but you will not live.[32]

It is again the Outsider's credo: Salvation lies in extremes. But he cannot make any suggestions about Ellie's alternative to marrying

Mangan; her statement that her soul needs to eat just like her body is unanswerable. Yet Shotover is certain of one thing: there must be more consciousness, more purpose and direction; not merely in the individual, but in our whole civilisation, if it is not to smash. Mazzini Dunn, Ellie's idealist father, comments that in politics one can drift as much as one likes: nothing happens.

> SHOTOVER: At sea nothing happens to the sea. Nothing happens to the sky . . . Nothing happens, except something not worth mentioning.
> ELLIE: What is that, O Captain, my captain?
> SHOTOVER (*savagely*): Nothing but the smash of the drunken skipper's ship on the rocks, the splintering of her rotten timbers, the tearing of her rusty plates, the drowning of the crew like rats in a trap.
> ELLIE: Moral: dont take rum.
> SHOTOVER: That is a lie, child. Let a man drink ten barrels of rum a day, he is not a drunken skipper until he is a drifting skipper. Whilst he can lay his course and stand on his bridge and steer it, he is no drunkard. It is a man who lies drinking in his bunk and trusts to Providence that I call the drunken skipper, though he drank nothing but the waters of the River Jordan.[33]

Again, Shaw's meaning is plain: the Outsider must find a direction and commit himself to it, not lie moping about the meaninglessness of the world.

After *Heartbreak House*, Shaw prepared himself for the great effort: the attempt to treat the Outsider's problems in their widest context. He tried to do this in *Back to Methuselah*. Unfortunately, he still had the terrible habit of mixing farce and seriousness, and the play is too painful a mixture of these to be his masterpiece. Nevertheless, as always with Shaw, the ideas are alive, no matter how uncertain the artistic achievement may be. It does not provide a complete solution; there are many things that can be added to it in the light of Toynbee and Whitehead. Nevertheless, it is, taken as a whole, Shaw's most important achievement.

His long Preface has a very simple theme, one which has already been treated many times in the course of this book: the rise of ma-

terialism, and the need for a new religion. The Preface — one of
Shaw's most lucid and witty pieces of writing — speaks of the unbelief of the Victorian era, and the rise of Darwinism and Marxism.
Shaw points out that Darwin tried to reduce life to a mere biological mechanism, but that Lamarck had advanced a far more sensible theory of evolution long before Darwin. Lamarck suggested that
species evolve because they want to evolve; Darwin thought they
evolved automatically, because their conditions altered. Finally,
Shaw makes the crucial statement: '. . . I had always known that
civilisation needs a religion as a matter of life or death.' He asks
the question: 'What religion?' and admits that he himself finds a
religious attitude easy enough to accept. This is the religious attitude which I outlined in *The Outsider*. Shaw calls it 'Vitalism.'
But how is this religion to be made universal? Is it to be taught in
schools? Are children to be told about Lamarck and Darwin instead
of about Jesus? No: for the legends and stories of saints are essential to religion, and so is a Church. But, Shaw asks, why not pool
all the religious legends of the world, and teach schoolchildren not
only about Jesus but about Gautama and Zarathustra and Krishna
too? In science, he points out, you can take the truth and leave the
myth: you do not have to believe that Newton lay down in an
orchard before you can believe the theory of gravitation. But most
Churches nowadays are insisting upon the mythical elements as being vital to the truth of their religion: the Vicarious Atonement,
the Assumption of the Virgin, and all the rest. The consequence
is that the educated man becomes a sceptic, and declares that his
religion is humanity.

Since Shaw propounded this idea, many thinkers have taken it
up: notably Aldous Huxley and Arnold Toynbee. Huxley has also
argued that there is a kernel of truth common to all religions, out
of which a new world religion can be manufactured. Toynbee has
recently expounded the same view in his *Historian's Approach to
Religion*.

Now no good Catholic or Hindu could be blamed for rejecting
this idea as inadequate. It is difficult to think of such an ersatz religion as anything other than a sort of thin soup. No one who examines the problem closely can fail to agree that there is nothing to
be gained by trying to manufacture a new religion — especially in

our intellectual workshops. Yet the alternatives are too awful to contemplate. Any honest person who considers the problem is bound to feel the need to take up some 'attitude': to *commit* himself. And this is just what the very nature of the problem makes it almost impossible to do.

In *Methuselah*, Shaw tries strenuously to define our dilemma. Like Whitehead in *Science and the Modern World*, he opens with an attack on scientific materialism. '. . . People were unable to understand . . . why I habitually derided Neo-Darwinism as a ghastly idiocy, and would fall on its professors slaughterously in public discussions.' [34] He then goes on to speak of the appalling results of Darwinian materialism in politics — he is referring to the 1914 war — and points out, like Toynbee, that civilisations invariably collapse at the point where man's power outruns his religion. 'What hope is there, then, of human improvement? According to the Neo-Darwinists, to the Mechanists, no hope whatever, because improvement can only come through some senseless accident. . . . But this dismal creed does not discourage those who believe that the impulse that produces evolution is creative. They have observed the simple fact that the will to do anything can and does, at a certain pitch of intensity set up by conviction of its necessity, create and organise new tissue to do it with. To them therefore mankind is by no means played out yet.' [35]

Now Shaw introduces the most important idea of the play: 'Among other matters apparently changeable at will is the duration of human life. Weismann, a very clever and suggestive biologist who was unhappily reduced to idiocy by Neo-Darwinism, pointed out that death is not an eternal condition of life, but an expedient introduced to provide for continual renewal without overcrowding.' This suggestion is developed in the play itself. Shaw's diagnosis can be summarised: Human beings are fools because they have no time to be wise. They are thrown down into the world, not knowing who they are or what they are supposed to do. Some of them instinctively feel that life should have a purpose and meaning, and manage to imbue their own lives with a certain direction. These we call men of genius. But the majority take the world much as they find it, and are contented if they can keep alive and well fed, and live and die as their parents lived and died. These are the In-

siders. They are necessary to keep the race moving — to provide
the solid bedrock of stability and ordinariness that life builds on.
(Thomas Mann had such an admiration for them that they are the
heroes of many of his books.) Even the men of genius — or the
Outsiders, who are men of genius in embryo — never have enough
time to really settle down in the world with a serene sense of purpose, and to set out to create more consciousness for the human race
in full knowledge of what they are doing. For the strength of the
Outsider and the man of genius lies in his inner life, and the world
is a complicated place which demands a great deal of attention.
Often, by the time an Outsider has fought his battles, and developed courage and certainty, and has started to feel 'at home in the
world,' it is time for him to leave it. There are two obvious remedies, not mutually exclusive: to become mature much younger, or
to live much longer. And maturity does not mean mere technical
accomplishment. It means the *real* maturity — the maturity of
which Goethe talked in *Wilhelm Meister* — the ability to grasp the
meaning and purpose of human existence. In *Methuselah,* Shaw en-
visages the human race achieving both these ends.

But even if the Outsiders succeeded in solving their Outsider
problems and then extending their term of life to apply their new
sense of purpose — what about the Insiders? In his play, Shaw
solves the problem by making the Insiders gradually die out as
superfluous. But the real problem would be for the Outsiders, as
usual, to find some way to persuade the Insiders to understand the
problems and their solution. An Outsider-Prophet invented Christianity, but the Church found its own means of making Christianity
acceptable to the masses. And in his Preface, Shaw recognises that
it would be no solution if the Outsiders all went off on to an island
(as they do in the play) and left the Insiders to their own devices.
The difference between the Insider and Outsider is the difference
between a man capable of thinking of nothing but personal appetites
and ambitions, and the man driven by something greater than his
own personality. The problem of the Outsiders has always been to
persuade the Insiders to obey the same laws as Outsiders, and for this
purpose they have constructed religions with their laws and commandments. The aim of the Church has always been to persuade
men to behave as if they were something greater than a bundle of

appetites and perceptions. In the twentieth century, science has told man that he is just that and no more. The effects are not immediate and catastrophic; they simply lead to a slow disintegration of our society. But even if the Outsider recognises that scientific materialism is the real villain (the materialism symbolised by Boss Mangan in *Heartbreak House*), the problem of how to uproot it and replace it still remains. Shaw says, with admirable insight: 'As long as the Church of England preaches a single doctrine that the Brahman, the Buddhist, the Mussulman, the Parsee, and all the other sectarians . . . cannot accept, it . . . will remain what it is at present . . . a danger to the State, and an obstruction to the fellowship of the Holy Ghost!' [36] But his solution is too simple: 'What we should do, then, is to pool our legends and make a delightful stock of religious folklore on an honest basis for all mankind. With our minds freed from pretence and falsehood we could enter into the heritage of all the faiths.' [37] If some council of Vitalists were convened to discuss the problems of our society, they might well agree that the ideal would be to create a new Church, whose intellectual foundations could be left to the Outsider-philosophers, and whose legends could be drawn from every source from the *Popol-Vuh* to the *Prometheus Unbound*. They would then be left with the question of how to bring it home to the ordinary man. In ancient India, the priests could leave this to the average man's fear of nature. The Buddha appealed to an Outsider-sense that the world is a den of misery, and that only religious discipline can save man from it. Christian thinkers relied on the same feeling (early Christians were, after all, mainly oppressed minorities), but also produced Jesus as the Saviour, and an after-life of bliss. Mahometanism promised its followers a sensual paradise after death. In the twentieth century, the scientists have replaced the priests as interpreters of the universe. The relation between Outsiders and Insiders is no longer simplified by the intellectual superiority of the Outsiders; on the contrary, the modern Outsider has no intellectual pretensions in comparison with the Insider scientist and philosopher. He is only distinguished by his sense of 'anguish,' the frustrated longing for spiritual purpose and certainty. Shaw's solution in *Methuselah* is so rudimentary that it ignores most of these difficulties.

Yet even so — even if Shaw does not reveal himself as a systematic thinker in the sense that Kant or Hegel are — he brings the insight of a great artist and poet to the problems which he considers. Certain matters he expresses with brilliant and staggering finality: for instance, the important religious question of discipline, self-control:

As there is no place in Darwinism for free will, or any other sort of will, the Neo-Darwinists held that there is no such thing as self-control. Yet self-control is just the one quality of survival value which Circumstantial Selection must invariably . . . develop in the long run. Uncontrolled qualities may be selected for survival and development for certain periods and under certain circumstances. For instance, since it is the ungovernable gluttons who strive the hardest to get food and drink, their efforts would develop their strength and cunning in a period of such scarcity that the utmost they could do would not enable them to over-eat themselves. But a change of circumstances involving a plentiful supply of food would destroy them. We see this very thing happening often enough in the case of the healthy and vigorous poor man who becomes a millionaire by one of the accidents of our competitive commerce, and immediately proceeds to dig his grave with his teeth. But the self-controlled man survives all such changes of circumstance, because he adapts himself to them, and eats neither as much as he can hold nor as little as he can scrape along on, but as much as is good for him. What *is* self-control? *It is nothing but a highly developed vital sense, dominating and regulating the mere appetites.* To overlook the very existence of this supreme sense; to miss the obvious inference that it is the quality that distinguishes the fittest to survive . . .; all this, which the Neo-Darwinians did in the name of Natural Selection, shewed the most pitiable want of mastery of their own subject, the dullest lack of observation of the forces upon which Natural Selection works. [My italics.] [38]

Here, in a single sentence, Shaw has defined the word 'religion' in the sense in which the Outsider understands it: a highly developed vital sense, dominating the mere appetites. For the poet and visionary, the need for this domination of the appetites is so self-evident that it requires no explanation. For the 'average sensual man,' there is no reason for dominating the appetites beyond the limits set by ordinary worldly prudence. Knowing nothing of visions, or of any way of regarding himself other than as a mere unit of the social body, he has no reason to exercise a will to self-change. True religion means to accept as a norm for all human beings the deepest insights of the prophets and visionaries.

The story of *Back to Methuselah* is so well known that I need waste very few words summarising it. In the first of its five long acts, Adam and Eve decide to set a limit to their term of life, because living for eternity would be intolerable. Already the problem of original sin is present: they cannot bear to live with their own personalities for all eternity. The Outsider's accents begin to echo even in the Garden of Eden: 'I am tired of myself. And yet I must endure myself, not for a day . . . but for ever.' [39] Adam wants to escape from himself, like all the Outsiders of the previous volume, and in order to accomplish this, he decides to die. He has chosen the wrong road — the road of Villiers de l'Isle-Adam's *Axel*. He does not realise that the way of escape from personality must lie forward, not backward. But Eve knows there is another way out of the time-trap: the way of the artist and visionary. She speaks of some of her children who are weaklings and cowards, and yet have a strange power of creation. 'They have not will enough to create instead of dreaming; but the serpent said that every dream could be willed into creation by those strong enough to believe in it.' [40] Adam would like to shed his personality every year, as a snake sheds its skin; Eve's son Enoch has given up his personality to do the will of the Voice that he hears in the hills. Adam impatiently tells her to stop talking and go on with her work — otherwise she will starve. Eve answers: 'Man need not always live by bread alone. There is something else. We do not yet know what it is; but some day we shall find out; and then we will live on that alone. . . .' [41]

The second act jumps forward to 1920, when two brothers have decided that man can live far longer than his average seventy-five years when he understands that only by doing this can civilisation be saved. Dramatically, this act is dull and fatiguing to read; it is devoted mainly to satirising two politicians based on Lloyd George and Asquith. But the 'Gospel of the Brothers Barnabas' is of supreme importance. Franklyn Barnabas predicts a new religion of creative evolution, 'a religion that has its intellectual roots in science and philosophy just as mediaeval Christianity had its intellectual roots in Aristotle,' and the coming of a new type of man who will live for three hundred years. The third act, set two hundred and fifty years later, is a satire on a few British government officials who discover — to their horror — that two of their colleagues — a man and a woman — are over two hundred years old. Again, the satire is no longer witty. In fact, the middle three acts of this play are a justification of Tolstoy's criticism of Shaw — that he lost effect by trying to be funny. The fourth act is almost completely superfluous; it establishes nothing except that the long-livers have now formed their own community. The satire on the 'short-livers' has now become downright tiresome; it has not even the occasional magnificent lines and speeches that make the previous two acts bearable. It is perhaps the appalling boredom of this fourth act which has blinded critics to the greatness of the act that follows it: for almost without exception this last act of the play has been condemned by its critics. This should not prejudice us; for *As Far As Thought Can Reach* is undoubtedly one of the greatest things that Shaw ever wrote.

The time has moved forward thirty thousand years. The world has regained the simplicity of Ancient Greek civilisation. A group of youths and maidens dance in front of a temple. That morning they will have a birth ceremony: a girl is to be born out of an egg. When she is born, she will be as fully developed as a girl of twenty. The youths and girls have nothing else to do but amuse themselves with dancing and games and fine arts — or science, if their bent happens to lie that way. As they dance, an Ancient walks among them in deep meditation — a naked and hairless old man, many centuries old. They crowd around him and ask whether his life of meditation does not bore him. He tells them gravely: 'One moment of the ecstasy of life as we live it would strike you dead.' [42] They agree among themselves that when they reach four years old — the age at which all desire for physical pleasure disappears — they will kill themselves. They cannot imagine any other pleasures than those connected with the body and emotions. A few minutes later we are shown this process of maturing when a sculptor exhibits his latest work: everyone is horrified that he has made nothing but busts of Ancients, but he tells them the legend of Michelangelo, who began by filling the Sistine Chapel with paintings of beautiful naked men and women, but ended by painting prophets and sybils, 'whose majesty was that of the mind alone at its intensest.'

(Inevitably, one is reminded of the lines from Yeats's 'Under Ben Bulben':

> Michael Angelo left a proof
> On the Sistine Chapel roof,
> Where but half-awakened Adam
> Can disturb globe-trotting Madam
> Till her bowels are in heat,
> Proof that there's a purpose set
> Before the secret working mind:
> Profane perfection of mankind.[43]

It is strange that Yeats, who disliked Shaw's work so much, should have come so close to echoing the ideas of *Back to Methuselah*.)

Pygmalion, a scientific prodigy, has manufactured a pair of human beings. He explains that life, like electricity, is conducted by certain kinds of matter of fine organisation. The only difficulty about making life in the laboratory is therefore simply that of making highly organised organic matter. Once the matter is made, it lives automatically. Pygmalion's prodigies get out of hand and accidentally kill their creator; but when the Ancient lays his hand on their heads and tries to raise them to a higher level of life, they die of spiritual exhaustion. Like the human beings of our own age, they lack the will power for self-change.

Their deaths lead to the most interesting scene of this act: the attempt of the Ancients to explain to the young people what the process of maturing actually means. These remarks are an extension of what Tanner said in *Man and Superman*: that the artist's task is to create more consciousness. 'You use a glass mirror to see your face: you use works of art to see your soul.' [44] The artist attempts to give himself greater intensity of life by using art as a sort of crutch for his will power. 'It leads,' the Ancient says, 'to the truth that you can create nothing but yourself.' [45] This is the task in which the Ancients are continually engaged: self-creation. Their purpose can be expressed in a single sentence: Make perfect your will. The Ancients no longer need works of art or literature to act as a crutch to the will; they have 'a direct sense of life,' and can transform their physical shapes by an act of will. They never sleep; they ceased to need sleep at the age of four, when the intellectual world became so exciting that sleep became a tiresome interruption of the delight of thought. (It will be recalled that the *Bhagavad-Gita* credits Arjuna with this same power, and frequently refers to him as 'the conqueror of sleep.') But, they explain, the problem is still that they are slaves of their bodies, and completely reliant upon them. When they have achieved sufficient will power, they hope to be able to master the body completely to the point of ceasing to be at the mercy of accidental death: then they will be immortal. The play ends with the ghosts of Adam and Eve reviewing the history of mankind, and wondering where it will end. Then Lilith, the primeval mother (Ramakrishna's Kali), makes her famous speech, with its phrase: '. . . their life does not fail them even in the hour of their destruction.' [46] The Outsider's problem is, ultimately, the problem of the failure of life: the problem of the escape from personality. In *Methuselah*, Shaw has come closer than any other writer to diagnosing this problem and looking towards a solution.

Strangely enough, this last act of Shaw's play is the one that has excited most condemnation from critics of his thought; and the condemnation is always of the same nature: horror at his conception of the Ancient. The usual epithets applied to the Shavian Ancient are 'dreary,' 'repellent,' 'heartless,' 'abstract.' For the critics who have a grudge against Shaw because of his 'lack of heart,' the Ancient seems to be the culminating insult; they find him as incomprehensible as a late Beethoven quartet would be to a lover of Ivor Novello. Other critics attack the concept of the Ancient from the D. H. Lawrence–Walt Whitman point of view, declaring that it is insane to regard the body as totally unimportant. Here again, I think, there is a misconception; the Ancients are not 'contemners of the body,' any more than Nietzsche's Zarathustra was. Their complete power over it is like an athlete's power over his body: a means to intenser life.

Together with the third act of *Man and Superman*, the last act of *Methuselah* is Shaw's supreme achievement. It is a contribution to world literature the importance of which may not be realised fully for many centuries, for it has the power of vision combined with a deceptive clarity of expression. At the end of the *Methuselah* preface, Shaw expressed the hope that younger hands might soon leave his own work far behind. It may be that younger men will be able to go further than Shaw by standing on his shoulders; but it is unlikely that *Methuselah* will ever be left behind as a work of the religious imagination.

After *Methuselah*, Shaw produced no more important plays. *Saint Joan*, his next play, is certainly very fine theatre; it is also the play by which he is known to many readers who otherwise find his cast of mind unsympathetic. This in itself is enough to make any lover of Shaw suspicious of it. For me, it is as far below Shaw's best work — *Major Barbara* or *Heartbreak House* — as Shakespeare's *King Lear* (in my opinion, at any rate) is below *Hamlet*. The trial scene reaches greatness as drama; but in retrospect, the whole play seems to have nothing to say.

But for readers who may have been misled by the dreary satire of *Methuselah* into believing that Shaw had lost his talent for comedy, the next play is a triumphant disproof. *The Apple Cart* remains Shaw's best comedy, for it has enough seriousness in it to make it weightier than any of his other comedies. Once again, the play is based on the principle of the clash of wills: this time, King Magnus is pitted against his Prime Minister and cabinet. The play has no 'message' in the sense that the middle-period comedies have, but at least Shaw had proved that a man can still be writing at his best at the age of seventy-four, unlike Ibsen, who drained himself dry and completely exhausted his imagination by writing *When We Dead Awaken* at seventy-two.

In the remaining quarter of a century of his life, Shaw wrote eight more full-length plays, and eleven playlets. Some of these are simply not worth reading — a category into which, so far, none of Shaw's work has fallen. Some are interesting ideas that are carelessly handled. For instance, *The Simpleton of the Unexpected Isles* is about the Last Judgement, and really about the question of what constitutes the value of a human being in the 'eyes of God' or the Life Force. When the Angel sounds the trump of the Last Judgement, the useless people simply vanish into thin air. 'The useless people, the mischievous people, the selfish somebodies and the noisy nobodies, are dissolving into space. . . . The lives which have no use, no meaning, no purpose, will fade out. We shall have to justify our existences or perish.' [47] Shaw is really letting his Outsider's impatience with Insiders have full rein; but he does not try to express precisely what it is that justifies the existence of human beings. The Outsider has a deep sense that all human beings are failures; that if there were really a Last Judgement in which every man had to demonstrate that he had lived his life with the fullest possible exercise of his will power and sense of purpose, we would all dissolve into space.

Of these later plays, at least one touches a completely new note. *Too True to Be Good* is a strange mixture of bad comedy and the intellectual tragedy of the postwar period. On the surface, it is just an attempt to write about 'the younger generation,' the generation which Evelyn Waugh was then portraying so brilliantly. On this level, the play is a disappointing farce, which drags on for two acts, with a caricature of T. E. Lawrence thrown in for good measure. But in the third act, an old man appears — the father of one of the 'young people' — and makes long speeches in which, for the first time, the world of the modern Outsider begins to appear in Shaw — the world which Sartre and Aldous Huxley describe.

> Yes, sir; the universe of Isaac Newton . . . has crumbled . . . before the criticism of Einstein. Newton's universe was the stronghold of rational Determinism. . . . Everything was calculable: everything happened because it must. . . . And now — now — what is left of it? . . . All is caprice: the calculable world has become incalculable. . . .[48]

These are the accents of *Mind at the End of its Tether:*

> A frightful queerness has come into life. . . . Hitherto, events have been held together by a certain logical consistency, as the heavenly bodies have been held together by gravitation. Now it is as if that cord had vanished. . . .[49]

Shaw's Elder speaks with the same tones:
'Nothing can save us from a perpetual headlong fall into a bot-

tomless abyss but a solid footing of dogma; and we no sooner agree
to that than we find that the only trustworthy dogma is that there
is no dogma. As I stand here I am falling into that abyss, down,
down, down. We are all falling into it. . . . ' [50] And at the end of
the play, the son of the Elder delivers a long sermon on the loss of
faith and belief caused by the war, and on the demoniacal desire of
the younger generation to strip life naked. (Shaw may be thinking
of Joyce's *Ulysses* or the many other realistic novels that followed
it.) This last act is a curious mixture of greatness and low comedy.
It shows that Shaw had it in him to write a great play about the
entre deux guerres period. Reading this play, it is impossible not to
wish, with Tolstoy, that Shaw had known when to drop his sense
of humour. In his later years, Shaw was, in many ways, a disappointed man, for his effect on his age was far less than he might
have hoped. But it was his own fault; if he had continued to write
with the seriousness of the last part of *Methuselah*, his influence on
his age might have been as great as Dostoevsky's. His power of rising to heights of prophetic greatness always ran in double harness
with a sense of humour that sometimes became puerile. (It may be
that this type of humour is peculiarly Irish: James Joyce is said to
have possessed it, but at least he kept it for his private life.)

After a decade of these appalling comedies, many of Shaw's admirers wished he would stop writing. But with his usual unpre-
dictability, he suddenly produced another extremely fine play, *In
Good King Charles's Golden Days*.

Once again, the play is based on the great Shavian principle of
the clash of wills. The scene is Sir Isaac Newton's house; King
Charles comes to visit him, then George Fox, Sir Godfrey Kneller
(Shaw wanted a painter — Rembrandt would have been ideal, but
his dates did not fit, and Kneller's did), and various mistresses of
the king. Without perhaps fully realising it, Shaw was treating a
situation that symbolised the whole problem of Western culture;
for with George Fox, the religious rebel, and Isaac Newton, the
unconscious originator of so much modern scepticism, he had
touched on the problem of the bifurcation of nature: Fox and Newton represent different aspects of the decline of the Church and the
new epoch of humanism. By throwing in Charles — the Don Juan
figure — Shaw had also unconsciously symbolised the whole of his

own temperament: the thinker, the prophet, the libertine and lover of life.

After *Good King Charles*, there is only one more full-length play, *Buoyant Billions*, written when Shaw was ninety-one. By the standards of the plays of the 'thirties, it is a good play. It also contains something of Shaw's last word on the Outsider question. As the play opens, a father asks his son what he intends to do with his life. The son replies: 'Be a world-betterer,' and explains that world-bettering is the profession of the practical idealist — of Ruskin, Plato, Jesus, Gautama, Luther, William Morris. In this choice of examples, we immediately see the Outsider theme reappearing; Ruskin, the mixture of melancholy aesthete and practical socialist, followed by a number of religious rebels, and finally Morris, the man who managed to lead an enviably balanced life between romantic Outsiderism and practical creativeness.

But Shaw does nothing in particular with his theme. The rest of the play seems to have no connection whatever with it. The potential rebel meets a girl in the middle of the jungle, and follows her back to London trying to persuade her to marry him. She is the daughter of old Bill Buoyant, the millionaire, and the last act of the play is a long discussion between all the members of Buoyant's family in his house. The only interesting member of this family is Secondborn, the mathematical amateur, who has the tremendous line: 'I don't want to be happy. I want to be alive and active.' [51] And Secondborn ends the play by talking in a vein reminiscent of the Shavian Ancient:

And who dares say that mathematics and reasoning are not passions? Mathematic perception is the noblest of all the faculties! This cant about their being soulless, dead, inhuman mechanisms is contrary to the plainest facts of life and history. What has carried our minds further than mathematical foresight? . . . God is not Love: Love is not Enough: the appetite for more truth, more knowledge, for measurement and precision, is far more universal: even the dullest fools have some glimmer of it. . . . Mathematical passion alone has no reaction: our pleasure in it promises a development in which life will be an intellectual ecstasy surpassing the ecstasies of saints. [52]

Shaw's last play, a brief parable called *Why She Would Not,*
deals again with the theme of *Major Barbara:* that man must strive
for social efficiency; for otherwise, all the Outsider's spiritual efforts
count for nothing. At the end, Shaw was unrelenting: his last hero
is completely heartless, but the heartlessness is the ecstasy of a man
whose final loyalty is to life itself, the paradoxical destroyer and
creator symbolised in the Hindu goddess Kali.

Considering Shaw's output since the First World War, it is not
surprising that he failed to have any great influence on the generations that grew up during the war. The first decade of this century
had an atmosphere of slightly irresponsible optimism, but the war
refined artistic sensibility, which in some ways reverted to the
nostalgic mood of the 'nineties. Shaw, Chesterton, Wells, Belloc,
were all 'personalities' stating their convictions. Wilfred Owen,
Joyce, Eliot, Pound, Hemingway, all tried to efface their personalities in their art, and to write again as sensitive recording-instru-
ments. 1900 to 1914 was a prose epoch. 1918 to 1930 was an epoch
of poetry, where the ideal was 'negative capability.' It was natural
that it should be felt that Shaw lacked this negative capability. The
appalling plays of the 'thirties underlined that impression.

But it was not true. The negative capability *was* there — the intense concern with the Outsider's problems (which, I have tried to
show, was really the central preoccupation of the postwar writers).
No doubt if Shaw had died after *Major Barbara,* he would have
been ready for reassessment by the nineteen-twenties, and Eliot
would have pointed out that *John Bull's Other Island* has a profoundly religious standpoint. But Shaw went on, dragging a reputation for being a mere prose writer in an age where all literary art
was supposed to aspire towards poetry.

What of our own age? 'Prose' is reappearing; convictions are
again being affirmed. But this is not therefore merely a return swing
of the pendulum. It is rather a time of digestion; a time for considering the first fifty years of our century as a whole. For the first
time, Shaw can be seen clearly in his relation to Wells on the one
side, and Eliot and Joyce on the other. And it can be seen at once
that he belongs to something far greater than a 'prose' epoch of the
twentieth century. He stands in relation to Goethe and Nietzsche
and Kierkegaard as an existentialist thinker, whose central preoccu-

pations were education (*Bildung*) and religion.

It is difficult to summarise Shaw's contribution to the Outsider problem: it covers so many aspects. He began as a romantic Outsider with a strong practical trait; that is to say, he began as a confirmed Outsider with a strong conviction that the Outsider's problems can be solved. He was lucky in being born with a singularly healthy outlook; he was not subject to moods of deep pessimism. His first apprenticeship was under Dickens and Fielding, Shakespeare and Mozart; his second under Marx and Henry George. If he had been brought up on Wagner and Schiller, Stendhal and Flaubert, his writing would be more acceptable to our age; at least his affinity with Nietzsche and Kierkegaard would be less difficult to grasp. His minor works might have gained, and the novels of his twenties would not have been so bad; but his major work might have lost by it. He was trained in a classical school, and his writing has a classical hardness of outline. Eliot, Joyce and Pound all revolted against romanticism in the end, and became 'neo-classicists' without seeing that Shaw had been a neo-classicist for fifty years. Shaw was always in revolt. At ninety, when he wrote *Buoyant Billions*, he was still irritated by the sloppiness of thought which confused weakness with humanity and sentimentality with intuition, which considered the aim of human life to be happiness, and thought of 'intellect' as a barren and inhuman faculty. He was still fighting the battles that had defeated Nietzsche sixty years before.

In the last analysis, Shaw failed. He towers over the 'successful' writers of his age; nevertheless, the works of his last twenty-five years represent a slow decline, much as he had insisted that men should live longer in order to become greater. Where did the failure lie? At some point in his life, he ceased to develop; and the point can be placed roughly after *Back to Methuselah*. Development — by the existentialist definition — means a steady surmounting of difficulties, the slow absorbing of complexities. Up to *Methuselah*, Shaw had developed his Outsider theme to the point of recognising the need for a new religion: to seeing that the Outsider problem finally becomes a problem of history and civilisation. After *Methuselah*, he relaxed on his laurels and was content to repeat himself. His next major work was his *Intelligent Woman's Guide to Socialism* (1928), a rehashing of all his Fabian pamphlets. In a chapter on 'The Natural Limit to Liberty,' he begins by saying: 'Once for all, we are not born free; and we never can be free. When all the human tyrants are slain or deposed there will still be the supreme tyrant that can never be slain or deposed, and that tyrant is nature.' [53] Admittedly, he is now talking about socialism, and not about ultimate human aims; so it cannot be objected that he is retreating from his gospel in *Back to Methuselah*. Yet his friend Wells had only recently written his own vast summary, *The Outline of History*, and there is no good reason why, after the *Guide to Socialism*, Shaw should not have ventured into the realms of historical philosophy to investigate the religious questions which he raises in *Methuselah*. Alternatively, he might have turned to the study of subjective freedom (as distinguished from social freedom) and developed Captain Shotover's mysticism. Instead, he relaxed for twenty years, and wrote with a carelessness that steadily reduced his reputation among serious writers.

When Shaw is read in the light of the existentialist thinkers, a new philosophical position arises from his work as a whole, a position of which he himself was probably unconscious. It is this: that although the ultimate reality may be irrational, *yet man's relation to it is not.* Existentialism means the recognition that life is a tiny corner of casual order in a universe of chaos. All men are aware of that chaos; but some insulate themselves from it and refuse to face it. These are the Insiders, and they make up the overwhelming majority of the human race. The Outsider is the man who has faced chaos. If he is an abstract philosopher — like Hegel — he will try to demonstrate that chaos is not really chaos, but that underlying it is an order of which we are unaware. If he is an existentialist, he acknowledges that chaos *is* chaos, a denial of life — or rather, of the conditions under which life is possible. If there is nothing but life and chaos, then life is permanently helpless — as Sartre and Camus think it is. But if a rational relation can somehow exist between them, ultimate pessimism is avoided, as it must be avoided if the Outsider is to live at all. It is this contribution which makes Shaw the key figure of existentialist thought.

CHAPTER NINE

WITTGENSTEIN AND WHITEHEAD

Ludwig Wittgenstein was born in Vienna in 1889. He came of a remarkable family. His father was an engineer who became an Undershaft figure in the iron and steel industry of Austria, a man of intelligence and powerful character. His mother had the temperament of an artist; sensitive, highly musical, a close friend of Brahms, she made the Wittgenstein home a centre of culture in Vienna. Ludwig was the youngest of a family of eight, all of them gifted. He was educated at home until he was fourteen, then went to school at Linz for three years. An interest in science had developed since his childhood, and when he left school, he decided to study engineering. He had always shown an ability to make things with his hands (he had constructed a sewing machine when he was a small boy); in his adolescence, this developed into an interest in aeroplanes. (The Wright brothers had made the first machine-propelled flight in 1903, when Wittgenstein was fourteen.) When he was nineteen, and had finished his engineering studies in Berlin, he came to England and registered as a research student in engineering at Manchester University. He remained there for three years and conducted many experiments in aeronautics, including some on the jet reaction engine. Soon, his interests switched to the mathematical problems involved in the design of the propeller, and from there to pure mathematics. He patented some of his inventions in aeroplane design. Yet in spite of his interest in scientific problems, the years of study were not happy. His friend Von Wright (to whose biographical article I am indebted in the following pages) mentions that Wittgenstein probably lived on the border of mental illness, and was always afraid of being driven across it. It is possible that his interest in science and mathematics may have been a deliberate attempt on his part to counterbalance certain 'morbid' tendencies of his mind. The great clarity of all his major writings seems to have a positive *fear* of obscurity and indefiniteness underlying it. Schopenhauer's *World as Will and Idea* influenced him greatly as a very young man, and encouraged in him the same kind of romantic outlook that it had encouraged in Nietzsche. And, like Nietzsche, he turned to the clean, precise outlines of scientific knowledge as an antidote. (Nietzsche, of course, studied philology.)

But one of the major influences on Wittgenstein's development was a reading of Bertrand Russell's *Principles of Mathematics*. Russell had conceived the idea that mathematics and logic are ultimately the same thing. This led him to the notion that philosophy might one day be reduced to a set of mathematical symbols. Kierkegaard, of course, had attacked such an idea half a century before; for if truth is subjectivity — that is, intensity of insight — it is obviously impossible to arrive at it by logic alone. However, Wittgenstein knew nothing of Kierkegaard, and he was intoxicated by Russell's idea. He went to Jena to meet another philosopher who had the same notion — Frege — and was advised by him to go and study under Russell at Cambridge.

In 1912, he was admitted to Trinity College. Cambridge was a hive of intellectual activity. Russell and Alfred North Whitehead had just finished their immense *Principia Mathematica*, and G. E. Moore was at the height of his powers. G. H. Hardy, one of the finest mathematicians of the time, was there, and J. M. Keynes, the economist, who, according to Russell, had 'one of the sharpest intellects I have come across.' With his Teutonic seriousness and his tendency to gloom and introspection, Wittgenstein found Cambridge difficult to understand: it was full of an atmosphere of belief in progress and free thinking. There is a story that Wittgenstein was once having coffee with Russell and Moore, when Russell turned to Moore and said suddenly: 'You don't like me, Moore, do

you?' Moore pondered on this for a moment, and replied: 'No.'
The discussion then turned to other topics. Wittgenstein found
the whole business a little mad. This division of the mind into neat
compartments was beyond his comprehension.

He did not devote himself entirely to mathematics. Music still
remained one of his chief interests — he had been soaked in it
throughout his childhood — and he carried out experiments con-
cerning rhythm in music, hoping it would throw some light on the
problems of aesthetics. In 1913, he went to Norway, and lived on a
farm for a year. Like his fellow countryman Lenau (the romantic
poet, who died insane in 1850), he had a pathetic belief in the
'simple life' (although he never went quite so far as to consider the
backwoods of America as a suitable home for a philosopher). In the
1914–18 war, he fought on the Eastern front, and later in Northern
Italy. When he was taken prisoner in 1918, he was carrying in his
knapsack the manuscript of his most famous book, the *Logisch-
Philosophische Abhandlung*, the *Discussion of Logic-Philosophy*
(whose English translation was given the ponderous title *Tractatus
Logico-Philosophicus* at the suggestion of Moore). The manuscript
was sent to Russell, and also to Keynes and Frege. Russell published
an English translation (with an introduction that infuriated Wittgenstein) in 1922. An attempt at a summary of the *Discussion* must
be left until I have finished speaking of Wittgenstein's life.

When Wittgenstein came out of the army in 1919, one of the
first things he did was to give away all his money. His father's death
in 1912 had placed him in possession of a considerable fortune.
(There had been a period when he was making Rilke an allowance
— anonymously — although he professed not to admire his poetry,
claiming that it was artificial.) He then decided to become a schoolmaster; and actually did teach for six years in various remote villages
in Austria.

It is difficult to understand the full psychological process that lay
behind this action; perhaps one day, letters may be published which
will give us a complete insight into it. One reason is certainly that
during the war he lost faith in the 'logic philosophy' of Russell, and
began to brood on the problems of personality, free will, and the
meaning of life and death. (The consequence is that the *Discussion*
is divided into two types of thinking, and only the earlier parts deal

with logic.) But he had also read Tolstoy's later works, and been greatly influenced by them, and had begun to study the Gospels. In the *Discussion*, he had come to the conclusion that he had solved all the problems of philosophy. No doubt he felt that the next stage was spiritual exercise, a semi-religious self-discipline. His motive in becoming a schoolmaster must have had something in common with T. E. Lawrence's in entering the R.A.F.

Six years of schoolmastering taught him that, in giving away his fortune, he had only deprived himself of leisure. His experiment in living among uneducated villagers was as unsuccessful as Van Gogh's Borinage episode. They were trivial and annoying, and in 1926, he gave up schoolmastering for ever. He was now without money, or means of supporting himself. One of his first thoughts was to enter a monastery — a wish that came to him many times in his life. He actually did go to work as a gardener's assistant in a monastery near Vienna; but decided that his vocation was not for the religious life. He was now completely an Outsider, not knowing what to do or where he belonged. Luckily, one of his sisters came to the rescue, and asked him to design and build a house for her in Vienna. He spent two years on this task, and the result was a severely beautiful structure in concrete, glass and steel. During these two years, Wittgenstein also became interested in sculpture, and developed considerable skill in the modelling of busts.

In spite of his self-chosen seclusion, Wittgenstein was not completely cut off from the philosophical life of his time. A young Cambridge student, Frank Ramsey (who had done a brilliant review of the *Discussion*) came out to see him, and a Viennese professor, Moritz Schlick, was deeply influenced by the *Discussion* and personal contact with him; Schlick belonged to the 'Vienna circle' of thinkers, the original logical positivists. But Wittgenstein himself was never a logical positivist. (Logical positivism — I should mention for uninformed readers — is a kind of Marxist materialism in philosophy.)

A lecture by Brouwer, the 'intuitionist' mathematician (intuitionism might be roughly described as mathematical logical positivism), revived Wittgenstein's interest in philosophy, and in 1929, he returned to Cambridge. He obtained a Ph.D. by presenting the *Discussion* as a thesis, and in 1930 was made a Fellow of Trinity.

During the next few years, he rejected many of the ideas of the *Discussion*, and began to build up an entirely new theory of language. This, like the *Discussion*, became the basis of the school of philosophy known as 'linguistic analysis.' Wittgenstein has the unique distinction of being the founder of two out of the three most important schools of thought in the past thirty years. The third, of course, is existentialism; and, as I shall attempt to show, his whole outlook was far closer to this than to either of the other two.

In 1935, he considered settling down in Russia, but the idea was dropped — perhaps on account of Stalin's purges. But he visited Russia, and then visited Norway again, where he spent a year living alone in a hut. He began to write his second book, the *Philosophical Investigations*. He made several attempts to plan this book, but finally gave up, and left it as a series of notes and aphorisms (published posthumously in 1953). It is interesting to remember that German romantic philosophy in the nineteenth century tended to express itself in this way (Novalis's philosophical fragments, for instance), and that Kierkegaard chose the title *Philosophical Fragments* (or *Crumbs*) for one of his books to emphasise how much he disliked huge systematic books.

In 1937, Wittgenstein succeeded Moore to the chair of philosophy at Cambridge. But he was a highly unorthodox professor. He gave his lectures in his rooms, and by all accounts they were not lectures, but discussions which he led. He never wore a tie, but usually dressed in an old tweed jacket, or a leather lumber jacket with a zip over a soft shirt. He disliked Cambridge and the artificial life there (he once told Karl Britton that when he heard one undergraduate saying 'Oh, really?' to another, he knew he was back in Cambridge). He never ate at high table — he could not bear the smart conversation; on the one occasion when he dined there, he left with his hands over his ears, groaning 'But they don't even *enjoy* doing it.' His rooms in Whewells Court were barely furnished with a bed, a small table and a deck-chair, and he had no books (he felt that the reading of books simply stopped people from thinking for themselves). Moore and Russell still failed to feel much sympathy for his 'Teutonic seriousness,' and Moore attended his discussion groups wearing an expression of disapproval. (He later admitted that he understood very little of what was said.) He was developing his idea that what is usually called philosophy is actually a misunderstanding of language. In the *Investigations*, he says: 'Philosophy is a battle against the bewitchment of our senses by means of language.' [1] What he was trying to do in philosophy had something in common with what James Joyce was trying to do in literature. Joyce did not want to write novels and extend his range through creation of situations; he wanted to find a new *way* of writing novels, and plot and situation would have impeded him; he was experimenting with language. So it was with Wittgenstein. The *Discussion* was his *Ulysses*: a sort of machine gun with which he mowed down all previous philosophical techniques. It would have been an anticlimax for him to start philosophising along the same lines as Russell, or even Whitehead. Instead, he concentrated on the problem of a *new way* of philosophising, a new and rigorous use of language, a revitalising of the language of philosophy. In the *Investigations*, he is still laying the foundations *before* the act of philosophising.

He was not happy as a Cambridge don; he considered giving up his position in order to conduct music. When the war came, he accepted it as a relief from lecturing, and came to London during the blitz. There, he took a job as a hospital porter at Guy's. Later, he went up to Newcastle, and worked in a medical laboratory there. (There had been a time in the 'thirties when he had decided to give up philosophy and study medicine; but the idea came to nothing.)

In the Easter of 1947, he gave his last lectures at Cambridge, and once again thought about going into seclusion. This time, he decided on Ireland — the west coast, near Galway. There he lived in a cottage, and continued work on the *Investigations*. People who knew him there speak of his curious power over birds; a Galway resident has told me of seeing Wittgenstein with his head and shoulders covered with birds, which flew off when he approached.

Life in the cottage was too strenuous as winter came on, and in late 1948, he moved to a Dublin hotel, where he finished the *Investigations*. In 1949, he went to the United States on a visit, and then returned to Cambridge. There it was discovered that he was suffering from a cancer. He died in April, 1951; the last years of his life had been spent in constant work, which continued up to a few days before his death. At the date of writing (1957), only one volume besides the *Investigations* has been published.

I have already said that Wittgenstein believed that his *Discussion* had solved all the problems of philosophy. A brief examination of the book will show why he thought so.

There are, as I have said, two lines of thought in the *Discussion*. The first is a result of his study of Russell and Frege. There would be no point in trying to summarise this aspect here, but his conclusions can be stated briefly. All significant propositions, he maintains, are 'truth functions' of elementary propositions. (A 'truth function' of a simple proposition is a proposition whose truth depends only on the truth of the simple proposition: i.e. if the simple proposition is 'Hitler is dead,' then the 'truth function' is a sentence like 'There is no Füehrer of Germany now that Hitler is dead.') This led Wittgenstein to define 'logical truth' as tautology.

However, this aspect of the *Discussion* is not important here, and I mention it only for the sake of completeness. What is more important about the *Discussion* is that it sets limits to philosophy.

Wittgenstein does this by defining language as a *picture* of reality. In other words, what is not real cannot be said.

He then asks: What is real? and answers: All the *facts* of the universe. He begins the book 'The world is everything that is the case,' (i.e. the world is everything of which one can say 'This is true' — the world is all the *facts* in the universe).

He then goes on (proposition 6.41 — the *Discussion* is divided into numbered propositions for clarity):

> The sense of the world must lie outside the world. In the world everything is as it is and happens as it does happen. *In* it there is no value . . .
>
> Hence also there can be no ethical propositions. Propositions cannot express anything higher. It is clear that ethics cannot be expressed. . . .
>
> 6.423. Of the will as the subject of the ethical we cannot speak.[2]

In other words, language has no business trying to express propositions about ethics, the Will, or life and death. If the meaning of the world lies outside the world, then it cannot be expressed in language, which only expresses what is *in* the world.

Wittgenstein goes on to express certain thoughts about death, immortality, and kindred subjects:

> Death is not an event of life. Death is not lived through.
> If by eternity is understood not endless temporal duration but timelessness, then he lives eternally who lives in the present.[3]

With these last words, the *Discussion* moves into the realm of the mystical. 'Living in the present' does not mean Epicureanism; it means those moments experienced by Dostoevsky's characters, when a single moment seems to be a million years. Wittgenstein goes on to deny the concept of the immortality of the soul (in the Christian sense), and asks: 'Is a riddle solved by the fact that I survive for ever?'[4] He is, of course, attacking only what can be called 'naïve Christianity,' the spiritualist notion that life goes on unaltered in another world after death. When Dante confesses that it is quite impossible to express the beatific vision in words, he is saying something with which Wittgenstein would agree completely. Or, as a certain logical positivist has expressed it: 'What can't be said can't be said, and it can't be whistled either.' (John Tanner, it will be remembered, raises the same point with Enry Straker in the second act of *Man and Superman*.) Wittgenstein asks:

> Is this eternal life not as enigmatic as our present one? The solution of the riddle of life in space and time lies *outside* space and time. . . .
> Not *how* the world is, is the mystical, but *that* it is.[5]

This is the mysticism of Kirilov in *The Devils:* the mere existence of *anything* is a mystical fact — a leaf, a grain of sand. Wittgenstein goes on:

> The feeling of the world as a limited whole is the mystical feeling.
> For an answer which cannot be expressed the question too cannot be expressed.
> *The riddle* does not exist.
> If a question can be put at all, then it *can* also be answered. . . .

We feel that even if *all possible* scientific questions be answered, the problems of life have still not been touched at all. Of course there is then no question left, and just this is the answer.

The solution of the problem of life is seen in the vanishing of this problem.

(Is not this the reason why men to whom . . . the sense of life became clear, could not then say wherein this sense consisted?)

There is indeed the inexpressible. This *shows* itself; it is the mystical.

[Note this doctrine of the mystical which *shows* itself although it cannot be expressed.]

The right method of philosophy would be this. To say nothing except what can be said, i.e. the propositions of natural science, i.e. something that has nothing to do with philosophy: and then always, when someone else wished to say something metaphysical, to demonstrate to him that he had given no meaning to certain signs in his propositions. This method would be unsatisfying to the other — he would not have the feeling that we were teaching him philosophy — but it would be the only strictly correct method.

My propositions are elucidatory in this way: he who understands me finally recognises them as senseless, when he has climbed out through them, on them, over them. (He must so to speak throw away the ladder, after he has climbed up on it.)

He must surmount these propositions; then he sees the world rightly.

Whereof one cannot speak, thereof one must be silent.[6]

This is the last sentence of the *Discussion*. I have quoted the last three pages fairly fully, but omitting to number the paragraphs. It is not a long book — barely eighty pages long. In these eighty pages, however, Wittgenstein has managed to say more than most philosophers in eight hundred. His paragraph about 'throwing away the ladder' is obviously an attempt to anticipate an objection: that if all statements about the meaning of the world are nonsense, are not Wittgenstein's statements in the *Discussion* also nonsense? His admission that this is so does not ring true. If a statement is *really* nonsense, it is like a ladder with no rungs, and one could not climb up it anyway. And if one can climb up it to some higher state of wisdom, then it is certainly not nonsense in the sense that Wittgenstein says metaphysics is nonsense. His statement bears some resemblance to the Buddhist doctrine of repeating the Sutras until their meaning is quite clear, and then no longer having to repeat them. Certainly, as a professor of philosophy, Wittgenstein tried to do what Nietzsche declared to be his own aim: to provoke people to think, not merely to accept what he told them.

Let me briefly summarise Wittgenstein's argument in the *Discussion* in order to try to elucidate these paragraphs. Language is a picture of reality — just as a picture of the stork on a Guinness advertisement is a representation of a real stork. Therefore, language can only picture what actually *is*. And what 'is'? All the facts in the world; that is, not just all the things in the universe, but every possible combination of those things.

If there is a meaning of life, it must lie outside life; that is, it must lie in life considered as a whole. Therefore, all metaphysics (which talks about God, purpose, good and evil, and so on) is meaningless: it cannot be expressed in language. This does not mean that 'God does not exist,' or 'There is no such thing as sin.' It only means that if one uses the word 'God' in a logical sentence, it promptly takes the logic out of the sentence, and renders it meaningless.

The sentence 'The riddle does not exist' (i.e. the 'riddle of life') has been seized on with delight by logical positivists as being a justification for considering all questions about the meaning of life as nonsense. They are ignoring the fact that two paragraphs earlier, Wittgenstein speaks of the riddle quite plainly: 'Is this eternal life not as enigmatic as our present one? The solution of the riddle . . . lies outside space and time.' And his last sentence implies that, as Dante says, a point comes where one cannot use words any more. A logical positivist has quoted this last sentence 'Whereof one cannot speak, thereof one must be silent,' and added: 'That's all right — provided we're agreed that *there's nothing to be silent about*.' Now Wittgenstein has stated very plainly that there is something to be silent about. The logical positivist was merely making a statement about his own temperament — an Insider temperament — and was trying to assert that it ought to fit the whole world. (This argument is considered at length by William James in *The Varieties of Religious Experience.*)

The logical positivist interpretation of the *Discussion*, then, insists on ignoring Wittgenstein's plain statement that the 'mystical' does exist. But what about the other interpretation — the existentialist? Does this fit the *Discussion* any better?

It does, as soon as it becomes apparent that there are certain sentences which must be added to the *Discussion*. The *Discussion* is about the scope of language. (Incidentally, Wittgenstein changed his mind about language being a 'picture of reality' in the *Investigations*.) It assumes that philosophy can only be conducted in language, and that there are certain things which language cannot express. In this, Wittgenstein is obviously partly right. For instance, Kierkegaard set out to attack Hegel's ponderous System because it was inhuman and cold, but wrote a great ponderous inhuman book about it himself (the *Unscientific Postscript*), thus defeating his own purposes. Heidegger tried to 'systematise' existentialism, and has created an anomaly, an 'existentialist system' which is more unreadable than Hegel.

In fact — and this is what I am trying to emphasise — the only way one can talk about the problems of 'meaning' in life is by *showing* them in terms of living people. Jaspers is a better existentialist than Heidegger, for at least he keeps his attention focussed on *men* like Van Gogh, Nietzsche, and Dostoevsky. Let me be even more explicit. One cannot *talk* about the real issues of life: one can only *show* them. Critical language, discursive language, has no meaning other than its logical meaning. But consider Coleridge's *Kubla Khan*, Rilke's Orpheus sonnets, Eliot's *Ash Wednesday*. This language has a meaning quite apart from the 'logical syntax' of the sentences. 'True poetry can communicate before it is understood,' Eliot wrote in his essay on Dante. And one can go further, and say: What true poetry can communicate cannot be expressed in ordinary language.

But there is a still more important point to be made here, and it is this: poetry can present certain mystical issues, but it cannot investigate them. It can only show them in the way that a flash of lightning lights up a landscape. Now Dostoevsky manages to convey far more of such issues in *Crime and Punishment* and *The Brothers*

Karamazov than even Dante was able to express in the *Commedia*, simply because, by examining them in terms of a number of Outsiders, he is able to *show* the reader insights which he could not have expressed if he had been writing a philosophical treatise.

True existentialism cannot be communicated in ordinary logical language; it can only be expressed in the drama, in poetry (and it is no coincidence that Eliot has stated that all great poetry is dramatic in essence), in the novel. True existentialism is the dramatic investigation of human nature through the medium of art. The true existentialist philosopher is the 'artist-philosopher' of whom Shaw spoke in *Man and Superman*.

Only one more statement need be added to complete the circle of this argument: A philosophy which is not existentialist is only half a philosophy; it is philosophy without arms or legs. *All European philosophy since the seventeenth century has been a half-measure.* An abstract philosopher is a half-man.

All this is implied clearly in the *Discussion*. It is ironical, under the circumstances, that the *Discussion* has become the textbook of the most bloodless half-philosophy of the twentieth century.

This is partly Wittgenstein's own fault. He did not fully understand the implications of his own book. Consider, for instance, his sentence about the meaning of life lying outside life, and being therefore unknowable. What does it really mean? One could say, with perfect truth, that the *shape* of a gasometer is only visible from outside the gasometer. The shape of the gasometer cannot be *in* the gasometer. Neither can the meaning of life be in life. This is true enough. But this does not mean that a man in a gasometer would have to go outside to see the shape of the gasometer. All he would have to do would be to turn on the light inside. The shape would be as visible from inside as outside. So the meaning of life can be discerned, by mystical intuition, from inside.

It is a commonplace of *any* religious philosophy that a point comes where one has to stop talking and start submitting to *discipline*. Wittgenstein came to maturity under the influence of Russell, who has always fostered the innocent belief that one can talk one's way to the depths of the universe; that logic is all-sufficient. The *Discussion* was Wittgenstein's revolt against this view, as, indeed, was his life itself, with all the dissatisfaction and constant change, the fear of mental illness, the endless desire to try new ways of self-expression. Engineer, scientist, mathematician, schoolteacher, monk, architect, sculptor, doctor, musician, workman . . . Wittgenstein demonstrates perfectly that the Outsider's problem is the problem of self-expression. At the end of the *Discussion*, he knew it was time to stop talking and start *doing*, submitting to the Outsider's discipline. But like Van Gogh, Lawrence, and Nijinsky, his 'doing' was not satisfactory.

Wittgenstein was a creator *manqué*. That was his problem. If he had gone on from the *Discussion* to write a *Brothers Karamazov*, to discipline himself until he achieved *samadhi* like Ramakrishna, to strive to achieve a state of self-remembering, like Ouspensky, he would have followed the road to self-expression. He knew, as clearly as Gurdjieff knew, that the only purpose of knowledge is to *be more*. He expresses this sense in *Philosophical Investigations*, where he refuses to 'philosophise,' but instead conducts a long and painstaking examination into language, the instrument of philosophy. He knew that a point comes where a man can use words brilliantly, but cannot *change himself*. Knowledge, like art, has only one purpose: to show man his own face. When a schoolboy first learns how to use his mind, he uses it ecstatically; he revels in the power of his intellect. In this stage, the free use of his intellect helps to change him, to develop him. But if he remains a clever schoolboy, brilliant in mind, but immature emotionally and physically, he is worse off than a ploughman, who at least leads a well-balanced life.

The twentieth century has produced this 'clever schoolboy' type of writer in abundance. (Bertrand Russell, Arthur Koestler, Aldous Huxley, are examples, but it would be unfair to pretend that they are the only examples.) And the 'clever schoolboy' is a fitting image for Western civilisation, brilliant in mind, but immature in all other things. We are too 'clever' in the worst sense of the word. When Shakespeare praised Brutus with the words 'This was a man,' he understood the basic condition of life — that it must be complete and balanced. And in order to survive, a civilisation has to be complete and balanced, too. Abstract philosophy is a symbol of Western civilisation. The Outsider is the man who revolts instinctively against abstraction, against our infant-prodigy civilisation. The

Outsider is the man who yearns for a return to ancient standards — the standards which recognise that 'cleverness' is of the intellect alone, that wisdom is a complex of intellect, emotions and body.

Wittgenstein, like all the Outsiders whom we have considered, must ultimately be reckoned a failure. The measure of how far he failed lies in the fact that the two schools which are associated with his teaching are logical positivism and linguistic analysis. Linguistic analysis devotes its time to analysing what the philosophers of the past have said, and objecting: 'But you cannot say that,' or 'That is meaningless . . .' A recognition that abstract philosophy is basically a half-measure would save the linguistic analysts all this effort. There is no point in flogging a dead horse. But Wittgenstein himself failed because he could never resist the temptation of intellect. Intellect never wholly satisfied him, and he was always restless; yet he had to return to philosophising, to analysing, because it was the path of least resistance for his mind. Intellect on its own is a triviality. Wittgenstein never completely surrendered to that triviality; but he never had the strength and insight to put it behind him. After admitting that the really important things cannot be talked about, he went on talking for the rest of his life.

This is not intended to minimise Wittgenstein's importance. He is one of the most important European thinkers since Descartes. Like Nietzsche, he always felt that he was writing for a new type of man. It is certainly true that his significance is not yet fully realised, and will not be until everything he ever wrote is published, and an exhaustive biography produced.

Alfred North Whitehead was born twenty-eight years before Wittgenstein; nevertheless, I have chosen to speak of him later because his philosophy covers a wider ground than Wittgenstein's, and can be better understood in the light of what has been said about the *Discussion*. On the other hand, I do not propose to try to give a complete picture of Whitehead's thought. His philosophy is difficult and technical, and no purpose would be served by trying to present it fully here.

There seems to be very little to tell about Whitehead's life; what little there is, he has recounted himself in half a dozen pages of autobiographical notes at the beginning of the volume on him in

the 'Library of Living Philosophers.' He was born in 1861 at Rams-
gate, Kent, the son of a Protestant clergyman. His childhood was
spent in contact with the idyllic world of a Trollope cathedral
town; in his autobiographical notes he manages to evoke the pic-
turesque background against which he grew up: Richborough
castle, built by the Romans, Ebbes Fleet, where the Saxons and
Augustine landed, and the sixteenth- and seventeenth-century houses
of Sandwich. He attended Sherborne school from the age of fifteen
— a school which can claim Alfred the Great as a pupil, and which
has 'one of the most magnificent abbeys in existence, with tombs of
Saxon princes.' Four years later, he went up to Trinity College,
Cambridge. Unlike Wittgenstein, he loved the place, and remained
there for thirty years, first as a student, then as a don. He became a
Fellow of Trinity in 1885, and, a little later, a senior lecturer in
mathematics. One of his pupils was Bertrand Russell. He married
in 1890, and the marriage was unusually successful. The White-
heads lived in the Mill House at Grantchester — next door to the
Old Vicarage, later to be the home of Rupert Brooke. In 1910, they
moved to London, and from then until 1924, Whitehead taught first
at University College, and then at the Imperial College of Science
in Kensington. In 1924, he was invited to Harvard University. He
lived and taught there until his death at the age of eighty-six in 1947.
His life, on the whole, was serene and untroubled — the ideal life for
a philosopher.

Whitehead's true stature is by no means fully recognised today,
even in America, his adopted country. In England, most of his
works are out of print, with the exceptions of *Science and the
Modern World* and *Adventures of Ideas* (which can be obtained in
Penguins) and a volume of his essays.

Whitehead's greatness lies in the fact that he began as a typical
'abstract philosopher,' and gradually rejected 'abstractionism,' until
he became one of the broadest and most profound minds since
Plato.

His writing can be divided into three periods: a mathematical
period, a scientific period, a religious and metaphysical period. It
is with the last of these that we are mainly concerned; but a brief
summary of the first two may be found useful at this point.

His first book, published when he was thirty-seven, was the

Universal Algebra. It was not (as one might suppose from the title) a textbook for schools, but an attempt to invent a way of performing logical operations by means of symbols. Leibniz had first conceived this idea, reasoning that if the rules of thought could be expressed by algebraic symbols, all logical thinking might eventually be accomplished by means of those symbols. Leibniz never carried through this idea, but a century and a half later, a self-educated English schoolmaster named Boole invented symbolic logic in a book called *The Laws of Thought.* Inspired by him, and by a German called Grassmann, Whitehead tried to invent a set of symbols, whose purpose was that "all serious thought which is not philosophy . . . or imaginative literature, shall be mathematics. . . .'[7] It is worth noting that Whitehead does *not* include philosophy. Unlike Russell, he did not think that philosophy should be nothing but glorified logic.

His second major work was a paper called *Mathematical Concepts of the Material World,* which contains some remarkable anticipations of Einstein's general relativity theory. (Whitehead's paper was read at the Royal Society in 1905, the year in which Einstein's first paper on relativity appeared.)

In 1903, Russell had written his book *Principles of Mathematics,* which covered some of the same ground as the *Universal Algebra,* and now Russell and Whitehead decided to collaborate on producing a volume to systematise this idea of an algebra of logic. For the next six years, they worked in close harmony, producing the immense *Principia Mathematica.* Russell and Whitehead believed that mathematics is simply a branch of logic, and that consequently all mathematical concepts can be reduced to logic. This the *Principia Mathematica* professes to do. But as the book is of extreme complexity, and even expert mathematicians find it difficult to follow, it is impossible to know whether or not it really succeeded. An example of the kind of logical problem which Russell and Whitehead had to surmount (a very famous problem which Russell was the first to recognise) is called the problem of sets that are members of themselves. (A set simply means a collection of objects: a tea set is a collection of tea things; an underwear set is a collection of underwear.) There are two kinds of sets, which can be called ordinary and extraordinary. An extraordinary set is a set that contains itself as one of its own members. For instance 'The set of all phrases of eight words' contains itself as a member, for it contains eight words. But this kind of set is unusual. Most sets do not contain themselves as members: the set of all square objects, the set of all obscene words, and so forth. These are ordinary sets. Now consider the set of *all ordinary sets,* and call it C. Is C a member of itself? If the answer is No, then it cannot be the set of *all* ordinary sets. But if the answer is Yes, then C is an extraordinary set, and contains itself as a member. And this is contrary to the definition, which said that C was the set of all ordinary sets only.

This kind of problem is not particularly profound or important; another famous example is Epimenides's paradox: If I say I lie and I do lie, then I tell the truth; If I say I lie and really tell the truth, then I lie. Such exercises represent a game which most mathematicians have ceased to play.

From 1919 until 1922, Whitehead produced three books: *The Principles of Natural Knowledge, The Concept of Nature,* and *The Principle of Relativity.* These are his three 'scientific books.' They were an attempt to construct a philosophy of Nature; and he defined Nature as 'that which we observe . . . through the senses.' In other words, Whitehead treated Nature in the way which is anathema to the existentialist, behaving as if it were something at the other end of a telescope. This method, which is natural to the scientist (for whom nature *is* something at the other end of a telescope — or microscope) is the method of 'abstract philosophy.' For Blake and Wordsworth, Nature was a living entity, which could only be understood if it was regarded as in some way a reflection of God, or the human spirit. Whitehead ploughed on with his analyses of space and time and four-dimensional geometry, doing his best to create a complete philosophy of Nature, treating nature as the scientist treats it. But he soon began to find all kinds of difficulties arising. He discovered that, sooner or later, the philosopher *has* to start talking about the mind observing Nature. In this limited space, it is impossible to explain how this came about (apart from which, the three books in question are full of mathematical terminology, and questions about space and time, objects and events, which would be comprehensible only to a reader with special knowledge of his earlier books). All that need be said here is that Whitehead came to feel that a purely scientific approach to philosophy is an impossibility. His curious, probing mind began to ask questions about the role of the human observer in Nature. In the *Principles of Natural Knowledge*, he had written: '. . . none of our perplexities as to Nature will be solved by having recourse to the consideration that there is a mind knowing it.' [8] But more and more, in the course of the investigation, he found that the idea of 'a mind knowing it' could not be kept out. Not only that, but that there can be no idea of Nature without the idea of a mind knowing it.

Where exactly does Whitehead's 'theory of relativity' differ from Einstein's? This question cannot be answered without assuming some slight knowledge of Einstein's theory. It will be remembered that Einsteinian relativity talks about 'the curvature of space,' and other similar concepts; in fact, it claims that space can only be adequately understood by a mathematician. (These ideas of the curvature of space, and the notion that space is 'twisted' around the objects that exist in it, have been popularised by Jeans and Eddington — also the idea that space is really only the relation between material bodies, not a 'thing' in its own right.) Whitehead felt that the whole idea of 'points' in space is inadequate — you cannot mark a 'point' in space with your fountain pen, as you can mark a point on a sheet of paper. So for these 'points' of Einstein, he substituted the idea of *events*, and elaborated a theory of space as the relation between events. This is all that can be said without becoming unintelligible; but the idea is not particularly important for what I shall have to say about Whitehead. If Whitehead's ideas ever become widely accepted, though, it may be necessary to revise Einstein's theory completely.

In *The Principle of Relativity*, Whitehead made a particularly important statement about the 'bifurcation of nature.' He comments that when the scientist knocks a molecule to pieces, he does not see a molecule, but a flash of light. The same scientist will then say: 'Yes, this is what *I* saw happening [the flash of light], but what really happened is. . . .' He is making a sharp bifurcation (division) of the world into things as they really are and things as they seem. Whitehead protests: 'Nature is . . . a totality including individual experiences, so that we must reject the distinction between nature as it really is and experiences of it which are purely psychological.

Our experiences of the apparent world are nature itself.' [9] [My italics.]

We now come to Whitehead's most important period, his metaphysical period, which lasted until the end of his life. This is the period where Whitehead's thought can throw some light on the problems of the Outsider.

In *Science and the Modern World*, the first book he wrote after becoming a Harvard professor, he launches his attack on 'abstract philosophy' — an attack which was not to cease for the remaining quarter of a century of his life. He states: 'My theme is the energising of a state of mind in the modern world . . . and its impact upon other spiritual forces.' [10] The phrase 'energising of a state of mind' is particularly apt in this connection. That is just what happened when science began to develop: it gave the scientists tremendous mental energy — the energy of idealism — the ideal of man becoming godlike through knowledge. What Whitehead sets out to show in *Science and the Modern World* is just why mankind has not become 'godlike' through science.

Even on the surface, *Science and the Modern World* is an unusual book; one does not expect to find Milton, Shelley, Wordsworth, the Bible, quoted in a volume on philosophy; but from the beginning of this book, Whitehead's mind ranges as freely through literature and philosophy as Toynbee's. (Whitehead and Toynbee have a great deal in common as thinkers.) Its argument is one which has now appeared many times in the course of this book, that the result of placing too much weight on intellect alone is lopsided confusion. If Whitehead had been acquainted with Spengler and Toynbee, he might have added that this confusion is the direct cause of the decline of our civilisation.

He puts the problem with unexampled clarity. Scientific materialism ends with the view that there is no mind, only matter, and 'spirit' is an outcome of matter. Berkeley went to the other extreme, and said there was no matter, only mind. Berkeley was a bishop, and he was attempting to refute the materialistic view of the universe. The truth, Whitehead says, lies between the two. Complete materialism denies that man has any free will. It asserts that the human body and the human mind are subject to the 'laws of nature,' and that nature is dead. There is only one clear logical alternative:

to state that nature is alive, that the human body is more alive, and that the human mind is more alive still; that life pervades the whole of nature as the 'ether' was once supposed to pervade the whole of space. (This, of course, is the Shavian view, expressed in *Back to Methuselah*.) Whitehead denies that his doctrine of 'organism' (this is what he calls his idea) is the same thing as 'vitalism.' But he is only denying the validity of Bergson's vitalism, in which life squeezes its way into matter through the tiny gap called 'living bodies.' (A man is a 'higher being' simply because he is a bigger hole than an animal.) Whitehead conceives the whole of nature as a single organism, like one living body — as Shaw does in *Methuselah* — and all events in it as 'biological cells.' (He speaks of events rather than objects because he thinks of nature as a *four-dimensional* continuum.)

What Whitehead is attempting to do in *Science and the Modern World* is to assert that the poets are right, and the scientists wrong. The 'nature' that Wordsworth lóved and worshipped is closer to the reality than the 'nature' that Newton talks about. But Whitehead is not willing to leave it at that. He wants to build an unassailable 'scientific' doctrine of nature which conforms to the insights of poets like Shelley and Wordsworth. This is the essence of his 'philosophy of organism.'

It can hardly have failed to strike readers that Whitehead's aim and my own (in *The Outsider*) have a great deal in common. Both views begin with a rejection of scientific materialism (and its natural rejection of religion) and an appeal to the *psychological foundations* of common sense. One cannot ignore half of life for the purposes of science, and then claim that the results of science give a full and adequate picture of the meaning of life. All discussions of 'life' which begin with a description of man's place on a speck of matter in space, in an endless evolutionary scale, are bound to be half-measures, because they leave out most of the experiences which are important to us as human beings. The general feeling of the scientist — the 'abstract philosopher' who would like to tie up the universe into a neat parcel — is that 'art' is irrelevant, a mere meaningless by-product of our animal functions. Compare this attitude with that of Beethoven, who said, 'He who understands my music will not be tormented by the ordinary difficulties of life.' Beethoven felt that he, as a man, had used music to gain a certain power over his own life — over the complexity of his own experience — and that his music, apprehended intuitively, would teach other people to gain the same mastery.

And here we come to one of the most important concepts in Whitehead, the concept which forms his link with existentialism, and with the idea of *Bildung* in Goethe (and Goethe, it must be remembered, also believed that all nature is a single living organism) — Whitehead's idea of *prehension*. This can be best defined by quoting a passage from his last book, *Modes of Thought:*

> . . . the notion of life implies a certain absoluteness of self-enjoy-ment. This must mean a certain immediate individuality, which is a complex process of *appropriating into a unity of existence* the many data presented as relevant by the physical processes of nature. Life implies the absolute, individual self-enjoyment aris-ing out of this process of appropriation. I have, in my recent writings, used the word 'prehension' to express this process of appropriation. Also I have termed each individual act of imme-diate self-enjoyment an 'occasion of experience.' I hold that these unities of existence, these occasions of experience, are the really real things which . . . compose the evolving universe, ever plung-ing into the creative advance.[11] [My italics.]

Prehension, in other words, is the act of reaching out to grasp experience. That 'hunger for experience' of which Henry James speaks in Isabel Archer and Milly Theale is a prehensive hunger. Wilhelm Meister's process of self-education was a process of pre-hension. Prehension is that act of the soul, reaching out like an octopus to digest its experience. When Evan Strowde asked 'How can the spirit of man gain power over his prosperity?' he might have expressed himself, 'How can the spirit of man prehend his prosperity?' Prehension is the act of gaining power over experience. The only question in which existentialism is interested with regard to a human being is: Master or slave? Master of his own complexity, or the slave of it? Prehension is the most fundamental activity of life. Man is a higher type of creature than the amoeba simply be-cause he has developed a greater power of prehension: an ability to master his own chaos. When, in *Methuselah*, Pygmalion's male creature (whom he had made in his laboratory) dies with the words: 'I am discouraged. Life is too heavy a burden,' he is confessing his inability to make an act of prehension of the complex world of A.D. 31,920. Shaw's term 'discouragement' (which first occurs in the fourth part of the *Methuselah* cycle) is the natural counterpart of Whitehead's prehension.

Prehension, then, is the most fundamental term of an existentialist philosophy. It means the same as Goethe's *Bildung*, but it has a far wider meaning than the term 'education.' Education means a conscious addition to knowledge. *Bildung* has a far wider sense of 'growing to maturity.' To a large extent, this growing to maturity is unconscious; the amount of conscious effort most of us *make* to grow is minimal. But Elijah's protest about being no wiser than his fathers (with which I began this book) underlines the fact that man grows for a limited period only, and then stops; *beyond that, a conscious effort of prehension is needed*. And what man 'prehends' are the actual units of his living experience, which Whitehead calls 'events,' or 'occasions of experience.'

In 1926, Whitehead produced one of his shortest, yet most important books, *Religion in the Making*. He states his aim in the first paragraph — to consider the justification for belief in doctrines of religion. He goes on to draw attention to the difference between religion and arithmetic. Arithmetic dawned on the mind of man over a long period as a simple form of objective truth: 'One cow plus two cows makes three cows.' But religion never 'dawned' as objective truth; it was always an internal condition in man. One can hold mathematical truths at arm's length and look at them; but religion is tangled up with man's insides, and man never knows himself as well as he knows that one and one make two. Religion is man's relation to life and death, and is a function of the parts of him that he knows least about: the will, the sense of purpose:

> Religion is force of belief cleansing the inward parts. For this reason the primary religious virtue is sincerity, a penetrating sincerity. . . . Religion is the art and the theory of the internal life of man. . . .[12]

Whitehead denies that religion is primarily a social fact, and asserts its real significance in Outsider terminology:

... most psychology is herd-psychology. But all collective emotions leave untouched the awful ultimate fact, which is *the human being, consciously alone with itself*, for its own sake. ... Religion is what the individual does with his own solitariness. ... Thus religion is solitariness; and if you are never solitary, you are never religious.[12] [My italics.]

And finally, at the conclusion of one of the most penetrating studies of religion since James's *Varieties of Religious Experience*, Whitehead writes: 'God is that function in the world by reason of which our purposes are directed to ends which in our own consciousness are impartial as to our own interests. He is that element in life in virtue of which judgement stretches beyond facts of existence to values of existence.'[13] The 'facts of existence,' that 'irreducible and stubborn fact' which he wrote about at the beginning of *Science and the Modern World*, comprise the element that makes for meaninglessness — as when Sartre's Roquentin sat on the bench and felt that it was grotesque, shapeless, nameless. If the mind had lost its power of prehension, all nature would look like that seat; failure of prehension is '*la nausée.*' God is expressed in nature as this endless effort of prehension. This effort of prehension is not, as Whitehead points out, anything to do with our immediate personal needs; it is for something altogether greater. A man becomes great in so far as he expresses the will of God, which is an eternal act of prehension in life.

Whitehead's major statement of his position is made in the immense volume *Process and Reality*, published in 1929. This is by far Whitehead's most important book, but one which it is impossible to summarise in a study as brief as this. He begins with his well-known statement that 'philosophy is the endeavour to frame a coherent, logical, necessary system of general ideas in terms of which every element of our experience can be interpreted.'[14] Note the phrase '*every* element' — that is, not just the things we can reason about, but the sensation of listening to music, the effect of a painting, those moments of which Proust speaks when the past is suddenly evoked by a casual word or action. Whitehead never thought of philosophy as a strictly limited field, as Wittgenstein did. He declared that philosophy should be the critic of abstractions, serving to keep abstractions in their proper place, and 'completing them by comparison with more concrete intuitions of the universe.'[15] And in *Modes of Thought*, he states what he means by 'concrete intuitions':

> Nothing can be omitted, experience drunk and experience sober, experience sleeping and experience waking, experience drowsy and experience wide-awake, experience self-conscious and experience self-forgetful, experience intellectual and experience religious and experience sceptical, experience anxious and experience care-free, experience anticipatory and experience retrospective, experience happy and experience grieving, experience dominated by emotion and experience under self-restraint, experience in the light and experience in the dark, experience normal and experience abnormal.[16]

Wittgenstein's retort to this would be, probably, that so far no language has been invented which could incorporate all these things into a philosophy. He might agree, though, (and Whitehead certainly would) that the novelist is better qualified to absorb all this experience than the philosopher. Shakespeare or Tolstoy have come far closer to it than Hegel.

After *Science and the Modern World*, Whitehead's most readable book is *Adventures of Ideas*. The knotty, difficult prose of *Process and Reality* is dropped, and once again there is an abundance of illustration from literature, philosophy, and many other sources. The book is an application of Whitehead's philosophy of organism to various fields of practical human experience; there is a long section on sociology, and another on civilisation. It is not an easy book to read — nothing Whitehead wrote ever was — but it shows Whitehead extending his field steadily, taking a widening interest in all sorts of subjects apart from philosophy. After this, Whitehead had only one more major work ahead of him, *Modes of Thought* (1938), a restatement of the way in which his views had developed since *Science and the Modern World*. It contains the passage I quoted above about 'experience,' which shows Whitehead taking a view of philosophy which is broader than any conception since Plato. We cannot imagine Descartes,

Leibniz, or Kant writing such a passage, although it would not surprise us in Goethe.

Whitehead's final position can be taken from an essay called *Immortality*, delivered in 1941 at the Harvard Divinity School. It is not, as one might suppose, an attempt to prove that man has an immortal soul, or survives after death. Whitehead states that the world in which we live is a world of chaos, purposelessness, mortality. It is the World of Value which is the timeless world. Plato's works mean as much to us today as when he wrote them 2500 years ago, although Plato the man is dead. Men have this power of transmitting value which is greater than their individual physical selves: 'Creation aims at Value, whereas Value is saved from the futility of abstraction by its impact upon the process of Creation. But in this fusion, Value preserves its Immortality. In what sense does creative action derive Immortality from Value? This is the topic of our lecture.'[17]

Now Whitehead begins to state the views which we find in Spengler: that the philosopher must be the man of action. Whitehead develops the idea in his own calm, slightly demure way, so that it does not seem to express the same notion as Spengler's angry self-assertion. But it does, nevertheless:

> The notion of Effectiveness cannot be divorced from the understanding of the World of Value. The notion of a purely abstract self-enjoyment of values apart from any reference to effectiveness in action was the fundamental error prevalent in Greek philosophy . . . and . . . is not unknown in the modern world of learning.[18]

Although he uses a very different terminology, Whitehead is making the same point as Undershaft:

> Value is saved from the futility of abstraction by its impact upon . . . Creation.

He restates his notion of organism with complete clarity: 'The misconception which has haunted philosophic literature throughout the centuries is the notion of "independent existence." There is no such mode of existence; every entity is only to be understood in terms of the way in which it is interwoven with the rest of the Universe.' [19]

Whitehead goes on to say that 'personal identity' is the fusion of the World of Value with the World of Activity; in fact, the human being is a manifestation of the world of value in the world of activity; and the greater the man, the more 'value' he manifests.

This 'world of value' of which Whitehead speaks is the concept of life in Shaw. For Shaw, life is all-pervasive in space and time, but can only manifest itself by inserting itself into matter and by imposing its own world of order and pattern on the chaos of matter. The fact that there are 'laws of nature' at all is a manifestation of life. If life did not pervade space and time, the universe of matter would be *tohu bohu*, complete chaos. The fact that the earth circles around the sun is a manifestation of life. This is also Whitehead's concept of organism.

Whitehead's analysis now begins to touch on the realms of the 'mystical':

> Our sense-experiences are superficial, and fail to indicate the massive self-enjoyment derived from internal bodily functioning. Indeed human experience can be described as a flood of self-enjoyment, diversified by a trickle of conscious memory and conscious anticipation.[20]

Whitehead's way of expressing it is so flat and matter-of-fact that the startling content of this sentence is likely to escape us. In Dostoevsky's *The Devils*, Kirilov had expressed the same idea: that at a certain moment, he knew that everything was good, and had stopped the clock to remind himself of the recognition. In Camus's *L'Etranger*, Meursault knows, on the point of death, that 'I had been happy, and I was happy still.' Whitehead has put his finger on the essence of all the sudden moments of illumination:

> While on the shop and street I gazed
> My body of a sudden blazed;
> And twenty minutes more or less
> It seemed, so great my happiness,
> That I was blessèd and could bless.[21]

Whitehead goes on to summarise the role of memory and anticipation. Without memory, life is a flat train of events; a man without memory would be no better than an imbecile. But as soon as there is memory, no matter how faint, 'there is a reaction against mere . . . material domination. Thus the universe is material in proportion to the restriction of memory and anticipation.' [22] Memory is the instrument of man's consciousness; memory, as Proust knew, is the key to prehension. The struggle of life to assert itself into the world of activity by means of memory and consciousness is the ultimate definition of the ideal of heroism. The heroic is the struggle of Value against the unmeaning. The Outsider's lust for the heroic is the lust of life itself.

Whitehead ends his lecture by re-emphasising the principles of his idea of organism. He asserts that there are no such things as 'independent existences,' and no such thing as 'the adequate description of a finite fact.' Everything is tied up with everything else. He fires off one big gun into the air, when its target might well have been Marxism or logical positivism:

Much philosophic thought is based upon the *faked adequacy* of some account of various modes of human experience. . . .

Understand that I am not denying the importance of the analysis of experience: far from it. The progress of human thought is derived from the progressive enlightenment produced thereby. What I am objecting to is the absurd trust in the adequacy of our knowledge. The self-confidence of learned people is the comic tragedy of civilisation.

There is not a sentence which adequately states its own meaning. There is always a background of presupposition which defies analysis by reason of its infinitude.[23] [My italics.]

He finishes with a summary of his whole life's thought:

The conclusion is that Logic, conceived as an adequate analysis of the advance of thought, is a fake. It is a superb instrument, but it requires a background of common sense. . . .

My point is that the final outlook of Philosophic thought cannot be based upon the exact statements which form the basis of special sciences.

The exactness is a fake.[24]

Since the seventeenth century, this bogy of abstract thought has reigned unchallenged. The twentieth century tried to turn it into an algebra; and Whitehead was one of the men involved in the attempt. He has also been the man who has shown that abstract thought is inadequate. He was not, like Blake, a 'mere poet'; he was a mathematician and scientist of formidable qualifications. It is one of the miracles of the history of philosophy that a man who began as an 'abstract philosopher' should have ended by expressing the attitude of the prophetic visionary.

Whitehead's thought is extremely difficult, and his prose style is not always all that could be asked; consequently, the foregoing summary is bound to seem puzzling. I am also conscious that I have not succeeded in making Whitehead's thought seem attractive to readers who approach it for the first time. Nevertheless, it is my own conviction that he will one day be regarded as the outstanding philosopher of the twentieth century; and the attempt to present him in summary had to be made. England is always singularly unfair to its thinkers; if Whitehead had been a German, he would have had a special department of some university dedicated to expounding his thought.

What is surprising — even in view of the English indifference to metaphysics — is that no one has noticed that Whitehead has created his own kind of existentialism; and that it is fuller and more adequate than that of any Continental thinker. He was his own Hegel and Kierkegaard rolled into one. *Science and the Modern World* is the *Unscientific Postscript* of the twentieth century — with the additional advantage of being readable.

Whitehead continues the dialectic of Dostoevsky's beetle-man; the anti-rationalist argument. But Whitehead does not dismiss logic, in spite of his assertion that it is a fake. He states its function with precision in one of his earliest books, the *Introduction to Mathematics* in the Home University Library. It is a way of taking shortcuts, a way of saving valuable creating-time:

> It is a profoundly erroneous truism . . . that we should culti-
> vate the habit of thinking of what we are doing. . . . Civilisation
> advances by extending the number of important operations which
> we can perform without thinking about them. Operations of

thought are like cavalry charges in a battle — they are strictly limited in number, they require fresh horses, and must only be made at decisive moments.[25]

Logic is meant to save time, and to give us additional freedom — but here Zarathustra's question arises: Freedom for what? The mere logical philosopher hoards time as a miser hoards money, and his logic is directed to no other purpose; but unfortunately, time saved cannot be spent later. Without creation, all time is waste.

I began this book by admitting that 'the Outsider' is of interest to me because of my own obsession with the problems of mental strain, of extreme psychological states; yet during the course of this book, I have moved further and further away from questions of human psychology into the realm of ideas. I am aware that, in doing this, I have left the problems of a Van Gogh, a Dostoevsky and a Nijinsky far behind. And yet there is a kind of logic in this. The chief problem of life is not to learn how to think correctly, but simply to live. The thinking capacity cannot march forward on its own. Like a mountain guide, it is tied by a double rope to its companions, the emotions and the body. It can go so far and no further. Then the other two have to be induced to follow it before it can advance. At the end of *The Outsider*, I still had a great deal of rope left; I have now gone as far as my two companions will allow.

The Outsider was an attempt to argue the thesis that *man is not complete without a religion*. The inspiration of the book was William James's *Varieties of Religious Experience*. James had also, in his own way, attempted to do what Pascal, Hulme and Whitehead have attempted. His argument amounts to this: Man is at his most complete when his imagination is at its most intense. Imagination is the power of prehension; without it, man would be an imbecile, without memory, without forethought, without power of interpreting what he sees and feels. The higher the form of life, the greater its power of prehension; and in man, prehension becomes a conscious faculty, which can be labelled imagination. If life is to advance yet a stage higher, beyond the ape, beyond man the toiler or even man the artist, it will be through a further development of the power of prehension. This craving for greater intensity of imagination is the religious appetite.

Naturally, this is always bound up with the idea of the heroic. Even the heroism of Hemingway's novels has an ultimate religious significance.

This is the point at which I began *The Outsider*. My thesis was that religion begins with the stimulus which heroism supplies to the imagination. The Outsiders of the early chapters were men with hunger for heroism, stranded in an unheroic age. Their 'abnormalities' as Outsiders were their attempts to manufacture their own 'heroism.' Roquentin's complaint was that 'There's no adventure,' and he implied that this is necessarily true in a modern civilisation.

I tried to show that the craving for greater intensity of imagination (which means precisely the same as greater intensity of life: 'to have life more abundantly') takes the form of a search for the heroic. This craving for the heroic was quite plainly visible in the lives of Van Gogh, T. E. Lawrence, Rimbaud, Gauguin. (Guido Ruggiero referred to Gauguin and Rimbaud as 'existentialist saints,' and stated — with complete accuracy — that existentialism treats life in the manner of a thriller.) Hector Hushabye in *Heartbreak House* is the symbol of the hero in the modern age — mollycoddled by a highly efficient technical civilisation, driven to act out his heroism in imagination — the hero become the buffoon.

I tried to show the way in which heroism is the basis of the lives of all great religious figures. When George Fox left his Leicestershire home to tramp the roads as an itinerant preacher, he was inspired by the heroic example of Jesus. It was Jesus's value as a hero which made him the centre around which Dostoevsky's work revolved. The saint's self-torture, his renunciation of the world, is also heroic.

Nietzsche knew that the ideal of 'universal peace' is a false ideal; man will always attempt to create opportunities for the heroic. The wars of the twentieth century are the expression of a widespread subconscious craving. Kierkegaard was right when he said that boredom is the real evil of the world. A religion is the receptacle of the heroic, the symbol of man's need to strive for prehension. Failure of religion and world wars are inevitable companions.

This was the theme of *The Outsider*. The book ended with a question: What can be done? But it also indicated plainly the direction which the argument had to take. (One American reviewer stated that my next critical book would undoubtedly be my own 'recipe for a new religion.')

The analysis, in this book, has been forced to widen its scope. The Outsider had to be considered as a phenomenon of modern civilisation. The conclusion arrived at is that he is a symptom of a civilisation in decline; but that at least, he is a healthy sign.

I believe every civilisation reaches a moment of crisis, and that Western civilisation has now reached its moment. I believe that this crisis presents its challenge: Smash, or go on to higher things. So far, no civilisation has ever met this challenge successfully. History is the study of the bones of civilisations that failed, as the pterodactyl and the dinosaur failed.

In the second part of this book, I have tried to show *why* the Western world has reached its moment of crisis. I have tried to show how religion, the backbone of civilisation, hardens into a Church that is unacceptable to Outsiders, and the Outsiders — the men who strive to become visionaries — become the Rebels. In our case, the scientific progress that has brought us closer than ever before to conquering the problems of civilisation, has also robbed us of spiritual drive; and the Outsider is doubly a rebel: a rebel against the Established Church, a rebel against the unestablished church of materialism. Yet for all this, he is the real spiritual heir of the prophets, of Jesus and St. Peter, of St. Augustine and Peter Waldo. The purest religion of any age lies in the hands of its spiritual rebels. The twentieth century is no exception.

Nietzsche and Shaw both believed that the force behind life aims at the creation of higher and higher types of men — and ultimately, at the Superman, or Saint, or god. They believed that life aims at this god-creation slowly and inevitably, as a glacier moves. But the conclusions of the present book point to a different pattern. Every time a civilisation reaches its moment of crisis, it is capable of creating some higher type of man. Its successful response to the crisis *depends* upon the creation of a higher type of man. Not necessarily the Nietzschean Superman, but some type of man with broader consciousness and a deeper sense of purpose than ever before. Civilisation cannot continue in its present muddling, shortsighted way, producing better and better refrigerators, wider and wider cinema screens, and steadily draining men of all sense of a life of the spirit. The Outsider is nature's attempt to counterbalance this death of purpose. The challenge is immediate, and demands response from every one of us who is capable of understanding it.

Under the circumstances, it would be merely silly to speak of 'remedies.' It is too early even to speak of a final diagnosis. In the most important chapter of *The Outsider*, 'The Attempt to Gain Control,' I spoke of three types of discipline: the intellectual, the physical and the emotional, epitomised by T. E. Lawrence, Nijinsky and Van Gogh. Our civilisation, it would seem, is suffering from Lawrence's disease: too much intellect, and the consequent starvation of the emotional and physical factors. Existentialism is a protest on behalf of completeness, of balance. But it is difficult enough to prescribe for the individual Outsider; almost impossible to prescribe for the civilisation. Nevertheless, existentialism clearly plays the same role in the twentieth century that Christianity played in the Roman Empire in the first century. The parallel cannot be pressed. It is only suggested as a bulwark against complete pessimism.

The solution, as always, is for the individual Outsider to continue to try to bring new consciousness to birth. The circumstances are at least less depressing than they might be. Compared to the situation after the First World War, they seem distinctly hopeful. There is a taste of intellectual revolt in the air. And yet the burden remains upon the individual Outsider. There can be no easy 'engagement' — even if the situation is unprecedentedly serious. If our age *does* stand on the edge of a last decline, like Greek civilisation in Plato's time, the Outsider can only watch it with scientific curiosity, and continue — like Plato — to meditate on less immediate problems. This detachment is the basic condition of survival; it is the sign of ultimate optimism:

> All things fall and are built again,
> And those that build them again are gay.[26]

Yeats had written of three old Chinamen looking down on the dissolution of a civilisation; their attitude is the answer to the Outsider's question of engagement:

> On all the tragic scene they stare.
> One asks for mournful melodies;
> Accomplished fingers begin to play.
> Their eyes mid many wrinkles, their eyes,
> Their ancient, glittering eyes, are gay.

NOTES

Wherever British and American editions are both cited, page references are to the British edition.

An Autobiographical Introduction

page 11. 1. Shaw, G. B.: *Complete Plays* (London, Odhams, 1951), p. 362.

page 12. 2. Ibid., p. 387.

page 13. 3. Eliot, T. S.: *Collected Poems* (London, Faber, 1936; New York, Harcourt, 1936), p. 94.

page 16. 4. Ibid., p. 72.

page 17. 5. *The Bible of the World*, ed. Robert O. Ballou (London, Routledge and Kegan Paul, 1940; New York, Viking, 1939), p. 481.

page 22. 6. Brooke, Rupert: *Collected Poems, with a Memoir* (London, Sidgwick & Jackson, 1929; New York, Dodd, Mead, 1930, under the title *Collected Poems*), p. 109.

page 26. 7. Blake, William: *Poetry and Prose* (London, Nonesuch Edition, 1949), p. 413.

PART ONE
Chaper One

page 39. 1. Eliot, T. S.: *Collected Poems* (ed. cit.), p. 157.

page 41. 2. Yeats, W. B.: *Collected Poems* (London, Macmillan, 1950; New York, Macmillan, 1951), p. 268.

page 42. 3. Shaw, G. B.: *Complete Plays* (ed. cit.), p. 411.

page 44. 4. Ibid., p. 440.

page 46. 5. Nietzsche: *The Joyful Wisdom*, tr. T. Common (London, Foulis, 1910), p. 106.

6. Blake, William: *Poetry and Prose* (ed. cit.), p. 290.

page 49. 7. Wydenbruck, Nora: *Rilke: Man and Poet* (London, Lehmann, 1949; New York, Appleton, 1950), p. 39.

page 55. 8. Blake: *Poetry and Prose* (ed. cit.), p. 183.

9. Rilke, R. M.: *The Notebook of Malte Laurids Brigge*, tr. John Linton (London, Hogarth Press, 1930; New York, Norton, 1949), p. 21.

page 57. 10. Ibid., p. 76.
 11. Ibid., p. 72.
page 58. 12. Rilke: *Duino Elegies*, tr. J. B. Leishman and Stephen Spender (London, Hogarth Press, 1939; New York, Norton, 1939), p. 25.
page 59. 13. Ibid., p. 25.
 14. Yeats: *Collected Poems* (ed. cit.), p. 358.
 15. Rilke: *Sonnets to Orpheus*, tr. J. B. Leishman (London, Hogarth Press, 1936), p. 19.
 16. Goethe: *Faust*, Part Two, Act V, Scene 7, tr. A. G. Latham (London, Dent, 1928; New York, Dutton, 1928).
 17. Rilke: *Duino Elegies* (ed. cit.), p. 85.
page 60. 18. Ibid., p. 87.
 19. Ibid., p. 91.
page 62. 20. Ibid., p. 154.
 21. Ibid., p. 157.
page 63. 22. Rilke: *Sonnets to Orpheus*, tr. J. B. Leishman (London, Hogarth Press, 1946), p. 49.
page 64. 23. Yeats: *Collected Poems* (ed. cit.), p. 278.
page 65. 24. Synge, J. M.: *Plays, Poems and Prose* (London, Everyman's Library, 1954), p. 219.
page 68. 25. Rimbaud, Arthur: *The Drunken Boat: Thirty Six Poems by Arthur Rimbaud*, tr. Brian Hill (London, Hart-Davis, 1952), p. 19.
page 69. 26. Ibid., p. 27.
page 70. 27. tr. Anthony Hartley, *The Penguin Book of French Verse: III* (Penguin, 1957), p. 247.
page 71. 28. Rimbaud: *The Drunken Boat* (ed. cit.), p. 25.
page 72. 29. Ibid., p. 29.
page 77. 30. tr. Colin Wilson.
page 80. 31. Rimbaud: *A Season in Hell*, tr. Norman Cameron (London, Lehmann, 1949), p. 41.
page 81. 32. Mizener, Arthur: *The Far Side of Paradise* (London, Eyre and Spottiswoode, 1951; Boston, Houghton, 1951), p. 5. (Quoted from *The Romantic Egotist*.)
page 82. 33. Fitzgerald, F. Scott: *The Crack-Up* (New York, New Directions, 1945), p. 15.
 34. Ibid., p. 15.
page 83. 35. Mizener: op. cit., p. 126.
 36. Fitzgerald: *The Crack-Up* (ed. cit.), p. 13.
page 84. 37. Fitzgerald, F. Scott: *The Great Gatsby* (New York, Scribner, 1925), Ch. III.
page 85. 38. Brooke, Rupert: op. cit., p. lxxviii.
 39. Mizener: op. cit., p. 104.
page 86. 40. Brooke, Rupert: op. cit., p. xviii.
 41. Ibid., p. liii.
page 87. 42. Fitzgerald: *The Crack-Up* (ed. cit.), p. 72.
page 88. 43. Ibid., p. 69.
 44. Ibid., p. 20.
page 90. 45. Ibid., p. 69.
 46. Hemingway, Ernest: *The First Forty-Nine Stories* (London, Cape, 1944), p. 78.

Chapter Two

page 93. 1. Spengler, Oswald: *The Decline of the West*, tr. C. F. Atkinson (London, Allen & Unwin, 1934; New York, Knopf, 1945), p. 3.
page 100. 2. Ibid., p. 7.
        3. Ibid., p. 61.
page 101. 4. Ibid., p. 43.
        5. Ibid., p. 43.
        6. Ibid., p. 44.
page 103. 7. Ibid., p. 186.
        8. Ibid., p. 186.
page 105. 9. Ibid., p. 21.
       10. Ibid., p. 21.
page 109. 11. Sophocles: *Seven Plays*, tr. Sir George Young (London, Everyman's Library, 1906; New York, Dutton, 1906), p. 11.
page 110. 12. Toynbee, Arnold: *A Study of History* (London and New York, Oxford, 1955), Vol. X, p. 107.
page 111. 13. Ibid., Vol. I, p. 281.
page 115. 14. Ibid., Vol. IV, p. 127.
page 116. 15. Hesse, Hermann: *Steppenwolf*, tr. Basil Creighton (London, Secker, 1929; New York, Holt, 1929), p. 96.
page 119. 16. Toynbee: op. cit., Vol. X, p. 129.
page 122. 17. Ibid., Vol. X, p. 130.
page 123. 18. Ibid., Vol. X, p. 139.
       19. Ibid., Vol. IX, p. 634.
       20. Ibid., Vol. IX, p. 411 ff.
page 124. 21. Ibid., Vol. IX, p. 608.
page 125. 22. Shaw, G. B.: *Prefaces* (London, Odhams, 1938), p. 63.
       23. Toynbee: op. cit., Vol. IX, p. 612.
       24. Ibid., Vol. IX, p. 641.

PART TWO

Introduction

page 132. 1. Eliot, T. S.: *Collected Poems* (ed. cit.), p. 127.
page 137. 2. Shaw, G. B.: *Prefaces* (ed. cit.), p. 560.
page 140. 3. Nietzsche: *The Dawn of Day*, tr. Johanna Volz (London, Fisher Unwin, 1903), p. 59.
page 147. 4. Blake: op. cit., p. 121.
       5. Yeats: *Collected Poems* (ed. cit.), p. 272.

Chapter One

page 151. 1. Lawrence, D. H.: *Lady Chatterley's Lover*, Ch. XII.
page 154. 2. *Confessions of Jacob Boehme*, ed. W. Scott Palmer (London, Methuen, 1954), p. 3.
page 155. 3. Ibid., p. 1.
       4. Boehme: *The Signature of All Things* (London, Everyman's Library, 1934; New York, Dutton, 1934), p. 15.
page 156. 5. Boehme: *Morgenröte*, xiii: 136.
page 163. 6. Boehme: *Six Theosophic Points*, tr. J. R. Earle (London, Constable, 1919), p. 5.

page 165.   7. Boehme: *Morgenröte*, xiii: 27.
             8. *Confessions of Jacob Boehme* (ed. cit.), p. 13.
             9. Ibid., p. 25.
           10. Ibid., p. 8.
page 167. 11. Ibid., p. 17.
           12. Nietzsche: *The Antichrist*, tr. W. Kaufmann (New York, Viking, 1954), p. 570 ff.
page 168. 13. *Confessions of Jacob Boehme* (ed. cit.), p. 10.

Chapter Two

page 176.   1. Yeats, W. B.: *Autobiographies* (London, Macmillan, 1955; New York, Macmillan, 1953, under the title *The Autobiography*), p. 90.
            2. Ibid., p. 154.
            3. Ibid., p. 155.

Chapter Three

page 185.   1. Bishop, Morris: *Pascal* (London, Bell, 1937; New York, Reynal, 1936), p. 173.
page 188.   2. Ibid., p. 234.
page 191.   3. Blake: op. cit., p. 110.
page 193.   4. Pascal: *Pensées* (London, Everyman's Library, 1954; New York, Dutton, 1954), p. 14.

Chapter Four

page 199.   1. Trobridge: *Swedenborg* (London, Swedenborg Society, 1945; New York, Swedenborg Foundation, 1947), p. 226.
page 205.   2. Sigstedt: *The Swedenborg Epic* (London, Allen & Unwin, 1952; New York, Bookman Associates, 1953), p. 221.
            3. Swedenborg: *Apocalypsis Revelata*, xii: 15.
page 207.   4. Yeats: *Collected Poems* (ed. cit.), p. 386.

Chapter Five

page 210.   1. Quoted by Henri Talon: *William Law* (London, Rockliff, 1948; New York, Harper, 1949), p. 13.
page 212.   2. Law, William: *A Serious Call to a Devout and Holy Life* (London, Methuen, 1950), p. 4.
page 213.   3. Ibid., p. 209.
            4. Ibid., p. 179.
            5. Ibid., p. 12.
page 214.   6. Ibid., p. 8.
            7. Ibid., p. 163.
page 215.   8. Ibid., p. 55.
page 216.   9. Ibid., p. 25.
           10. Blake: op. cit., p. 124.

Chapter Six

page 224.   1. Newman: *Prose and Poetry*, ed. Geoffrey Tillotson (London, Hart-Davis, 1957; Cambridge, Harvard University Press, 1957), p. 579.

page 226. 2. Ibid., p. 90.
3. Ibid., p. 102.
4. Ibid., p. 150.
page 227. 5. Ibid., p. 757.
page 230. 6. Newman: *A Grammar of Assent* (London and New York, Long-mans, Green, 1947), p. 328.
7. *The Bible of the World* (ed. cit.), p. 455.
page 231. 8. Newman: *Prose and Poetry* (ed. cit.), p. 100.

Chapter Seven

page 233. 1. Kierkegaard, Søren: *A Kierkegaard Anthology*, ed. Robert Bretall (London, Oxford, 1947; Princeton, Princeton University Press, 1946), p. 10.
page 234. 2. Ibid., p. 22.
page 235. 3. Ibid., p. 33.
page 237. 4. Kierkegaard: *The Concept of Dread*, tr. Walter Lowrie (London, Oxford, 1944; Princeton, Princeton University Press, 1944), p. 156.
5. Nietzsche: *The Joyful Wisdom* (ed. cit.), p. 7.

Chapter Eight

page 244. 1. Blake: op. cit., p. 108.
page 245. 2. Eliot, T. S.: *Selected Essays* (London, Faber, 1932; New York, Harcourt, 1932), p. 287.
3. Yeats: *Collected Poems* (ed. cit.), p. 208.
4. Brooke, Rupert: op. cit., p. 79.
page 248. 5. Shaw: *Prefaces* (ed. cit.), p. 673.
6. Ibid., p. 680.
page 249. 7. Shaw: *Complete Plays* (ed. cit.), p. 411.
page 252. 8. Shaw: *Prefaces* (ed. cit.), p. 670.
page 253. 9. Ibid., p. 662.
page 254. 10. Ibid., p. 145.
page 255. 11. Shaw: *Selected Prose*, ed. Diarmuid Russell (London, Constable, 1953; New York, Dodd, 1952), p. 489.
12. Ibid., p. 489.
13. Shaw: *Back to Methuselah* (World's Classics: London, Oxford, 1946; New York, Oxford, 1947), p. 286.
page 256. 14. Shaw: *Selected Prose* (ed. cit.), p. 590.
page 257. 15. Shaw: *Complete Plays* (ed. cit.), p. 30.
page 258. 16. Ibid., p. 133.
page 259. 17. Ibid., p. 257.
page 260. 18. Ibid., p. 281.
19. Ibid., p. 291.
page 262. 20. Ibid., p. 337.
page 263. 21. Ibid., p. 381.
22. Ibid., p. 385.
page 264. 23. Ibid., p. 386.
page 265. 24. Ibid., p. 403.
25. *Don Giovanni*, Act II, Scene 5.
page 266. 26. Shaw: *Complete Plays* (ed. cit.), p. 789.

page 267. 27. *Song of God: Bhagavad-Gita*, tr. Swami Prabhavananda and Christopher Isherwood (London, Phoenix, 1951; New York, Harper, 1951), p. 40.

page 268. 28. Shaw: *Complete Plays* (ed. cit.), p. 491.
29. Ibid., p. 502.

page 269. 30. Ibid., p. 699.

page 272. 31. Ibid., pp. 773 ff.
32. Ibid., p. 790.

page 273. 33. Ibid., p. 800.

page 275. 34. Shaw: *Prefaces* (ed. cit.), p. 502.
35. Ibid., p. 506.

page 277. 36. Ibid., p. 539.
37. Ibid., p. 540.

page 278. 38. Ibid., p. 526.

page 279. 39. Shaw: *Complete Plays* (ed. cit.), p. 277.
40. Ibid., p. 867.
41. Ibid., p. 869.

page 280. 42. Ibid., p. 939.

page 281. 43. Yeats: *Collected Poems* (ed. cit.), p. 399.
44. Shaw: *Complete Plays* (ed. cit.), p. 957.
45. Ibid., p. 957.

page 282. 46. Ibid., p. 962.

page 284. 47. Ibid., p. 1,245.
48. Ibid., p. 1,157.
49. Wells, H. G.: *Mind at the End of Its Tether* (London, Heinemann, 1945), p. 4.

page 285. 50. Shaw: *Complete Plays* (ed. cit.), p. 1,157.

page 286. 51. Ibid., p. 1,381.
52. Ibid., p. 1,389.

page 289. 53. Shaw: *The Intelligent Woman's Guide to Socialism and Capitalism* (London, Constable, 1928; New York, Garden City, 1931), p. 319.

Chapter Nine

page 295. 1. Wittgenstein, Ludwig: *Philosophical Investigations* (London, Blackwell, 1953; New York, Macmillan, 1953), p. 47.

page 296. 2. Wittgenstein, Ludwig: *Tractatus Logico-Philosophicus* (London, Routledge and Kegan Paul, 1949; New York, Harcourt, 1933), p. 183.

page 297. 3. Ibid., p. 185.
4. Ibid., p. 185.
5. Ibid., p. 185.

page 298. 6. Ibid., pp. 187 ff.

page 305. 7. Whitehead, Alfred North: *A Treatise on Universal Algebra* (Cambridge, The University Press, 1898), p. viii.

page 307. 8. Whitehead: *An Enquiry into the Principles of Natural Knowledge* (Cambridge, The University Press, 1925), p. vii.

page 308. 9. Whitehead: *The Principle of Relativity* (Cambridge, The University Press, 1922), p. 62.

10. Whitehead: *Science and the Modern World* (Cambridge, The University Press, 1927; New York, Macmillan, 1925), p. 4.

page 310. 11. *Alfred North Whitehead: An Anthology*, ed. Northrop and Gross (Cambridge, The University Press, 1953; New York, Macmillan, 1955), p. 907.

page 311. 12. Ibid., p. 472.

page 312. 13. Ibid., p. 527.

14. Ibid., p. 567.

page 313. 15. Ibid., p. 442.

16. Ibid., p. 845.

page 314. 17. *The Philosophy of A. N. Whitehead*, ed. Schilpp (Evanston, Northwestern University, 1941), p. 686.

18. Ibid., p. 686.

page 315. 19. Ibid., p. 687.

20. Ibid., p. 694.

21. Yeats: *Collected Poems* (ed. cit.), p. 284.

page 316. 22. *The Philosophy of A. N. Whitehead* (ed. cit.), p. 695.

23. Ibid., p. 698.

24. Ibid., p. 700.

page 318. 25. Whitehead: *An Introduction to Mathematics* (London and New York, Oxford, Home University Library, 1948), p. 41.

page 321. 26. Yeats: *Collected Poems* (ed. cit.), p. 339.

INDEX